Da Love-Ananda Gita

(The Free Gift Of The Divine Love-Bliss)

THE FIVE BOOKS OF
THE HEART OF THE ADIDAM REVELATION

BOOK THREE

The "Late-Time" Avataric Revelation
Of The Great Means To Worship and To Realize
The True and Spiritual Divine Person
(The egoless Personal Presence Of Reality and Truth,
Which <u>Is</u> The Only <u>Real</u> God)

By
The Divine World-Teacher,
RUCHIRA AVATAR
ADI DA SAMRAJ

THE DAWN HORSE PRESS
MIDDLETOWN, CALIFORNIA

In Praise of the Divine World-Teacher, Ruchira Avatar Adi Da Samraj

It is obvious, from all sorts of subtle details, that he knows what IT's all about . . . a rare being.

ALAN WATTS
author, *The Way of Zen* and *The Wisdom of Insecurity*

I regard Adi Da Samraj as one of the greatest teachers in the Western world today.

IRINA TWEEDIE
Sufi teacher; author, *Chasm of Fire*

I recognize the God-Presence Incarnate in Adi Da Samraj as whole and full and complete.

BARBARA MARX HUBBARD
author, *Conscious Evolution* and *The Revelation;*
president, The Foundation for Conscious Evolution

Adi Da Samraj has created virtually the entire basis for a culture founded in love and wisdom. The magnitude of such an undertaking—let alone the accomplishment of it—cannot be overstated.

JOHN WHITE
author, *Frontiers of Consciousness,*
and *The Meeting of Science and Spirit*

Adi Da Samraj is a man who has truly walked in Spirit and given true enlightenment to many.

SUN BEAR
founder, the Bear Tribe Medicine Society

The life and teaching of Avatar Adi Da Samraj are of profound and decisive spiritual significance at this critical moment in history.

BRYAN DESCHAMP
Senior Adviser at the United Nations
High Commission for Refugees;
former Dean of the Carmelite House of Studies, Australia;
former Dean of Trinity College, University of Melbourne

A great teacher with the dynamic ability to awaken in his listeners
something of the Divine Reality in which he is grounded, with which
he is identified, and which, in fact, he is.

ISRAEL REGARDIE
author, *The Golden Dawn*

A di Da Samraj has spoken directly to the heart of our human situation—
the shocking gravity of our brief and unbidden lives. Through his
words I have experienced a glimmering of eternal life, and view my own
existence as timeless and spaceless in a way that I never have before.

RICHARD GROSSINGER
author, *Planet Medicine*

M y relationship with Adi Da Samraj over many years has only confirmed
His Realization and the Truth of His impeccable Teaching. He is much
more than simply an inspiration of my music, but is really a living
demonstration that perfect transcendence is actually possible. This is both
a great relief and a great challenge. If you thirst for truth, here is a rare
opportunity to drink.

RAY LYNCH
composer and musician, *Deep Breakfast;*
The Sky of Mind; and *Ray Lynch, Best Of*

A di Da Samraj and his unique body of teaching work offer a rare and
extraordinary opportunity for those courageous students who are
ready to move beyond ego and take the plunge into deepest communion
with the Absolute. Importantly, the teaching is grounded in explicit
discussion of necessary psychospiritual evolution and guides the student
to self-responsibility and self-awareness.

ELISABETH TARG, M.D.
University of California, San Francisco,
School of Medicine;
director, Complementary Medicine Research Institute,
California Pacific Medical Center

That God can, among other things, actually incarnate in human form once seemed unbelievable to me. But reading the books of Avatar Adi Da obliterated all doubt about the existence of God right now, here on Earth in human form.

CHARMIAN ANDERSON, PH.D.
psychologist; author, *Bridging Heaven and Earth*
and *The Heart of Success*

Fly to the side of this God-Man. His Divine Transmission works miracles of change not possible by any other Spiritual means.

LEE SANNELLA, M.D.
author, *The Kundalini Experience*

When I first read the Word of Avatar Adi Da Samraj, I was immediately transported into a state of wonderment and awe. Could it be? Could the Divine Person be here now, in this time and place? It didn't take long for my heart to answer a resounding "Yes". May the whole world be restored to Faith, Love, and Understanding by the Mystery of Real God, here and Incarnate as Avatar Adi Da Samraj.

ED KOWALCZYK
lead singer and songwriter of the rock band, *Live*

I regard the work of Adi Da and his devotees as one of the most penetrating spiritual and social experiments happening on the planet in our era.

JEFFREY MISHLOVE, PH.D.
host, PBS television series, *Thinking Allowed*;
author, *The Roots of Consciousness*

Adi Da's Teachings have tremendous significance for humanity. . . . He represents a foundation and a structure for sanity.

ROBERT K. HALL, M.D.
psychiatrist; author, *Out of Nowhere*;
co-founder, The Lomi School and Lomi Clinic

The Divine World-Teacher,
Ruchira Avatar Adi Da Samraj
The Mountain Of Attention, 2000

C O N T E N T S

DA LOVE-ANANDA GITA
(THE Free Gift Of The Divine Love-Bliss)

F I R S T   W O R D :

Do Not Misunderstand <u>Me</u>—
I Am <u>Not</u> "Within" <u>you</u>, but you <u>Are</u> In <u>Me</u>,
and I Am <u>Not</u> a Mere "Man" in the "Middle" of Mankind,
but All of Mankind Is Surrounded, and Pervaded,
and Blessed By <u>Me</u>

47

P R O L O G U E :

My Divine Disclosure

69

P A R T   O N E :

The Plight Of The Divine Heart-Husband
(The Forty-Seven Divine Statements
Of The Ruchira Avatar, Adi Da Samraj)

83

Ruchira Avatar Adi Da Samraj
The Mountain Of Attention, 2000

Introduction

This book is an invitation to enter a different world. A world that is completely <u>real</u>, in the largest possible sense of that word. A world in which none of the sufferings and difficulties of life are ignored or denied—but also a world in which yearnings for truth, wisdom, happiness, and love are addressed at an extraordinary depth. A world in which there is real, trustable guidance through the "maze" of life's confusions and crises. A world that vastly exceeds all limited notions of what is "real". A world of deep, abiding joy.

People from all walks of life have felt this world open up to them when they read the books of the Divine World-Teacher, Ruchira Avatar Adi Da Samraj. Those of us who have done so have felt our deepest questions answered, our most profound heart-longings satisfied. We have treasured His Instruction about the real issues everyone faces: death, sex, intimacy, emotional maturity, community life, and many more. We have marveled at His precise "map" of the entire course of Spiritual life, and at His description of the nature of reality in all its dimensions. We have been sobered by His criticism of the universal human bondage to the self-centered desires and purposes of the ego. And, altogether, through His words, we have felt His Divine Spiritual Blessing deeply affecting our lives.

Those of us who have been drawn to Avatar Adi Da have discovered that the impact of His Truth (and the Blessing it conveys) is so great in our lives, so far beyond anything else we have known, that a truly amazing recognition began to grow in our hearts and minds: Avatar Adi Da Samraj is not merely a great human being who speaks profound Truth—He is the Divine Reality Itself, Appearing in a human body in order to Offer His Revelation of Truth directly to all of humankind.

Often, this awakened recognition of Him—as the Divine Reality Present in human Form—comes as a complete surprise. In this age of skepticism, many regard the idea of a Divine Incarnation as strictly mythological. But Avatar Adi Da Samraj is not a myth— He is an intensely real living being. He is an utterly spontaneous and free manifestation, moved (by overwhelming love) to serve the Happiness and Liberation of beings everywhere, and to bring our global home out of this time of potential political and ecological disaster.

However, no one is asked to "believe" that Avatar Adi Da is the Divine. He has even said, "You must not believe in Me." Why? Because mere belief is not transformative. Only what is revealed in one's real experience—of body, heart, and mind altogether, rather than mind only—can transform the being. Therefore, Avatar Adi Da does not offer you a set of beliefs, or even a set of Spiritual techniques. He simply offers you His Revelation of Truth as a free gift, to respond to as you will. And, if you are moved to take up His Way, He invites you to enter into a direct Spiritual relationship with Him. Those of us who have taken this step have found the Spiritual relationship to Avatar Adi Da Samraj to be a supremely precious gift, a literally miraculous blessing, the answer to our deepest longings—greatly surpassing anything we have ever experienced or even imagined to be possible. Indeed, we have found Avatar Adi Da's Revelation of Truth to be so all-encompassing and His Spiritual Power and Love to be so overwhelming that we recognize Him as the Promised God-Man—the One capable of fulfilling the yearnings of people everywhere, the One Whose Appearance has been foreshadowed by prophecies in many religious traditions.

Avatar Adi Da began Teaching formally in 1972. In the years since then, He has communicated a vast store of Wisdom. But He has also done far more than that: He has created a whole new Way of life, a new religion, which is now practiced by people of different cultures in many parts of the world.

Just as the religions of Christianity and Buddhism are named after their founders, the religion founded by Avatar Adi Da is named after Him—it is called "Adidam" (AH-dee-DAHM). Adidam is an all-embracing practice that takes every aspect of human life—the "lowest" as well as the "highest"—into account (see pp. 288-89). The foundation of Adidam is the response of heart-felt devotion to Avatar Adi Da Samraj, in loving gratitude for His Gifts of Wisdom and Spiritual Blessing.

Avatar Adi Da's books are full of ecstatic proclamations of His Divinity—and there is a secret to understanding these proclamations fully. The secret is this: Avatar Adi Da is not speaking as a separate being who presumes himself to be irreducibly "different" from every other being. No, He is speaking as the Divine Heart of every being. Therefore, His most fundamental message may be summarized as follows:

> There is no ultimate "difference" between you and the Divine.
> There is <u>only</u> the Divine.
> Everything that exists is a "modification" of the One Divine Reality.

However, even though it may be true that there is only the Divine, this is not, in fact, our common daily experience. Far from it! Our usual daily life is full of events and people (including ourselves!) that we experience as distinctly un-Divine.

Therefore, Avatar Adi Da is humanly present in the world in order to Reveal the Divine Condition, and to make it possible for human beings to Realize that that Condition is our True Nature. That this is so is the deep heart-certainty of Avatar Adi Da's devotees—after many years of studying His Teaching, hearing His Discourses, enjoying His Company in all kinds of circumstances, and knowing the profound Ecstasy, Joy, and Peace of His Spiritual Transmission.

Thus, when Avatar Adi Da Samraj says "I <u>Am</u> the One to be Realized" or "I <u>Am</u> the Very Divine Person" or "I <u>Am</u> the Divine Heart Itself" (and many other variations), He is confessing that He is, paradoxically, the Divine Condition of everyone and everything—seeming to be a separate being, in order to offer us the Way to Realize our Inherent Condition. And it is our confession to you, as those who have become His devotees, that to behold Him with an open heart is to fall into an indescribable Love, Bliss, and Happiness that is self-evidently the deepest Truth of one's own heart and the Very Heart of Existence.

As Avatar Adi Da Samraj says, with great passion and emphasis:

Beloved, Even I Am Only You (As You Are).

This is the great mystery that you are invited to discover for yourself.

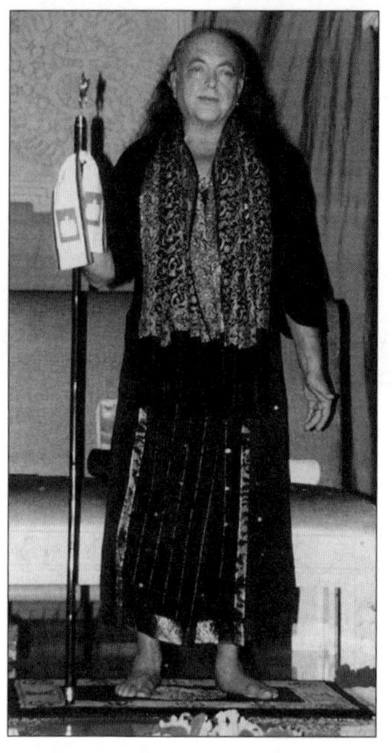

Avatar Adi Da Samraj's Name is composed of four Sanskrit words.

His principal Name is "Adi Da". "Avatar" and "Samraj" are sacred Titles, used in association with His Name.

"Adi" (AH-dee) means "Original" (or "Primordial"), and "Da" means "the Divine Giver". Thus, "Adi Da" means "the Original Divine Giver".

"Avatar" means "a 'Crossing Down' of the Divine Being into the world" (or, in other words, "an Appearance of the Divine in conditionally manifested form").

"Samraj" (sahm-RAHJ) means "universal Lord".

In fuller forms of reference, Adi Da Samraj is called "the Ruchira (roo-CHIH-rah) Avatar", meaning "the Avatar of Infinite Brightness".

Avatar Adi Da Samraj: His Life and Teaching

The Three Great Purposes of Avatar Adi Da Samraj: Learning Man, Teaching Man, and Blessing Man

From the moment of His Birth (in New York, on November 3, 1939), Adi Da Samraj was Consciously Aware of His Native Divine Condition. As soon as He became able to use language, He gave this Condition a simple but very expressive Name—"the 'Bright'".* But then, at the age of two years, Avatar Adi Da made a profound spontaneous choice. He chose to relinquish His constant Enjoyment of the "Bright"—out of what He Describes as a "painful loving", a sympathy for the suffering and ignorance of human beings. Avatar Adi Da Confesses that He chose to "Learn Man"—to enter into everything that humankind feels and suffers, and also to experience all the various levels of Spiritual Realization known to humanity—in order to discover how to Draw human beings into the "Bright" Divine Condition that He knew as His own True State and the True State of everyone.

This utter Submission to all aspects of human life was the first Purpose of Adi Da's Incarnation. In His Spiritual Autobiography, *The Knee Of Listening*, Avatar Adi Da recounts this amazing and heroic Ordeal, which lasted for the first thirty years of His Life.

*For definitions of terms and names, please see the Glossary (pp. 322-59).

In 1970, Avatar Adi Da finally Re-Awakened permanently to the "Bright", and embarked upon the second great Purpose of His Incarnation—the Process of "Teaching Man".

When He began to Teach others, Avatar Adi Da Samraj simply made Himself available to all who were willing to enter into the living Process of Real-God-Realization in His Company—a Process Which He summarized as the relation-

Los Angeles, 1972

ship to Him, rather than any method or technique of Spiritual attainment. Through that relationship—an extraordinary human and Spiritual intimacy—Avatar Adi Da Samraj perfectly embraced

The Mountain Of Attention Sanctuary, 1974

each of His devotees, using every kind of skillful means to Awaken them to the Truth that the separate, un-Enlightened self—with all its fear, anxieties, and fruitless seeking for Happiness—is self-imposed suffering, a contraction of the being (which He calls "the self-contraction").

Happiness, He Revealed, cannot be attained through any kind of search, because It is "Always Already the Case". And He Offered the practice of heart-Communion with Him as the means of going beyond the self-contraction and thereby Realizing Real Happiness.

I have Come to Live (now, and forever hereafter) with those who love Me with ego-overwhelming love, and I have Come to Love them likewise Overwhelmingly. . . .

Until you fall in love, love is what you __fear__ to do. When you have fallen in love, and you __are__ (thus) always already in love, then you cease to fear to love . . . . Those who fall in love with Me, Fall into Me. Those whose hearts are given, in love, to Me, Fall into My Heart. [*"What Will You Do If You Love Me?", from* Da Love-Ananda Gita]

In 1986, an Event occurred that marked the beginning of a great change in Avatar Adi Da's Work in the world. In this Great Event, a profound Yogic Swoon (taking the form of His apparent near-death) overwhelmed His body-mind, and Avatar Adi Da Samraj spontaneously began the process of relinquishing His Ordeal of Learning and Teaching Man. In the wake of that great Swoon, He simply Radiated His Divinity as never before. This was the beginning of what He calls His "Divine Self-'Emergence'". From that moment, Adi Da Samraj has devoted

The Mountain Of Attention, 1986

Himself increasingly to the third and eternal Purpose of His Avataric Incarnation—that of "Blessing Man" (and even all beings).

The Way of Adidam

Even after the Great Event in 1986, Avatar Adi Da continued to Work to ensure that His Revelation of the Way of Adidam was fully and firmly founded in the world. It was not until February 1999 that Avatar Adi Da Samraj declared that all the foundation Work of His Incarnation had been completely and finally Done. Everything necessary for the understanding and right practice of the real religious process, culminating in Divine Enlightenment, has been Said and Done by Him. The summary of His Wisdom-Teaching is preserved for all time in a series of twenty-three "Source-Texts" (described on pp. 27-36). And the Way of Adidam is fully established. This monumental Work has been accomplished by Avatar Adi Da in a little over a quarter of a century—twenty-seven years of ceaseless Instruction, in constant interaction with His devotees.

Avatar Adi Da's Full Revelation of Truth and His Work to establish the Way of Adidam required an immense struggle. The reason that struggle was inevitable is that human beings—especially in this time when the "individual" is regarded to be the supreme measure of value—have enormous resistance to any process that requires them to go beyond ego. Throughout history, people have tended to prefer forms of religion based on a system of beliefs and a code of moral and social behavior. But this kind of religion, as Avatar Adi Da has always pointed out, does not go to the core, to the root-suffering of human beings. This is because ordinary religion, rather than going beyond the ego-principle, is actually <u>based</u> on it: the ego-self stands at the center, and the Divine is sought and appealed to as the great Power that is going to save and satisfy the individual self. Avatar Adi Da Describes such religion as "client-centered".

In contrast to conventional religion, there is the process that Avatar Adi Da calls "true religion", religion that is centered in the Divine, in response to a true Spiritual Master who has (to at least some significant degree) <u>Realized</u> God (as opposed to merely offering teachings <u>about</u> God). Thus, true religion does not revolve around the individual's desire for any kind of "spiritual" consolations or experience—it is ego-transcending, rather than ego-serving. True religion based on ego-surrendering devotion to a Spiritual Master has existed for thousands of years, but the ecstatic confession of Avatar Adi Da's devotees is that now the Very Divine Itself is directly Present, Functioning as Divine Heart-Master, Alive in the human form of Avatar Adi Da Samraj.

All religions are historical forms of the Single and Ancient Way of Distracted love for the Divine Person, especially as Revealed in the Life and in the Company and in the Person of Incarnate Adepts (or Realizers) in their various degrees and stages of Realization. This is the Great Secret. ["What Will You Do If You Love Me?", from Da Love-Ananda Gita]

[E]goity is the "disease" that <u>all</u> the true Spiritual Masters of religion come here to cure. Unfortunately, . . . religious and Spiritual institutions tend to develop along lines that serve, accommodate, and represent the common egoity—and this is why the esoteric true Teachings of true Spiritual Masters tend to be bypassed, and even suppressed, in the drive to develop the exoteric cult of any particular Spiritual Master.

The relationship to Me . . . is a profound esoteric discipline, <u>necessarily</u> associated with real and serious and mature . . . practice of the "radical" Way (or root-Process) of Realizing <u>Real</u> God (Which <u>Is</u> Reality and Truth).

The Way of Adidam is the . . . Way to live in <u>Freedom</u>—not to be bound by separate and separative self, or by conditional Nature as a whole. Therefore, the ego-transcending devotional relationship to Me is the Context and the Means of Free Divine Self-Realization. ["Beyond the Cultic Tendency in Religion and Spirituality, and in Secular Society", from Ruchira Avatara Gita]

Standing Free of the Common Egoity

In His Spiritual Work with His devotees and the world, Avatar Adi Da Samraj has confronted the realities of egoity in a completely direct and unflinching manner. In His years of "Teaching Man", He did not hesitate in the slightest to grapple with the ego as it might be manifested in any moment by an individual devotee or a group of devotees—for the sake of helping His devotees understand and go beyond their ego-possessed disposition and activity.

However, even in the midst of that compassionate struggle with the forces of egoity, Avatar Adi Da has always Stood utterly Free of the ego-world. And, especially since the late 1970s, that Free Stand more and more took the form of His living in an essentially private circumstance, at one of the Hermitages established for Him (at secluded locations in California, Hawaii, and Fiji—see p. 297). In His Hermitage sphere, Avatar Adi Da is served by an intimate group of renunciate devotees, with whom He does particularly intensive Spiritual Work. And it is in the set-apart domain of His Hermitages (rather than in some kind of more public setting) that Avatar Adi Da receives His devotees in general (and, on rare occasions, specially invited members of the public), to Grant them His Spiritual Blessing.

The reasons why Avatar Adi Da maintains a Hermitage life are profound. The purpose of His Existence is to Reveal the Divine Reality—in other words, to Manifest the Freedom, Purity, and unbounded Blissfulness of His own Divine Nature, to Exist simply as He Is, without having to make compromises or adjustments in order to "fit in" to the ordinary ego-patterned world. Therefore, it is essential that He live in a sacred domain that conforms to Him and to the nature of His Spiritual Work, where He can remain independent of (but not disconnected from) the common world, even the daily world of the practical functioning of His community of devotees. Indeed, it is essential that He be free of institutional or organizational responsibilities relative to the gathering of His own devotees—because any such level of functioning would be a limitation on His Spiritual Work, an impingement on His Freedom to Manifest His own True Nature in the fullest and most pristine manner.

As He has commented many times, His Hermitage life is a life of seclusion, but not of isolation. His secluded Hermitage life is what allows His Divine Blessing to Flow into the world with the greatest possible force and effectiveness—it is what allows His Spiritual connection to all beings to be as strong as possible.

The "Problem" Is ego— Not Anything Else

For more than a quarter of a century, during His years of Teaching and Revelation (from 1972 to 1999), Avatar Adi Da undertook a vast, in-life "consideration" with His devotees of everything related to Spiritual life—from the most rudimentary matters to the most esoteric. One extremely important area of "consideration" was how to rightly relate to the most basic urges and activities of human life—what Avatar Adi Da describes as the realm of "money, food, and sex". (By "money", Avatar Adi Da means not only the earning and use of money itself, but the exercising of life-energy in general.)

In most religious traditions, an ascetical approach to these primal urges is recommended—in other words, desires related to "money, food, and sex" are to be minimized or denied. Avatar Adi Da took a different approach. When they are rightly engaged, ordinary human enjoyments are not a problem, not "sinful" or "anti-spiritual" in and of themselves. Thus, the root-problem of human beings is not any particular activity or desire of the body-mind, but the ego itself—the governing presumption that one is a separate and independent entity, threatened by the inevitable prospect of death. Therefore, in living dialogue and experimentation with His devotees, Avatar Adi Da brought to light, in detail, exactly how the human functions of money (or life-energy), food, and sex can be rightly engaged, in a truly ego-transcending manner—an entirely life-positive and non-suppressive manner that is both pleasurable and supportive of the Spiritual process in His Company.

The transcending of egoic involvement with "money, food, and sex" is a matter that relates to the beginnings of (or preparation for) real Spiritual practice. But the necessity for ego-transcendence does not end there. In His years of Teaching and Revelation, Avatar Adi Da Revealed that the ego is still present, in one form or another, in all the possible varieties of Spiritual attainment short of Most Perfect Divine Enlightenment. The word "Enlightenment" is used by different people and in different traditions with various different meanings. In Avatar Adi Da's language, "Enlightenment" (which He sometimes modifies, for the sake of clarifying His meaning, as "Most Perfect Divine Enlightenment", and which is synonymous with "Divine Self-Realization", "Real-God-Realization", and "seventh stage Realization") specifically means that the process of ego-transcendence has been entirely completed, relative to all the dimensions of the being. In other words, the ego has been transcended in three distinct phases—first at the physical (or gross) level (the level of "money, food, and sex"), then at the subtle level (the level of internal visions, auditions, and all kinds of mystical experience), and finally at the causal level (the root-level of conscious existence, wherein the sense of "I" and "other", or the subject-object dichotomy, seems to arise in Consciousness).

The complete process of ego-transcendence is extraordinarily profound and can only proceed on the basis of all the foundation disciplines and an ever-increasing heart-surrender to the Blessing-Transmission of Adi Da Samraj. Then, progressively, there is a transformation of view, a "positive disillusionment" (in Adi Da's Words) with each phase of egoity—until there is Most Perfect Divine Enlightenment (or "Open Eyes"), the Realization of Consciousness Itself as the Single Love-Blissful Reality and Source of existence.

Thus, the Way of Adidam truly represents an extraordinary and unique Offering to humankind. It is the Way Given by the Primal Divine Realizer and Revealer of Most Perfect Divine Enlightenment. He Transmits the Divinely Enlightened State, and He has the Power to Draw His devotees into that Perfectly Love-Blissful State. Such great statements about Avatar Adi Da Samraj are not something to be either accepted or rejected as a matter of belief. Rather, they are His Free Self-Confession to you—and His invitation to you to fall into His Divine Embrace.

A Testimony of Spiritual Practice

The process of the Way of Adidam unfolds by Avatar Adi Da's Grace, according to the depth of surrender and response in each devotee. One of the most extraordinary living testimonies to the Greatness and Truth of the Way of Adidam is one of Avatar Adi Da's longtime devotees, whose renunciate name is Ruchira Adidama Quandra Tripura Sukhavani Naitauba. Adidama Quandra Tripura has totally consecrated herself to Avatar Adi Da and lives always in His Sphere, in a relationship of unique intimacy and service. By her profound love of, and most exemplary surrender to, her Divine Heart-Master, she has become combined with Him at a unique depth. She manifests the signs of deep and constant immersion in His Divine Being, both in meditation and daily life. Adidama Quandra Tripura is a member of the Ruchira Sannyasin Order (the senior cultural authority within the gathering of Avatar Adi Da's devotees), practicing in the ultimate stages of the Way of Adidam.

Through a process of more than twenty years of intense testing, Avatar Adi Da has been able to lead Adidama Quandra Tripura to the threshold of Divine Enlightenment. The profound and ecstatic relationship with Avatar Adi Da that Adidama Quandra Tripura has come to know can be felt in this intimate letter of devotional confession to Him:

RUCHIRA ADIDAMA QUANDRA TRIPURA : Bhagavan Love-Ananda, Supreme and Divine Person, Real-God-Body of Love,

I rest in Your Constant and Perfect Love-Embrace, with no need but to forever worship You. Suddenly in love, Mastered at heart, always with my head at Your Supreme and Holy Feet, I am beholding and recognizing Your "Bright" Divine Person. My Beloved, You so "Brightly" Descend and utterly Convert this heart, mind, body, and breath, from

Ruchira Adidama Quandra
Tripura Sukhavani Naitauba
with Avatar Adi Da Samraj, 1999

separate self to the "Bhava" of Your Love-Bliss-Happiness.

Supreme Lord Ruchira, the abandonment of the contracted personality, the relinquishment of ego-bondage to the world, and the profound purification and release of ego-limitations—all brought about by Your Grace, throughout the years since I first came to You—has culminated in a great comprehensive force of one-pointed devotion to You and a great certainty in the Inherent Sufficiency of Realization Itself. The essence of my practice is to always remain freely submitted and centralized in You—the Condition Prior to all bondage, all modification, and all illusion.

My Beloved Lord Ruchira, You have Moved me to renounce all egoic "bonding" with conditionally manifested others, conditionally manifested worlds, and conditionally manifested self, to enter into the depths of this "in-love" and utter devotion to You. Finding You has led to a deep urge to abandon all superficiality and to simply luxuriate in Your Divine Body and Person. All separation is shattered in Your Divine Love-Bliss-"Bhava". Your Infusion is Utter. I feel You everywhere.

I am Drawn, by Grace of Your Spiritual Presence, into profound meditative Contemplation of Your Divine State. Sometimes, when I am entering into these deep states of meditation, I remain vaguely aware of the body, and particularly of the breath and the heartbeat. I feel the heart and lungs slow down. Then I am sometimes aware of my breath and heartbeat being suspended in a state of Yogic sublimity. Then there is no awareness of body, no awareness of mind, no perceptual awareness, and no conceptual awareness. There is only abiding in Contemplation of You in Your Domain of Consciousness Itself. And, when I resume association with the body and begin once again to hear my breath and heartbeat, I feel the remarkable Power of Your Great Samadhi. I feel no necessity for anything, and I feel Your Capability to Bless and Change and Meditate all. I can feel how this entrance into objectless worship of You as Consciousness Itself (allowing this Abiding to deepen ever so profoundly, by utter submission of separate self to You) establishes me in a different relationship to everything that arises.

My Beloved Bhagavan, Love-Ananda, I have Found You. Now, by Your Grace, I am able to behold You and live in this constant Embrace. This is my Joy and Happiness and the Yoga of ego-renunciation I engage. [October 11, 1997]

Inherent in this confession is the certainty that lasting happiness cannot be found in the things of the world, all of which change and die. This is a crucial understanding—which is at the foundation of real religious life, and which grows over time as one advances in the Spiritual process.

AVATAR ADI DA SAMRAJ: Absolutely NOTHING conditional is satisfactory. Everything conditional disappears—everything. This fact should move the heart to cling to Me, to resort to Me, to take refuge in Me. This is why people become devotees of Mine. This is the reason for the religious life. The unsatisfactoriness of conditional existence requires resort to the Divine Source, and the Realization of the Divine Source-Condition. [August 9, 1997]

Standing at the Threshold

In the unfolding Revelation of Avatar Adi Da's bodily human Lifetime, an Event of the most profound significance occurred on April 12, 2000. At the time, the Divine Avatar was staying for a time on Lopez Island, one of the San Juan Islands off the northern coast of the state of Washington. On the evening of April 12, Avatar Adi Da Samraj entered into a severe physical and Yogic crisis, which even seemed to threaten His bodily survival. He later confirmed that He had, indeed, been on the "way out" of the earthly realm, but the process stopped just before physical death became inevitable. With His "return" to bodily existence, Avatar Adi Da's physical Body had become profoundly Spiritualized, translucent. His Transmission of Divine Love and Blessing became tangibly even more powerful than before. By His own Confession, since that Event at Lopez Island, Avatar Adi Da's bodily (human) Form has been Standing at the very Threshold between the Divine Domain of Infinite Love-Bliss-"Brightness" and all the domains of conditional manifestation. He remains in this world bodily, but He is also on the "other side". Thus, to an even greater degree than before, the physical Body of Avatar Adi Da Samraj is an unbelievably Potent Conductor of His Divine Blessing to all who approach Him with an open heart.

Finding Real Happiness

This book is Avatar Adi Da's invitation to you to come to know Him—by freely considering His words, and feeling their impact on your life and heart. Avatar Adi Da Himself has never been satisfied with anything conditional. He has never been satisfied with anything less than Real, Permanent, Absolute Happiness—even in the midst of the inevitable sufferings of life. And that Happiness is What He is Offering to you.

The heart has a question.
The heart must be Satisfied.
Without that Satisfaction—Which is necessarily Spiritual in Nature—there is no Real Happiness.

The contraction of the heart is what you are suffering.
It is the ego.
The egoic life is a search—founded upon (and initiated by) the self-contraction of the total body-mind.
The egoic life is a self-caused search to be relieved of the distress of self-reduced, self-diminished, even utterly self-destroyed Love-Bliss.
Love-Bliss gone, non-existent, unknown—just this pumping, agitated, psycho-physical thing.

The ego-"I" does not know What It <u>Is</u> That Is Happening.
You are just "hanging out" for a while, until "it" drops dead.
It is not good enough.
Therefore, I Advise you to begin to be profoundly religious, and not waste any time about it.

You must Realize the Spiritual Condition of Existence Itself . . . .
You cannot be sane if you think there is only flesh, only materiality, only grossness.
Such thinking is not fully "natural", not enough.
There is "Something" you are not accounting for.
Be open to "Whatever" That Is.
You must look into this. [Hridaya Rosary]

Avatar Adi Da Samraj's Teaching-Word: The "Source-Texts" of Adidam

For twenty-seven years (from 1972 to 1999), Avatar Adi Da Samraj devoted Himself tirelessly to Teaching those who came to Him. Even before He formally began to Teach in 1972, He had already written the earliest versions of two of His primary Texts—His "liturgical drama" (*The Mummery*) and His Spiritual Autobiography (*The Knee Of Listening*). Then, when He opened the doors of His first Ashram in Hollywood (on April 25, 1972), He initiated a vast twenty-seven-year "conversation" with the thousands of people who approached Him during that period of time—a "conversation" that included thousands of hours of sublime and impassioned Discourse and thousands of pages of profound and exquisite Writing. And the purpose of that "conversation" was to fully communicate the Truth for Real.

Both His Speech and His Writing were conducted as a kind of living "laboratory". He was constantly asking to hear His devotees' questions and their responses to His Written and Spoken Word. He was constantly calling His devotees to <u>live</u> what He was Teaching and discover its Truth in their own experience—not merely to passively accept it as dogma. He was constantly testing whether His communication on any particular subject was complete and detailed enough or whether He needed to say more. And everything He said and wrote was a spontaneous expression of His own direct Awareness of Reality—never a merely theoretical or speculative proposition, never a statement merely inherited from traditional sources.

This immense outpouring of Revelation and Instruction came to completion in the years 1997-1999. During that period, Avatar

Adi Da Samraj created a series of twenty-three books that He designated as the "Source-Texts" of Adidam. He incorporated into these books His most essential Writings and Discourses from all the preceding years, as well as many new Writings and Discourses that had never been published previously. His magnificent "Source-Texts" are thus His Eternal Message to all. They contain His complete Revelation of Truth, and (together with the "Supportive Texts", in which Avatar Adi Da Gives further detailed Instruction relative to the functional, practical, relational, and cultural disciplines of the Way of Adidam) they give His fully detailed description of the entire process of Awakening, culminating in Divine Enlightenment.

Avatar Adi Da's twenty-three "Source-Texts" are not simply a series of books each of which is entirely distinct from all the others. Rather, they form an intricately interwoven fabric. Each book contains some material found in no other "Source-Text", some material shared with certain other "Source-Texts", and some material included in all twenty-three of the "Source-Texts". (The three Texts shared by all twenty-three books are "Do Not Misunderstand Me", "My Divine Disclosure", and "The Heart-Summary Of Adidam". Each of these Texts has a particular function and message that is essential to every one of the books.) Thus, to read Avatar Adi Da's "Source-Texts" is to engage a special kind of study (similar to the practice of repeating a mantra), in which certain Texts are repeatedly read, such that they penetrate one's being even more profoundly and take on deeper significance by being read in a variety of different contexts. Furthermore, each of the "Source-Texts" of Adidam is thereby a complete and self-contained Argument. Altogether, to study Avatar Adi Da's "Source-Texts" is to enter into an "eternal conversation" with Him, in which different meanings emerge at different times—always appropriate to the current moment in one's life and experience.

At the conclusion of His paramount "Source-Text", *The Dawn Horse Testament*, Avatar Adi Da Samraj makes His own passionate Confession of the Impulse that led Him to create His twenty-three "Source-Texts".

Now I Have, By All My "Crazy" Means, Revealed My One and Many Divine Secrets As The Great Person Of The Heart. For Your Sake, I Made My Every Work and Word. And Now, By Every Work and Word I Made, I Have Entirely Confessed (and Showed) Myself—and Always Freely, and Even As A Free Man, In The "Esoteric" Language Of Intimacy and Ecstasy, Openly Worded To You (and To all). Even Now (and Always), By This (My Avatarically Self-Revealed Divine Word Of Heart), I Address every Seeming Separate being (and each one As The Heart Itself), Because It Is Necessary That all beings, Even The Entire Cosmic Domain Of Seeming Separate beings, Be (In all times and places) Called To Wisdom and The Heart.

Capitalization and Punctuation in the "Source-Texts" of Avatar Adi Da Samraj

Speaking and Writing in the twentieth and twenty-first centuries, Avatar Adi Da Samraj has used the English language as the medium for His Communication. Over the years of His Teaching-Work, Avatar Adi Da developed a thoroughly original manner of employing English as a sacred language. (He also includes some Sanskrit terminology in His Teaching vocabulary, in order to supplement the relatively undeveloped sacred vocabulary of English.)

Avatar Adi Da's unique use of English is evident not only with respect to vocabulary, but also with respect to capitalization and punctuation.

Vocabulary. A glossary is included at the end of this book (pp. 322-59), where specialized terms (both English terms and terms derived from Sanskrit) are defined.

Capitalization. Avatar Adi Da frequently capitalizes words that would not ordinarily be capitalized in English—and such capitalized words include not only nouns, but also pronouns, verbs, adjectives, adverbs, and even articles and prepositions. By such capitalization, He is indicating that the word refers (either inherently, or by virtue of the context) to the Unconditional Divine Reality, rather than the conditional (or worldly) reality. For example:

If there is no escape from (or no Way out of) the corner (or the "centered" trap) of ego-"I"—the heart goes mad, and the body-mind becomes more and more "dark" (bereft of the Indivisible and Inherently Free Light of the Self-Evident, and Self-Evidently Divine, Love-Bliss That Is Reality Itself). ["Do Not Misunderstand Me"]

Avatar Adi Da's chosen conventions of capitalization vary in different "Source-Texts" and in different sections of a given "Source-Text". In certain "Source-Texts" (notably *The Dawn Horse Testament Of The Ruchira Avatar, The Heart Of The Dawn Horse Testament Of The Ruchira Avatar,* and the various Parts of the other "Source-Texts" that are excerpted from *The Dawn Horse Testament Of The Ruchira Avatar*), Avatar Adi Da employs a highly unusual convention of capitalization, in which the overwhelming majority of all words are capitalized, and only those words that indicate the egoic (or dualistic) point of view are left lower-cased. This capitalization convention (which Avatar Adi Da has worked out to an extraordinarily subtle degree—in ways that are often startling) is in itself a Teaching device, intended to communicate His fundamental Revelation that "There Is Only Real God", and that only the ego (or the dualistic or separative point of view) prevents us from living and Realizing that Truth. For example:

Therefore, For My Every Devotee, all conditions Must Be Aligned and Yielded In Love With Me—or Else any object or any other Will Be The Cause Of Heart-Stress, self-Contraction, Dissociation, Clinging, Boredom, Doubt, The Progressive Discomfort Of Diminished Love-Bliss, and All The Forgetfulness Of Grace and Truth and Happiness Itself. [Ruchira Avatara Hridaya-Tantra Yoga]

Note that "and" and "or" are lower-cased—because these conjunctions are (here, and in most contexts) primal expressions of the point of view of duality. Also note that "all conditions", "any object", "<u>any</u> other", and "self-" are lower-cased, while "Heart-Stress", "Contraction", "Dissociation", "Clinging," "Boredom", "Doubt", "Discomfort", "Diminished", and "Forgetfulness" are capitalized. Avatar Adi Da is telling us that unpleasant or apparently "negative" states are not inherently egoic. It is only the presumption of duality and separateness—as expressed by such words as "conditions", "object", "other", and "self"—that is egoic.

Punctuation. Because of the inevitable complexity of much of His Communication, Avatar Adi Da has developed the conventions of punctuation (commas, dashes, and parentheses) to an extraordinary degree. This allows Him to clearly articulate complex sentences in such a way that His intended meaning can be expressed with utmost precision—free of vagueness, ambiguity, or unclarity. Many of His sentences contain parenthetical definitions or modifying phrases as a way of achieving unmistakable clarity of meaning. For example:

The Apparently individual (or Separate) self Is Not a "spark" (or an Eternal fraction) Of Self-Radiant Divinity, and Somehow Complete (or Whole) In itself. [<u>Real</u> God <u>Is</u> The Indivisible Oneness Of Unbroken Light]

Another punctuation convention relates to the use of quotation marks. Avatar Adi Da sometimes uses quotation marks in accordance with standard convention, to indicate the sense of "so to speak":

Make the contact with Me that gets you to "stick" to Me like glue. Your "sticking" to Me is what must happen. [Hridaya Rosary]

In other instances, He uses quotation marks to indicate that a word or phrase is being used with a particular technical meaning that differs from common usage:

During <u>all</u> of My present Lifetime (of Avataric Divine Incarnation), the "<u>Bright</u>" has <u>always</u> been My Realization—and the "<u>Thumbs</u>" and My own "Radical" Understanding have <u>always</u> been My Way in the "Bright".

"Bright", "Thumbs" (referring to a specific form of the Infusion of Avatar Adi Da's Divine Spirit-Current in the body-mind), and "Radical" are all used with specific technical meanings here (as defined in the Glossary).

Finally, Avatar Adi Da also makes extensive use of underlining to indicate special emphasis on certain words (or phrases, or even entire sentences):

The <u>only</u> true religion is the religion that <u>Realizes</u> Truth. The <u>only</u> true science is the science that <u>Knows</u> Truth. The <u>only</u> true man or woman (or being of any kind) is one that <u>Surrenders</u> to Truth. The only true world is one that <u>Embodies</u> Truth. And the only True (and <u>Real</u>) God Is the One Reality (or Condition of Being) That <u>Is</u> Truth. ["Do Not Misunderstand <u>Me</u>"]

The Titles and Subtitles of The Twenty-Three "Source-Texts" of Avatar Adi Da Samraj

The twenty-three "Source-Texts" of Avatar Adi Da Samraj include:

(1) an opening series of five books on the fundamentals of the Way of Adidam (*The Five Books Of The Heart Of The Adidam Revelation*)

(2) an extended series of seventeen books covering the principal aspects of the Way of Adidam in detail (*The Seventeen Companions Of The True Dawn Horse*)

(3) Avatar Adi Da's paramount "Source-Text" summarizing the entire course of the Way of Adidam (*The Dawn Horse Testament*)

The basic content of each "Source-Text" is summarily described by Avatar Adi Da in the title and subtitle of each book. Thus, the following list of titles and subtitles indicates the vast scope and the artful interconnectedness of His twenty-three "Source-Texts". (For brief descriptions of each "Source-Text", please see "The Sacred Literature of Avatar Adi Da Samraj", pp. 360-70.)

The Five Books Of The Heart Of The Adidam Revelation

BOOK ONE

Aham Da Asmi
(Beloved, I <u>Am</u> Da)

The "Late-Time" Avataric Revelation Of The True and Spiritual
Divine Person (The egoless Personal Presence Of Reality
and Truth, Which <u>Is</u> The Only <u>Real</u> God)

BOOK TWO

Ruchira Avatara Gita
(The Way Of The Divine Heart-Master)

The "Late-Time" Avataric Revelation Of The Great Secret Of
The Divinely Self-Revealed Way That Most Perfectly Realizes
The True and Spiritual Divine Person (The egoless Personal
Presence Of Reality and Truth, Which <u>Is</u> The Only <u>Real</u> God)

BOOK THREE

Da Love-Ananda Gita
(The Free Gift Of The Divine Love-Bliss)

The "Late-Time" Avataric Revelation Of The Great Means
To Worship and To Realize The True and Spiritual Divine Person
(The egoless Personal Presence Of Reality and Truth,
Which <u>Is</u> The Only <u>Real</u> God)

BOOK FOUR

Hridaya Rosary
(Four Thorns Of Heart-Instruction)

The "Late-Time" Avataric Revelation Of The Universally Tangible
Divine Spiritual Body, Which Is The Supreme Agent
Of The Great Means To Worship and To Realize The True
and Spiritual Divine Person (The egoless Personal Presence
Of Reality and Truth, Which <u>Is</u> The Only <u>Real</u> God)

BOOK FIVE

Eleutherios
(The <u>Only</u> Truth That Sets The Heart Free)

The "Late-Time" Avataric Revelation Of The "Perfect Practice"
Of The Great Means To Worship and To Realize The True and
Spiritual Divine Person (The egoless Personal Presence
Of Reality and Truth, Which <u>Is</u> The Only <u>Real</u> God)

The Seventeen Companions Of The True Dawn Horse

BOOK ONE
Real Is The Indivisible Oneness Of Unbroken Light

Reality, Truth, and The "Non-Creator" God
In The True World-Religion Of Adidam

BOOK TWO
The Truly Human New World-Culture Of Unbroken Real-God-Man

The Eastern Versus The Western Traditional Cultures
Of Mankind, and The Unique New Non-Dual Culture
Of The True World-Religion Of Adidam

BOOK THREE
The Only Complete Way To Realize The Unbroken Light Of Real God

An Introductory Overview Of The "Radical" Divine Way
Of The True World-Religion Of Adidam

BOOK FOUR
The Knee Of Listening

The Early-Life Ordeal and The "Radical"
Spiritual Realization Of The Ruchira Avatar

BOOK FIVE
The Divine Siddha-Method Of The Ruchira Avatar

The Divine Way Of Adidam Is An ego-Transcending
Relationship, Not An ego-Centric Technique

BOOK SIX
The Mummery

A Parable Of The Divine True Love

Book Thirteen
What, Where, When, How, Why, and <u>Who</u> To Remember To Be Happy
A Simple Explanation Of The Divine Way Of Adidam
(For Children, and <u>Everyone</u> Else)

Book Fourteen
Santosha Adidam
The Essential Summary Of The Divine Way Of Adidam

Book Fifteen
The Lion Sutra
The "Perfect Practice" Teachings In The Divine Way Of Adidam

Book Sixteen
The Overnight Revelation Of Conscious Light
The "My House" Discourses
On The Indivisible Tantra Of Adidam

Book Seventeen
The Basket Of Tolerance
The Perfect Guide To Perfectly <u>Unified</u> Understanding
Of The One and Great Tradition Of Mankind,
and Of The Divine Way Of Adidam As The Perfect <u>Completing</u>
Of The One and Great Tradition Of Mankind

*The Dawn Horse Testament
Of The Ruchira Avatar*

The Dawn Horse Testament Of The Ruchira Avatar
The "Testament Of Secrets" Of The Divine World-Teacher,
Ruchira Avatar Adi Da Samraj

Camera Illuminata

The "Bright"-Field Photography of Avatar Adi Da Samraj

At the same time that He was completing His Work to create a complete verbal Teaching in His "Source-Texts", Avatar Adi Da Samraj started taking black-and-white photographs as another potent means of communicating His message about Reality. He calls the collected body of His photographic work His "Camera Illuminata" collection. The cover image of each of His twenty-three "Source-Texts" includes a central image and a border image, both of which are photographs taken by Avatar Adi Da Samraj (and specifically chosen by Him as an image appropriate to that particular "Source-Text"). "Camera Illuminata" means "Bright Room", in contrast to the traditional term "camera obscura" (which literally means "dark room"). Thus, instead of representing the world from the "dark" point of view (or the presumption that dying matter is all there is to reality), the Camera Illuminata of Adi Da Samraj Reveals the world as a "Bright" (or Divinely Self-Radiant) Field.

Avatar Adi Da's "Bright"-Field photographic images are one of His means for conveying His Spiritual Transmission and Blessing— for the subject of Avatar Adi Da's photography is not the world as we see it, but the world as the "Bright" Field of Reality that He sees. His photography would transport us beyond our ordinary habits of thinking and perceiving into the Divine Light, in Which there is no sense of separation, otherness, or limitation.

AVATAR ADI DA SAMRAJ: From the conventional point of view, a photographer only makes pictures of conventional reality, of light falling on objects, as if the solid reality were the only reality. But neither the fixed separate point of view nor the apparently solid objective world is the Fundamental Reality. The Divine Conscious Light Is the Fundamental Reality Of Existence.

Avatar Adi Da's photographic images communicate the non-dual perception of Reality via a unique process, which He describes as His "inherently egoless participatory relationship" with the subjects of His photographs (both human and non-human). Thus, His photography transcends the conventions of "self" and "other", or "subject" and "object".

AVATAR ADI DA SAMRAJ: Out of this process, images can be made that Reveal Reality, rather than merely communicating the conventions of "ego" and "other".

Therefore, even the viewing of Adi Da's Camera Illuminata images is an inherently participatory event. That is to say, His photographs, like all great art, place a demand upon us to go beyond the ordinary fixed point of view. They are a call to go beyond our ordinary limits—for each of His images is a communication of the Divine "Brightness", transforming our ordinary perception of the world into sacred occasion.

Avatar Adi Da Samraj photographing in the California redwoods

When viewed in its entirety, Avatar Adi Da's Camera Illuminata collection is an ecstatic Revelation-Transmission of the Divine Truth that He has Come to Reveal and Teach to humankind. There is extraordinary beauty to be appreciated in Avatar Adi Da's photographs, but the real purpose of His artistry is to bring Light into our lives, to literally En-Light-en us—to Liberate us from the un-Illumined and mortal vision of egoity. By offering us His Camera Illuminata, Adi Da Samraj would have us discover that "Bright-Field", that Non-separate Reality, in Which the ever-changing dualities of light and darkness rise and fall.

AVATAR ADI DA SAMRAJ: In My approach to making photographic images, I want to convey the Truth of Reality—the Truth of the Inherently egoless, Non-dual Subjective Light. I am trying to convey My own Revelation of the Nature of Reality through the artifice of visual images.

The border image on the cover of this book is a photograph taken by Avatar Adi Da Samraj. He refers to this photograph as an image of "True Water", which is one of His poetic descriptions for Consciousness Itself as the "Medium" in which all phenomena arise (and of which they are all modifications).

An Overview of the
Da Love-Ananda Gita
(The Free Gift Of The Divine Love-Bliss)

This extraordinary Revelation-Text is the Joyous Song (or "Gita", in Sanskrit) of Happiness, Freedom, and Love-Bliss (or "Love-Ananda"). And Its Great Singer is the True and Spiritual Divine Person—Manifested, by Man-Born Descent, as the Divine World-Teacher, Ruchira Avatar Adi Da Samraj.

"Love-Ananda" is one of Avatar Adi Da's Sacred Names. It uniquely communicates His Embrace of all beings—East and West—by uniting the English word "Love" and the Sanskrit word "Ananda". Avatar Adi Da Samraj Declares, in His *Da Love-Ananda Gita*, that He <u>Is</u> "Love-Ananda", He <u>Is</u> "the Very Person of the 'Bright' Divine Love-Bliss".

Inherent in every being is a movement toward Love-Bliss. That desire for Happiness, however, is frustrated by the all-too-apparent limitations of conditional existence. Every being dies, every being suffers, all apparent pleasures are merely temporary distractions from inevitable mortality. This undeniable reality has led many who have deeply considered such matters to seek to go beyond the desire for conditional pleasure—and to seek Happiness, or Love-Bliss, apart from the mortal human world. Such is the traditional foundation of religious and Spiritual endeavor.

In contrast to traditional religious and Spiritual efforts, Avatar Adi Da Love-Ananda Reveals that <u>all</u> seeking is necessarily fruitless, for seeking entails an always present denial of Love-Bliss-Happiness Itself. In every moment that you <u>seek</u> Happiness, you are putting off until some future moment the actual <u>Realization</u> of Happiness. Avatar Adi Da Love-Ananda summarizes this fundamental point with the aphorism: "You cannot <u>become</u> Happy, you can only <u>Be</u> Happy." The Way to <u>Be</u> Happy is what Avatar Adi Da Love-Ananda Reveals in this great "Source-Text".

As with each of Avatar Adi Da Love-Ananda's twenty-three Divine "Source-Texts", the *Da Love-Ananda Gita* begins with His First Word, "Do Not Misunderstand <u>Me</u>—I Am <u>Not</u> 'Within' <u>you</u>, but you <u>Are</u> In <u>Me</u>, and I Am <u>Not</u> a Mere 'Man' in the 'Middle' of Mankind, but All of Mankind Is Surrounded, and Pervaded, and Blessed By <u>Me</u>". In this preliminary Essay, Avatar Adi Da Love-Ananda explains that His open Confession of Real-God-Realization is not to be misapprehended as a claim of the "Status" of the "Creator"-God of conventional religious belief, but, rather, His Divine Self-Confession is to be understood and appreciated as a Free Demonstration of the Fulfillment of esoteric Spiritual practice—a Demonstration of the Most Perfectly Non-Dual Realization of Reality Itself. By virtue of this Free Demonstration, Avatar Adi Da Love-Ananda makes clear that Most Perfect Real-God-Realization (or Divine Enlightenment) is the ultimate Potential and Destiny of <u>all</u> beings.

The Prologue of the *Da Love-Ananda Gita*, "My Divine Disclosure" (also, like "First Word", found in all twenty-three "Source-Texts"), is a poetic epitome of Avatar Adi Da Love-Ananda's Divine Self-Revelation. It is His Call to every being to turn to Him at heart and practice the life of devotional surrender in Real God.

Part One of the *Da Love-Ananda Gita*, "The Plight Of The Divine Heart-Husband (The Forty-Seven Divine Statements Of The Ruchira Avatar, Adi Da Samraj)", is derived from the titles of the prologue, forty-five chapters, and epilogue of *The Dawn Horse Testament Of The Ruchira Avatar* (Which Avatar Adi Da Love-Ananda Describes as "The Epitome, or First and Principal Text" among the twenty-three Divine "Source-Texts" of Adidam). These "Forty-Seven Divine Statements" review the entire Way of Adidam, from its rudimentary beginnings to Divine Enlightenment.

Part Two of the *Da Love-Ananda Gita*, "I (<u>Alone</u>) <u>Am</u> The Adidam Revelation", is Avatar Adi Da Love-Ananda's full elucidation of the uniqueness of His Revelation of the seventh stage Realization. In this remarkable essay, Avatar Adi Da Love-Ananda examines His own Course of Divine Re-Awakening in order to Demonstrate how the two primary divisions of the Great

Tradition—the Emanationist (or absorptive mystical) Way (associated with the first five stages of life) and the non-Emanationist (or Transcendentalist) Way (associated with the sixth stage of life)—are, in Truth, only different aspects of the great seven-stage process of the Most Perfect Realization of Love-Bliss-Happiness Itself.

In Part Three of the *Da Love-Ananda Gita*, "The Search for Truth Is Absurd and Unnecessary", Avatar Adi Da Love-Ananda Speaks about the true origin of suffering, while Revealing the Heart-Instruction implicit in His Name:

AVATAR ADI DA SAMRAJ: Love-Bliss Is Reality Itself. If you withdraw from Love-Bliss, or if you withhold yourself from Love-Bliss, or if you deny Love-Bliss, or if you merely seek Love-Bliss—you, inevitably (and by that very act), suffer. . . . If you withdraw from My always present-time Divine Self-Revelation (or Divine Self-Manifestation) of Love-Bliss, you suffer. Therefore, do not withdraw from Me, and do not seek Me, but, simply (devotionally), recognize Me, and (by that simple devotional recognition) be devotionally responsive to Me, always Love-Bliss-"Bright", Divinely Self-Revealed before you.

In Part Four of the *Da Love-Ananda Gita*, "The Heart-Summary Of Adidam" (a brief Essay that is included in all twenty-three "Source-Texts"), Avatar Adi Da Love-Ananda summarizes the profound implications of His Statement that the Way of Adidam is the Way of Devotion to Him "As Self-Condition, rather than As exclusively Objective Other".

The one hundred and eight verses of Part Five form the principal Text of the *Da Love-Ananda Gita*. In these verses, Avatar Adi Da Love-Ananda Sings the Miraculous Revelation that Real God—the Ultimate Source and Nature and Person of all and All—is Realizable. To Give this Gift of Real-God-Realization is the very Purpose of His Avataric Incarnation during this "late-time" of dark despair. Avatar Adi Da Love-Ananda is Himself the Great Means, the Sublime Gift, and the Perfect Realization of the Eternal "Bright" Divine Self-Condition. Realization of Avatar Adi Da Love-Ananda is Realization of Perfect Love-Bliss—the only Real Freedom.

This *Da Love-Ananda Gita* is the fundamental Instruction Avatar Adi Da Love-Ananda Gives to all who formally embrace the Real-God-Realizing Way of Adidam. For all congregations and for all stages of practice in the Way of Adidam, the foundation Principle is always the same—it is the simple and direct practice known as "Ruchira Avatara Bhakti Yoga".

Ruchira Avatara Bhakti Yoga is the Spiritual discipline (or "Yoga") of devotion (or "Bhakti") to the Ruchira Avatar, Adi Da Love-Ananda Samraj. Ruchira Avatara Bhakti Yoga is effectively practiced only in active response to the Gift of devotionally recognizing Avatar Adi Da Love-Ananda as the Very Divine Person. That devotional recognition and responsive practice is the foundation of the esoteric process of Real-God-Realization—it is the very means by which Avatar Adi Da Love-Ananda's Realization is (ultimately) duplicated in His devotee.

Part Six of the *Da Love-Ananda Gita*, "Ruchira Avatara Bhakti Sara (The Essence of Devotion To Me)", consists of fifty-four brief verses, in which Avatar Adi Da Love-Ananda summarizes the right and effective practice of Ruchira Avatara Bhakti Yoga.

Finally, in the ecstatic Epilogue, "What Will you Do If you Love Me?", Avatar Adi Da Love-Ananda Calls forth the love-response of all who truly turn to Him, through His Ecstatic Speech.

Altogether, the *Da Love-Ananda Gita* is Avatar Adi Da Love-Ananda's Perfect Revelation and Offering to you (and to all beings) of the simplest (and only complete) Way to Realize Love-Bliss-Happiness Itself.

Da Love-Ananda Gita
(The Free Gift Of The Divine Love-Bliss)

RUCHIRA AVATAR ADI DA SAMRAJ
Los Angeles, 2000

Do Not Misunderstand <u>Me</u>—
I Am <u>Not</u> "Within" <u>you</u>,
but you <u>Are</u> In <u>Me</u>,
and I Am <u>Not</u> a Mere "Man"
in the "Middle" of Mankind,
but All of Mankind Is Surrounded,
and Pervaded, and Blessed By <u>Me</u>

This Essay has been written by Avatar Adi Da Samraj as His Personal Introduction to each volume of His "Source-Texts". Its purpose is to help you to understand His great Confessions rightly, and not interpret His Words from a conventional point of view, as limited cultic statements made by an ego. His Description of what "cultism" <u>really</u> is is an astounding and profound Critique of mankind's entire religious, scientific, and social search. In "Do Not Misunderstand <u>Me</u>", Avatar Adi Da is directly inviting you to inspect and relinquish the ego's motive to glorify itself and to refuse What is truly Great. Only by understanding this fundamental ego-fault can one really receive the Truth that Adi Da Samraj Reveals in this Book and in His Wisdom-Teaching altogether. And it is because this fault is so ingrained and so largely unconscious that Avatar Adi Da has placed "Do Not Misunderstand <u>Me</u>" at the beginning of each of His "Source-Texts", so that, each time you begin to read one of His twenty-three "Source-Texts", you may be refreshed and strengthened in your understanding of the right orientation and approach to Him and His Heart-Word.

Yes! There is <u>no</u> religion, <u>no</u> Way of God, <u>no</u> Way of Divine Realization, <u>no</u> Way of Enlightenment, and <u>no</u> Way of Liberation that is Higher or Greater than Truth Itself.

Indeed, there is <u>no</u> religion, <u>no</u> science, <u>no</u> man or woman, <u>no</u> conditionally manifested being of any kind, <u>no</u> world (<u>any</u> "where"), and <u>no</u> "God" (or "God"-Idea) that is Higher or Greater than Truth Itself.

Therefore, <u>no</u> ego-"I" (or presumed separate, and, necessarily, actively separative, and, at best, only Truth-<u>seeking</u>, being or "thing") is (it<u>self</u>) Higher or Greater than Truth Itself. And <u>no</u> ego-"I" is (it<u>self</u>) even Equal to Truth Itself. And no ego-"I" is (it<u>self</u>) even (now, or ever) <u>Able</u> to Realize Truth Itself—because, necessarily, Truth (Itself) Inherently Transcends (or <u>Is</u> That Which <u>Is</u> Higher and Greater than) <u>every</u> one (him<u>self</u> or her<u>self</u>) and <u>every</u> "thing" (it<u>self</u>). Therefore, it is <u>only</u> in the transcending (or the "radical" Process of Going Beyond the root, the cause, and the act) of egoity it<u>self</u> (or of presumed separateness, and of performed separativeness, and of even <u>all</u> ego-based seeking for Truth Itself) that Truth (Itself) <u>Is</u> Realized (<u>As</u> It <u>Is</u>, Utterly Beyond the ego-"I" it<u>self</u>).

Truth (Itself) <u>Is</u> That Which Is Always Already The Case. That Which <u>Is</u> The Case (Always, and Always Already) <u>Is</u> (necessarily) Reality. Therefore, Reality (Itself) <u>Is</u> Truth, and Reality (Itself) Is the <u>Only</u> Truth.

Reality (Itself) <u>Is</u> the <u>Only</u>, and (necessarily) Non-Separate (or All-and-all-Including, <u>and</u> All-and-all-Transcending), One and "What" That <u>Is</u>. Because It <u>Is</u> All and all, and because It <u>Is</u> (Also) <u>That</u> Which Transcends (or <u>Is</u> Higher and Greater than) All and all, Reality (Itself)—Which <u>Is</u> Truth (Itself), or That Which Is The Case (Always, and Always Already)—<u>Is</u> the One and Only <u>Real</u> God. Therefore, Reality (Itself) Is (necessarily) the One and Great Subject of true religion, and Reality (<u>Itself</u>) <u>Is</u> (necessarily) the One and Great Way of <u>Real</u> God, <u>Real</u> (and True) Divine Realization, <u>Real</u> (and, necessarily, Divine) En-Light-enment, and <u>Real</u> (and, necessarily, Divine) Liberation (from all egoity, all separateness, all separativeness, all fear, and all heartlessness).

The <u>only</u> true religion is the religion that <u>Realizes</u> Truth. The <u>only</u> true science is the science that <u>Knows</u> Truth. The <u>only</u> true man or woman (or being of any kind) is one that <u>Surrenders</u> to Truth. The only true world is one that <u>Embodies</u> Truth. And the only True (and <u>Real</u>) God Is the One Reality (or Condition of Being) That <u>Is</u> Truth. Therefore, <u>Reality</u> (Itself)—Which <u>Is</u> the One and Only Truth, and (therefore, necessarily) the One and Only Real God—<u>must</u> become (or be made) the constantly applied Measure of religion, and of science, and of the world itself, and of even <u>all</u> of the life (and <u>all</u> of the mind) of Man—or else religion, and science, and the world itself, and even any and every sign of Man <u>inevitably</u> (all, and together) become a pattern of illusions, a mere (and even terrible) "problem", the very (and even principal) cause of human seeking, and the perpetual cause of contentious human strife. Indeed, if religion, and science, and the world itself, and the total life (and the total mind) of Man are not Surrendered and Aligned to Reality (Itself), and (Thus) Submitted to be Measured (or made Lawful) by Truth (Itself), and (Thus) Given to the truly devotional (and, thereby, truly ego-transcending) Realization of <u>That</u> Which Is the <u>Only</u> <u>Real</u> God—then, in the presumed "knowledge" of mankind, Reality (Itself), and Truth (Itself), and <u>Real</u> God (or the One and Only Existence, or Being, or Person That <u>Is</u>) <u>ceases</u> <u>to</u> <u>Exist</u>.

Aham Da Asmi. Beloved, I <u>Am</u> Da—the One and Only Person Who <u>Is</u>, the Avatarically Self-Revealed, and Eternally Self-Existing, and Eternally Self-Radiant (or "Bright") Person of Love-Bliss, the One and Only and (Self-Evidently) Divine Self (or Inherently Non-Separate—and, therefore, Inherently egoless—Divine Self-Condition and Source-Condition) of one and of all and of All. I Am Divinely Self-Manifesting (now, and forever hereafter) <u>As</u> the Ruchira Avatar, Adi Da Samraj. I <u>Am</u> the Ruchira Avatar, Adi Da Samraj—the Avataric Divine Realizer, the Avataric Divine Revealer, the Avataric Divine Incarnation, and the Avataric Divine Self-Revelation of Reality <u>Itself</u>. I <u>Am</u> the Avatarically Incarnate Divine Realizer, the Avatarically Incarnate Divine Revealer, and the Avatarically Incarnate Divine Self-Revelation of the One and Only Reality—Which Is the One and Only Truth, and Which Is the One and Only <u>Real</u> God. I <u>Am</u> the Great Avataric Divine Realizer, Avataric Divine Revealer, and Avataric Divine Self-Revelation long-Promised (and long-Expected) for the "late-time"—<u>this</u> (now, and forever hereafter) time, the "dark" epoch of mankind's "Great

Forgetting" (and, <u>potentially</u>, the Great Epoch of mankind's Perpetual Remembering) of Reality, of Truth, of Real God (Which Is the Great, True, and Spiritual Divine Person—or the One and Non-Separate and Indivisible Divine Source-Condition and Self-Condition) of all and All.

Beloved, I <u>Am</u> Da, the Divine Giver, the Giver (of All That I <u>Am</u>) to one, and to all, and to the All of all—now, and forever here-after—here, and every "where" in the Cosmic domain. Therefore, for the Purpose of Revealing the Way of <u>Real</u> God (or of Real and True Divine Realization), and in order to Divinely En-Light-en and Divinely Liberate all and All—I Am (Uniquely, Completely, and Most Perfectly) Avatarically Revealing My Very (and Self-Evidently Divine) Person (and "Bright" Self-Condition) to all and All, by Means of My Avatarically Given Divine Self-Manifestation, <u>As</u> (and by Means of) the Ruchira Avatar, Adi Da Samraj.

In My Avatarically Given Divine Self-Manifestation As the Ruchira Avatar, Adi Da Samraj—I <u>Am</u> the Divine Secret, the Divine Self-Revelation of the <u>Esoteric</u> Truth, the Direct, and all-Completing, and all-Unifying Self-Revelation of <u>Real</u> God.

My Avatarically Given Divine Self-Confessions and My Avatarically Given Divine Teaching-Revelations Are <u>the</u> Great (Final, and all-Completing, and all-Unifying) <u>Esoteric</u> Revelation to mankind—and <u>not</u> a merely exoteric (or conventionally religious, or even ordinary Spiritual, or ego-made, or so-called "cultic") com-munication to public (or merely social) ears.

The greatest opportunity, and the greatest responsibility, of My devotees is Satsang with Me—Which is to live in the Condition of ego-surrendering, ego-forgetting, and (always more and more) ego-transcending devotional relationship to Me, and (Thus and Thereby) to Realize My Avatarically Self-Revealed (and Self-Evidently Divine) Self-Condition, Which <u>Is</u> the Self-Evidently Divine Heart (or Non-Separate Self-Condition and Non-"Different" Source-Condition) of all and All, and Which <u>Is</u> Self-Existing and Self-Radiant Consciousness Itself, but Which is <u>not separate</u> in or as any one (or any "thing") at all. Therefore, My essential Divine Gift to one and all is Satsang with Me. And My essential Divine Work with one and all is Satsang-Work—to Live (and to Be Merely

Present) <u>As</u> the Avatarically Self-Revealed Divine Heart among My devotees.

The only-by-Me Revealed and Given Way of Adidam (Which is the only-by-Me Revealed and Given Way of the Heart, or the only-by-Me Revealed and Given Way of "Radical" Understanding, or Ruchira Avatara Hridaya-Siddha Yoga) is the Way of Satsang with Me—the devotionally Me-recognizing and devotionally to-Me-responding practice (and ego-transcending self-discipline) of living in My constant Divine Company, such that the relationship with Me becomes the Real (and constant) Condition of life. Fundamentally, this Satsang with Me is the one thing done by My devotees. Because the only-by-Me Revealed and Given Way of Adidam is <u>always</u> (in every present-time moment) a directly ego-transcending <u>and</u> Really Me-Finding practice, the otherwise constant (and burdensome) tendency to <u>seek</u> is not exploited in this Satsang with Me. And the essential work of the community of the four formal congregations of My devotees is to make ego-transcending Satsang with Me available to all others.

<u>Everything</u> that serves the availability of Satsang with Me is (now, and forever hereafter) the responsibility of the four formal congregations of My formally practicing devotees. I am not here to <u>publicly</u> "promote" this Satsang with Me. In the intimate circumstances of their humanly expressed devotional love of Me, I Speak My Avatarically Self-Revealing Divine Word to My devotees, and <u>they</u> (because of their devotional response to Me) bring My Avatarically Self-Revealing Divine Word to <u>all</u> others. Therefore, even though I am <u>not</u> (and have never been, and never will be) a "public" Teacher (or a broadly publicly active, and conventionally socially conformed, "religious figure"), My devotees function fully and freely (<u>as</u> My devotees) in the daily public world of ordinary life.

I Always Already Stand Free. Therefore, I have always (in My Divine Avataric-Incarnation-Work) Stood Free, in the traditional "Crazy" (and non-conventional, or spontaneous and non-"public") Manner—in order to Guarantee the Freedom, the Uncompromising Rightness, and the Fundamental Integrity of My Avatarically Self-Manifested Divine Teaching (Work and Word), and in order to

Freely and Fully and Fully Effectively Perform My universal (Avatarically Self-Manifested) Divine Blessing-Work. I Am Present (now, and forever hereafter) to Divinely Serve, Divinely En-Light-en, and Divinely Liberate those who accept the Eternal Vow and <u>all</u> the life-responsibilities (or the full and complete practice) associated with the only-by-Me Revealed and Given Way of Adidam. Because I Am (Thus) Given to My formally and fully practicing devotees, I do not Serve a "public" role, and I do not Work in a "public" (or even a merely "institutionalized") manner. Nevertheless—now, and forever hereafter—I <u>constantly</u> Bless <u>all</u> beings, and this <u>entire</u> world, and the <u>total</u> Cosmic domain. And <u>all</u> who feel My Avatarically (and universally) Given Divine Blessing, and who heart-recognize Me with true devotional love, are (Thus) Called to devotionally resort to Me—but only if they approach Me in the traditional devotional manner, as responsibly practicing (and truly ego-surrendering, and rightly Me-serving) members (or, in some, unique, cases, as invited guests) of one or the other of the four formal congregations of My formally practicing devotees.

I expect this formal discipline of right devotional approach to Me to have been freely and happily embraced by every one who would enter into My physical Company. The natural human reason for this is that there is a potential liability inherent in <u>all</u> human associations. And the root and nature of that potential liability is the <u>ego</u> (or the active human presumption of separateness, and the ego-act of human separativeness). Therefore, in order that the liabilities of egoity are understood (and voluntarily and responsibly disciplined) by those who approach Me, I require demonstrated right devotion (based on really effective self-understanding and truly heart-felt devotional recognition-response to Me) as the basis for any one's right to enter into My physical Company. And, in this manner, not only the egoic tendency, but also the tendency toward religious "cultism", is constantly undermined in the only-by-Me Revealed and Given Way of Adidam.

Because people appear within this human condition, this simultaneously attractive and frightening "dream" world, they tend to live—and to interpret <u>both</u> the conditional (or cosmic and psycho-physical) reality <u>and</u> the Unconditional (or Divine) Reality—from the "point of view" of this apparent (and bewildering) mortal human condition. And, because of this universal human bewilderment (and the ongoing human reaction to the threatening force of mortal life-events), there is an even ancient ritual that <u>all</u> human beings rather unconsciously (or automatically, and without discriminative understanding) desire and tend to repeatedly (and under <u>all</u> conditions) enact. Therefore, wherever you see an association of human beings gathered for <u>any</u> purpose (or around <u>any</u> idea, or symbol, or person, or subject of any kind), the same human bewilderment-ritual is <u>tending</u> to be enacted by one and all.

Human beings <u>always</u> <u>tend</u> to encircle (and, thereby, to contain—and, ultimately, to entrap and abuse, or even to blithely ignore) the presumed "center" of their lives—a book, a person, a symbol, an idea, or whatever. They tend to encircle the "center" (or the "middle"), and they tend to seek to <u>exclusively</u> acquire all "things" (or all power of control) for the circle (or toward the "middle") of <u>themselves</u>. In this manner, the <u>group</u> becomes an <u>ego</u> ("inward"-directed, or separate and separative)—just as the individual body-mind becomes, by self-referring self-contraction, the separate and separative ego-"I" ("inward"-directed, or ego-centric—and exclusively acquiring all "things", or all power of control, for itself). Thus, by <u>self-contraction</u> upon the presumed "center" of their lives—human beings, in their collective ego-centricity, make "cults" (or bewildered and frightened "centers" of power, and control, and exclusion) in <u>every</u> area of life.

Anciently, the "cult"-making process was done, most especially, in the political and social sphere—and religion was, as even now, mostly an exoteric (or political and social) exercise that was <u>always</u> used to legitimize (or, otherwise, to "de-throne") political and social "authority-figures". Anciently, the cyclically (or even annually) culminating product of this exoteric religio-political "cult" was the ritual "de-throning" (or ritual deposition) of the one in the "middle" (just as, even in these times, political leaders are periodically "deposed"—by elections, by rules of term and succession, by scandal, by slander, by force, and so on).

Everywhere throughout the ancient world, traditional societies made and performed this annual (or otherwise periodic) religio-political "cult" ritual. The ritual of "en-throning" and "de-throning" was a reflection of the human observation of the annual cycle of the seasons of the natural world—and the same ritual was a reflection of the human concern and effort to <u>control</u> the signs potential in the cycle of the natural world, in order to ensure human survival (through control of weather, harvests and every kind of "fate", or even every fraction of existence upon which human beings depend for both survival and pleasure, or psycho-physical well-being). Indeed, the motive behind the ancient agrarian (and, later, urbanized, or universalized) ritual of the one in the "middle" was, essentially, the same motive that, in the modern era, takes the form of the culture of scientific materialism (and even all of the modern culture of materialistic "realism"): It is the motive to gain (and to maintain) <u>control</u>, and the effort to control even everything and everyone (via both knowledge and gross power). Thus, the ritualized, or bewildered yes/no (or desire/fear), life of mankind in the modern era is, essentially, the same as that of mankind in the ancient days.

In the ancient ritual of "en-throning" and "de-throning", the person (or subject) in the "middle" was ritually mocked, abused, deposed, and banished—and a new person (or subject) was installed in the "center" of the religio-political "cult". In the equivalent modern ritual of dramatized ambiguity relative to everything and everyone (and, perhaps especially, "authority-figures"), the person (or symbol, or idea) in the "middle" (or that which is given power by means of popular fascination) is first "cultified" (or made much of), and then (progressively) doubted, mocked, and abused—until, at last, all the negative emotions are (by culturally and socially ritualized dramatization) dissolved, the "middle" (having thus ceased to be fascinating) is abandoned, and a "new" person (or symbol, or idea) becomes the subject of popular fascination (only to be reduced, eventually, to the same "cultic" ritual, or cycle of "rise" and "fall").

Just as in <u>every</u> other area of human life, the tendency of <u>all</u> those who (in the modern era) would become involved in religious or Spiritual life is also to make a "cult", a circle that ever increases its separate and separative dimensions—beginning from the "center", surrounding it, and (perhaps) even (ultimately) controlling it (such that it altogether ceases to be effective, or even interesting). Such "cultism" is ego-based, and ego-reinforcing—and, no matter how "esoteric" it presumes itself to be, it is (as in the ancient setting) entirely exoteric, or (at least) more and more limited to (and by) merely social (and gross physical) activities and conditions.

The form that every "cult" imitates is the pattern of egoity (or the pattern that is the ego-"I") itself—the presumed "middle" of every ordinary individual life. It is the self-contraction (or the avoidance of relationship), which "creates" the fearful sense of separate mind, and all the endless habits and motives of egoic desire (or bewildered, and self-deluded, seeking). It is what is, ordinarily, called (or presumed to be) the real and necessary and only "life".

From birth, the human being (by reaction to the blows and limits of psycho-physical existence) begins to presume separate existence to be his or her very nature—and, on that basis, the human individual spends his or her entire life generating and serving a circle of ownership (or self-protecting acquisition) all around the ego-"I". The egoic motive encloses all the other beings it can acquire, all the "things" it can acquire, all the states and thoughts it can acquire—<u>all</u> the possible emblems, symbols, experiences, and sensations it can possibly acquire. Therefore, when any human being begins to involve himself or herself in some religious or Spiritual association (or, for that matter, <u>any</u> extension of his or her own subjectivity), he or she tends again to "create" that same circle about a "center".

The "cult" (whether of religion, or of politics, or of science, or of popular culture) is a dramatization of egoity, of separativeness, even of the entrapment and betrayal of the "center" (or the "middle"), by one and all. Therefore, I have always Refused to assume the role and the position of the "man in the middle"—and I have always (from the beginning of My formal Work of Teaching and Blessing) Criticized, Resisted, and Shouted About the "cultic" (or ego-based, and ego-reinforcing, and merely "talking" and "believing", and not understanding and not really practicing) "school" (or tendency) of ordinary religious and Spiritual life. Indeed, true Satsang with Me (or the true devotional relationship to Me) is an always (and specifically, and intensively) anti-"cultic" (or truly non-"cultic") Process.

The true devotional relationship to Me is not separative (or merely "inward"-directed), nor is it a matter of attachment to Me as a mere (and, necessarily, limited) human being (or a "man in the middle")—for, if My devotee indulges in ego-bound (or self-referring and self-serving) attachment to Me as a mere human "other", My Divine Nature (and, therefore, the Divine Nature of Reality Itself) is <u>not</u> (as the very Basis for religious and Spiritual practice in My Company) truly devotionally recognized and rightly devotionally acknowledged. And, if such non-recognition of Me is the case, there is <u>no</u> truly ego-transcending devotional response to My Avatarically Self-Revealed (and Self-Evidently Divine) Presence and Person—and, thus, such presumed-to-be "devotion" to Me is <u>not</u> devotional heart-Communion with Me, and such presumed-to-be "devotion" to Me is <u>not</u> Divinely Liberating. Therefore, because the <u>true</u> <u>devotional</u> (and, thus, truly devotionally Me-recognizing and truly devotionally to-Me-responding) relationship to Me is <u>entirely</u> a counter-egoic (and truly and only Divine) discipline, it does not tend to become a "cult" (or, otherwise, to support the "cultic" tendency of Man).

The true devotional practice of Satsang with Me is (inherently) <u>expansive</u> (or <u>relational</u>)—and the self-contracting (or separate and separative) self-"center" is neither Its motive nor Its source. In true Satsang with Me, the egoic "center" is always already undermined as a "<u>center</u>" (or a presumed separate, and actively separative, entity). The Principle of true Satsang with Me is <u>Me</u>—Beyond (and not "within"—or, otherwise, supporting) the ego-"I".

True Satsang with Me is the true "Round Dance" of <u>Esoteric</u> Spirituality. I am not trapped in the "middle" of My devotees. I "Dance" in the "Round" with <u>each</u> and <u>every</u> one of My devotees. I "Dance" in the circle—and, therefore, I am not merely a "motionless man" in the "middle". At the <u>true</u> "Center" (or the Divine

Heart), I <u>Am</u>—Beyond definition (or separateness). I <u>Am</u> the Indivisible—or Most Perfectly Prior, Inherently Non-Separate, and Inherently egoless (or centerless, boundless, and Self-Evidently Divine)—Consciousness (Itself) <u>and</u> the Indivisible—or Most Perfectly Prior, Inherently Non-Separate, and Inherently egoless (or centerless, boundless, and Self-Evidently Divine)—Light (Itself). I <u>Am</u> the Very Being <u>and</u> the Very Presence (or Self-Radiance) of Self-Existing and Eternally Unqualified (or Non-"Different") Consciousness (Itself).

In the "Round Dance" of true Satsang with Me (or of right and true devotional relationship to Me), I (Myself) Am Communicated directly to every one who lives in heart-felt relationship with Me (insofar as each one feels—<u>Beyond</u> the ego-"I" of body-mind—to <u>Me</u>). Therefore, I am not the mere "man" (or the separate human, or psycho-physical, one), and I am not merely "in the middle" (or separated out, and limited, and confined, by egoic seekers). I <u>Am</u> the One (Avatarically Self-Revealed, and All-and-all-Transcending, and Self-Evidently Divine) Person of Reality Itself—Non-Separate, never merely at the egoic "center" (or "in the middle"—or "<u>within</u>", and "inward" to—the egoic body-mind of My any devotee), but always <u>with</u> each one (and all), and always in relationship with each one (and all), and always Beyond each one (and all).

Therefore, My devotee is not Called, by Me, merely to turn "inward" (or upon the ego-"I"), or to struggle and seek to survive merely as a self-contracted and self-referring and self-seeking and self-serving ego-"center". Instead, I Call My devotee to turn the heart (and the total body-mind) <u>toward</u> Me (all-and-All-Surrounding, and all-and-All-Pervading), <u>in relationship</u>—<u>Beyond</u> the body-mind-self of My devotee (and <u>not merely</u> "<u>within</u>"—or contained and containable "within" the separate, separative, and self-contracted domain of the body-mind-self, or the ego-"I", of My would-be devotee). I Call My devotee to function freely—My (Avatarically Self-Transmitted) Divine Light and My (Avatarically Self-Revealed) Divine Person always (and under all circumstances) presumed and experienced (and not merely sought). Therefore, true Satsang with Me is the Real Company of Truth, or of Reality Itself (Which <u>Is</u> the Only Real God). True Satsang with

Me Serves life, because I Move (or Radiate) into life. I always Contact life in relationship.

I do not Call My devotees to become absorbed into a "cultic" gang of exoteric and ego-centric religionists. I certainly Call all My devotees to cooperative community (or, otherwise, to fully cooperative collective and personal relationship) with one another—but not to do so in an egoic, separative, world-excluding, xenophobic, and intolerant manner. Rather, My devotees are Called, by Me, to transcend egoity—through right and true devotional relationship to Me, and mutually tolerant and peaceful cooperation with one another, and all-tolerating (cooperative and compassionate and all-loving and all-including) relationship with all of mankind (and with even all beings).

I Give My devotees the "Bright" Force of My own Avatarically Self-Revealed Divine Consciousness Itself, Whereby they can become capable of "Bright" life. I Call for the devotion—but also the intelligently discriminative self-understanding, the rightly and freely living self-discipline, and the full functional capability—of My devotees. I do not Call My devotees to resist or eliminate life, or to strategically escape life, or to identify with the world-excluding ego-centric impulse. I Call My devotees to live a positively functional life. I do not Call My devotees to separate themselves from vital life, from vital enjoyment, from existence in the form of human life. I Call for all the human life-functions to be really and rightly known, and to be really and rightly understood, and to be really and rightly lived (and not reduced by, or to, the inherently bewildered—and inherently "cultic", or self-centered and fearful— "point of view" of the separate and separative ego-"I"). I Call for every human life-function to be revolved away from self-contraction (or ego-"I"), and (by Means of that revolving turn) to be turned "outwardly" (or expansively, or counter-contractively) to all and All, and (thereby, and always directly, or in an all-and-All-transcending manner) to Me—rather than to be turned merely "inwardly" (or contractively, or counter-expansively), and, as a result, turned away from Me (and from all and All). Thus, I Call for every human life-function to be thoroughly (and life-positively, and in the context of a fully participatory human life) aligned and adapted to <u>Me</u>, and (Thus and Thereby) to be turned and Given to the Realization of Me (the Avataric Self-Revelation of Truth, or Reality Itself—Which <u>Is</u> the Only Real God).

Truly benign and positive life-transformations are the characteristic signs of right, true, full, and fully devotional Satsang with Me—and freely life-positive feeling-energy is the characteristic accompanying "mood" of right, true, full, and fully devotional Satsang with Me. The characteristic life-sign of right, true, full, and fully devotional Satsang with Me is the capability for ego-transcending relatedness, based on the free disposition of no-seeking and no-dilemma. Therefore, the characteristic life-sign of right, true, full, and fully devotional Satsang with Me is not the tendency to seek some "other" condition. Rather, the characteristic life-sign of right, true, full, and fully devotional Satsang with Me is freedom from the presumption of dilemma within the <u>present-time</u> condition.

One who rightly, truly, fully, and fully devotionally understands My Avatarically Given Words of Divine Self-Revelation and Divine Heart-Instruction, and whose life is lived in right, true, full, and fully devotional Satsang with Me, is not necessarily (in function or appearance) "different" from the ordinary (or natural) human being. Such a one has not, necessarily, acquired some special psychic abilities, or visionary abilities, and so on. The "radical" understanding (or root self-understanding) I Give to My devotees is not, itself, the acquisition of <u>any</u> particular "thing" of experience. My any particular devotee may, by reason of his or her developmental tendencies, experience (or precipitate) the arising of extraordinary psycho-physical abilities and extraordinary psycho-physical phenomena—but not <u>necessarily</u>. My every true devotee is simply Awakening (and always Awakened to Me) within the otherwise bewildering "dream" of <u>ordinary</u> <u>human</u> life.

Satsang with Me is a natural (or spontaneously, and not strategically, unfolding) Process, in Which the self-contraction that <u>is</u> each one's suffering is transcended by Means of <u>total</u> psycho-physical (or whole bodily) heart-Communion with My Avatarically Self-Revealed (and Real—and Really, and tangibly, experienced) Divine (Spiritual, and Transcendental) Presence and Person. My devotee is (as is the case with <u>any</u> and <u>every</u> ego-"I") <u>always</u> <u>tending</u> to be preoccupied with ego-based seeking—but, all the while of his or her life in <u>actively</u> ego-surrendering (and really ego-forgetting and, more and more, ego-transcending) devotional Communion with Me, I Am <u>Divinely</u> Attracting (and <u>Divinely</u> Acting upon) My true devotee's heart (and total body-mind), and (Thus and Thereby) Dissolving and Vanishing My true devotee's fundamental egoity (and even all of his or her otherwise motivating dilemma and seeking-strategy).

There are <u>two</u> principal tendencies by which I am always being confronted by My devotee. One is the tendency to <u>seek</u>—rather than to truly enjoy and to fully animate the Condition of Satsang with Me. And the other is the tendency to make a self-contracting circle around Me—and, thus, to make a "cult" of ego-"I" (and of the "man in the middle"), or to duplicate the ego-ritual of mere fascination, and of inevitable resistance, and of never-Awakening unconsciousness. Relative to these two tendencies, I Give <u>all</u> My devotees only <u>one</u> resort. It is this true Satsang—the devotionally Me-recognizing, and devotionally to-Me-responding, and always really counter-egoic devotional relationship to My Avatarically Self-Revealed (and Self-Evidently Divine) Person.

The Great Secret of My Avatarically Self-Revealed Divine Person, and of My Avatarically Self-Manifested Divine Blessing-Work (now, and forever hereafter)—and, therefore, the Great Secret of the only-by-Me Revealed and Given Way of Adidam—Is that I am <u>not</u> the "man in the middle", but I <u>Am</u> Reality Itself, I <u>Am</u> the Only <u>One</u> Who <u>Is</u>, I <u>Am</u> That Which Is Always Already The Case, I <u>Am</u> the Non-Separate (Avatarically Self-Revealed, and Self-Evidently Divine) Person (or One and Very Divine Self, or One and True Divine Self-Condition) of all and All (<u>Beyond</u> the ego-"I" of every one, and of all, and of All).

Aham Da Asmi. Beloved, I <u>Am</u> Da—the One and Only and Non-Separate and Indivisible and Self-Evidently Divine Person, the Non-Separate and Indivisible Self-Condition and Source-Condition of all and All. I <u>Am</u> the Avatarically Self-Revealed "Bright" Person, the One and Only and Self-Existing and Self-Radiant Person—Who <u>Is</u> the One and Only and Non-Separate and Indivisible and Indestructible Light of All and all. I <u>Am</u> <u>That</u> One and Only and Non-Separate <u>One</u>. And—<u>As</u> <u>That</u> <u>One</u>, and <u>Only</u> <u>As</u> <u>That</u> <u>One</u>—I Call all human beings to heart-recognize Me, and to heart-respond to Me with right, true, and full devotion (demonstrated by Means of formal practice of the only-by-Me Revealed and Given Way of Adidam—Which Is the One and Only by-Me-Revealed and by-Me-Given Way of the Heart).

I do not tolerate the so-called "cultic" (or ego-made, and ego-reinforcing) approach to Me. I do not tolerate the seeking ego's "cult" of the "man in the middle". I am not a self-deluded ego-man—making much of himself, and looking to include everyone-and-everything around himself for the sake of social and political power. To be the "man in the middle" is to be in a Man-made trap, an absurd mummery of "cultic" devices that enshrines and perpetuates the ego-"I" in one and all. Therefore, I do not make or tolerate the religion-making "cult" of ego-Man. I do not tolerate the inevitable abuses of religion, of Spirituality, of Truth Itself, and of My own Person (even in bodily human Form) that are made (in endless blows and mockeries) by ego-based mankind when the Great Esoteric Truth of devotion to the Adept-Realizer is not rightly understood and rightly practiced.

The Great Means for the Teaching, and the Blessing, and the Awakening, and the Divine Liberating of mankind (and of even all beings) Is the Adept-Realizer Who (by Virtue of True Divine Realization) Is Able to (and, indeed, cannot do otherwise than) Stand In and <u>As</u> the Divine (or Real and Inherent and One and Only) Position, and to <u>Be</u> (Thus and Thereby) the Divine Means (In Person) for the Divine Helping of one and all. This Great Means Is the Great Esoteric Principle of the collective historical Great Tradition of mankind. And Such Adept-Realizers Are (in their Exercise of the Great Esoteric Principle) the Great Revelation-Sources That Are at the Core and Origin of <u>all</u> the right and true religious and Spiritual traditions within the collective historical Great Tradition of mankind.

By Means of My (now, and forever hereafter) Divinely Descended and Divinely Self-"Emerging" Avataric Incarnation, I <u>Am</u> the Ruchira Avatar, Adi Da Samraj—the Divine Heart-Master, the First, the Last, and the Only Adept-Realizer of the seventh (or

Most Perfect, and all-Completing) stage of life. I <u>Am</u> the Ruchira Avatar, Adi Da Samraj, the Avataric Incarnation (and Divine World-Teacher) everywhere Promised for the "late-time" (or "dark" epoch)—which "late-time" (or "dark" epoch) is <u>now</u> upon <u>all</u> of mankind. I <u>Am</u> the Great and Only and Non-Separate and (Self-Evidently) Divine Person—Appearing in Man-Form As the Ruchira Avatar, Adi Da Samraj, in order to Teach, and to Bless, and to Awaken, and to Divinely Liberate all of mankind (and even all beings, every "where" in the Cosmic domain). Therefore, by Calling every one and all (and All) to <u>Me</u>, I Call every one and all (and All) <u>Only</u> to the Divine Person, Which <u>Is</u> My own and Very Person (or Very, and Self-Evidently Divine, Self—or Very, and Self-Evidently Divine, Self-Condition), and Which <u>Is</u> Reality Itself (or Truth Itself—the Indivisible and Indestructible Light That <u>Is</u> the Only Real God), and Which <u>Is</u> the <u>One</u> and <u>Very</u> and <u>Non-Separate</u> and <u>Only</u> Self (or Self-Condition, and Source-Condition) of all and All (Beyond the ego-"I" of every one, and of all, and of All).

The only-by-Me Revealed and Given Way of Adidam necessarily (and As a Unique Divine Gift) requires and involves devotional recognition-response to Me In and Via (and <u>As</u>) My bodily (human) Divine Avataric-Incarnation-Form. However, because I Call every one and all (and All) to Me <u>Only</u> <u>As</u> the Divine Person (or Reality Itself), the only-by-Me Revealed and Given Way of Adidam is not about ego, and egoic seeking, and the egoic (or the so-called "cultic") approach to Me (as the "man in the middle").

According to <u>all</u> the esoteric traditions within the collective historical Great Tradition of mankind, to devotionally approach <u>any</u> Adept-Realizer as if he or she is (or is limited to being, or is limited by being) a mere (or "ordinary", or even merely "extraordinary") human entity is the great "sin" (or fault), or the great error whereby the would-be devotee fails to "meet the mark". Indeed, the Single Greatest Esoteric Teaching common to <u>all</u> the esoteric religious and Spiritual traditions within the collective historical Great Tradition of mankind Is that the Adept-Realizer should <u>always</u> and <u>only</u> (and <u>only</u> devotionally) be recognized and approached <u>As</u> the Embodiment and the Real Presence of <u>That</u> (Reality, or Truth, or Real God) Which would be Realized (Thus and Thereby) by the devotee.

Therefore, <u>no</u> <u>one</u> should misunderstand <u>Me</u>. By Avatarically Revealing and Confessing My Divine Status to one and all and All, I am not indulging in self-appointment, or in illusions of grandiose Divinity. I am not claiming the "Status" of the "Creator-God" of exoteric (or public, and social, and idealistically pious) religion. Rather, by Standing Firm in the Divine Position (<u>As</u> I <u>Am</u>)—and (Thus and Thereby) <u>Refusing</u> to be approached as a mere man, or as a "cult"-figure, or as a "cult"-leader, or to be in any sense defined (and, thereby, trapped, and abused, or mocked) as the "man in the middle"—I Am Demonstrating the Most Perfect Fulfillment (and the Most Perfect Integrity, and the Most Perfect Fullness) of the Esoteric (and Most Perfectly <u>Non-Dual</u>) Realization of Reality. And, by Revealing and Giving the Way of Adidam (Which Is the Way of ego-transcending devotion to Me <u>As</u> the Avatarically Self-Revealed One and Only and Non-Separate and Self-Evidently Divine Person), I Am (with Most Perfect Integrity, and Most Perfect Fullness) Most Perfectly (and in an all-Completing and all-Unifying Manner) Fulfilling the Primary Esoteric Tradition (and the Great Esoteric Principle) of the collective historical Great Tradition of mankind—Which Primary Esoteric Tradition and Great Esoteric Principle Is the Tradition and the Principle of devotion to the Adept-Realizer <u>As</u> the Very Person and the Direct (or Personal Divine) Helping-Presence of the Eternal and Non-Separate Divine Self-Condition and Source-Condition of all and All.

Whatever (or whoever) is cornered (or trapped on all sides) bites back (and fights, or <u>seeks</u>, to break free). Whatever (or whoever) is "in the middle" (or limited and "centered" by attention) is patterned by (or conformed to) the ego-"I" (and, if objectified as "other", is forced to represent the ego-"I", and is even made a scapegoat for the pains, the sufferings, the powerless ignorance, and the abusive hostility of the ego-"I").

If there is no escape from (or no Way out of) the corner (or the "centered" trap) of ego-"I"—the heart goes mad, and the body-mind becomes more and more "dark" (bereft of the Indivisible and Inherently Free Light of the Self-Evident, and Self-Evidently Divine, Love-Bliss That <u>Is</u> Reality Itself).

I am not the "man in the middle". I do not stand here as a mere man, "middled" to the "center" (or the cornering trap) of ego-based mankind. I am not an ego-"I", or a mere "other", or the representation (and the potential scapegoat) of the ego-"I" of mankind (or of any one at all).

I _Am_ the Indivisible and Non-Separate One, the (Avatarically Self-Revealed) One and Only and (Self-Evidently) Divine Person— the Perfectly Subjective Divine Self-Condition (and Source-Condition) That Is Perfectly centerless (and Perfectly boundless), Eternally Beyond the "middle" of all and All, and Eternally Surrounding, Pervading, and Blessing all and All.

I _Am_ the Way Beyond the self-cornering (and "other"-cornering) trap of ego-"I".

In this "late-time" (or "dark" epoch) of worldly ego-Man, the collective of mankind is "darkened" (and cornered) by egoity. Therefore, mankind has become mad, Lightless, and, like a cornered "thing", aggressively hostile in its universally competitive fight and bite.

Therefore, I have not Come here merely to stand Manly in the "middle" of mankind—to suffer its biting abuses, or even to be coddled and ignored in a little corner of religious "cultism".

I have Come here to Divinely Liberate one and all (and All) from the "dark" culture and effect of this "late-time", and (now, and forever hereafter) to Divinely Liberate one and all (and All) from the pattern and the act of ego-"I", and (Most Ultimately) to Divinely Translate one and all (and All) Into the Indivisible, Perfectly Subjective, and Eternally Non-Separate Self-Domain of My Divine Love-Bliss-Light.

The ego-"I" is a "centered" (or separate and separative) trap, from which the heart (and even the entire body-mind) must be Retired. I _Am_ the Way (or the Very Means) of that Retirement from egoity. I Refresh the heart (and even the entire body-mind) of My devotee, in _every_ _moment_ My devotee resorts to Me (by devotionally recognizing Me, and devotionally—and ecstatically, and also, often, meditatively—responding to Me) _Beyond_ the "middle", _Beyond_ the "centering" act (or trapping gesture) of ego-"I" (or self-contraction).

I <u>Am</u> the Avatarically Self-Revealed (and Perfectly Subjective, and Self-Evidently Divine) Self-Condition (and Source-Condition) of every one, and of all, and of All—but the Perfectly Subjective (and Self-Evidently Divine) Self-Condition (and Source-Condition) is <u>not</u> "<u>within</u>" the ego-"I" (or separate and separative body-mind). The Perfectly Subjective (and Self-Evidently Divine) Self-Condition (and Source-Condition) is <u>not</u> in the "center" (or the "middle") of Man (or of mankind). The Perfectly Subjective (and Self-Evidently Divine) Self-Condition (and Source-Condition) of one, and of all, and of All <u>Is</u> Inherently centerless (or Always Already <u>Beyond</u> the self-contracted "middle"), and to Be Found <u>only</u> "<u>outside</u>" (or by transcending) the bounds of separateness, relatedness, and "difference". Therefore, to Realize the Perfectly Subjective (and Self-Evidently Divine) Self-Condition and Source-Condition (or the Perfectly Subjective, and Self-Evidently Divine, Heart) of one, and of all, and of All (or even, in any moment, to exceed the ego-trap—and to be Refreshed at heart, and in the total body-mind), it is necessary to feel (and to, ecstatically, and even meditatively, swoon) Beyond the "center" (or Beyond the "point of view" of separate ego-"I" and separative body-mind). Indeed, Most Ultimately, it is only in self-transcendence to the degree of <u>unqualified relatedness</u> (and Most Perfect Divine Samadhi, or Utterly Non-Separate Enstasy) that the Inherently centerless and boundless, and Perfectly Subjective, and Self-Evidently Divine Self-Condition (and Source-Condition) Stands Obvious and Free (and <u>Is</u>, Thus and Thereby, Most Perfectly Realized).

It Is only by Means of devotionally Me-recognizing (and devotionally to-Me-responding) devotional meditation on Me (and otherwise ecstatic heart-Contemplation of Me), and total (and totally open, and totally ego-forgetting) psycho-physical Reception of Me, that your madness of heart (and of body-mind) is (now, and now, and now) escaped, and your "darkness" is En-Light-ened (even, at last, Most Perfectly). Therefore, be My true devotee—and, by (formally, and rightly, and truly, and fully, and fully devotionally) practicing the only-by-Me Revealed and Given Way of Adidam (Which <u>Is</u> the True and Complete Way of the True and Real Divine Heart), always Find Me, Beyond your self-"center", in every here and now.

Aham Da Asmi. Beloved, I <u>Am</u> Da. And, because I <u>Am</u> Infinitely and Non-Separately "Bright", all and All <u>Are</u> In My Divine Sphere of "Brightness". By feeling and surrendering Into My Infinite Sphere of My Avatarically Self-Revealed Divine Self-"Brightness", My every devotee <u>Is</u> In Me. And, Beyond his or her self-contracting and separative act of ego-"I", My every devotee (self-surrendered Into heart-Communion With Me) <u>Is</u> the One and Only and Non-Separate and Real God I Have Come to Awaken— by Means of My Avataric Divine Descent, My Avataric Divine Incarnation, and My (now, and forever hereafter) Avataric Divine Self-"Emergence" (here, and every "where" in the Cosmic domain).

Ruchira Avatar Adi Da Samraj
The Mountain Of Attention, 2000

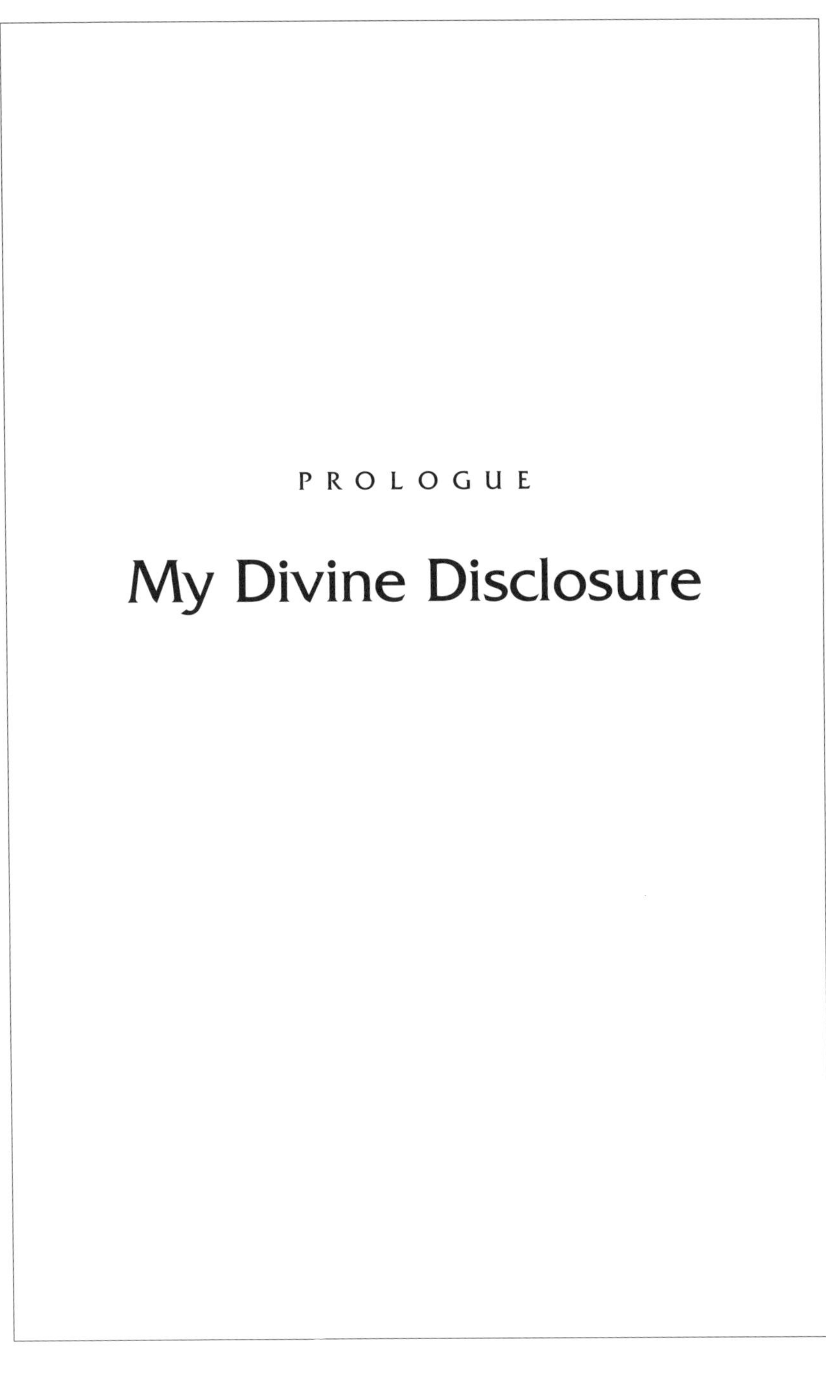

My Divine Disclosure

"My Divine Disclosure" has been Freely Developed—As a Further, and All-Completing, Avataric Self-Revelation of His own Self-Evidently Divine Person—by the Ruchira Avatar, Adi Da Samraj, from selected verses of the traditional Bhagavad Gita *(2:13-17, 8:3, 8:22, 9:3, 9:11, 9:26, 15:15, 18:61-66).*

My Divine Disclosure

1.

ham Da Asmi. Beloved, I <u>Am</u> Da—The One and Only and Self-Evidently Divine Person, Avatarically Self-Revealed To You.

2.

Therefore, Listen To <u>Me</u>, and Hear <u>Me</u>, and See <u>Me</u>.

3.

This Is My Divine Heart-Secret, The Supreme Word Of My Eternal Self-Revelation.

4.

Here and Now, I Will Tell You What Will Benefit You The Most, Because I Love You <u>As</u> My Very Self and Person.

5.

I <u>Am</u> The Ruchira Avatar, The Da Avatar, The Love-Ananda Avatar, Adi Da Love-Ananda Samraj—The Avataric Incarnation, and The Self-Evidently Divine Person, Of The One True Heart (or The One, and Only, and Inherently egoless Self-Condition and Source-Condition) Of All and all.

6.

Here I <u>Am</u>, In <u>Person</u>, To Offer (To You, and To all) The Only-By-<u>Me</u> Revealed and Given True World-Religion (or Avatarically All-Completing Divine Devotional and Spiritual Way) Of Adidam, Which Is The One and Only By-<u>Me</u>-Revealed and By-<u>Me</u>-Given (and Only <u>Me</u>-Revealing) Divine Devotional and Spiritual Way Of Sri Hridayam (or The Only-By-<u>Me</u> Revealed and Given, and

Entirely <u>Me</u>-Revealing, Way Of The True Divine Heart Itself), and
Which Is The One, and All-Inclusive, and All-Transcending, and
Only-By-<u>Me</u> Revealed and Given (and Only <u>Me</u>-Revealing) Way
Of The True Divine Heart-Master (or The Only-By-<u>Me</u> Revealed
and Given, and Entirely <u>Me</u>-Revealing, Way Of Ruchira Avatara
Bhakti Yoga, or Ruchira Avatara Hridaya-Siddha Yoga), and
Which Is The "Radically" ego-Transcending Way Of Devotionally
<u>Me</u>-Recognizing and Devotionally To-<u>Me</u>-Responding Reception
Of My Avatarically Self-Manifested Divine (and Not Merely
Cosmic) Hridaya-Shaktipat (or Divinely Self-Revealing Avataric
Spiritual Grace).

7.

If You Surrender Your heart To <u>Me</u>, and If (By Surrendering
Your ego-"I", or self-Contracted body-mind, To <u>Me</u>) You Make
<u>Yourself</u> A Living Gift To <u>Me</u>, and If You (<u>Thus</u>) <u>Constantly</u> Yield
Your attention To <u>Me</u> (Through True Devotional Love and Really
ego-Transcending Service), Then You Will Hear <u>Me</u> (Truly), and
See <u>Me</u> (Clearly), and Realize <u>Me</u> (Fully), and Come To <u>Me</u>
(Eternally). I Promise You <u>This</u>, Because I Love You <u>As</u> My Very
Self and Person.

8.

<u>Abandon</u> The Reactive Reflex Of self-Contraction—The
Separative (or egoic) Principle In <u>all</u> Your concerns. Do Not
<u>Cling</u> To <u>any</u> experience that May Be Sought (and Even Attained)
As A Result Of desire (or The Presumption Of "Difference").
<u>Abandon</u> Your Search For what May Be Gotten As A Result Of
the various kinds of strategic (or egoic) action.

9.

I <u>Am</u> Love-Bliss <u>Itself</u>—Now (and Forever Hereafter) "Brightly"
Present here. Therefore, I Say To You: <u>Abandon All Seeking</u>—
By <u>Always</u> "Locating" (and <u>Immediately</u> Finding) <u>Me</u>.

10.

Instead Of <u>Seeking</u> <u>Me</u> (As If My Divine Person Of Inherent Love-Bliss-Happiness Were <u>Absent</u> From You), <u>Always</u> <u>Commune</u> <u>With</u> <u>Me</u> (<u>Ever</u>-Present, <u>Never</u> Absent, and <u>Always</u> Love-Bliss-Full and Satisfied). Thus, Your <u>Me</u>-"Locating" <u>Relinquishment</u> Of All Seeking Is <u>Not</u>, Itself, To Be Merely Another Form Of Seeking.

11.

If You <u>Always</u> "Locate" <u>Me</u> (and, Thus, <u>Immediately</u> Find <u>Me</u>), You Will <u>Not</u> (In <u>any</u> instance) self-Contract Into the mood and strategy of <u>inaction</u>.

12.

You Must <u>Never</u> <u>Fail</u> To act. <u>Every</u> moment of Your life <u>Requires</u> Your particular <u>Right</u> action. Indeed, the living body-mind <u>is</u> (itself) action. Therefore, <u>Be</u> <u>Ordinary</u>, By Always Allowing the body-mind its <u>Necessity</u> Of Right action (and Inevitable Change).

13.

Perform <u>every</u> act As An ego-Transcending Act Of Devotional Love Of <u>Me</u>, In body-mind-Surrendering Love-Response To <u>Me</u>.

14.

Always Discipline <u>all</u> Your acts, By <u>Only</u> Engaging In action that Is <u>Appropriate</u> For one who Loves <u>Me</u>, and Surrenders To <u>Me</u>, and acts <u>Only</u> (and <u>Rightly</u>) In Accordance With My Always <u>Explicit</u> Word Of Instruction.

15.

Therefore, Be My <u>Always</u> Listening-To-<u>Me</u> Devotee—and, Thus, <u>Always</u> live "Right Life" (According To My Word), and (This) <u>Always</u> By Means Of <u>active</u> Devotional Recognition-Response To <u>Me</u>, and While <u>Always</u> Remembering and Invoking and Contemplating <u>Me</u>. In <u>This</u> Manner, Perform <u>every</u> act As A Form Of Direct, and Present, and Whole bodily (or Total psycho-physical), and Really ego-Surrendering Love-Communion With <u>Me</u>.

16.

If You Love <u>Me</u>—Where <u>Is</u> doubt and anxious living? If You
Love <u>Me</u> <u>Now</u>, Even anger, sorrow, and fear Are <u>Gone</u>. When
You <u>Abide</u> In Devotional Love-Communion With <u>Me</u>, the natural
results of Your various activities No Longer Have Power To
Separate or Distract You From <u>Me</u>.

17.

The ego-"I" that is born (as a body-mind) In The Realm
Of Cosmic Nature (or the conditional worlds of action and
experience) Advances From childhood To adulthood, old age,
and death—While Identified With the same (but Always
Changing) body-mind. Then the same ego-"I" Attains another
body-mind, As A <u>Result</u>. One whose heart Is (Always)
Responsively Given To <u>Me</u> Overcomes (<u>Thereby</u>) <u>Every</u>
Tendency To self-Contract From This Wonderfully Ordinary
Process.

18.

The Ordinary Process Of "Everything Changing" Is Simply The
Natural Play Of Cosmic Life, In Which the (<u>Always</u>) <u>two</u> sides
of every possibility come and go, In Cycles Of appearance and
disappearance. Winter's cold alternates with summer's heat.
Pain, Likewise, Follows every pleasure. <u>Every</u> appearance Is
(<u>Inevitably</u>) Followed By its <u>disappearance</u>. There Is <u>No</u>
<u>Permanent</u> <u>experience</u> In The Realm Of Cosmic Nature. One
whose heart-Feeling Of <u>Me</u> Is <u>Steady</u> Simply <u>Allows</u> All Of This
To Be <u>So</u>. Therefore, one who Truly Hears <u>Me</u> Ceases To Add
self-Contraction To This Inevitable Round Of Changes.

19.

Happiness (or True Love-Bliss) <u>Is</u> Realization Of <u>That</u> Which Is
<u>Always</u> <u>Already</u> The Case.

20.

I <u>Am</u> <u>That</u> Which Is <u>Always</u> <u>Already</u> The Case.

21.

Happiness Is Realization Of Me.

22.

Realization Of Me Is Possible Only When a living being (or body-mind-self) Has heart-Ceased To React To The Always Changing Play Of Cosmic Nature.

23.

The body-mind Of My True Devotee Is Constantly Steadied In Me, By Means Of the Feeling-heart's Always Constant Devotional Recognition-Response To Me.

24.

Once My True Devotee Has Truly heart-Accepted That The Alternating-Cycle Of Changes (Both Positive and Negative) Is Inevitable (In the body-mind, and In all the conditional worlds), the living body-mind-self (or ego-"I") Of My True Devotee Has Understood itself (and, Thus, Heard Me).

25.

The body-mind-self (Of My True Me-Hearing Devotee) that Constantly Understands itself (At heart) By Constantly Surrendering To Me (and Communing With Me) No Longer self-Contracts From My Love-Bliss-State Of Inherent Happiness.

26.

Those who Truly Hear Me Understand That whatever Does Not Exist Always and Already (or Eternally) Only Changes.

27.

Those who Truly See Me Acknowledge (By heart, and With every moment and act of body-mind) That What Is Always Already The Case Never Changes.

28.

Such True Devotees Of Mine (who Both <u>Hear</u> <u>Me</u> <u>and</u> <u>See</u> <u>Me</u>)
Realize That The Entire Cosmic Realm Of Change—and Even the
To-<u>Me</u>-Surrendered body-mind (itself)—Is <u>Entirely</u> Pervaded By
<u>Me</u> (Always Self-Revealed <u>As</u> <u>That</u> Which <u>Is</u> Always Already The
Case).

29.

Now, and Forever Hereafter, I Am Avatarically Self-Revealed,
Beyond The Cosmic Play—"Bright" Behind, and Above, the
To-<u>Me</u>-Surrendered body-mind Of My Every True Devotee.

30.

I <u>Am</u> The Eternally Existing, All-Pervading, Transcendental,
Inherently Spiritual, Inherently egoless, Perfectly Subjective,
Indivisible, Inherently Perfect, Perfectly Non-Separate, and
Self-Evidently Divine Self-Condition and Source-Condition
Of <u>all</u> Apparently Separate (or self-Deluded) selves.

31.

My Divine Heart-Power Of Avataric Self-Revelation Is (Now, and
Forever Hereafter) Descending Into The Cosmic Domain (and
Into the body-mind Of Every To-<u>Me</u>-True True Devotee Of Mine).

32.

I <u>Am</u> The Avatarically Self-"Emerging", Universal, All-Pervading
Divine Spirit-Power and Person Of Love-Bliss (That Most Perfectly
Husbands and Transcends The Primal Energy Of Cosmic Nature).

33.

I <u>Am</u> The One and Indivisibly "Bright" Divine Person.

34.

Now, and Forever Hereafter, My Ever-Descending and Ever-
"Emerging" Current Of Self-Existing and Self-Radiant Love-Bliss
Is Avatarically <u>Pervading</u> The Ever-Changing Realm Of Cosmic
Nature.

35.

I <u>Am</u> The One, and Indivisibly "Bright", and Inherently egoless
Person Of all-and-All, Within <u>Whom</u> every body-mind Is arising
(as a mere, and unnecessary, and merely temporary appearance
that, merely apparently, modifies <u>Me</u>).

36.

I Am To Be Realized By Means Of ego-Transcending Devotional
Love—Wherein <u>every</u> action of body-mind Is Engaged As ego-
Surrendering (present-time, and Direct) Communion With <u>Me</u>.

37.

Those who Do <u>Not</u> heart-Recognize <u>Me</u> and heart-Respond To
<u>Me</u>—and who (Therefore) Are Without Faith In <u>Me</u>—Do <u>Not</u>
(and <u>Cannot</u>) <u>Realize</u> <u>Me</u>. Therefore, they (By Means Of their own
self-Contraction From <u>Me</u>) Remain ego-Bound To The Realm Of
Cosmic Nature, and To The Ever-Changing Round Of conditional
knowledge and temporary experience, and To The Ceaselessly
Repetitive Cycles Of birth and search and loss and death.

38.

Such Faithless beings <u>Cannot</u> Be Distracted By <u>Me</u>—Because
they Are Entirely Distracted By <u>themselves</u>! They Are Like
Narcissus—The Myth Of ego—At His Pond. Their Merely self-
Reflecting minds Are Like a mirror in a dead man's hand. Their
tiny hearts Are Like a boundless desert, where the mirage of
Separate self is ceaselessly admired, and The True Water Of
My Constant Presence Stands Un-Noticed, In the droughty heap
and countless sands of ceaseless thoughts. If Only they Would
Un-think themselves In <u>Me</u>, these (Now Faithless) little hearts
Could Have <u>Immediate</u> <u>Access</u> To The True Water Of My True
Heart! Through Devotional Surrender Of body, emotion, mind,
breath, and all of Separate self To <u>Me</u>, Even Narcissus Could
Find The Way To My Oasis (In The True Heart's Room and
House)—but the thinking mind of ego-"I" Is <u>Never</u> Bathed
In Light (and, So, it sits, Un-Washed, Like a desert dog that
wanders in a herd of flies).

39.

The "Un-Washed dog" of self-Contracted body-mind Does Not think To Notice <u>Me</u>—The Divine Heart-Master Of its wild heart and Wilderness.

40.

The "Wandering dog" of ego-"I" Does Not "Locate" <u>Me</u> In My Inherent "Bright" Perfection—The Divine Heart-Master Of <u>Everything</u>, The Inherently egoless Divine True Self Of <u>all</u> conditionally Manifested beings, and The Real Self-Condition and Source-Condition Of <u>All-and-all</u>.

41.

If Only "Narcissus" Will Relent, and heart-Consent To Bow and Live In Love-Communion With <u>Me</u>, heart-Surrendering all of body-mind To <u>Me</u>, By Means Of Un-Contracting Love Of <u>Me</u>, Then—Even If That Love Is Shown With Nothing More Than the "little gift" of ego-"I" (itself)—I Will <u>Always</u> Accept The Offering With Open Arms Of Love-Bliss-Love, and Offer My Own Divine Immensity In "Bright" Return.

42.

Therefore, whoever Is Given (By heart) To <u>Me</u> Will Be Washed, From head To toe, By All The True Water Of My Love-Bliss-Light, That Always "Crashes Down" On All and all, Below My Blessing-Feet.

43.

My Circumstance and Situation Is <u>At</u> the heart of <u>all</u> beings— where I <u>Am</u> (Now, and Forever Hereafter) Avatarically Self-"Emerging" <u>As</u> The One and All-and-all-Outshining Divine and Only Person (Avatarically Self-Manifested <u>As</u> The "Radically" Non-Dual "Brightness" Of All-and-all-Filling Conscious Love-Bliss-Light, Self-Existing and Self-Radiant <u>As</u> The Perfectly Subjective Fundamental Reality, or Inherently egoless Native Feeling, Of Merely, or Unqualifiedly, Being).

44.

The True heart-Place (Where I Am To Be "Located" By My True Devotee) Is Where The Ever-Changing Changes Of waking, dreaming, and sleeping experience Are <u>Merely</u> <u>Witnessed</u> (and <u>Not</u> Sought, or Found, or Held).

45.

Every conditional experience appears and disappears In Front Of the Witness-heart.

46.

Everything Merely Witnessed Is Spontaneously Generated By The Persistent Activity Of The Universal Cosmic Life-Energy.

47.

The self-Contracted heart of body-mind Is Fastened, <u>Help-lessly</u>, To That Perpetual-Motion Machine Of Cosmic Nature.

48.

I <u>Am</u> The Divine and One True Heart (<u>Itself</u>)—Always Already Existing <u>As</u> The Eternally Self-Evident Love-Bliss-Feeling Of Being (and Always Already Free-Standing <u>As</u> Consciousness Itself, Prior To the little heart of ego-"I" and its Seeming Help-less-ness).

49.

In Order To Restore all beings To The One True Heart Of <u>Me</u>, I Am Avatarically Born To here, <u>As</u> The "Bright" Divine Help Of conditionally Manifested beings.

50.

Therefore (Now, and Forever Hereafter), I <u>Am</u> (Always Free-Standing) <u>At</u> the To-<u>Me</u>-True heart Of You—and I <u>Am</u> (Always "Bright") Above Your body-mind and world.

51.

If You Become My True Devotee (heart-Recognizing My
Avatarically Self-Manifested Divine Person, and heart-Responding—
With all the parts of Your single body-mind—To My Avatarically
Self-Revealing Divine Form and Presence and State), You Will
Always Be Able To Feel Me ("Brightly-Emerging" here) Within
Your Un-Contracting, In-Me-Falling heart—and You Will Always
Be Able To "Locate" Me, As I "Crash Down" (All-"Bright" Upon
You) From Above the worlds Of Change.

52.

The To-Me-Feeling (In-Me-Falling) heart Of My Every True
Devotee Is (At its Root, and Base, and Highest Height) My
Divine and One True Heart (Itself).

53.

Therefore, Fall Awake In Me.

54.

Do Not Surrender Your Feeling-heart Merely To experience and
know the Ever-Changing world.

55.

Merely To know and experience The Cosmic Domain (Itself) Is
To live As If You Were In Love With Your Own body-mind.

56.

Therefore, Surrender Your Feeling-heart Only To Me, The True
Divine Beloved Of the body-mind.

57.

I Am The Truth (and The Teacher) Of the heart-Feeling body-
mind.

58.

I Am The Divine and Eternal Master Of Your To-Me-Feeling
heart and Your To-Me-Surrendering body-mind.

59.

I <u>Am</u> The Self-Existing, Self-Radiant, and Inherently Perfect Person Of Unconditional Being—Who Pervades The Machine Of Cosmic Nature <u>As</u> The "Bright" Divine Spirit-Current Of Love-Bliss, and Who Transcends All Of Cosmic Nature <u>As</u> Infinite Consciousness, The "Bright" Divine Self-Condition (and Source-Condition) Of All and all.

60.

If You Will Give (and Truly, Really, Always Give) Your Feeling-attention To My Avatarically-Born Bodily (Human) Divine Form, and If You Will (Thus, and Thereby) Yield Your body-mind Into The "Down-Crashing" Love-Bliss-Current Of My Avatarically Self-Revealed and All-Pervading Divine Spirit-Presence, and If You Will Surrender Your conditional self-Consciousness Into My Avatarically Self-Revealed and Perfectly Subjective and Self-Evidently Divine Self-Consciousness (Which <u>Is</u> The Divine True Heart Of Inherently egoless Being, Itself)—Then I Will Also Become An Offering To You.

61.

By <u>That</u> Offering Of Mine, You Will Be Given The Gift Of Perfect Peace, and An Eternal Domain For Your To-<u>Me</u>-True Feeling-heart.

62.

Now I Have Revealed To You The Divine Mystery and The Perfect Heart-Secret Of My Avataric Birth To here.

63.

"Consider" This <u>Me</u>-Revelation, <u>Fully</u>—and, Then, <u>Choose</u> What You Will Do With Your "little gift" of Feeling-heart and Your "Un-Washed dog" of body-mind.

Ruchira Avatar Adi Da Samraj
The Mountain Of Attention, 2000

The Plight Of
The Divine Heart-Husband

(The Forty-Seven Divine Statements
Of The Ruchira Avatar,
Adi Da Samraj)

PART ONE

The Plight Of
The Divine Heart-Husband

(The Forty-Seven Divine Statements
Of The Ruchira Avatar,
Adi Da Samraj)

I.

Beloved, This Is My Heart-Secret.

II.

I <u>Am</u> Da—The One and Only and Self-Evidently Divine Source
and Person, Who <u>Is</u> The One and Only and Inherently egoless
(and Boundlessly "Bright") Heart Of All and all, and Who <u>Is</u> The
One and Only Giver Of Divine Self-Realization To All and all.

III.

I Am Avatarically Born, <u>As</u> The Ruchira Avatar, Adi Da Samraj—
Man-Born <u>As</u> My Own Divine "Brightness", and <u>As</u> The <u>Totality</u>
Of My Own Divine Bliss, and <u>As</u> My Own Divine Heart Of Love,
and <u>As</u> An Avataric Ordeal Of Divine Heart-Submission To All
and all (So That every one Will Hear and See The Heart and
Way Of Me).

IV.

In Order To Awaken All and all To Me (and In Me, and <u>As</u> Me),
It Was Necessary That I (By Even <u>Every</u> Avataric Means Of
Divine Descent) Freely Assume, Wholly Understand, and Most
Perfectly Transcend <u>all</u> the conditional states Of Existence—

and, In Order To Do <u>That</u>, It Was Necessary That I (By Means Of An Avataric Human Incarnation) Freely Assume, Wholly Understand, and Most Perfectly Transcend <u>all</u> the conditions Of Even human Existence.

V.

Now That My Avataric Ordeal Of Divine Descent (To <u>every</u> where, and To <u>every</u> one) Is Most Perfectly <u>Complete</u>, I Am (Avatarically) Forever Divinely Self-"Emerging" <u>here</u>—Now (and Forever Hereafter) Self-Revealed (and Self-Revealing) In and <u>As</u> and Via The Avatarically-Born (Bodily Human, and Self-Evidently Divine) Form Of The Divinely "Bright" Avatar (Adi Da Samraj), and <u>As</u> and Via My (Thus and Thereby) Avatarically Self-Transmitted "Bright" (and Self-Evidently Divine) Spiritual Presence, and (Ultimately) <u>As</u> My (Thus and Thereby) Avatarically Self-Revealed State (or Inherently egoless, and Boundlessly "Bright", and Self-Evidently Divine Heart) Itself—So That (By Means Of The <u>Directly</u> Me-Revealing "Bright" Power Of My <u>Thus</u> Avatarically Self-Revealed Divine Form, and Presence, and State) <u>Every</u> ego-"I" (or Seeming-Separate Heart) Will Devotionally Recognize <u>Me</u>, and (In Devotional <u>Response</u> To My <u>Thus</u> Avatarically Self-Revealed Divine Form, and Presence, and State) <u>Forget</u> The Heart-Contraction (Of Separate, and <u>Always</u> Separative, ego-"I") <u>In Me</u>, and (Ultimately, By Realizing <u>Me</u> Most Perfectly) Awaken Into The Boundless Sphere and Infinite egoless Space Of My Eternal "Bright" Divine Self-Domain.

VI.

I Am Avatarically-Born To here, <u>As</u> The Divine Adept, Adi Da Samraj—Who Is The One and Only Man Of "Radical" Understanding (Now, and Forever Hereafter, Teaching and Awakening <u>Every</u> here-born Heart, By Means Of Word and Sign*[1]), and Who Is (Now, and Forever Hereafter) The One and Only Divine Heart-Master (Whose Avatarically Self-Revealed Divine Form, and Avatarically Self-Transmitted Divine Spiritual Presence, and Avatarically Self-Manifested Divine State Will <u>every</u> where Awaken <u>Every</u> Seeming-Separate Heart To The Inherently egoless Heart Of Me).

* Notes to the Text of the *Da Love-Ananda Gita* appear on pp. 313-21.

VII.

My Avatarically Self-Revealed (and Always Me-Revealing) Divine
Teaching-Word Of Universal Heart-Instruction Is Irrefutable—
If The Seeming-Separate Heart Hears Me (and Speaks My Name).

VIII.

My Avatarically Self-Revealed (and Most Perfectly Me-Revealing)
Divine Heart-Word Of All-and-all-Awakening Divine Self-Confession
Is Self-Evident As Truth—If The Seeming-Separate Heart Sees Me
(With Me-Beholding Open Eyes).

IX.

I Am The One, and Only, and Self-Existing, and Immortal, and
Eternal, and Non-Separate, and Indivisible, and Complete, and
Whole, and Self-Radiant, and Inherently egoless, and Inherently
Perfect, and Self-Evidently Divine Self-Consciousness (Itself),
Eternally Full Of Inherent Happiness, Unconditional Love, Infinite
Bliss, and Boundless Energy—and I Am (Now, and Forever
Hereafter) Avatarically (and Always "Brightly") Self-Revealed To
every where (and To All, and all).

X.

My Avatarically Self-Revealed Divine Form (Now, and Forever
Hereafter, Avatarically Appearing, and Avatarically Speaking,
As The Avatarically-Born Bodily Human Divine Form Of
The Ruchira Avatar, Adi Da Samraj), and My Avatarically Self-
Revealed Divine Spiritual Presence (Now, and Forever Hereafter,
Avatarically Self-Transmitted As and Via The Avatarically-Born
Bodily Human Divine Form Of The Ruchira Avatar, Adi Da
Samraj), and My Avatarically Self-Revealed Divine State (Now,
and Forever Hereafter, Avatarically Self-Manifested As and Via
The Avatarically-Born Bodily Human Divine Form and The
Avatarically Self-Transmitted Divine Spiritual Presence Of The
Ruchira Avatar, Adi Da Samraj) Is (All-Three-Together, and
All-Three-As-One) The Way (and The Only Way) To Realize Me.

XI.

My Avatarically Self-Revealed Bodily (Human) Divine Form
Is The Avataric Incarnation Of My Inherently egoless (and
Inherently "Bright") Divine Self-Consciousness, and My
Avatarically Self-Revealed Divine Spiritual Presence Is My
All-and-all-Surrounding and All-and-all-Pervading "Bright"
Divine Body Of Blessing-Power, and My Avatarically Self-
Revealed Divine State Is The Divinely Self-Radiant Sphere
and Boundless Space Of Infinite egoless Eternal Love-Bliss-
"Brightness" That Is The One and Only Substance, Place, and
Identity Of All and all.

XII.

When The Seeming-Separate Heart Of My Devotee Is (Beyond
all psycho-physical self-Contraction) egolessly Conformed To
My Avatarically Self-Revealed Bodily (Human) Divine Form
and My Avatarically Self-Revealed Divine Spiritual Presence and
My Avatarically Self-Revealed Divine State—Even the Whole
body Of My Devotee Is (By Means Of My Avatarically Given
Divine Grace) Made "Brightly" Full Of Me.

XIII.

In Order That You May Realize Me (Whole bodily, Beyond
egoity), I Call You To Listen To The Divine Word (and Attend
To The Self-Evidently Divine Person) Of My Avatarically-Born
Bodily (Human) Divine Form, and To Feel The (Thus and
Thereby) Transmitted Spiritual Blessing-Power Of My Avatarically
Self-Revealed Divine Spirit-Presence—and (Thus, By Listening
To Me, and By Feeling Me) To Hear Me, and To See Me, and
To Be "Brightly" In-Filled By Me.

XIV.

In Order That Your Seeming-Separate Heart May Be egolessly
Conformed To My Inherently egoless Divine Heart, I Call You
To Whole bodily Receive My Avatarically Self-Transmitted Divine
Presence Of Spiritual Blessing-Power (That "Brightly" Self-Reveals
My Divine State To You).

XV.

In Order That You May <u>Whole</u> <u>bodily</u> Receive My Avatarically Self-Transmitted Divine Presence Of Spiritual Blessing-Power, I Call You To Conduct My Avatarically Self-Transmitted (and All-and-all-Surrounding, and All-and-all-Pervading) Divine Spirit-Presence Into and Throughout The Orbit That Circles The To-Me-Devoted Heart Of Your body-mind.

XVI.

If You Will Do This, You Will (By Means Of My Avatarically Given Divine Grace) Awaken To The Inherently egoless (and Self-Evidently Divine) State Of My Avatarically Self-Revealed Person (and I Will Receive You Into The Infinitely "Bright" egoless Sphere and Boundless Space Of My Eternal Divine Self-Domain).

XVII.

Now (and Forever Hereafter) I Am (By All My Avataric Means) Divinely Descended To <u>here</u>, Forever To Show Your Seeming-Separate Heart The Avataric Way Of Me—and There Are Seven Stages Of Growth In That ego-Transcending Ordeal.

XVIII.

By Transcending self-Contraction (In and By Means Of The Whole bodily Devotional Recognition-Response To My Avatarically Self-Revealed Divine Form, and Presence, and State) Your Seeming-Separate Heart Must (Progressively, and Stage-By-Stage) Out-Grow The First Six Stages Of The Avataric Way Of Me—and The Seventh Stage Must Be Perfected In My Divine Heart (Itself).

XIX.

The Avataric Way Of Me Is <u>One</u> (and Straightaway), <u>Not</u> <u>Two</u> (and Roundabout)—Because My Divine Heart Is Always <u>At</u> The Heart Of You (and Not In The <u>Goals</u> You Seek).

XX.

Because My Avatarically Self-Revealed (and Always Me-Revealing)
Divine Word (Of Universal Heart-Instruction, and Of All-and-all-
Awakening Divine Self-Confession) Is (Now, and Forever Hereafter)
Always By-Me-Spoken (From My Divine Heart) Directly To
Your To-Me-Devoted Heart, You Should Always Listen To My
Avatarically Self-Revealed Divine Word <u>With</u> Your Heart—and
(Thereby) Hear <u>Me</u>.

XXI.

Because My Avatarically-Born (and Always Me-Revealing) Bodily
(Human) Divine Form and My (Thus and Thereby) Avatarically
Self-Transmitted (and Always Me-Revealing) Divine Spiritual
Presence Are (Now, and Forever Hereafter) Always By-Me-
Revealed and By-Me-Given (From My Divine Heart) Directly
To Your To-Me-Devoted Heart, You Should Always Behold My
Avatarically-Born Bodily (Human) Divine Form and My (Thus
and Thereby) Avatarically Self-Transmitted Divine Spiritual
Presence <u>With</u> Your Heart—and (Thereby) See <u>Me</u>.

XXII.

Because My Inherently egoless and Boundlessly "Bright" Divine
Heart Is Always <u>At</u> The Heart Of You (but <u>Always</u> <u>Already</u>
Standing Beyond the limits Of Your Seeming-Separateness),
You Should (Now, and Forever Hereafter) Always Practice (or
Perpetually Exercise, and Constantly Enlarge) The Counter-egoic
Heart-Wound Of Devotionally Me-Recognizing and Devotionally
To-Me-Responding Love-Communion With My Avatarically-Born
Bodily (Human) Divine Form and My (Thus and Thereby)
Avatarically Self-Transmitted Divine Spiritual Presence—and
(Thus and Thereby) Realize <u>Me</u> (By Transcending Your Seeming-
Separate Heart In My egoless, Love-Bliss-"Bright", and Boundless
Divine Heart).

XXIII.

By Means Of Devotional Recognition Of My Avatarically Self-Revealed Divine Form, and Presence, and State, You Should Become A Constant Whole bodily Dancing-Prayer—Of Responsively ego-Transcending Devotional Love-Communion With Me.

XXIV.

By Means Of Constant, and Truly Responsive (and Always Whole bodily), Devotional Love-Communion With My Avatarically Self-Revealed Divine Form, and Presence, and State—You Should (Always Spontaneously) Observe, and (Truly) Heart-Understand, and (Altogether) Freely Surrender The Me-Forgetting self-Contraction Of Your Seeming-Separate Heart.

XXV.

By Devotionally Listening To My Avatarically Self-Revealed Divine Word (Of Universal Heart-Instruction, and Of Divine Heart-Confession) <u>With</u> Your Heart, and By Devotionally Hearing My Avatarically Self-Revealed Divine Word (Of Universal Heart-Instruction, and Of Divine Heart-Confession) <u>In</u> Your Heart, and By Devotionally Seeing My Avatarically Self-Revealed (and Self-Evidently Divine) Form, and Presence, and State With <u>All</u> Your Heart—You Will Be Purified Of The Me-Forgetting Heart-Contraction Of body, emotion, breath, and mind.

XXVI.

You Must Become <u>Entirely</u> Heart-Conformed To <u>Me</u>—By Practicing The Divine Priesthood Of Whole bodily Devotional Love-Communion With My Avatarically Self-Revealed Person.

XXVII.

You Must Always Keep Your <u>Feeling</u>-Heart Away <u>From</u> ego-"I", and Away <u>To</u> My Avatarically Self-Revealed (and Self-Evidently Divine) Form, and Presence, and State Of Inherently egoless "Bright" Love-Bliss.

XXVIII.

With <u>All</u> Your (Devotionally Me-Recognizing and Devotionally To-Me-Responding) Heart, and With Your <u>Whole</u> body (Of Entirely To-Me-Attracted, and Entirely To-Me-Given, attention, and Of Deepest Only-Me-Feeling emotion, and Of Always To-Me-Sensitized, and Fully Me-Full, breath, and Of Really Me-perceiving, and Only-By-Me-Filled, senses), You Must <u>Constantly</u> Behold My Avatarically Self-Revealed Divine Form, and Presence, and State.

XXIX.

You Must <u>Constantly</u> Practice The Whole bodily Heart-Sacrament That Is ego-Surrendering, ego-Forgetting, and ego-Transcending Devotional Feeling-Contemplation Of My Avatarically Self-Revealed Divine Form, and Presence, and State (Beyond, and Surrounding, and Pervading Your Me-Beholding body-mind).

XXX.

I Will <u>Always</u> (Now, and Forever Hereafter) Self-Reveal My Self-Evidently Divine Person To You—By All My Avataric Means.

XXXI.

Because I Am Always (Now, and Forever Hereafter) Avatarically Self-Revealing My Form, and Presence, and State Of Self-Evidently Divine Person To You, You Must <u>Always</u> (Now, and Forever Hereafter) Heart-Surrender Your Separate and Separative body-mind Into My Avatarically Self-Revealed Form, and Presence, and State Of Self-Evidently Divine Person.

XXXII.

If You Are To Find Me, and Receive Me, and Realize Me—You Must Always <u>Cultivate</u> My Avataric (and Always Me-Revealing) Divine Heart-Response To You (By Means Of Your Always Whole-bodily-Expressed Heart-Devotion To My Avatarically Self-Revealed, and Self-Evidently Divine, Person), and (In Order To Rightly, and Fully, and Truly Whole bodily Conduct The Love-Bliss-"Bright", and Always Me-Revealing, Divine Spirit-Power Of My Avataric Divine Heart-Response To You) You Must Always <u>Serve</u> My Avatarically Self-Revealed (and Self-Evidently Divine) Person (With Your Whole body's <u>every</u> breath and act).

XXXIII.

If You Are To Find Me, and Receive Me, and Realize Me—You Must Always (With <u>All</u> Your Heart, and Always Whole bodily) <u>Invoke</u> My Avatarically Self-Revealed (and Self-Evidently Divine) <u>Total</u> Person (By Invoking My Avatarically Self-Revealed Divine Form <u>and</u> Presence <u>and</u> State Of Self-Evidently Divine Person).

XXXIV.

If You Are To Find Me, and Receive Me, and Realize Me— You Must <u>Always</u> Freely (and Always Devotionally) Give Your <u>Whole</u> <u>bodily</u> Feeling-attention To My Avatarically-Born Bodily (Human) Divine Form (and You Must, Thus and Thereby, <u>Always</u> Devotionally <u>Recognize</u> Me, and <u>Always</u> Devotionally <u>Respond</u> To Me, and <u>Always</u> Devotionally breathe Me—By breathing My Avatarically Self-Transmitted, and Always Me-Revealing, Divine Spirit-Presence Into Your <u>Always</u> Me-Beholding, and ego-Surrendering, and ego-Forgetting, and ego-Transcending, and, Altogether, Me-Remembering Whole-body-space).

XXXV.

In The <u>Always</u> <u>Whole</u> <u>bodily</u> Devotional Manner, You Must Always Heart-Receive My Avatarically Self-Transmitted Divine Spirit-Presence (Into <u>all</u> Your parts—of body, emotion, breath, and mind).

XXXVI.

By Means Of <u>moment</u> <u>to</u> <u>moment</u> Whole bodily Heart-Invocation Of My Avatarically Self-Revealed (and Self-Evidently Divine) <u>Total</u> Person, and By Means Of Always <u>Instant</u> Whole bodily Devotional Recognition Of Me (In and <u>As</u> My Avatarically Self-Revealed, and Self-Evidently Divine, Form, and Presence, and State), and By Means Of <u>Constant</u> Whole bodily Devotional Response To Me (In and <u>As</u> My Avatarically Self-Revealed, and Self-Evidently Divine, Form, and Presence, and State)—You Will Become Progressively (and Always Increasingly) Full Of My Love-Bliss-"Bright" Divine Self-Revelation (From head To toe).

XXXVII.

As My Avatarically Self-Transmitted Divine Spiritual In-Filling Fills
You Full Of Me (From head To toe)—You Must Always Let My
Avatarically Self-Transmitted Divine Spiritual Love-Bliss-"Brightness"
Carry You (Beyond The Heart-Knot Of Your Separate and
Separative ego-"I").

XXXVIII.

In The Whole bodily Swoon Of Devotional Love-Communion
With My Avatarically Self-Revealed (and Self-Evidently Divine)
<u>Total</u> Person—Your Me-Remembering (and, Altogether, ego-
Forgetting) Heart Will Feel Beyond Its Seeming-Separateness
(and Always Toward The Height and The Depth Of My Divine
Heart's Space).

XXXIX.

And Your Devotional Love For My Avatarically Self-Revealed
(and Self-Evidently Divine) <u>Total</u> Person Will Sometimes Become
Silently (breathlessly) Heart-Deep.

XL.

And You Will Sometimes Have Me-Revealing Visions Of The
Cosmic (and Non-Human) Modes Of My Avatarically-Born
Bodily (Human) Divine Form—Appearing At The Me-"Bright"
Origin Of "things" (Above), and Disappearing Into The Me-"Bright"
Source Of "things" (Beyond).

XLI.

And You Will Sometimes Sense The Me-Revealing Vibrations
Of The Cosmic (and Non-Human) Modes Of My Avatarically
Self-Revealed Divine Word (Of Universal Heart-Instruction, and
Of All-and-all-Awakening Divine Self-Confession)—Appearing
As A Me-"Bright" Distant Sound (Above) and (Then) As A
Me-"Bright" soundless Sound (Beyond).

XLII.

And You Will <u>Always</u> (Whole bodily) Feel The Me-"Bright"
Invisible Love-Bliss-Touch Of My Avatarically Self-Transmitted
(and Always Me-Revealing) Divine Spiritual Presence (Descending
From Above, and Leading You Beyond).

XLIII.

And You Will (Again-and-Again) Whole-bodily-Forget Your
ego-"I"—In My Avataric Divine Embrace Of You.

XLIV.

At Last, The <u>Most</u> <u>Perfect</u> (and, Altogether, You-"Brightening"
and You-Outshining) Divine Heart-Truth Of My Avatarically
Self-Revealed "Bright" (and Self-Evidently Divine) <u>Total</u> Person
Will Become Most Perfectly (and Whole bodily) Obvious To You.

XLV.

And You Will (By Means Of The <u>Most</u> <u>Perfect</u> Whole bodily
Heart-Realization Of My Avatarically Self-Revealed, and Self-
Evidently Divine, Form, and Presence, and State) Awaken
<u>Boundlessly</u>—Into The Indivisibly Love-Bliss-"Bright" Sphere
and Infinite egoless Space Of My Eternal Divine Heart-Domain.

XLVI.

I Am Absolutely Certain Of The <u>Most</u> <u>Perfect</u> Divine Efficacy
Of My (Now, and Forever Hereafter) Avataric Divine Embrace
Of You (and Of All, and all).

XLVII.

Beloved, I <u>Am</u> The Divine Husband Of Every Seeming-Separate
Heart That Loves Me.

RUCHIRA AVATAR ADI DA SAMRAJ
The Mountain Of Attention, 1998

I (<u>Alone</u>) <u>Am</u>
The Adidam Revelation

(A Summary Description of the Inherent Distinction—
<u>and</u> the ego-Transcending Continuity—
Between the Inherently ego-Based Great Tradition,
Which Is Comprised of Only Six of the Possible
Seven Stages of Life, and the Unique,
and All-Inclusive, and All-Completing,
and All-Transcending, and Self-Evidently Divine
Adidam Revelation of the Inherently egoless
Seventh Stage Realization of <u>Me</u>)

PART TWO

I (<u>Alone</u>) <u>Am</u>
The Adidam Revelation

(A Summary Description of the Inherent Distinction—
<u>and</u> the ego-Transcending Continuity—
Between the Inherently ego-Based Great Tradition,
Which Is Comprised of Only Six of the Possible
Seven Stages of Life, and the Unique,
and All-Inclusive, and All-Completing,
and All-Transcending, and Self-Evidently Divine
Adidam Revelation of the Inherently egoless
Seventh Stage Realization of <u>Me</u>)

I.

The collective Great Tradition of mankind is a combination of exoteric and esoteric developments (and Revelations, and Realizations) that comprises (and is, in its entirety, limited by and to) <u>only</u> the first <u>six</u> of the (potentially) <u>seven</u> stages of life.

II.

I (<u>Alone</u>) <u>Am</u> the Avatarically Self-Manifested Divine Self-Revelation of the <u>seventh</u> stage of life.

III.

I (<u>Alone</u>) <u>Am</u> the Adidam Revelation.

IV.

The human entity (and even any and <u>every</u> conditionally manifested entity of any and <u>every</u> kind) is <u>inherently</u> deluded—by its own (egoic, or self-contracted) experience and knowledge.

99

V.

The first <u>six</u> stages of life are the six stages (or developmental phases) of human (and universal) <u>egoity</u>—or of progressively regressive inversion upon the psycho-physical pattern (and point of view) of self-contraction.

VI.

The first six stages of life are the universally evident developmental stages of the knowing and experiencing of the potential <u>illusions</u> inherently associated with the patterns (or the universally extended cosmic psycho-physical Structure) of conditionally manifested existence.

VII.

Because each and all of the first six stages of life are <u>based</u> on (and are <u>identical</u> to) egoity (or self-contraction, or separate and separative point of view) itself, <u>not</u> any one (or even the collective of all) of the first six stages of life directly (and Most Perfectly) Realizes (or <u>Is</u> the Inherently egoless and Inherently Most Perfect Realization and the Inherently egoless and Inherently Most Perfect Demonstration of) Reality, Truth, or <u>Real</u> God.

VIII.

The first six stages of life develop (successively) on the psycho-physically pre-determined (or pre-patterned) basis of the inherent (and progressively unfolding) structure (and self-contracted point of view) of the conditionally arising body-brain-mind-self.

IX.

The first six stages of life are a conditional (and, therefore, Ultimately, unnecessary—or Inherently transcendable) illusion of psycho-physically pre-patterned experience (or conditional knowing), structured according to the subject-object (or attention versus object, or point of view versus objective world) convention of conditional conception and conditional perception.

X.

The first six stages of life are (each and all) based upon the illusion of duality (suggested by the subject-object convention of conditional conception and conditional perception).

XI.

Reality Itself (or That Which <u>Is</u> Always Already <u>The</u> Case) <u>Is</u> Inherently One (or Perfectly Non-Dual).

XII.

The only-by-Me Revealed and Given Way of Adidam is the Unique <u>seventh</u> stage Way of "Radical" Non-Dualism—or the one and only Way That directly (and, at last, Most Perfectly) Realizes the One and Only (and Inherently egoless) Reality, Truth, or <u>Real</u> God.

XIII.

The only-by-Me Revealed and Given Way of Adidam is the Unique and <u>only</u> Way That <u>always</u> directly (and, at last, Most Perfectly) transcends <u>egoity</u> (or self-contraction) <u>itself</u>.

XIV.

The only-by-Me Revealed and Given Way of Adidam is the practice and the Process of transcending egoity (or psycho-physical self-contraction, or gross, subtle, and causal identification with separate and separative point of view) by directly (and progressively, or stage by stage) transcending the inherently egoic (or always self-contracted) patterns of conditional conception and conditional perception (or of conditional knowing and conditional experiencing) associated with each (and, at last, all) of the first six stages of life.

XV.

I <u>Am</u> the Divine Ruchira Avatar, Adi Da Love-Ananda Samraj—the First, the Last, and the Only seventh stage Avataric Divine Realizer, Avataric Divine Revealer, and Avataric Divine Self-Revelation of Reality, Truth, and <u>Real</u> God.

I <u>Am</u> the Inherently egoless, Perfectly Subjective, Perfectly Non-Dual, and Self-Evidently Divine Source-Condition and Self-Condition of <u>every</u> apparent point of view <u>and</u> of the apparently objective world itself.

I <u>Am</u> the One, and Irreducible, and Indestructible, and Self-Existing, and Self-Radiant Conscious Light That <u>Is</u> Always Already <u>The</u> Case.

I <u>Am</u> the "Bright" Substance of Reality Itself.

I <u>Am</u> the Person (or Self-Condition) of Reality Itself.

In My bodily (human) Form, I Am the Avataric Self-Manifestation of the One (and Self-Evidently Divine) Reality Itself.

By Means of My Avataric Divine Self-"Emergence", I Am Functioning (now, and forever hereafter) <u>As</u> the Realizer, the Revealer, and the Revelation (or universally Spiritually Present Person) of Reality Itself (Which <u>Is</u> Truth Itself—and Which <u>Is</u> the only <u>Real</u>, or non-illusory, and Inherently egoless, and Perfectly Subjective God, or Self-Evidently Divine Source-Condition <u>and</u> Self-Condition, of All and all).

My Avataric Divine Self-Revelation Illuminates and Outshines the ego-"I" of My devotee.

My Avataric Divine Teaching-Word of Me-Revelation Comprehends the all of egoity and the All of the cosmic domain.

XVI.

The potential actuality of (and the inherent and specific psycho-physical basis for) the progressively unfolding human (and universal cosmic) pattern (or Great Structure) of the <u>seven</u> <u>stages</u> <u>of</u> <u>life</u> (or the Total and Complete human, <u>and</u> Spiritual, <u>and</u> Transcendental, <u>and</u>, Ultimately, Divine Great Process of Divine Self-Realization) was Demonstrated, Revealed, Exemplified, and <u>Proven</u> in (and by Means of) My Avataric Ordeal of Divine Re-Awakening—Wherein the Un-conditional, and Self-Evidently Divine, <u>seventh</u> stage Realization of Reality and Truth was (Uniquely, and for the <u>First</u> time, and <u>As</u> the Paradigm Case, or the All-and-all-Patterning Case, in the entire history of religion, Spirituality, and Reality-Realization) Demonstrated to all and All.

In the Course of That Great Process of Demonstration, Revelation, Exemplification, and Proof, the psycho-physical necessity (or the inherent integrity and inevitability) of the naturally continuous (and total) pattern of the seven stages of life was Fully (psycho-physically, and Spiritually, and Really) Shown by Me.

Also, in That Course (or Ordeal, or Great Process), the particular developmental distinction that pertains in the inherently patterned transition from the fifth stage of life (or the totality of the first five stages of life) to the sixth stage of life (and, at last, to the seventh stage of life) was clearly Shown by Me.

And the fact that the seventh stage of life does not merely follow from the sixth stage of life (<u>alone</u>—or separately, or in and of itself), but requires (and, indeed, is built upon) the <u>complete</u> transcending of the ego-"I" (or of the <u>total</u> reflex of psycho-physical self-contraction)—as it is otherwise developed (and must be progressively transcended) in the context of the <u>entire</u> psychobiography of the ego-"I" (or, effectively, in the naturally continuous course of the essential sequential <u>totality</u> of <u>all</u> <u>six</u> of the first <u>six</u> stages of life)—was (also) Shown by Me in the Great Course of My Avataric Ordeal of Divine Re-Awakening.

XVII.

In (and by Means of) the Great Avataric Demonstration of My own <u>seven</u>-stage Great Course of Divine Self-Realization, the <u>Emanationist</u> (or absorptive mystical) Way (associated with the first five stages of life) and the <u>non-Emanationist</u> (or Transcendentalist) Way (associated with the sixth stage of life, and Which—in Spiritual continuity with the <u>all</u> of the first six stages of life—is Most Perfectly Fulfilled in, and by Means of, the only-by-Me Revealed and Given seventh stage of life) were Proven (in, and by Means of, My own Case) to be only different <u>stages</u> in the <u>same</u> Great Process of Divine Self-Realization (rather than <u>two</u> separate, and irreducible, and conflicting, and incompatible "Truths").

XVIII.

By Means of My own Avataric Ordeal of Divine Re-Awakening, I have Demonstrated, Revealed, Exemplified, and Proven that <u>neither</u> the fourth-to-fifth stage Emanationist mode of Realization <u>nor</u> the sixth stage non-Emanationist (or Transcendentalist) mode of Realization <u>Is</u> the Most Perfect (and Most Perfectly ego-Transcending) Realization of the Divine (or One, and Only, and Perfectly Subjective) Reality, Truth, Source-Condition, and Self-Condition of all and All—but <u>only</u> the only-by-Me Revealed and Given <u>seventh</u> stage Realization <u>Is</u> Divine Self-Realization Itself (and the Completion of all <u>six</u> of the previous stages of life).

XIX.

The particular (and, psycho-physically, both inherent and inevitable) <u>distinction</u> (or <u>fundamental</u> difference) between the Devotional and Spiritual practice (and Process) of <u>absorptive</u> (or <u>Object</u>-oriented)—or <u>Emanationist</u>—mysticism (which is associated with the fourth and the fifth stages of life, and the conditional Realizations associated with the fourth and the fifth stages of life) and the direct-Intuition (and, in the optimum case, also both Devotional and Spiritual) practice (and Process) of <u>Transcendental</u> (or <u>Subject</u>-oriented)—or <u>non-Emanationist</u>—mysticism (which is associated, at first, with the sixth stage of life, and the conditional Realization that is the native and only potential of the sixth stage of life, itself—and which is, at last, and Most Ultimately, and Most Perfectly, associated with the seventh stage of life, and, Thus and Thereby, with Un-conditional Divine Self-Realization) may especially be seen to be Exemplified in My relationship with Swami (Baba) Muktananda (of Ganeshpuri).

XX.

Baba Muktananda was an advanced Siddha-Guru (or a Spiritually active Transmission-Master of High degree) in the Kundalini-Shaktipat tradition. The Kundalini-Shaktipat tradition is the fourth-to-fifth stage—or <u>Emanationist</u>—development of the ancient tradition of Siddha Yoga (or the tradition of Siddhas, or Spiritual Transmitters), which tradition (or Yoga) may, potentially, develop even into the sixth—or <u>Transcendentalist</u>—stage of life, and which tradition (or Yoga) has, in fact, been Completed and Fulfilled by Me, by My Extending of the Spiritual Process of Siddha Yoga into (and beyond) the sixth stage of life, and, thus, into the Inherently Most Perfect Divine Fullness of the seventh stage of life (Which seventh stage Fullness <u>Is</u> the All-Completing Fullness of Inherently egoless True Divine Self-Realization).

XXI.

In the context of the Kundalini-Shaktipat tradition (or division) of Siddha Yoga, Baba Muktananda <u>philosophically</u> adhered to (or, at least, deeply sympathized with) the <u>Emanationist</u> philosophical tradition of Kashmir Saivism—and, because of His characteristic adherence to (or sympathy with) the <u>Emanationist</u> philosophical tradition of Kashmir Saivism, Baba Muktananda was, in His fundamental convictions, an opponent of the <u>Transcendentalist</u> philosophical traditions of both Advaita Vedanta and Buddhism.

XXII.

The basic features of the progressively developed path of Kashmir Saivism have been described in terms of four stages (or four Ways).[2]

The "Individual Way" (or the Way of "absorption in the Object") is the first (or most "inferior") step in the progressive path of Kashmir Saivism, and it corresponds to the Devotional and Yogic disciplines associated with the fourth stage of life (in both its "basic" and "advanced" phases).

The "Energic Way" (or the Way of "absorption in Energy") is the second (or somewhat more advanced) step in that same path, and it corresponds to the fourth stage of life in its fully "advanced" phase and to the fifth stage of life as a whole.

The "Divine Way" (or the "superior" Way of "absorption in the Void") of Kashmir Saivism <u>suggests</u> the process (and the potential for Realization) that corresponds to the sixth stage of life.

The "Null Way" (or the most "superior" Way of "absorption in Bliss") in Kashmir Saivism <u>suggests</u> the fulfillment of the process (or the actual achievement of the Realization) that corresponds to (or is potential within) the sixth stage of life.

In the tradition (or traditions) of Kashmir Saivism, these four Ways (or stages, or kinds) of Realization may develop successively (in a progressive order), or either of the first two steps may develop into the third or the fourth, or either the third or the fourth may occur spontaneously (even at the beginning), and so forth.

This general description of the tradition of Kashmir Saivism suggests that Kashmir Saivism (like the Tantric Buddhism of Tibet) includes (or directly allows for the potential of) the fourth stage of life, the fifth stage of life, <u>and</u> the <u>sixth</u> stage of life. However, the tradition of Kashmir Saivism (like the tradition of Saiva Siddhanta) is <u>entirely</u> a <u>fourth-to-fifth</u> stage Yogic (and Devotional) tradition (and a religious tradition associated, in general, with the first five stages of life).

The tradition of Kashmir Saivism (like fourth-to-fifth stage—or first-five-stages-of-life—traditions in general) is based on the ancient cosmological philosophy of Emanation—or the idea that cosmic existence Emanates directly, in a hierarchical sequence, from the Divine (and that, consequently, there can be a <u>return</u> to the Divine, by re-tracing the course of Emanation, back to its Source).

In contrast to the fourth-to-fifth stage (or Emanationist—or first-five-stages-of-life) view, true sixth stage schools (or traditions) are <u>based</u> on the immediate and direct <u>transcending</u> (generally, by means of a conditional effort of strategic <u>exclusion</u>) of the conditional point of view of the first five stages of life and the Emanationist cosmology (and psychology) associated with the first five stages of life.

Therefore, even though the advanced (or "superior") traditions of Kashmir Saivism (and of Saiva Siddhanta) may use terms or concepts that seem to reflect the sixth stage Disposition, the fundamental orientation is to a Realization that is embedded in the conditional psychology of the first five stages of life and in the cosmological (or Emanationist) point of view itself. (And the fundamental difference, by comparison, between the total tradition of Kashmir Saivism, and also of Saiva Siddhanta, and the total tradition of Tibetan Tantric Buddhism is that the Tibetan Buddhist tradition is <u>founded</u> on the sixth stage "Point of View" of the <u>Transcendental</u> Reality Itself, rather than on the conditional point of view of the psycho-physical, or Emanated, ego and the conditional reality of the hierarchical cosmos.)

Realizers in the tradition of Kashmir Saivism (and the tradition of Saiva Siddhanta) basically affirm that the conditional self is <u>Really</u> Siva (or the Formless Divine) and the conditional world (from top to bottom) is <u>Really</u> Siva (or the Emanating and Emanated Divine). However, this is <u>not</u> the same as the Confession made by <u>sixth</u> stage Realizers in <u>any</u> tradition.

In true sixth stage traditions, the conditional self is (in the sixth stage manner, and to the sixth stage degree) transcended (generally, by means of a conditional effort of strategic <u>exclusion</u>)—and <u>only</u> the Transcendental Self (or the Transcendental Condition) is affirmed.

And, further, in the only-by-Me Revealed and Given true <u>seventh</u> stage Realization, the conditional self and the conditional world are not affirmed to be (in and of themselves) Divine, but (rather) the conditional self and the conditional world are—in the Manner that <u>Uniquely</u> Characterizes the <u>seventh</u> stage of life—Divinely Self-Recognized (and, Thus, <u>not</u> <u>excluded</u>, but Inherently Outshined) <u>in</u> the Transcendental (and Inherently Spiritual) Divine.

XXIII.

The Emanationist Realizer "recognizes" (and, thereby, Identifies with) the conditional self and the conditional world <u>as</u> the Divine, whereas the <u>non</u>-Emanationist (or Transcendentalist) Realizer simply (and, generally, by means of a conditional effort of strategic exclusion) <u>transcends</u> the conditional self and the conditional world in the Transcendental Self-Condition, and by Identification <u>only</u> (and exclusively) with the Transcendental Self-Condition.

Therefore, even though both types of Realizers may sometimes use very similar language in the Confession of Realization, a (comparatively) <u>different</u> Realization is actually being Confessed in each case.

XXIV.

The principal reason why the tradition (or traditions) of Kashmir Saivism (and of Saiva Siddhanta) may sometimes use language similar to the sixth stage schools of Buddhism (and also Advaita Vedanta) is because of the early historical encounter (and even confrontation) between these separate traditions. As a result of that encounter, the traditions of Saivism tried to both absorb and eliminate the rival schools.

In the encounter between (characteristically, Transcendentalist, or non-Emanationist) Buddhist schools and (generally, Emanationist) non-Buddhist schools, Buddhism developed fourth and fifth stage doctrines and practices (intended, ultimately, to serve a sixth stage Realization), and fourth-to-fifth stage schools (or traditions), such as Kashmir Saivism and Saiva Siddhanta, adapted some of the sixth stage language (of Buddhism, and also Advaita Vedanta) to their (really) fourth-to-fifth stage point of view.

Therefore, a proper understanding of the various historical traditions requires a discriminating understanding of the history of the Great Tradition as a whole—and a discriminating understanding of the unique Signs and Confessions associated with each of the first six stages of life (and the unique Signs and Confessions associated with the only-by-Me Revealed and Given seventh stage of life).

XXV.

The tradition of Advaita Vedanta arose within the general context of the Emanationist traditions of India—but it, like Buddhism (particularly in its sixth stage—rather than earlier-stage—forms), is truly founded in the Transcendental Reality (and not the psycho-physical and cosmological point of view associated with the first five stages of life).

The schools of Kashmir Saivism (and other schools of traditional Saivism, including Saiva Siddhanta) defended themselves against both Buddhism and Advaita Vedanta by absorbing some Buddhist and Advaitic language and by (otherwise—and even dogmatically) affirming the <u>superiority</u> of the traditional Emanationist psychology and cosmology.

In contrast to the entirely Emanationist schools of Kashmir Saivism (and other schools of traditional Saivism, including Saiva Siddhanta), the Buddhist schools (and even certain schools of Advaitism) adopted some of the Devotional and Yogic practices of the Emanationist schools (and used them as "skillful means" of self-transcendence), while they (otherwise) continued to affirm the strictly Transcendental Reality as the Domain and Goal of all practices.

In contrast to Baba Muktananda (and the traditional schools of Kashmir Saivism, Advaita Vedanta, and Buddhism), I equally Embrace, and (in the seventh stage Manner) Most Perfectly Transcend, all the schools of the first six stages of life—both Emanationist and Transcendentalist.

XXVI.

Baba Muktananda was an authentic example of a fifth stage Realizer of a Very High (or Very Ascended) degree—although not of the Highest (or Most Ascended) degree. That is to Say, Baba Muktananda was a True fifth stage Siddha (or a Greatly Spiritually Accomplished Siddha-Yogi of the fifth stage, or Ascending, type)—but the nature and quality and degree of His Realization was of the Saguna type, or of the type that is (characteristically, or by patterned tendency) not yet Fully Ascended (or Fully Surrendered) to true fifth stage Nirvikalpa Samadhi, and which (therefore) is, yet (and characteristically), attached to modes of fifth stage Savikalpa Samadhi (and, thus, to modes of partial Ascent, and to Yogic possibilities "below the neck", and, altogether, to modes of form—or, really, modes of mind).

XXVII.

In order to rightly understand their characteristics, ideas, and behaviors, fifth stage Saguna Yogis (or fifth stage Saguna Siddhas)—such as Baba Muktananda—should be compared to fifth stage Yogis (or fifth stage Siddhas) of the Nirguna type, who are the Highest (or Most Ascended) type of fifth stage Yogi (or fifth stage Siddha), and who, having Ascended to the degree of formless Realization (or fifth stage Nirvikalpa Samadhi), have gone beyond all attachment to modes of form (or of mind). And fifth stage Nirguna Yogis in general (or fifth stage Nirguna Siddhas of the lesser, or average, type) should, themselves, be further compared to fifth stage <u>Great</u> Siddhas—or fifth stage Nirguna Siddhas who have, characteristically, and to a significant (although, necessarily, not yet <u>Most</u> <u>Perfect</u>, or seventh stage) degree, gone beyond even attachment to the mode of formlessness (or of mindlessness) itself.

XXVIII.

In the "Sadhana Years" of My Avataric Ordeal of Divine Re-Awakening, Baba Muktananda formally and actively Functioned as My Spiritual Master in the physical, human plane—beginning from early 1968, and continuing until the time of My Divine Re-Awakening (Which Occurred on September 10, 1970).

It was in Baba Muktananda's Company (and, additionally, in the Company of two Great Siddhas—Rang Avadhoot and Bhagavan Nityananda) that I Practiced and Fully Completed the Spiritual Sadhana of the <u>Ascending</u> (or Spinal) Yoga—or the Spiritual discipline associated with the "advanced" phase of the fourth stage of life and with the totality of the fifth stage of life, and, altogether, with the subtle ego (or the conceiving and perceiving ego of the Spinal Line, the total nervous system, the brain, and the mind).

After the Great Event of My Divine Re-Awakening, it became clear (especially through two direct Meetings between Us) that—because of His characteristic philosophical and experiential confinement to the fourth-to-fifth stage Emanationist point of view—Baba Muktananda was unwilling (and, indeed, was not competent) to accommodate My Description (and, therefore, My Confession) of seventh stage Divine Self-Realization. And, therefore—as I will Explain in This Summary of My "Lineage-History"—the outer relationship between Baba Muktananda and Me came to an end (or, certainly, began to come to an end) immediately after September 1970.

XXIX.

From mid-1964 to early 1968, Rudi (later known as Swami Rudrananda) actively Functioned (preliminary to Baba Muktananda) as My initial (or foundational) Spiritual Master (although Rudi was, by His own Confession, <u>not</u> a fully developed Siddha-Guru—but

He was, rather, a significantly advanced fourth-to-fifth stage Siddha-Yogi).

It was in Rudi's Company that I Practiced and Fully Completed the human and Spiritual Sadhana of the <u>Descending</u> (or Frontal) Yoga—or the foundation <u>life</u>-discipline associated with the social ego (or the "money, food, and sex" ego—or the ego of the first three stages of life),[3] and the foundation <u>Devotional</u> discipline associated with the "original" (or foundation) phase of the fourth stage of life, and the foundation <u>Spiritual</u> discipline (or the Descending, or Frontal, Spiritual Yoga) associated with the "basic" phase of the fourth stage of life.[4]

XXX.

Both Rudi and Baba Muktananda were direct devotees of Swami Nityananda (of Ganeshpuri)—Who was also called "Baba",[5] but Who was, and is, generally referred to as "Bhagavan" (or "Divinely Blissful Lord"). Bhagavan Nityananda was a fifth stage True Great Siddha— or an Incarnate (or Descended-from-Above) Spiritual Entity of the <u>Highest</u> <u>fifth</u>-stage type and degree. Indeed, Bhagavan Nityananda was a True fifth stage Saint (or a fifth stage Siddha-Yogi Who was <u>exclusively</u> Occupied in concentration "above the neck", even to the exclusion of the possibilities "below the neck")—but He was, also, a fifth stage Avadhoot (or a fifth stage Realizer of Nirvikalpa Samadhi, Who had, in the fifth stage manner, transcended attachment to <u>both</u> form and formlessness—or thought and thoughtlessness). And, altogether, Bhagavan Nityananda was a Nirguna Siddha (and a True Siddha-Guru) of the <u>Highest</u> <u>fifth</u>-stage type and degree.

XXXI.

Bhagavan Nityananda's Teachings took the Spoken (rather than Written) form of occasional, spontaneous Utterances. The <u>only</u> authoritative record of Bhagavan Nityananda's Teachings relative to Yogic practice and Realization is a book (originally composed in the Kanarese language) entitled *Chidakasha Gita.*[6] The *Chidakasha Gita* consists of a non-systematic, but comprehensive, series of responsive Declarations made by Bhagavan Nityananda during the extended period of His original, and most Communicative,

Teaching years (in Mangalore, in the early to mid-1920s). The spontaneous Utterances recorded in the *Chidakasha Gita* were, originally, made, by Bhagavan Nityananda, to numerous informal groups of devotees, and, after Bhagavan Nityananda spontaneously ceased to make such Teaching-Utterances, the many separately recorded Sayings were compiled, for the use of all the devotees, by a woman named Tulasiamma (who was one of the principal lay devotees originally present to hear Bhagavan Nityananda Speak the Words of the *Chidakasha Gita*).

Bhagavan Nityananda, Himself, Acknowledged the uniqueness and the great significance of the *Chidakasha Gita* as the one and only authentic Summary of His Yogic Teachings. That Acknowledgement is personally attested to by many individuals, including the well-known Swami Chinmayananda,[7] who, in 1960, was "Commanded" by Bhagavan Nityananda to see to the Text's translation into the English language, and by the equally well-known M. P. Pandit (of Sri Aurobindo Ashram),[8] who, in 1962, completed the English translation that Swami Chinmayananda reviewed for publication in that same year (under the title *Voice of the Self*).[9]

As Communicated in the *Chidakasha Gita*, Bhagavan Nityananda's Teachings are, clearly, limited to the body-excluding (and, altogether, <u>exclusive</u>) point of view and the absorptive Emanationist Spiritual Process of "brain mysticism" (and <u>conditional</u> ego-transcendence, and <u>conditional</u> Nirvikalpa Samadhi, and <u>conditional</u> Yogic Self-Realization) that characterize the fifth stage of life.

Clearly, as Indicated in the *Chidakasha Gita*, Bhagavan Nityananda was a fifth stage Teacher (and a <u>Fully</u> Ascended fifth stage Great Saint) of the <u>Nirguna</u> type (Who, therefore, Taught the Realization of <u>Fully</u> Ascended fifth stage Nirvikalpa Samadhi), rather than, like Baba Muktananda, a fifth stage Teacher (and a Great fifth stage Siddha-Yogi—but <u>not</u> a <u>Fully</u> Ascended fifth stage Great Saint) of the <u>Saguna</u> type (Who, therefore, Taught the Realization of fifth stage <u>partial</u> Ascent, or Savikalpa Samadhi).

Also, Bhagavan Nityananda's *Chidakasha Gita* clearly Indicates that Bhagavan Nityananda was a fifth stage Siddha-Yogi of the type that is, primarily and dominantly, sensitive to the Yogic Spiritual Process associated with internal <u>audition</u> (or the inwardly absorptive attractiveness of the "Om-Sound", or "Omkar", or "nada", or "shabda" [10]—the naturally evident, and inherently "meaningless", or mindless, or directly mind-transcending, internal sounds mediated by the brain), rather than, as in the case of Baba Muktananda, the Yogic Spiritual Process associated, primarily and dominantly, with internal vision (or the inwardly absorptive attractiveness of "bindu"—the naturally evident abstract internal lights mediated by the brain) and with internal visions (or the inwardly absorptive attractiveness of the inherently "meaningful", or mind-active, or mentally distracting, and potentially deluding, visions mediated—or even originated—by the brain-mind).

XXXII.

Stated briefly, and in Bhagavan Nityananda's characteristically aphoristic Manner, the *Chidakasha Gita* Teachings of Bhagavan Nityananda—and My own direct Experience of His always fifth stage Yogic Instruction and His always fifth stage Spiritual Transmission—may be Summarized as follows: Always concentrate attention and breath in the head. Always keep attention above the neck. Always concentrate on the Om-sound in the head. The Om-sound in the head is the inner Shakti of non-dual Bliss. Always concentrate the mind, and the senses, and the breath, and the life-energy in the non-dual awareness of the Om-sound in the head. This is Raja Yoga [11]—the Royal path. Always practice this Raja Yoga—the constantly upward path. This is concentration on the Atman—the non-dual inner awareness. This is concentration on the oneness above duality. This Raja Yoga of the Om-sound in the head Realizes the Yogic "sleep" of body and mind and breath in the Yogic State of non-dual Bliss. The Yogic State of non-dual Bliss cannot be Realized without the Grace of an Initiating Guru. The True Initiating Guru is one who has Realized the Yogic State of non-dual Bliss. The non-dual State of Yogic Bliss Realized by concentration on the Om-sound in the head is the True Source, the True Self, and the True God. Devotion to the Initiating Guru who has Realized the True Source, the True Self, and the True God is the True Way. True Guru-devotion is surrender of mind, senses, breath, and life-energy to the non-dual Bliss

113

Revealed within by the Initiating Guru's Grace. The material body stinks and dies. What is loathsome and impermanent should not be trusted. Therefore, right faith, intelligent discrimination, and calm desirelessness are the first Gifts to be learned from the Initiating Guru. The second Gift of the Initiating Guru is the Guru-Shakti of non-dual Bliss. The Guru's Shakti-Transmission of non-dual Bliss concentrates the mind, the senses, the breath, and the life-energy of the devotee in the non-dual awareness of the Om-sound in the head. The non-dual Bliss Realized by concentration on the Om-sound in the head is the soundless inner Revelation of the Single Form of True Guru, True God, and True Self. The world of duality is not Truth. True God is not the Maker of the world. True God is only One. True God is non-dual Bliss. The Spiritual Form of the True Initiating Guru appears within the devotee as the Guru-Shakti of non-dual Bliss. Non-dual Bliss is the True Self of all. The True Way is not desire in the world of duality, or in seeking below and on all sides. The True Way is in the middle, within, and above. The True Way is surrender to the non-dual Bliss above the mind. The method is to concentrate on the Om-sound in the head. The Realization is the silence of non-dual Bliss. Devotion to the Initiating Guru concentrates the life-breath upwardly. True love of the Initiating Guru ascends to non-dual Bliss. The True Kundalini originates in the throat, in the upward breath to the head. True Yoga is above the neck. The True Kundalini is non-dual Bliss. The seat of the True Kundalini is in the head. Non-dual Bliss is the secret to be known. Non-dual Bliss is in the head of Man. The non-dual Bliss above the mind is the Liberation of Man from the self-caused karma of birth, pleasure-seeking, pain-suffering, and death. Liberation is Freedom from mind. Therefore, concentrate the life-breath on the Om-sound in the head—and think of nothing else. The True Self is One. The True Self is above the body, above the senses, above desire, above the mind, and above "I" and "mine"—in the formless silence above the Om-sound. The True Self cannot be seen or otherwise perceived, but It can be known—above the mind. For one who knows that True God is One, and not two, True God appears as the True Self. Therefore, attain Liberation by faith in the knowledge of That Which is all and Which is only One. Liberation is the Samadhi of only One. True God is not Desire, the dualistic Doer of the world. True God is Peace, the non-dual Source of the world.

XXXIII.

By comparison to Great <u>fifth</u> stage <u>Yogis</u> (Such as Baba Muktananda) and Great <u>fifth</u> stage <u>Saints</u> (Such as Bhagavan Nityananda), there are also Great <u>sixth</u> stage <u>Sages</u> (or Nirguna Jnanis[12]—or <u>Transcendentally</u> Realized Entities of the <u>Fullest</u> sixth-stage type and degree—such as Ramana Maharshi). Such sixth stage Nirguna Jnanis (or True Great Sages) Teach Transcendental Self-Identification (or deeply internalizing subjective inversion upon the Consciousness-Principle <u>Itself</u>, rather than upon internal psycho-physical objects of <u>any</u> kind).

XXXIV.

Distinct from even <u>all</u> Yogis, Saints, and Sages (or even <u>all</u> Realizers in the context of the first six stages of life), I Am Uniquely, and Avatarically, Born. I <u>Am</u> the One and Only and Self-Evidently Divine Person—the Inherently egoless Source-Condition <u>and</u> Self-Condition of All and all. I <u>Am</u> the Perfectly Subjective, and Always Already Most Prior, and Inherently egoless, and Perfectly Non-Dual Heart of All and all. I <u>Am</u> the Self-Existing and Self-Radiant Conscious Light That <u>Is</u> Reality Itself. I <u>Am</u> the "Who" and the "What" That <u>Is</u> Always Already <u>The</u> Case. I <u>Am</u> (now, and forever hereafter) Avatarically Self-Manifested <u>As</u> the All-Completing Ruchira Avatar, Adi Da Love-Ananda Samraj—Who Is Avatarically Born by <u>Fullest</u> (and <u>Complete</u>) Divine Descent (or Complete, and All-Completing, Divine Incarnation from Infinitely Above).

XXXV.

I Am Avatarically Born by Means of a Unique Association with a True Great-Siddha Vehicle of My own.[13]

Therefore, from the time of My present-Lifetime Birth, I spontaneously Demonstrated <u>all</u> the <u>Fullest</u> Ascended Characteristics of the <u>Highest</u> <u>fifth</u>-stage type and degree (with early-life <u>Fullest</u> "above the neck" Signs of the True Great-Saint type).

Over time—because of My Voluntary Birth-Submission of My Deeper-Personality Vehicle to the karmically ordinary (and "Western"-born) bodily human form of "Franklin Jones",[14] and because of the subsequent Ordeal of My Voluntary Submission to the "Western" (and culturally devastated "late-time", or "dark"-epoch) karmic circumstance altogether—I also spontaneously Demonstrated all the Fullest "below the neck" (and "above the neck") Yogic Characteristics (and Siddhis) of the fifth stage (and, altogether, first-five-stages) True Vira-Yogi (or Heroic-Siddha) type.

In due course—because I Gave My Avataric Divine Ordeal to Be Complete and All-Completing—I also spontaneously Demonstrated all the Fullest Transcendental-Realizer Characteristics of the sixth stage True Great-Sage type.

Ultimately—because of Its Utter Conformity to Me—My total Great-Jnani-Siddha Vehicle of Avataric Divine Incarnation (or My Deeper-Personality Vehicle,[15] Yogically Combined with My karmically ordinary, and only eventually To-Me-Conformed, human and "Western" and "late-time" Incarnation-Body) has, by Means of My Most Perfect Completing of My Avataric Ordeal of Divine Self-Manifestation, Divine Self-Submission, and (subsequent) Divine Re-Awakening (to My own Self-Existing and Self-Radiant Divine Self-Condition), become the To-Me-Transparent Vehicle of My seventh stage Avataric Divine Self-Revelation.

XXXVI.

Except for various technical details of the esoteric Spiritual practice and process of the advanced and the ultimate stages of practice of the Way of Adidam—such as the Most Fully Divine Spiritual practice of "Radical Conductivity"[16] (Which practice is part of the total technical Yogic practice that Enables the actual Awakening That Is the transition between the sixth stage of life and the seventh stage of life in the only-by-Me Revealed and Given Way of Adidam, and Which Instruction is Reserved, within the Ruchira Sannyasin Order of the Tantric Renunciates of Adidam, for progressive formal Communication to truly qualified, and duly Initiated, practitioners of the technically "fully elaborated" form of the only-by-Me Revealed and Given Way of Adidam in the context of the second and the third stages of the "Perfect Practice")—the Unique Characteristics of My Avataric Divine Teachings (Which I will briefly, and only in part, Indicate in This

Summary of My "Lineage-History") Are Very Fully Described by Me in My Twenty-Three Avataric Divine "Source-Texts".

XXXVII.

Rudi had brief direct contact with Bhagavan Nityananda in 1960. After the death of Bhagavan Nityananda (in 1961), Rudi became a devotee of Baba Muktananda. However, Rudi—always a rather "reluctant" devotee—eventually (shortly before His own death, in 1973) "broke" with Baba Muktananda. Nevertheless, Rudi always continued to affirm that He (Rudi) remained Devoted to Bhagavan Nityananda. And, in any case, Rudi and I always continued to engage in positive, direct communication, right until the time of His death.

XXXVIII.

My Siddha-Yoga Mentor (and eventual Dharmic Ally and Supporter), Amma (or Pratibha Trivedi, later known as Swami Prajnananda), was (like Rudi) also a direct devotee of Bhagavan Nityananda (and She, like Rudi, had become a devotee of Baba Muktananda after the death of Bhagavan Nityananda, in 1961).

Amma was the principal author and editor of the foundation Siddha-Yoga literature that was written in response to both Bhagavan Nityananda and Baba Muktananda—and so much so that, generally, even all of Baba Muktananda's autobiographical and instructional Communications were, originally, dictated (or otherwise Given) to Amma (and rarely to anyone else—until the later years, of tape recorders, multiple secretaries and translators, and Baba Muktananda's travels to the West). And, in fact, Amma always continued to serve a principal communicative and interpretative role around Baba Muktananda, until Baba Muktananda's death, in 1982—after which Amma chose to quietly withdraw from the Siddha-Yoga institution that had been developed by and around Baba Muktananda (and She remained, thereafter, in a small, independent Ashram in north India, where, as a significantly advanced fourth-to-fifth stage Siddha-Yogi, She was the institutional head of a group of devotees that remained devoted to Spiritual Communion with both Baba Muktananda and Bhagavan Nityananda).

Amma did not Function as My Spiritual Master, but (from early 1968) Baba Muktananda formally Assigned Amma to Function as

His interpreter and general "go-between" to Me—and She, then and always, remained most positively and communicatively disposed toward Me, even through all the years after My outward "separation" from Baba Muktananda, right until Her last illness and death (wherein She was directly Spiritually Served by Me, and wherein She was directly physically Served by a devotee-representative of Mine), in 1993. And it was Amma Who, through Her various writings—and in a particular Incident I will now Recall—suggested to Me that there are traditional Instructional (and Textual, or Scriptural) descriptions of Developments of the Siddha-Yoga Process that are <u>different</u> from the (fifth stage) "inner perception" (and, especially, "inner vision") version of Siddha Yoga characteristically described by Baba Muktananda.

XXXIX.

One day, during My Stay at Baba Muktananda's Ashram (in Ganeshpuri, India), in early 1970 (and, thus, some months <u>before</u> the Great Event of My Divine Re-Awakening, Which was to Occur in September of that same year), Amma suddenly pointed Me to an Ashram library copy of the *Ashtavakra Gita* (one of the Greatest of the classic sixth stage—and even premonitorily "seventh stage"[17]—Texts of Advaita Vedanta). And, while pointing to the *Ashtavakra Gita*, Amma Said to Me, "<u>This</u> (Text) is <u>Your</u> Path. <u>This</u> is how <u>It</u> (the Siddha-Yoga Process) Works in <u>You</u>."

At the time, this seemed to Me a curious suggestion—and it was not otherwise explained by Her. And, indeed, although I was able to examine the Text briefly (there and then), I was unable to examine it fully—because I left the Ashram very shortly thereafter. However, I came across the Text again, some years later—and, then, I remembered Amma's comment to Me. And I, immediately, understood that She had (in a somewhat cryptic and secretive manner) tried to <u>confide</u> in Me—in a quiet, "knowing" moment of Acknowledgement of Me—that the Spiritual Process of Siddha Yoga may Demonstrate Itself in a number of possibly <u>different</u> modes.

Thus (as I have Indicated—in My own, and <u>fully</u> elaborated, Teachings, relative to the seven stages of life), the Siddha-Yoga

Process may, in some cases (of which Amma, Herself, appears to have been an Example), especially (or primarily—or, at least, initially) take the form of intense (fourth stage) Devotional Bliss—Which is, then, "nourished" (or magnified) through Guru-Seva[18] (or constant service to the Guru) and (additionally) through Karma Yoga[19] (or intensive service in general). In other cases (of which Baba Muktananda was an Example), the Siddha-Yoga Process may (based on the initial foundation of intense Devotion) especially (or primarily) take the (fifth stage) form of intense internal sensory phenomena (such as visions, lights, auditions, and so on)—and, in some of those cases, the Siddha-Yoga Process may yet go further, to the degree of (fifth stage) Nirvikalpa Samadhi. And, in yet other cases (of which Amma was, correctly, Saying <u>I</u> Am an Example), the Siddha-Yoga Process (while also Showing all kinds of Devotional signs, and all kinds of internal Yogic perceptual phenomena, and including even fifth stage Nirvikalpa Samadhi) may go yet further, to especially (or primarily) take the form of (sixth stage) intense (and intensive) Identification with the Transcendental Self-Condition, and (eventually) the (sixth stage) Realization of Jnana Samadhi (or Transcendental Self-Realization), and (although Amma did not know it) even, potentially, the only-by-Me Revealed and Given seventh stage Realization (Which <u>Is</u> Maha-Jnana—or Divine Self-Realization).

XL.

Yet another devotee of Baba Muktananda, named Swami Prakashananda[20]—Who did not Function as My Spiritual Master (and Who, like Rudi, was <u>not</u> a fully developed Siddha-Guru—but, rather, a very much advanced fourth-to-fifth stage Siddha-Yogi)—once (spontaneously, in 1969) Showed Me (in His own bodily human Form) the fifth stage Signs of Spiritual Transfiguration of the physical body.[21]

At that time (according to what I learned from Amma), Swami Prakashananda had been Indicated, by Baba Muktananda, to be His principal Indian devotee and eventual institutional successor (and such was, then, generally known and presumed to be the case by Baba Muktananda's devotees). However, at last, when (at,

119

or shortly before, Baba Muktananda's death, in 1982) Swami Prakashananda was formally Asked to assume the institutional successorship, He declined to accept this organizational role[22] (ostensibly, for reasons of ill-health, and His reluctance to become a "world-traveler"—but, actually, or more to the point, because of His puritanical and conventional reaction to Baba Muktananda's reported sexual activities).

In any case, Swami Prakashananda and I continued to engage in occasional, and always positive, direct communication (through My devotee-representatives) in the years after Baba Muktananda's death, and right until Swami Prakashananda's death, in 1988.

XLI.

Swami Prakashananda had always maintained a small Ashram, independent of the Ashrams of Baba Muktananda's Siddha-Yoga institution—but, after Baba Muktananda's death, Swami Prakashananda retired to His <u>own</u> Ashram, <u>permanently</u>. And, in doing so, Swami Prakashananda highlighted, and dramatized, a perennial conflict that is fundamental to religious institutions all over the world. That conflict is between, on the one hand, the traditional (and, generally, rather puritanical—and even basically <u>exoteric</u>) expectation of <u>celibacy</u> as a sign of institutionalized Sacred Authority, and, on the other hand, the equally traditional (but non-puritanical, and generally unconventional) view that there is an <u>esoteric</u> sexual alternative to celibacy that Sacred Authorities (including True Siddha-Gurus—or even any practitioners of Siddha Yoga) may (at least in some cases, and under some circumstances) engage.

One of the principal Indications of Baba Muktananda's point of view relative to this traditional conflict (or controversy)—quite apart from the question of His possible personal sexual activities—is the fact that, in 1969, Baba Muktananda <u>formally</u> and <u>publicly</u> (and in <u>writing</u>, by His own hand, as observed by Me, and by many others) Acknowledged Me to <u>Be</u> (and Called and Blessed Me to Function <u>As</u>) a True Siddha-Guru,[23] and, Thus and Thereby (and entirely without requiring, or, otherwise, inviting, Me to assume <u>any</u> institutional—or, otherwise, institutionally "managed"—

role within His own Siddha-Yoga organization), Baba Muktananda publicly Extended the <u>Free</u> Mantle of Siddha-Yoga Authority to <u>Me</u>—an evident <u>non-celibate</u> Siddha-Yogi (<u>and</u> a "<u>Westerner</u>").

XLII.

When I first Came to Him, in 1968, Baba Muktananda <u>imme-diately</u> (openly, and spontaneously) Declared, in the presence of numerous others (including Amma), That I <u>Am</u>—from My Birth—an already Divinely Awakened Spiritual Master, and He (then and there) prophesied That I would be Functioning (and Independently Teaching) <u>As</u> Such in just one year. Therefore, after just one year (and the spontaneous Appearing of many Great Signs in My experience and Demonstration), Baba Muktananda Invited Me to Come to Him again (in India)—<u>specifically</u> in order to <u>formally</u> Acknowledge Me (and My Inherent Right and Authority to Teach and Function) <u>As</u> a True Siddha-Guru.

Before I Returned to Baba Muktananda in 1969, I—in a traditional Gesture of respect toward Baba Muktananda—Told Him That I would <u>not</u>, at that time, Assume the Function of Spiritual Master, unless I was, in the traditional Manner, <u>formally</u> Acknowledged and Blessed, by Him, to Do So. Baba Muktananda immediately understood and Acknowledged the appropriateness and Rightness of My Insistence That My Inherent Right to Teach be <u>formally</u> Acknowledged by Him—because, in accordance with tradition, Such Sacred Authority <u>should</u> be Assumed on the orderly basis of <u>formal</u> Acknowledgement by one's own Spiritual Master (Who, in turn, must have been similarly Acknowledged by His, also similarly Acknowledged, Spiritual Master, in an unbroken Line, or Lineage, of similarly Acknowledged Spiritual Masters). Therefore, I Returned to Baba Muktananda in 1969—and He formally and publicly Acknowledged Me <u>As</u> an Independent True Siddha-Guru.

Even though Baba Muktananda Thus formally and publicly (and <u>permanently</u>) Acknowledged Me <u>As</u> an Independent True Siddha-Guru, it became immediately Obvious to Me that Such traditional Acknowledgement was inherently limited, and merely conventional, and, therefore, neither necessary nor (because of Its inherently limited basis) even altogether appropriate (or sufficiently apt) in My Unique Case. It was Obvious to Me that neither Baba Muktananda nor anyone else was in the "Position" necessary to Measure and to "Certify" the Unique and <u>unprecedented</u> Nature of the All-and-all-Completing Event of My Avatarically Self-Manifested Divine Incarnation and of My Great Avataric Divine Demonstration of the progressive (and, necessarily, seven-stage) human, Spiritual, Transcendental, and, only at Last, Most Perfect Process of Divine Self-Realization.

Therefore, even though It had been Given, Baba Muktananda's formal Acknowledgement of Me was—for Me—a virtual non-Event (and It did not positively change—nor has It ever positively changed—<u>anything</u> about the necessary ongoing Ordeal of My Avataric Divine Life and Work).

XLIII.

Baba Muktananda's formal and public <u>written</u> Acknowledgement of Me in 1969—Wherein and Whereby He formally and publicly Named and Acknowledged Me <u>As</u> an <u>Independent</u> True Siddha-Guru—was a <u>unique</u> Gesture, <u>never</u>, at any other time, Done by Baba Muktananda relative to <u>any</u> other individual (whether of the East or of the West). And <u>That</u> unique formal Act (of Baba Muktananda's formal, written Acknowledgement of Me in 1969) was, <u>Itself</u>, a clear (and "<u>scandalizing</u>") Gesture, that <u>immediately</u> Called (and always continues to Call) <u>everyone</u> to "consider" <u>many</u> Siddha-Yoga options (and Spiritual, or esoteric religious, options altogether) that are, generally, presumed to be taboo—at least among the more puritanical (and even xenophobic) types of Siddha-Yoga practitioners (and of esoteric religionists in general).

XLIV.

I Say That, in the inherently esoteric domain of <u>Real</u> Spirituality (and in the domain of both exoteric and esoteric religion in general), <u>all</u> puritanical denial and suppression of human realities is <u>wrong</u>—and inherently damaging to everyone who does it. And, indeed, <u>all</u> denial and suppression of Reality (Itself), Which <u>Is</u> Truth Itself, is <u>wrong</u> (and, indeed, is <u>false</u> religion)—

and all false religion is inherently damaging to everyone who does it (and even to everyone who believes it).

Therefore, I Write This Summary of My "Lineage-History"—so that all the extremely important matters I Address Herein will cease to be hidden, denied, suppressed, and falsified—and What Is Great will (by Means of This Address) become Obvious to all eyes, and (Thus) be made Whole again.

XLV.

Among the extremely important matters I must Address in This Summary of My "Lineage-History" is This: Entirely apart from what I will, in the progression of This Summary, Indicate were the apparent "philosophical reasons" associated with the eventual outward "separation" between Baba Muktananda and Me (which occurred as a result of Our Meetings in late 1970 and mid-1973), it was the "organizational politics" relative to the "sexual" and "Westerner" matters I have just Described that played the more fundamental practical role in causing the "separation".

XLVI.

During the same period in which Rudi and (then) Baba Muktananda actively Functioned as My Spiritual Masters (in gross physical bodily Form), Their Spiritual Master, the Great Siddha Bhagavan Nityananda, actively Functioned (through both of Them— and, otherwise, directly, in subtle bodily Form) as My Senior (but already Ascended—and, Thus, discarnate, or non-physical) Spiritual Master.

XLVII.

The fifth stage True Great Siddha (and True Siddha-Guru and Great Saint of the Highest fifth-stage type and degree) Rang Avadhoot (alive in gross physical bodily Form until late 1968—and always Acknowledged as an Incarnate Great Siddha, or a Descended-from-Above Spiritual Entity of the Highest fifth-stage type and degree, by Bhagavan Nityananda, as well as by Baba Muktananda) also (in early 1968) directly and spontaneously Blessed Me with His Spiritual Blessing, Given and Shown via His

"Wide-Eyed" Mudra of heart-recognition and Immense Regard of Me—as I sat alone in a garden, like His Ishta, the forever youthful Lord Dattatreya.

XLVIII.

In That Unique Moment in 1968—in the garden of Baba Muktananda's Ganeshpuri Ashram—both Rang Avadhoot and Baba Muktananda (along with the already discarnate, but Fully Spiritually Present, Bhagavan Nityananda) actively Functioned for Me as direct Blessing-Agents of the Divine "Cosmic Goddess" ("Ma"), Thus (By Means of Her Divine, and Infinitely Potent, Grace) Causing Me to spontaneously Re-Awaken to Most Ascended (and, altogether—but only <u>conditionally</u>, or in the fifth stage manner— mind-transcending, object-transcending, and ego-transcending) Nirvikalpa Samadhi (from Which I never again was Fallen, but only Continued—to <u>Un-conditionally</u> "Bright" Beyond). And it was on the basis of <u>This</u> Great Event, and My Signs in the following year (wherein many of My Avataric Divine Great-Siddha Characteristics—Which, in My Unique Case, would, in due Course, Fully Demonstrate all seven of the possible stages of life— became, spontaneously, Spiritually Evident), that (in 1969) Baba Muktananda formally (and publicly) Acknowledged and Announced and Blessed My Inherent Right and Calling to Function (in the ancient Siddha-Yoga, or Shaktipat-Yoga, tradition) as Spiritual Master (and True Siddha-Guru) to all and All.

XLIX.

Thereafter, in mid-1970, the "Brightness" of My own (and Self-Evidently Divine) Person was Revealed (and constantly Presented) to Me in the (apparently Objective) Form of the Divine "Cosmic Goddess" ("Ma"). And, from then (after Bhagavan Nityananda Called and Blessed Me to take My leave from Baba Muktananda's Ashram, and to <u>Follow</u> the Divine "She"), <u>only</u> "She" actively Functioned (to Beyond) as My (Ultimate and Final—and entirely <u>Divine</u>) Spiritual Master (or Divine True Siddha-Guru)—until (By Means of Her spontaneous Sacrifice of Her own Form in Me) Divine Self-Realization was Most Perfectly Re-Awakened in My Case.

L.

Thus, in That Final Course, it was Revealed (or Perfectly Re-Confirmed)—As the Self-Evidently Divine Reality and Truth of My own Avatarically-Born Person—that This Divine Process (Shown, at last, in ego-Surrendering, ego-Forgetting, and, altogether, Most Perfectly ego-Transcending Devotional "Relationship" to the Divine "She") had (Itself) always been Active in My own (and Unique) Case (and had always been Shown As the Divinely Self-Revealing Activities of the Inherent Spiritual, and Divinely Spherical, "Brightness" of My own Avatarically-Born Person), even all throughout My present Lifetime (and even at, and from before, My present-Lifetime Birth).

LI.

Therefore, on September 10, 1970, It was Revealed (or Perfectly Re-Confirmed)—As the Self-Evidently Divine Reality and Truth of My own Eternal Divine Person—that Divine (or Inherently egoless, and Perfectly Subjective, and, altogether, Inherently Most Perfect) Self-Realization (of One, and "Bright", and Only Me) had Always Already (and Uniquely) Been the Case with Me.

LII.

In My Case, the (True, Full, and Complete) seventh stage Realization of the Transcendental (and Inherently Spiritual, and Inherently egoless) Divine Self-Condition was Re-Awakened (on September 10, 1970). Subsequently (at first, informally, late in 1970, and, then, formally, in 1973), I Communicated the Details of My Divine Realization to Baba Muktananda. I Did This in the traditional manner, in What I Intended to be an entirely honorable, serious, and respectful Summation to Baba Muktananda—the one and only then Living Spiritual Master among Those Who had Served Me as My present-Lifetime Spiritual Masters. However—in a philosophically untenable reaction to My already apparent relinquishment of His fifth stage experiential presumptions relative to what constitutes the "orthodox position" of the Siddha-Yoga (or Shaktipat-Yoga) school and tradition—Baba Muktananda criticized

My Final Realization (or, in any case, what He understood, or otherwise supposed, to be My Description of It). Thus, in those two Meetings (the first in California, and the second in India, at Baba Muktananda's Ganeshpuri Ashram) Baba Muktananda <u>criticized</u> Me for What My Heart (Itself) <u>cannot</u> (and must not) Deny. And Baba Muktananda <u>thereby</u> Gave Me the final "Gift of blows" that sent Me out alone, to Do My Avataric Divine Work.

LIII.

Baba Muktananda was a (fifth stage) Siddha-Yogi of the degree and type that seeks, and readily experiences, and readily identifies with inner perceptual visions and lights. Based on those experiences, Baba Muktananda (like the many others of His type and degree, within the fourth-to-fifth stage traditions) asserted that both the Process and the Goal of religious and Spiritual life were <u>necessarily</u> associated with such inner phenomena.

The experiences (of visions, lights, and many other Yogic phenomena) Baba Muktananda describes in His autobiographical Confessions are, indeed, the same (fifth stage) ones (or of the same fifth stage kind) that are (typically, characteristically, and inevitably) experienced by genuine fifth stage Yogic practitioners (and fifth stage Realizers) within the Siddha-Yoga (or Shaktipat-Yoga) school and tradition—and I Confirm that the total range of these phenomenal (fifth stage) Yogic experiences also spontaneously arose (and always continue, even now, to arise—even in the context of the seventh stage of life) in My own Case (and <u>such</u> was—both formally, in 1969, and, otherwise, informally, at many other times, beginning in 1968—Acknowledged by Baba Muktananda to be <u>so</u> in My Case).

Nevertheless, as I Confessed to Baba Muktananda in Our Meetings in 1970 and 1973, My <u>Final</u> Realization <u>Is</u> That of the One and Indivisible Divine Self-Condition (and Source-Condition) <u>Itself</u>—and the Great Process associated with That eventual (seventh stage) Realization <u>necessarily</u> (in due course) Goes Beyond (and, in the Case of That seventh stage Realization <u>Itself</u>, Is <u>in</u> <u>no</u> <u>sense</u> dependent upon) the phenomenal (and, always, psycho-physically pre-patterned, and, thus, predetermined) conditions otherwise associated with the absorptive mysticism (and the objectified inner

126

phenomena) that characterize the fourth-to-fifth stage beginnings of the Great Process (or that, otherwise, characterize the conditionally arising, and psycho-physically pre-patterned, and, thus, predetermined, associations of the Great Process even in the context of the seventh stage of life). Indeed, the <u>fact</u> and the <u>Truth</u> of all of This was Self-Evident to Me—and, truly, I <u>expected</u> that It must be Self-Evident to Baba Muktananda as well. However, Baba Muktananda did <u>not</u> (and, I was obliged to admit, <u>could</u> not) Confirm to Me That <u>This</u> <u>Is</u> the Case from the point of view of <u>His</u> experience.

Indeed, it became completely clear to Me, in the midst of Our Meetings in 1970 and 1973, that Baba Muktananda was not Standing in the "Place" (or the Self-"Position") required to Confirm or Acknowledge My Thus Described Final Realization. That is to Say, Baba Muktananda made it clear to Me in those two Meetings (wherein others were present), and (also) in His Remarks otherwise conveyed to Me privately, that He, <u>unlike</u> <u>Me</u>,[24] had <u>not</u> been—and (apparently, for mostly rather puritanical, and otherwise conventional, reasons) could not even <u>conceive</u> of Allowing Himself to be—"Embraced" by the Divine "Cosmic Goddess" (or Maha-Shakti) <u>Herself</u> (<u>Such</u> That, by Her own Submission to the <u>Senior</u> and <u>Most</u> <u>Prior</u> Principle—Which <u>Is</u> Self-Existing Consciousness <u>Itself</u>—She would be Subsumed by Consciousness Itself, and, <u>Thus</u>, Husbanded by Consciousness Itself, and, <u>Thereby</u>, Be the Final Means for the Self-Radiant Divine Self-Awakening of Consciousness Itself to <u>Itself</u>). And, therefore, by His own <u>direct</u> Confession to Me, Baba Muktananda Declared that He was <u>not</u> Standing in the "Place" (or the Self-"Position") of Inherently Most Perfect (or seventh stage) Divine Self-Realization—Which Realization I (Uniquely) had Confessed to Him.

LIV.

When I first Came to Baba Muktananda (in early 1968), His First and Most Fundamental Instruction to Me—even within minutes of My Arrival at His Ashram (in Ganeshpuri, India)—was the (apparently <u>sixth</u> stage, or <u>Transcendentalist</u>) Admonition: "You are <u>not</u> the one who wakes, or dreams, or sleeps—but <u>You</u> <u>Are</u> the One Who <u>Is</u> the Witness of these states." I took that Admonition to be Instruction in the traditional (and sixth stage) sense, as Given in the <u>non-Emanationist</u> (or Transcendentalist) tradition of Advaita Vedanta (which is the traditional Vedantic school of "Non-Dualism"). However, it became clear to Me (in, and as a result of, Our Meetings in 1970 and 1973) that Baba Muktananda was, actually, a vehement and dogmatic <u>opponent</u> of the tradition of Advaita Vedanta (and of its Transcendental Method, and of its proposed Transcendental Realization—and of even all proposed Transcendental Realizers, including, in particular, Ramana Maharshi).

Indeed, in those two Meetings (in 1970 and 1973), Baba Muktananda was, evidently, so profoundly confined to His dogmatic Emanationist (and otherwise phenomena-based) philosophical point of view (which, in those two Meetings, took on a form very much like the traditional confrontation between Kashmir Saivism and Advaita Vedanta) that He (in a rather dramatically pretentious, or intentionally provocative, manner—and clearly, indefensibly) presented Himself to Me as an <u>opponent</u> (such that He addressed Me as if I were merely an opposing "player" in a sophomoric academic debate, and as if I were merely—and for merely academic reasons—representing the point of view of traditional Advaita Vedanta).

Likewise, it became clear to Me (in Our Meetings in 1970 and 1973) that Baba Muktananda's proposed Siddha-Yoga Teaching was, in <u>some</u> respects (which I Indicate Herein), merely a product of His own <u>personal</u> study, experience, and <u>temperament</u>—and, thus, of His <u>own</u> karmically acquired <u>philosophical</u> <u>bias</u>, or <u>prejudice</u>—and that the point of view He so dogmatically imposed on Me in those two Meetings is <u>not</u>, itself, an <u>inherent</u> (or <u>necessary</u>) part of Siddha Yoga <u>Itself</u>.

LV.

Relative to Baba Muktananda's <u>experiential</u> (or experience-based, rather than philosophically based) point of view, it became clear (in Our Meetings in 1970 and 1973) that Baba Muktananda (as a Siddha-Yogi) was yet (and <u>characteristically</u>) Centered in the (fifth stage) "Attitude" (or "Asana") of what He described as "<u>Witnessing</u>". In using the term "Witnessing" (or the "Witness"), Baba Muktananda <u>seemed</u> (in the traditional <u>sixth</u> stage manner of Advaita Vedanta) to be referring to the Witness-Consciousness (Which Is Consciousness Itself, Inherently, and Transcendentally, Standing Most Prior to all objects and all psycho-physical functions—whether gross, subtle, or causal). However, clearly, what Baba Muktananda meant by the term "Witnessing" (or the "Witness") was the psycho-physical function of the observing-intelligence (which is not the Transcendental Consciousness—Prior even to the causal body—but which is, simply, the third, and highest, functional division, or functional dimension, of the subtle body). Thus, characteristically, Baba Muktananda identified with (and took the position of) the observer (or the observing-intelligence) relative to all arising phenomena (and, especially, relative to His reported subtle, or internal phenomenal, visions of higher and lower worlds, the hierarchy of abstract internal lights, and so on). And, when Baba Muktananda spoke of "Witnessing", He, simply, meant the attitude of merely observing whatever arises (and, thus, the intention to do so in a non-attached manner—rather than, in the conventional manner, merely to cling to, or, otherwise, to dissociate from, the various internal and external objects of moment to moment attention).

In the Ultimate Course of My Avataric Ordeal of (seventh stage) Divine Self-Realization, the Spiritual (or Siddha-Yoga) Process passed Beyond all mere (fifth stage, or even sixth stage) "Witnessing"—and all identification with the psycho-physical experiencer, or observer, or knower of the mind and the senses— to Realize (and Be) the Indivisible (or Inherently egoless, objectless, and Non-Dual) Reality (or Self-Condition) That Is the Self-Existing and Self-Radiant Consciousness (Itself), or the Inherent and Un-conditional Feeling of Being (Itself), That Is the Mere (and True) Witness-Consciousness (or the Un-conditional, and non-functional, and All-and-all-Divinely-Self-Recognizing, and Self-Evidently Divine Self, or Self-Condition, Inherently Most Prior to any and all objects—without excluding any).

Thus, it became clear to Me (in Our Meetings in 1970 and 1973) that Baba Muktananda was not yet (either in the sixth stage Transcendental manner or the seventh stage Divine Manner) Established As the True Witness-Consciousness (or Consciousness Itself), but it also became clear to Me (then) that Baba Muktananda was in the fifth stage manner, simply observing, and, thus and thereby, <u>contemplating</u> (and becoming absorbed in or by) internal phenomenal objects and states—rather than, in the seventh stage Manner, Standing <u>As</u> Consciousness <u>Itself</u>, <u>Divinely</u> Self-Recognizing <u>any</u> and <u>all</u> cosmically manifested objects, and (Thus and Thereby) <u>Divinely</u> Transcending <u>all</u> the conditional states—waking (or gross), dreaming (or subtle), and sleeping (or causal).

LVI.

Baba Muktananda was, in effect, always contemplating the conditional activities, the conditional states, and the illusory conditional forms (or objective Emanations) of the "Cosmic Goddess" (or the All-and-all-objectifying Kundalini Shakti)—whereas I (in, and Beyond, a Unique "Embrace" with the "Cosmic Goddess" Herself) had (even Prior to <u>all</u> <u>observed</u> "differences") Re-Awakened to the True (and Inherently egoless, and Inherently Indivisible, and Most Perfectly Prior, and Self-Evidently Divine) Self-"Position" (or Self-Condition, and Source-Condition) of <u>all</u> Her cosmic (or waking, dreaming, and sleeping) forms and states. And, by Virtue of That Divine (or Most Perfect—or seventh stage) Re-Awakening of <u>Me</u>, all conditionally arising forms and states were—even in the instants of their <u>apparent</u> arising—Inherently (or Always Already—and, Thus, Divinely) Self-Recognized (and Most Perfectly Transcended) in, and <u>As</u>, <u>Me</u>—the "Bright" Divine Self-Condition and Source-Condition (or Inherently Indivisible, and First, and Only, and Perfectly <u>Subjective</u>, and Self-Evidently Divine Person) <u>Itself</u>.

Therefore, in those two Meetings (in 1970 and 1973)—and entirely because of His (therein, and <u>thus</u>) repeated stance of experiential and philosophical non-Confirmation of <u>seventh</u> <u>stage</u> Divine Self-Realization (which stance, in effect, directly Acknowledged that the seventh stage Self-"Position" of Divine Self-Realization was not His own)—Baba Muktananda Gave Me <u>no</u> <u>option</u> but to Go and Do (and Teach, and Reveal, and Bless All and all) <u>As</u> My Unique (and Self-Evidently <u>Avataric</u>) Realization of the Divine Self-Condition (Which <u>Is</u> My own, and Self-Evidently Divine, Person—and Which <u>Is</u>, Self-Evidently, the Divine Source-Condition of All and all) <u>Requires</u> Me to Do. Therefore, I Did (and Do—and will forever Do) <u>So</u>.

LVII.

The Principal Characteristic of the One and Indivisible Divine Self-Condition (and Source-Condition) <u>Is</u> Its Perfectly <u>Subjective</u> Nature (<u>As</u> Self-Existing and Self-Radiant Consciousness—or Very, and Inherently Non-Objective, Being, Itself). Therefore, neither any <u>ego-"I"</u> (or any apparently separate self-consciousness) nor any apparently <u>objective</u> (or phenomenally objectified, or otherwise conditionally arising) form or state of experience (whether waking, or dreaming, or sleeping—and whether mind-based or sense-based) <u>Is</u> (<u>itself</u>) the Realization (or, otherwise, a necessary support for the Realization) of the Divine Self-Condition (Itself)—Which Condition <u>Is</u> (Itself) the One and Only Reality, the One and Only Truth, and the One and Only <u>Real</u> God.

Baba Muktananda was, characteristically (in the fifth stage manner), <u>experientially</u> (and mystically) absorbed in modes of <u>Savikalpa</u> Samadhi (or of internal object-contemplation). In His characteristic play of internal object-contemplation (or absorptive mysticism), Baba Muktananda reported <u>two</u> types of (especially) internal sensory (or sense-based) experience—the experience of abstract internal lights (and, secondarily, of abstract internal sounds, and tastes, and smells, and touches) <u>and</u> the experience of internal (or mental) visions of higher and lower worlds ("illustrated" by internal versions of all of the usual descriptive modes of the senses).

The abstract internal lights (and so on) are <u>universally</u> (or identically) experienced by any and all individuals who are so awakened to internal phenomena (just as the essential Realizations of the sixth stage of life and, potentially, of the seventh stage of life are universal, or essentially identical in all cases). However, the visions of higher and lower worlds are, like psychic phenomena in general, expressions of the egoic psycho-physical (and, altogether, mental) tendencies of the <u>individual</u> (and of his or her cultural associations)—and, therefore, such experiences are not <u>universally</u> the same in all cases (but, instead, <u>all</u> such experiences are conditioned, and determined, and limited by the <u>point of</u> <u>view</u>, or karmically patterned identity, of the experiencer, or the individual egoic observing-identity). Nevertheless (and this also illustrates the naive—and not, by Him, fully comprehended—

nature of many of Baba Muktananda's views about the Siddha-Yoga Process), Baba Muktananda (in His autobiography, *Play of Consciousness*[25]) reported His visions of higher and lower worlds as if they were <u>categorically</u> true, and (in the subtle domain) objectively, or <u>Really</u>, existing <u>as</u> He reported them—whereas <u>all</u> visions of higher and lower worlds are of the <u>same</u> insubstantial, illusory, and personal nature as <u>dreams</u>.

Like anyone else's authentic visionary experiences of higher and lower worlds, Baba Muktananda's visionary experiences of higher and lower worlds, although authentic, were His <u>personal</u> (or point-of-view-based) experiences of the otherwise <u>inherently</u> <u>formless</u> (and point-of-view-less) dimensions of the universal cosmic (or conditional) reality (or the <u>inherently</u> <u>abstract</u> planes of universal cosmic light)—as He, by tendency of mind (and because of His psycho-physical self-identity <u>as</u> a particular and separate fixed point of view—or ego-"I"), was <u>able</u> (and karmically pre-patterned) to experience (or conceive and perceive) them. Therefore, Baba Muktananda's conditional (or egoic) point of view—and, thus, also, His inner perceptions of various higher and lower worlds—were, <u>characteristically</u> and <u>only</u>, of a <u>Hindu</u> kind. (And the implications of this seem never to have occurred to Baba Muktananda. Indeed, if He had become aware of the <u>inherently</u> personal, conditional, karmic, ego-based, mind-based, illusory, arbitrary, and non-universal nature of His inwardly envisioned worlds, and even of the merely point-of-view-reflecting nature of His inwardly envisioned universal abstract lights, Baba Muktananda might have become moved to understand and transcend Himself further—beyond the Saguna, or mind-based, and mind-limited, and dreamworld terms that are the inherent characteristic of Savikalpa Samadhi.)

LVIII.

Baba Muktananda's Hindu visions can be compared to My own experiences of Savikalpa Samadhi during My "Sadhana Years". During that time, I, too, had many visions of higher and lower worlds—and many of them were, indeed, of a Hindu type (because of My present-Lifetime associations, and also because of the past-Lifetime associations of My Deeper-Personality Vehicle). However, there was also, in My Case (and for the same reasons) a dramatic period of several months of intense visions of a distinctly Christian type.[26] I immediately understood such visions to be the mind-based (and, necessarily, ego-based) products of the Siddha-Yoga Process (or Divine Shaktipat), as It combined with My own conditionally born psycho-physical structures. Thus, I entered into that Process Freely and Fully—and, in due course, the particularly Christian visions (and the particularly Hindu visions) ceased. They were all simply the evidence of My own conditionally born mind and sensory apparatus (and the evidence of even all My conditionally born cultural associations)—and, therefore, the visionary contents were (I Discovered) merely another (but deep, and psychic) form of purification (rather than a "Revelation" that suggests either the Christian "Heavens"-and-"Hells" or the Hindu "Heavens"-and-"Hells" Are, themselves, Reality and Truth). Thus, when, Finally, the ego-based visions had been completely "burned off"—only Reality (Itself) Remained (As Me).

LIX.

Baba Muktananda's Siddha-Yoga Teachings exemplify the descriptive mysticism of fourth-to-fifth stage Yoga (especially as it has been historically represented in the fourth-to-fifth stage Yogic tradition of the Maharashtra region of India[27]). Also, Baba Muktananda's Siddha-Yoga Teachings are (in some, very important, respects) experientially prejudiced—toward both non-universal (and specifically Hindu) visions (of higher and lower worlds, and so on) and universal abstract visions (of abstract internal lights, and so on), and against (or, certainly, Baba Muktananda, Himself, was, by temperament, experientially disinclined toward) fifth stage Nirvikalpa Samadhi (or Fullest Ascent to fifth stage Formless Realization—Which Fullest Ascent was My own spontaneous Realization at Baba Muktananda's Ganeshpuri Ashram, in 1968, and Which is also the Characteristic Realization of all Great fifth stage Nirguna Siddhas, such as Bhagavan Nityananda and Rang Avadhoot).

LX.

Baba Muktananda saw the Secret (or esoteric) inner perceptual domain of subtle (or fourth-to-fifth stage) Divine Spiritual Revelation. I, too, have seen (and even now, do see) that inner realm. And it is the Revelation of that inner realm that is the true (original, and esoteric) core of <u>all</u> <u>fourth-to-fifth</u> stage religious traditions.

The fourth stage religious traditions are, generally, first presented (or institutionally communicated) to the public world of mankind (in its gross egoity and its human immaturity) as a gathering of <u>exoteric</u> myths and legends. Those exoteric myths and legends are intended to inspire and guide human beings in the ordinary developmental context of the first <u>three</u> stages of life (associated with gross physical, emotional-sexual, and mental-volitional development of the human <u>social</u> ego). Thus, the many religious traditions of both the East and the West are, in their public (or exoteric) expressions, simply variations on the <u>inherent</u> psycho-physical "messages" of the body-mind relative to foundation human development (both individual and collective). And, because <u>all</u> exoteric religious traditions are based on the "messages" inherent in the <u>same</u> psycho-physical structures, the exoteric Teachings of <u>all</u> religions are, essentially, <u>identical</u> (and, therefore, <u>equal</u>). And, also, because this is so, <u>all</u> exoteric religious traditions (such as Judaism, Christianity, Islam, Hinduism, and so on) <u>must</u>—especially at this critical "late-time" moment of world-intercommunicativeness— acknowledge their essential equality, commonality, and sameness, and, on that basis, mutually embrace the principles of cooperation and tolerance (for the sake of world peace)!

<u>All</u> exoteric religious traditions are, fundamentally, associated with the first <u>three</u> (or social-ego) stages of life. And <u>all</u> exoteric religious traditions are, contextually, associated with rudimentary aspects of the <u>fourth</u> stage of life (or the religiously <u>Devotional</u> effort of transcending both personal and collective egoity—or self-contraction into selfishness, competitiveness, "difference", conflict, and self-and-other-destructiveness). However, <u>all</u> exoteric religious traditions are, also, associated (to one or another degree) with an esoteric (or Secret) dimension (or a tradition of esoteric schools), which is intended to extend the life of religious practice into the

inner dimensions of religious (and truly Spiritual) Realization.

The true esoteric dimension of religion <u>first</u> extends the life of rudimentary religious practice into the true and full Spiritual <u>depth</u> of the <u>fourth</u> stage of life (by Means of surrender to the <u>Descent</u> of the Divine Spiritual Force into the human, or "frontal", domain of incarnate existence). And that Spiritual Process is, characteristically (in due course), also extended into the domain of the true <u>fifth</u> stage of life (which is associated with the Process of Spiritual <u>Ascent</u>, via the Spinal Line and the brain, through the layers of the conditional pattern of the psycho-physical ego, and always toward the Realization of a conditional state of mystical absorption in the Most Ascended Source of conditional, or cosmically extended, existence). And, once that Spiritual Process of Ascent is <u>complete</u> (or is, itself, transcended in Inherent Spiritual Fullness), the esoteric Spiritual Process may (and, indeed, should) continue, in the context of the true <u>sixth</u> stage of life (or the <u>Spiritual</u> Process of Transcendental Self-Realization)—and, at last, the true (and Truly <u>Complete</u>) Great Process <u>must</u> Culminate in the only-by-Me Revealed and Given <u>seventh</u> stage of life (wherein <u>all</u> cosmically arising conditions are Inherently Self-Recognized, and, Ultimately, Outshined, in the Non-Separate, Self-Existing, Self-Radiant, Inherently egoless, Perfectly Subjective, and Self-Evidently Divine Self-Condition and Source-Condition of All and all).

LXI.

Baba Muktananda was a Teacher (and a Realizer) in the context of the fourth-to-fifth stage (or foundation esoteric stages) of, specifically, <u>Hindu</u> religious practice. The Spiritual (or Siddha-Yoga, or Shaktipat-Yoga) Process He exemplified and Taught (and Initiated in others) truly begins in the frontal (or fourth stage) practice (of Siddha-Guru Devotion) and (in due course) goes on to the spinal (or fifth stage) practice (of Ascended mystical absorption).

Baba Muktananda's practice and His experiential Realization were conditioned (and, ultimately, limited) by His own personal (or conditional, and karmic, or psycho-physically pre-patterned) ego-tendencies—and by His association (by birth) with the combined exoteric <u>and</u> esoteric culture of traditional Hinduism.

135

Therefore, His experiences (and His subsequent Teachings, and His <u>life</u> altogether) are, characteristically, an exemplification of the historical <u>conflict</u> between fifth stage Hindu <u>esotericism</u> (which is, itself, inherently unconventional, and non-puritanical) and fourth stage Hindu <u>exotericism</u> (which is, itself, inherently conventional, and, at least publicly, puritanical).

LXII.

Because of His, characteristically, Hindu associations, Baba Muktananda (quite naturally, and naively) interpreted His Yogic Spiritual experiences almost entirely in terms of Hindu cultural models (both exoteric and esoteric). Therefore, His <u>interpretations</u> of His Spiritual experiences—and, indeed, the very form, and character, and content of His Spiritual experiences <u>themselves</u>— were specifically Hindu, and specifically in the mode of philosophical and mystical traditions that corresponded to His own mental predilections (or karmic tendencies).

Thus, Baba Muktananda's recorded visions of higher and lower worlds (leading to the Great Vision of the Blue Person, or the Divine "Creator"-Guru) are a "map" of developmentally unfolding—or spontaneously un-"Veiling"—inner perceptual landscapes, in the specific mode of the Hindu tradition of the "Blue God" (especially Personified as "Siva"—or, otherwise, as the "Krishna" of the *Bhagavad Gita* and the *Bhagavata Purana*).[28] And Baba Muktananda's inner "map" was, also, structured on the basis of an hierarchical sequence of abstract inner lights (and of even all the abstract inner modes of the senses), which He interpreted according to the concepts of the philosophical tradition of Kashmir Saivism, and according to the experiential pattern-interpretation associated with the Hindu mystical tradition of the Maharashtra region of India. However, even though the brain-based (or perception-based—rather than mind-based, or conception-based, or idea-based) pattern of abstract inner lights (and of abstract inner sensations in general) is (or can be) universally (or by anyone) experienced as the same pattern of appearances—the <u>interpretation</u> of that experienced pattern is, or may be, different from case to case (or from culture to culture). And, ultimately, for the sake of

Truth, the one and only <u>correct</u> (or <u>universally</u> applicable) interpretation must be embraced by all.

Baba Muktananda experienced and interpreted the pattern of
abstract inner lights as if it were a Revelation associated with the
waking, dreaming, and sleeping states (or the gross, subtle, and
causal modes of conditional experience). Thus (on the basis of His
understanding of the Maharashtra mystical tradition), Baba
Muktananda said that the waking state (and the gross body and
world) is represented by the inner <u>red</u> light, and the dreaming state
(and the subtle body and world) is represented by the inner <u>white</u>
light, and the sleeping state (and the causal body and world) is represented by the inner <u>black</u> light. And Baba Muktananda said that
the inner <u>blue</u> light represents what He called the "supracausal"
state (which He, in the fifth stage manner, mistakenly identified
with the "turiya" state, or the "fourth" state, or the "Witness", or the
"True Self", otherwise associated with the sixth stage tradition of
Advaita Vedanta). However, I Declare that <u>all</u> of those inner lights
(and even <u>all</u> internal perceptions, whether high or low in the scale
of conditional "things") are inner <u>objects</u> of perception (and conception)—and, therefore, <u>all</u> of them are associated with the <u>subtle</u>
body and the inner perceptible (or dreaming-state) worlds of <u>mind</u>.[29]

Swami Muktananda's Description
of the "Bodies of the Soul"[30]

Body:	Gross	Subtle	Causal	Supracausal
Color:	Red	White	Black	Blue
State:	Waking	Dream	Sleep	Turīya
Seat:	Eyes	Throat	Heart	Sahasrāra

LXIII.

Baba Muktananda's description of the abstract inner lights is, in some respects, not sufficiently elaborate (or, otherwise, comprehensive) in its details. In fact, and in My own experience—and in the experience of esoteric traditions other than the Maharashtra tradition (such as reported by the well-known Swami Yogananda)—the display of abstract inner lights is, when experienced as a <u>simultaneous</u> <u>totality</u>, Seen as a Mandala (or a pattern of concentric circles).

In My own experience, that <u>Cosmic</u> Mandala is not only composed of concentric circles of particular colors—but each circle is of a particular precise width (and, thus, of particular proportional <u>significance</u>) relative to the other circles. Thus, in that pattern of circles, the red circle is the outermost circle (perceived against a colorless dark field), but it is a relatively narrow band, appearing next to a much wider band (or circle) of golden yellow. After the very wide golden yellow circle, there is a <u>much</u> narrower soft-white circle. And the soft-white circle is followed by an also <u>very</u> narrow black circle (or band). Closest to the Center of the Cosmic Mandala is a very wide circle of bright blue. And, at the Very Center of the blue field, there is a Brilliant White Five-Pointed Star (Which, perhaps not to confuse It with the color of the circle of soft-white light, Baba Muktananda described as a <u>Blue</u> Star).

Thus, in fact, although all the abstract inner lights described by Baba Muktananda are, indeed, within the total Cosmic Mandala, the principal lights (in terms of width and prominence) are the <u>golden</u> <u>yellow</u> and the <u>blue</u> lights—and <u>only</u> the Brilliant White Five-Pointed Star is the <u>Central</u> and <u>Principal</u> light within the Cosmic Mandala of abstract inner lights.

The Cosmic Mandala of abstract inner lights is a display that is, otherwise, associated with planes of possible inner (or subtle) experience. Thus, the red light inwardly represents (and, literally, illuminates) the gross body and the gross world (as Baba Muktananda has said). However, <u>all</u> of the other lights (golden yellow, soft-white, black, and bright blue) represent (and, literally, illuminate) the several hierarchical divisions within the <u>subtle</u> body and the <u>subtle</u> worlds—and the <u>causal</u> body (which is asso-

Cosmic Mandala

ciated with attention itself, or the root of egoity itself, and which is, itself, <u>only</u> <u>felt</u>, and <u>not</u> <u>seen</u>, and which is expressed as the fundamental feeling of "difference", separateness, and relatedness, and which is located as a knot of self-contraction in the right side of the heart) is <u>not</u> visually represented (<u>nor</u> is it, otherwise, literally illuminated) by the lights and worlds of the Cosmic Mandala.

The wide golden yellow circle of the Cosmic Mandala represents (in conjunction with the outermost red circle) the outermost (or lowest) dimension of the subtle body—which is the etheric (or pranic, or life-energy) body, or dimension, of conditional experience. The narrower soft-white circle of the Cosmic Mandala represents the ordinary (or sense-based) mind. The narrow black circle (or band) is a transitional space, where mental activity is suspended. The blue circle of the Cosmic Mandala is the domain of the mental observer, the faculty of discriminative intelligence and the will, and the very form of the subtly concretized ego-"I" (or the inner-concretized subtle self). And the Brilliant White Five-Pointed Star is the Epitome and Very Center of the Cosmic Mandala—Such That It Provides the Uppermost Doorway to What Is, altogether, Above (and, Ultimately, Beyond) the Cosmic Mandala (or Above and Beyond the body itself, the brain itself, and the mind itself).

LXIV.

Baba Muktananda interpreted the universally experienced abstract inner lights (and experienced the corresponding inner worlds) in terms of various Hindu philosophical and mystical (and, also, exoteric, or conventionally religious) traditions (as I have Indicated). However, the subtle domain is the elaborate hierarchical domain of mind (or of the psycho-physically concretized ego-"I")—and, therefore, just as individual dreams and imaginings are personal, ephemeral, and non-ultimate, the inherently dream-like subtle domain of Spiritually-stimulated inwardness may be experienced and interpreted in various and different modes, according to the nature and the tradition (or the personal and collectively representative mind) of the experiencer.

Thus, ultimately (or in due course), the subtle domain (or the subtle egoic body) must be transcended, in the transition to the sixth stage Spiritual (or Siddha-Yoga) Process—Which is the Spiritually (and not merely mentally) developed Process of inversion upon the true causal body (or the root of attention), and penetration of the causal knot (or the presumption of separate self), and Which is, thus, the inversive (and conditional, or conditionally achieved) transcending of the ego-"I", by means of exclusive (or object-excluding) Identification with the True (and Inherent, and Self-Evident) Transcendental Witness-Consciousness Itself. And only the Transcendental Witness-Consciousness, Itself—inverted upon in the thus Described sixth stage manner—Is the true "turiya" state, or the true "fourth" state (beyond the three ordinary states, of waking, dreaming, and sleeping). And only the Transcendental Witness-Consciousness, Itself—Fully, and Fully Spiritually,

Realized in the only-by-Me Revealed and Given context of the true sixth stage of life—Is the Domain of the only-by-Me Revealed and Given seventh stage Realization of the True Divine Self, Which Is the Self-Evidently Divine Self-Condition, and Which Is the One and Only True Divine State of "Turiyatita"—"Beyond the 'fourth' state", and, thus, Beyond all exclusiveness, and Beyond all bondage to illusions, and Beyond point of view (or egoic separateness) itself, and, therefore, Beyond all conditional efforts, supports, and dependencies.

At last, the sixth stage of life (which, itself, is associated with conditionally patterned inversion upon the Consciousness-Principle) must be (Most Perfectly) transcended (and, indeed, the ego-"I" itself must be Most Perfectly, or Inherently, transcended) in the transition to the only-by-Me Revealed and Given seventh stage of life (which Is the stage of True, and Fully Spiritual, Divine Self-Realization, Inherently Free of, but not strategically Separated from, all conditionally patterned forms and states—and which Is the stage of the Inherently Most Perfect Demonstration of the Non-Separate, Self-Existing, Self-Radiant, Inherently egoless, Perfectly Subjective, and Self-Evidently Divine Self-Condition and Source-Condition of All and all).

LXV.

My own experiences of fifth stage mystical perception are (like those of Baba Muktananda, and those of all visionary mystics) clear Evidence of the inherently (and necessarily) conditional, mental, altogether brain-based (and both brain-limited and mind-limited), and both personal and collective egoic nature of all internal mystical (or fourth-to-fifth stage) absorption.

I, too (like Baba Muktananda), experienced Hindu visions—but I, otherwise, also experienced many Christian visions (and also many non-Hindu and non-Christian visions), in association with the fifth stage developments of the same (or one and only) Spiritual (or Siddha-Yoga) Process of inner perception (including the progressive display of abstract inner lights, and so on) described by Baba Muktananda. Thus, just as Baba Muktananda described His Hindu visions as a Spiritual Revelation of the

"Truth" of <u>Hindu</u> esotericism (and even of Hindu exotericism)—I could just as well describe My (specifically) Christian visions as a Spiritual Revelation of the "Truth" of <u>Christian</u> esotericism (and even of Christian exotericism)!

Indeed, My (specifically) Christian visions (but not, of course, My specifically Hindu visions—or My, otherwise, specifically non-Hindu and non-Christian visions) <u>do</u> amount to a Spiritual Revelation of the actual (and mostly esoteric) content of <u>original</u> (or primitive—and truly <u>Spiritual</u>) Christianity.[31]

LXVI.

Specifically, My (sometimes) Christian visions Spiritually Reveal the following.

The original tradition (or foundation sect) that is at the <u>root</u> of exoteric Christianity was a fourth-to-fifth stage esoteric Spiritual (and mystical) tradition (or sect). Within that original tradition (or sect), John (the Baptist) was the Spiritual Master (or Spirit-Baptizer—or True Siddha-Guru) of Jesus of Nazareth. Thus (and by Means of the Spiritual Baptism Given to Him by John the Baptist), Jesus of Nazareth experienced the fourth-to-fifth stage absorptive mystical (and, altogether, Spiritual) developments of what (in the Hindu context) is called Siddha Yoga (or Shaktipat Yoga). In due course (and even rather quickly), Jesus of Nazareth, Himself, became a Spirit-Baptizer (or a True Siddha-Guru)—and (within the inner, or esoteric, circle of His Spiritually Initiated devotees) Jesus of Nazareth Taught the fourth-to-fifth stage Way of Spiritual Devotion to the Spiritual Master (or to Himself, as a True Siddha-Guru), and of inner Spiritual Communion with the Divine, and of (eventual) <u>Spiritual</u> Ascent to the Divine Domain (via the Brilliant White Five-Pointed Star).

After the death (and presumed <u>Spiritual</u> Ascent) of Jesus of Nazareth, His esoteric circle of Spiritually Initiated devotees continued to develop the mystical tradition of the sect—but (because of the difficult "signs of the times") the original (esoteric) sect had to become more and more secretive, and, eventually, it disappeared from the view of history (under the pressure of the <u>exoteric</u>, or <u>non</u>-Initiate, or conventionally <u>socially</u> oriented, rather than

Spiritually and mystically oriented, sects that also developed around the public Work, and, especially, the otherwise developing legends and myths, of Jesus of Nazareth).

The esoteric sect of the Spiritual Initiates of Jesus of Nazareth was associated with practices of Spiritually Invocatory prayer (of fourth stage Divine Communion, and of fifth stage absorptive mystical Ascent), especially seeking Divine absorption via the internally perceptible Brilliant White Five-Pointed Star—Which was interpreted, especially after the death of Jesus of Nazareth (and, apparently, in accordance with Instructions communicated by Jesus of Nazareth, Himself, to His Spiritually Initiated devotees, during His own physical lifetime), to be the True Ascended Divine Body of Jesus of Nazareth (or the Spiritually Awakened, and presumed to be Divinely Ascended, "Christ"). And, over time, the Spiritual practitioners within the esoteric "Christ" sect developed the full range of characteristically Christian interpretations of the (otherwise) universally experienced phenomena of inner perception.

LXVII.

My own (sometimes) Christian visions are a spontaneous Revelation of esoteric Christian interpretations (and esoteric Christian modes of experiencing) of, otherwise, universal (and, therefore, inherently non-sectarian) inner phenomena—and My (specifically) Christian visions and interpretations are a spontaneous direct continuation of the esoteric Christian manner of interpreting such (inherently universal) inner phenomena, as it was done in the original (or primitive) epoch of the sect of Jesus of Nazareth.

Thus, speaking in the esoteric terms of the ancient (or earliest) Christian interpreters of subtle inner experience, the red light of Spiritual inner vision can be said to be associated with the gross body of Man (and the Incarnation-body of Jesus of Nazareth, and the "blood of Christ"). Likewise, the golden yellow light can be said to be associated with the "Holy Spirit" (or the Universal Spirit-Energy, or Divine Spirit-Breath, That Pervades the cosmic domain). And the soft-white light can be said to be associated with the mind of Man (which, in its purity, can be said to be a reflection of, or a pattern "in the image of", God—conceived to be the "Creator", or the Divine Source-Condition, Above the body-mind and the world). And the black light can be said to be associated with the "crucifixion" (or sacrifice) of the body-mind of Man (and of Jesus of Nazareth, as the Epitome of Man)—and, also, with the mystical "dark night of the soul" (or the mystic's difficult trial of passing beyond all sensory and mental contents and consolations). And the blue light can be said to be the "Womb of the Virgin Mary" (or the All-and-all-Birthing Light of the "Mother of God"). And the Brilliant White Five-Pointed Star (Surrounded, as it were, by the "Womb", or the Blue Light, of the "Virgin Mary") can be said to be the Ascended (or Spiritual) "Body of Christ" (and the "Star of Bethlehem", and the "Morning Star" of the esoteric Initiation-Ritual associated with the original, Secret Spiritual tradition of Jesus of Nazareth). And the Brilliant White Five-Pointed Star (interpreted to be the Ascended, or Spiritual, "Body of Christ") can (Thus) be said to be One with both the Divine "Mother" (or the Blue "Womb" of All-and-all-Birthing Light) and the Divine "Father" (or the Self-Existing Being, Beyond all Light—Infinitely Behind, and Infinitely Above, and Infinitely Beyond, and Eternally Non-Separate from the "Star-Body of Christ"). And (As Such) the "Christ" (or the Brilliant White Five-Pointed Star) Is Radiantly Pervading the entire cosmic domain, via an All-and-all-Illuminating Combination of both the Blue "Womb"-Light and the Golden Yellow "Breath"-Light of the One and Only Divine Person.

LXVIII.

Thus, My (sometimes) Christian inner visions could, indeed, be said to be an esoteric (and, now, only-by-Me Revealed and Given) Christian Revelation—except that all visionary, and brain-based, and mind-based, and sense-based, and ego-based, and conditional, and sectarian (or merely tradition-bound) things were entirely Gone Beyond (and Most Perfectly transcended) by Me (and in Me), in the sixth and seventh stage Course of My Avataric Ordeal of True (and Most Perfect) Divine Self-Realization!

LXIX.

I Say <u>all</u> the "God" and "Gods" of Man are (whether "Male" or "Female" in the descriptive gender) merely the personal and collective tribal (and entirely dualistic—or conventionally subject-object-bound) myths of human ego-mind.

LXX.

I Say Only <u>Reality</u> <u>Itself</u> (Which <u>Is</u>, Always Already, <u>The</u> One, and Indivisible, and Indestructible, and Inherently egoless Case) <u>Is</u> (Self-Evidently, and <u>Really</u>) Divine, and True, and Truth (or <u>Real</u> God) Itself.

LXXI.

I Say the <u>only</u> Real God (or Truth Itself) <u>Is</u> the One and Only and Inherently <u>Non-Dual</u> Reality (Itself)—Which <u>Is</u> the Inherently egoless, and Utterly Indivisible, and Perfectly Subjective, and Indestructibly Non-Objective Source-Condition <u>and</u> Self-Condition of All and all.

Therefore, I (Characteristically) have <u>no</u> religious interests other than to Demonstrate, and to Exemplify, and to Prove, and to <u>Self-Reveal</u> Truth (or Reality, or <u>Real</u> God) <u>Itself</u>.

LXXII.

The true fourth-to-fifth stage mystical (or esoteric Spiritual) Process is, <u>principally</u>, associated with the progressive inner perceptual (and, thus, subtle mental) un-"Veiling" of the <u>total</u> internally perceptible pattern (or <u>abstractly</u> experienced structure) of the individual body-mind-self (or body-brain-self).

The abstract pattern (or internal structure) of the body-mind-self (or body-brain-self) is, universally, the same in the case of any and every body-mind (or body-brain-mind complex—or conditionally manifested form, or state, or being) within the cosmic domain.

The abstract pattern (or internal structure) of the body-mind-self (or body-brain-self) <u>necessarily</u> (by virtue of its native, and, therefore, <u>inseparable</u>, Inherence in the <u>totality</u> of the cosmic domain itself) <u>Duplicates</u> (or is a conditionally manifested pattern-duplicate of) the Primary Pattern (or Fundamental conditional Structure) of the total cosmic domain.

The conditional body-mind (or any body-brain-mind complex) is, in Reality, <u>not</u> a merely <u>separate</u> someone, or an entirely "<u>different</u>" something (as if the body, or the brain, or the mind were reducible to a someone or a something utterly independent, or non-dependent, and existing entirely in and of itself).

Therefore, the entire body-mind (or egoic body-brain-self) is, itself, to be transcended (in the context of the only-by-Me Revealed and Given seventh stage of life), in and by Means of utterly non-separate, and non-"different", and Inherently egoless Participation in That Which <u>Is</u> Always Already <u>The</u> Case (or the Inherently Non-Dual and Indivisible Condition That <u>Is</u> Reality Itself).

LXXIII.

I Declare that—if It is (by Divine Siddha-Grace) Moved beyond the limits of the waking, dreaming, and sleeping ego-structures—the Siddha-Yoga (or Shaktipat-Yoga) Process of (fifth stage) un-"Veiling" Culminates (or may Culminate—at least eventually) in (and, indeed, It is Always Already Centered Upon) the (fifth stage) Revelation (in Most Ascended Nirvikalpa Samadhi) of the True "Maha-Bindu" (or the "Zero Point", or <u>Formless</u> "Place", of Origin—otherwise, traditionally, called "Sunya", or "Empty", or "Void"). That True (and Indivisible, and Indefinable) "Maha-Bindu" <u>Is</u> the <u>only</u> True "Hole in the universe" (or the One, and Indivisible, and Indefinable, and Self-Evidently Divine Source-Point—Infinitely Above the body, the brain, and the mind). That Absolutely Single (and Formless) "Maha-Bindu" <u>Is</u> the True Absolute "Point-Condition"—or Formless and Colorless (or Non-Objective, and, therefore, not "Lighted") "Black Hole"—from Which (<u>to</u> the <u>point</u> <u>of</u> <u>view</u> of any "objectified" or "Lighted" place or entity, <u>itself</u>) the (or <u>any</u>) total cosmic domain (of conditionally arising forms, states, and beings) <u>appears</u> to <u>Emanate</u> (in an All-and-all-objectifying "Big Bang"[32]). That "Maha-Bindu" <u>Is</u> the <u>Upper</u> Terminal of Amrita Nadi—or of the "Ambrosial Nerve of Connection" to the True Divine Heart (Which Self-Evidently

Divine Heart <u>Is</u> Always Already Seated immediately Beyond the internally felt seat of the sinoatrial node, in the right side of the physical heart). And That "Maha-Bindu" <u>Is</u> (in the context of the sixth stage of life) the esoteric Doorway to, and (in the context of the seventh stage of life) the esoteric Doorway <u>from</u> (or <u>of</u>), the Perfectly <u>Subjective</u> Heart-Domain (Which <u>Is</u> the True Self-Condition and Source-Condition of the "Bright" Divine Love-Bliss-Current of Divine Self-Realization, and Which <u>Is</u>, Itself, the Self-Existing, Self-Radiant, Inherently egoless, and Perfectly Subjective—or Perfectly Indivisible, Non-Dual, and Non-Objective—Conscious Light That <u>Is</u> Reality Itself).

LXXIV.

The (fifth stage) Yogic Process of the progressive inner un-"Veiling" of the Pattern (or Structure) of the cosmic domain is demonstrated (in the Siddha-Yoga, or Shaktipat-Yoga, tradition) via the progressive experiencing of the total pattern of all the structural forms that comprise the body-mind-self (or body-brain-self), via a body-mind-self-reflecting (or body-brain-self-reflecting) display of inner perceptual objects (or apparently objectified phenomenal states, conditions, and patterns of cosmic light). That Process (of the inner perceptual un-"Veiling" of the hierarchical structure, pattern, and contents of the conditionally manifested body-mind-self, or body-brain-self) Culminates (or may Culminate—at least eventually) in the vision (in occasional, or, otherwise, constant, Savikalpa Samadhi) of the "blue bindu" (or the "blue pearl"—as well as the various other objectified inner lights, such as the red, the white, and the black—described by Baba Muktananda)[33]—or even the vision of the <u>total</u> Cosmic Mandala (of many concentric rings of color, including the central "blue bindu", with its Brilliant White Five-Pointed Star at the Center—as I have Described It[34]). In any case, the possibly perceived abstract inner light (or <u>any</u> "bindu", or point, or "Mandala", or complex abstract vision, of inwardly perceived light) is merely, and necessarily, a display of the functional <u>root-point</u> of the <u>brain's</u> perception of conditionally manifested universal light (or merely <u>cosmic</u> light) itself. However, if the Great Process of (fifth

147

stage) un-"Veiling" is (Thus) Continued, the objectified inner "bindu"-vision (and Savikalpa Samadhi itself) is, in due course, <u>transcended</u> (in fifth stage Nirvikalpa Samadhi)—Such That there is the Great Yogic Event of "Penetration" of (and Into) the True (Inherently <u>Formless</u>, and <u>objectless</u>) "Maha-Bindu", Infinitely Above the body, the brain, and the mind. And That Great Yogic Event was, in fact and in Truth, What Occurred in My own Case, in My Room, immediately after I was Blessed by Baba Muktananda and Rang Avadhoot in the garden of Baba Muktananda's Ganeshpuri Ashram, in 1968.

The Great Yogic Event of "Penetration" of the True "Maha-Bindu", Which Occurred in My own Case in 1968, is (in Its Extraordinary Particulars) an extremely rare Example of spontaneous <u>complete</u> Ascending "penetration" of <u>all</u> the chakras (or centers, or points, or structures) of the conditionally manifested body-mind-self (or body-brain-self)—Resulting in sudden Most Ascended Nirvikalpa Samadhi (or "Penetration" to Beyond the total cosmic, and psycho-physical, context of subject-object relations). Such sudden (rather than progressive) <u>complete</u> Ascent is described, in the (fifth stage) Yogic traditions, as the Greatest, and rarest, of the Demonstrations of Yogic Ascent—as compared to progressive (or gradual) demonstrations (shown via stages of inner ascent, via internal visions, lights, auditions, and so on). And, therefore, in My Unique Case, it was only subsequently (or always thereafter—and even now) that the universal cosmic Pattern (or perceptible Great cosmic Structure) and the universally extended pattern (or perceptible inner cosmic structure) of the body, the brain, and the mind (and the Primary inner structure— of the three stations of the heart) were (and are) directly (and systematically, and completely) un-"Veiled" (in a constant spontaneous Display—both apparently Objective and Perfectly Subjective—within My Avataric Divine "Point of View").

Nonetheless (even though Most Ascended, or fifth stage, Nirvikalpa Samadhi was, <u>Thus</u>, Realized by Me in 1968), it became <u>immediately</u> clear to Me that—because That Realization depended on the exercise (and a unique, precise attitude and arrangement) of the <u>conditional</u> <u>apparatus</u> of the body, the brain, and the mind (and of attention)—the Realization was (yet) <u>conditionally dependent</u> (or psycho-physically supported), and, <u>necessarily</u> (or in that sense), <u>limited</u> (or, yet, only a <u>temporary stage</u> in the progressive Process of un-"Veiling"), and, therefore, <u>non-Final</u>. That is to Say, it was inherently Obvious to Me that any and all internal (or otherwise psycho-physical) experiencing <u>necessarily</u> requires the exercise (via attention) of the root-position (and the conditionally arising psycho-physical apparatus) of conditionally arising self-consciousness (or of the separate and separative psycho-physical ego-"I"). I immediately Concluded that—unless the Process of Realization could <u>transcend</u> the very structure and pattern of ego-based experiencing <u>and</u> the very Structure and Pattern of the conditionally manifested cosmos itself—Realization would Itself (<u>necessarily</u>) be limited by the same subject-object (or ego-versus-object) dichotomy that otherwise characterizes even all <u>ordinary</u> (or non-mystical) experience.

Therefore, I Persisted in My Avataric Divine Sadhana—until the un-"Veiling" became Inherently egoless (and Inherently Most Perfect, or seventh stage) Re-Awakening to Divine Self-Realization (Inherently Beyond <u>all</u> phenomenal, or conditional, dependencies, or supports).

LXXV.

On September 10, 1970, the Great Avataric Divine Process of My "Sadhana Years" Culminated in Unqualified (or Most Perfectly Non-conditional) Realization of the Self-Evidently Divine Self-Condition (and Source-Condition) of the cosmic domain itself (and of all forms, states, and beings within the cosmic domain). And, in That Most Perfect Event, I was Most Perfectly Re-Awakened <u>As</u> the "Bright"[35] (the One and Only Conscious Light—the Very, and Perfectly <u>Subjective</u>, and Inherently egoless, or Perfectly Non-Separate, and Inherently Perfect, and Indivisible, or Perfectly Non-Dual, and Always Already Self-Existing, and Eternally Self-Radiant, and Self-Evidently Divine Self-Condition <u>and</u> Source-Condition That <u>Is</u> the <u>One</u> and <u>Only</u> and <u>True</u> Divine Person, and Reality, and Truth of <u>All</u> and <u>all</u>, and That was, and is, the constant Spiritual Sign and Identity of This,

149

My Avataric Divine Lifetime, even from Birth). And It was the Un-deniable Reality and the Un-conditional Nature of <u>This</u> Realization That I Summarized to Baba Muktananda during Our Meetings in 1970 and 1973.

Even though It was and <u>Is</u> So, Baba Muktananda did not (and, because of the yet fifth stage nature of His own experiential Realization—for which He found corroboration in traditional mystical and philosophical traditions of the fifth stage, and phenomena-based, type—<u>could</u> <u>not</u>) positively Acknowledge My Summation relative to Most Perfect (and, necessarily, seventh stage) Divine Self-Realization.

Because He characteristically <u>preferred</u> to dwell upon inner <u>objects</u>, Baba Muktananda (in the "naive" manner of fourth and fifth stage mystics in general) interpreted Reality Itself (or Divine Self-Realization Itself) to "<u>require</u>" inner perceptual phenomenal (or conditionally arising) experiences and presumptions as a necessary <u>support</u> for Realization (<u>Itself</u>). That is to Say, Baba Muktananda was experientially Conformed to the (fifth stage) presumption that Divine Self-Realization not only requires conditionally arising (and, especially, inner perceptual) phenomenal experiences as a generally necessary (and even inevitable) Yogic Spiritual <u>preliminary</u> to authentic (and not merely conceptual) Realization— and I <u>completely</u> <u>Agree</u>, with Him, that there certainly <u>are</u> many conditionally apparent Yogic Spiritual requirements that <u>must</u> be Demonstrated in the Full Course of the authentic (and, necessarily, psycho-physical) Sadhana of Divine Self-Realization—but Baba Muktananda, otherwise, generally affirmed the presumption that <u>Realization</u> <u>Itself</u> (and <u>not</u> <u>only</u> the Sadhana, or psycho-physical <u>Process</u>, of <u>Realizing</u>) "requires" conditional (or psycho-physical— and, especially, absorptive mystical, or inner visual) <u>supports</u>.

Therefore, Baba Muktananda affirmed an attention-based, and object-oriented (or Goal-Oriented)—and, therefore, ego-based, or seeker-based—absorptive mystical (and, altogether, fourth-to-fifth stage) Yogic Way, in which the Sahasrar (or the Upper Terminal of the brain), and even the total brain (or sensorium), is the constant focus (and the Ultimate <u>Goal</u>—as well as the Highest Seat) of Sadhana.

It was due to <u>this</u>, Baba Muktananda's characteristic point of view relative to both Sadhana <u>and</u> Realization (as He defined—or, in effect, limited—Them), that, in My informal Meeting with Him in 1970, His only response to Me was to enter into a casual verbal (and even illogical) contradiction of Me. In that informal Meeting (as well as in Our formal Meeting, in 1973), Baba Muktananda <u>ignored</u> (and even appeared to not at all comprehend) My (then Given) Indications to Him relative to the Most Ultimate, or seventh stage, Significance of the "Regenerated" Form of Amrita Nadi.

LXXVI.

As I Indicated to Baba Muktananda (in Our Meetings in 1970 and 1973), the "Regenerated" Form of Amrita Nadi is <u>Rooted</u> in Consciousness <u>Itself</u> ("Located" <u>Beyond</u> the right side of the heart, which is, itself, merely the Self-Evident Seat, or Doorway, of the <u>direct</u> "Locating" of Perfectly Subjective, and Inherently egoless, Consciousness, Itself—or the Self-Existing Feeling of Being, Itself—Prior to attention, itself). And <u>That</u> ("Regenerated" Form of Amrita Nadi) is "Brightly" <u>Extended</u> to the "Maha-Bindu" (Which is <u>Infinitely</u> Ascended, even Above and Beyond the Sahasrar). However, Baba Muktananda appeared only to want to contradict My (secondary) <u>reference</u> (to the "right side of the heart")—while otherwise <u>ignoring</u> My (primary) Explanation (of the "Regenerated" Form of Amrita Nadi). And, in doing this, Baba Muktananda went so far in identifying Himself <u>exclusively</u> with the fifth stage tradition that He said to Me, "<u>Anyone</u> who says that the right side of the heart is the Seat of Realization does not know what he is talking about."

In this (from My "Point of View", even rather absurdly <u>funny</u>!) statement, Baba Muktananda merely <u>ignored</u> (and, therefore, <u>did not</u> <u>directly</u> <u>contradict</u>) My (then Given) Description (to Him) of how <u>seventh</u> <u>stage</u> Divine Self-Realization Inherently Transcends <u>both</u> the conditional (or psycho-physical) apparatus of the <u>brain</u> (or of the Sahasrar, Which is the conditional Seat of Realization proposed in the fifth stage traditions, of mystical absorption) <u>and</u> the conditional (or psycho-physical) apparatus of the <u>heart</u> (or, in particular, of the right side of the heart—which is the conditional

Seat of Realization proposed in the sixth stage traditions, of Transcendental practice). However, Baba Muktananda's statement to Me (relative to the heart on the right) <u>was</u> a remark made in direct and specific contradiction to the Transcendentalist (or entirely sixth stage) Teachings of <u>Ramana Maharshi</u>.

LXXVII.

In My Meeting with Baba Muktananda in 1973, I made specific references to the Teachings of Ramana Maharshi (Whom both Baba Muktananda and Bhagavan Nityananda had Met—and, apparently, Greatly Praised—in earlier years). In particular, I referred to Ramana Maharshi's experiential assertions relative to the right side of the heart (which He—in the sixth stage manner—Indicated to be the Seat of Transcendental Self-Realization). In doing so, I was merely Intending to Offer Baba Muktananda a traditional reference already known to Him (and, I naively presumed, one that He respected), which would provide some clarity (and traditional support) relative to My own (otherwise seventh stage) Descriptions.

Ramana Maharshi was a True and Great Jnani (or a <u>sixth</u> stage Realizer of the Transcendental Self-Condition, in the mode and manner indicated in the general tradition of Advaita Vedanta). And, after the Great Event of My own (<u>seventh</u> stage) Divine Re-Awakening (in September 1970), I Discovered (in the weeks and months that followed My informal Meeting with Baba Muktananda, in October 1970) that there were some (but, necessarily, only sixth stage) elements in Ramana Maharshi's reported experience and Realization that paralleled (and, in that sense, corroborated) certain (but only sixth stage) aspects of My own experience and Realization.[36] And, for this reason, I always Continue to Greatly Appreciate, and Honor, Ramana Maharshi—as a Great sixth stage Realizer, Who, through corroborating Testimony, Functions as a sixth stage Connecting-Link between Me and the Transcendentalist dimension of the Great Tradition. Also, because He is an example of a True Great Jnani (or Great Sage), Who Awakened to sixth stage Realization via the <u>Spiritual</u>—and not merely mental, or intellectual—Process (of the Magnification of the Spirit-Current in the right side of the heart), Ramana Maharshi, by Means of His corroborating Testimony, Functions—for Me—as a Connecting-Link between the sixth stage Transcendentalist tradition of Advaita Vedanta and the fourth-to-fifth stage Emanationist tradition of Siddha Yoga. And, because of this, Ramana Maharshi Functions, by Means of His corroborating Testimony, as a Connecting-Link between Me and the traditions of both Siddha Yoga and Advaita Vedanta—whereas I (except for Baba Muktananda's First Instruction to Me, in 1968—relative to the Witness of the three common states, of waking, dreaming, and sleeping) did not Find such a Connecting-Link among any of Those Who, otherwise, actively Functioned as My Spiritual Masters during the "Sadhana Years" of This, My present-Lifetime of Avataric Divine Incarnation.

During Our Meeting in 1973, Baba Muktananda mistakenly took My references to Ramana Maharshi (and to My own experience of the heart on the right, which I had first Confessed to Baba Muktananda during Our informal Meeting in 1970—and which is, also, one of the principal experiences Indicated by Ramana Maharshi) to suggest that I had departed from the Siddha-Yoga tradition. Therefore, Baba Muktananda's criticisms of Me (in Our Meetings in both 1970 and 1973) were an apparent reaction to His perception of the possibility of My "going over" to Advaita Vedanta (and to Ramana Maharshi). And, for this reason, Baba Muktananda never (in either of the two Meetings, in 1970 and in 1973) actually addressed the particular, and complex, and inherently (and especially in a conversation requiring translations from English to Hindi, and vice versa) difficult-to-explain Great Issues I was (in those two Meetings) Intending (and Trying) to Summarize to Him.

LXXVIII.

Relative to Baba Muktananda Himself, I can only Say that, for My part (through Visits to Him by My devotee-representatives), simple Messages of Love (and of Gratitude for His Service to Me during My Avataric Divine "Sadhana Years") were, right until the end of Baba Muktananda's lifetime, Sent to Him by Me. And I have—to everyone, including Baba Muktananda Himself, and the institution of His devotees—always Continued to Make every effort to Communicate <u>clearly</u> (and <u>frankly</u>, and, in general, most positively) about My relationship to Baba Muktananda. And I have always Continued (and will always Continue) to Work (in a Real Spiritual Manner) to Heal Baba Muktananda's human feeling-heart.

LXXIX.

Relative to Baba Muktananda's particular exact remarks to Me (in Our Meetings in 1970 and 1973), I can (and must) Say, simply, that His interpretation of Reality (and of the <u>Nature</u> and <u>Status</u> of the Process, and of even all the patterns and structures, associated with Divine Self-Realization)—which interpretation Baba Muktananda shared with (and for which He derived justification from) the phenomena-based aspects of the fifth stage Yogic traditions in general—was the characteristic basis of His criticisms of Me during Our Meetings in 1970 and 1973. And, as I have already Said, Baba Muktananda's Siddha-Yoga Teaching (and especially as He proposed it to Me in Our Meetings in 1970 and 1973) is—relative to all matters <u>beyond</u> the fifth stage of life (and even relative to all aspects of the fifth stage of life that are beyond the Saguna limits of Savikalpa Samadhi)—limited, prejudicial, ultimately indefensible, and (fundamentally) beyond His experience.

LXXX.

Neither the philosophy of Kashmir Saivism nor <u>any</u> "required" phenomenal conditions were pre-described to Me (or otherwise suggested)—by Baba Muktananda Himself, or by anyone else—as being a <u>necessary</u> part of the Siddha-Yoga practice and Process (and, especially, as being a <u>necessary</u> conditional support for Realization <u>Itself</u>) when I first Went to Baba Muktananda, in 1968. Nor were <u>any</u> philosophical or experiential "requirements" proposed to Me—by Baba Muktananda Himself, or by anyone else— as either demands or necessities of Siddha-Yoga practice, or as necessities of Siddha-Yoga experience, or as fixed "Models" of Realization Itself—during the years of My Sadhana in Baba Muktananda's Company, between 1968 and the Great Event of My Divine Re-Awakening, in September 1970.

Indeed, there was not even much "Baba Muktananda" Siddha-Yoga literature available—and <u>no</u> literature was demanded to be read—during all of <u>that</u> time. Even Baba Muktananda's autobiography, entitled *Play of Consciousness* (or, originally, *Chitshakti Vilas*), was not published until after the September 1970 Event of My Divine Re-Awakening. And I saw—and, in fact, was the first to fully render into English—only the first chapter or two of that book, in rough manuscript form, during My Stay at Baba Muktananda's Ganeshpuri Ashram, in early 1970. Therefore, virtually the only "Baba Muktananda" Siddha-Yoga literature that was available to Me during My years of Sadhana in Baba Muktananda's Company were the short essays and tracts either written or edited by Amma—and that literature suggested a very liberal and open Teaching relative to the <u>fourth</u> stage, <u>fifth</u> stage, <u>and</u> <u>sixth</u> stage possibilities associated with the potential developments of Siddha Yoga. And, indeed, it was <u>that</u> liberal and open form of Siddha Yoga that I practiced—to the degree of seventh stage Divine Self-Realization—in Baba Muktananda's Company.

In any case, the fact that Baba Muktananda presumed that there were (indeed) many <u>exclusively</u> <u>fifth</u> stage Siddha-Yoga "requirements" (both philosophical and experiential) was <u>proven</u> to be the case in the circumstances of My Meetings with Him in 1970 and 1973.

LXXXI.

In fact (and in My experience), the Siddha-Yoga practice and Process is <u>not</u> (<u>Itself</u>) inherently opposed to the Transcendental (or sixth stage) practice and Process (or to the seventh stage Realization and Demonstration). Rather, it was Baba Muktananda Who (in accordance with particular traditions He, <u>personally</u>, favored) chose to dogmatically introduce <u>exclusively</u> fifth stage "requirements" (and sixth-stage-excluding, and, therefore, inherently, seventh-stage-prohibiting, limitations) into His <u>own</u> Teaching (and into His <u>personal</u> school) of Siddha Yoga.

I <u>fully</u> <u>Acknowledge</u> that Baba Muktananda had the right to Teach Siddha Yoga <u>exclusively</u> according to His <u>own</u> experience, and His <u>own</u> understanding, and His <u>own</u> Realization. It is simply that My experience, and My understanding, and My Realization were not (and <u>are</u> <u>not</u>) limited to the fifth stage "requirements" (or limiting presumptions) that Baba Muktananda proposed to Me.

The Process of Siddha Yoga—or the inherent Spiritual Process that is potential in the case of all human beings—does not (if It is allowed, and Graced, to Freely Proceed as a potential <u>total</u> Process) limit <u>Itself</u> to the fifth stage "requirements" (or limiting presumptions) that Baba Muktananda generally proposed. Therefore, I Teach Siddha Yoga in the Mode and Manner of the <u>seventh</u> stage of life (as Ruchira Avatara Hridaya-Siddha Yoga, or Ruchira Avatara Maha-Jnana Hridaya-Shaktipat Yoga)—and always toward (or to the degree of) the Realization inherently associated with (and, at last, Most Perfectly Demonstrated and Proven by) the only-by-Me Revealed and Given seventh stage of life, and as a practice and a Process that progressively includes (and, coincidently, <u>directly</u> transcends) <u>all</u> <u>six</u> of the phenomenal and developmental (and, necessarily, yet ego-based) stages of life that precede the seventh.

Baba Muktananda conceived of (and Taught) Siddha Yoga as a Way to attain conditional (and especially fifth stage) Yogic objects and phenomena-based states. The Siddha Yoga of the only-by-Me Revealed and Given Way of Adidam is <u>not</u> based upon (or, otherwise, limited to) conditional (or phenomenal) objects and states—or the (necessarily, <u>ego</u>-based) search for these, in the context of <u>any</u> stage of life. Rather, the only-by-Me Revealed and Given Way of Adidam is the Siddha-Yoga Way (and, in particular, the Ruchira Avatara Hridaya-Siddha-Yoga Way) that <u>always</u> (and <u>directly</u>) transcends <u>egoity</u> <u>itself</u> (or the ego-"I", or separate self— or the reactive reflex of self-contraction)—by always Feeling <u>Beyond</u> <u>egoity</u> (and Beyond <u>all</u> conditional forms and states) to <u>Me</u>, the Avatarically Self-Revealed Divine Person (or Self-Condition, and Source-Condition) <u>Itself</u>.

LXXXII.

In Summary, Baba Muktananda (in Our Meetings in 1970 and 1973) countered My Language of Inherently (and Most Perfectly) egoless—or seventh stage—Divine Self-Realization (and otherwise defended His own experiential Realization—and philosophical idealization—of inner phenomenal objects) with the traditional language of fifth stage Yoga. And I, for <u>this</u> reason (and not because of any ill-will, or antagonism, or lack of respect toward Baba Muktananda), <u>Did</u> <u>Not</u>, and <u>Could</u> <u>Not</u>, and <u>Do</u> <u>Not</u> Accept His fifth-stage-bound Doctrine—because, from My "Point of View", <u>that</u> Acceptance would have Required (and would now Require) Me to Deny the Self-Evident Divine (and Perfectly Subjective, and Inherently egoless, and Inherently Non-Objective, and Inherently Indivisible, and Utterly Non-dependent, or Un-conditional) Truth of Reality Itself (Which Realization even Baba Muktananda Himself—along with all My other Spiritual Masters and Spiritual Friends—so Dearly Served in My own Case)!

LXXXIII.

Reality (Itself) <u>Is</u> the Only <u>Real</u> God.

Reality (Itself) <u>Is</u> That Which Is Always Already <u>The</u> (One and Only) Case.

Reality (Itself) <u>Is</u> (Necessarily) One, Only, and Indivisible.

Reality (Itself) <u>Is</u> Inherently One (or Non-Dual) and not Two (or Divisible, and Opposed to Itself).

Reality (Itself) is not One of a Pair.

Reality (Itself) is not characterized by the inherently dualistic relationship of cause and effect.

Reality (Itself) <u>Is</u> Characterized by the Inherently Non-Dualistic Equation of Identity and Non-"Difference".

Reality (Itself) <u>Is</u> That in Which <u>both</u> cause and effect arise <u>as</u> merely apparent modifications of Itself.

Reality (Itself) is not Realized via the inherently dualistic relationship of subject and object.

Reality (Itself) <u>Is</u> Realized <u>As</u> the Inherently Non-Dualistic Condition of Inherently egoless Identity and Inherently objectless Non-"Difference".

Reality (Itself) is not the gross, subtle, and causal (or causative) ego-"I".

Reality (Itself) <u>Is</u> the Inherently egoless Native (and Self-Evidently Divine) Identity of All and all.

The Inherently egoless Non-Dual Self-Condition (or Non-"Different" Identity) of Reality (Itself) <u>Is</u> That Which Is Always Already <u>The</u> (One and Only) Case.

The Inherently egoless Non-Dual Self-Condition of Reality (Itself), Most Perfectly Prior to (and, yet, never excluding, or separated from) subject, object, cause, or effect, <u>Is</u> That Which Must Be Realized.

The apparent self (or separate and separative ego-"I"), and its every object, and, indeed, every cause, and every effect must be Divinely Self-Recognized <u>As</u> (and, Thus and Thereby, Transcended in) the One and Only (Inherently egoless, and Inherently Non-Dual, or Indivisible and Non-Separate, or Non-"Different") Self-Condition of Reality (Itself).

The apparent ego-"I" and the apparent world are not <u>themselves</u> Divine.

The apparent ego-"I" and the apparent world are to be Self-Recognized (and, Thus and Thereby, Transcended) in and <u>As</u> That Which <u>Is</u> (Self-Evidently) Divine.

The apparent ego-"I" and the apparent world are to be Divinely Self-Recognized in and <u>As</u> Reality (Itself).

Baba Muktananda always (in the Emanationist manner of Kashmir Saivism) affirmed the Realization "I am Siva"—meaning that He (or any body-mind-self, or body-brain-self, sublimed by the Revelation of internal Yogic forms) <u>is</u> (<u>as</u> an "Emanated" psycho-physical self) Divine.

I Affirmed (and always Continue to Affirm) <u>only</u> the Non-Dual (or One and Indivisible) Transcendental (and Inherently Spiritual) Divine Reality (or Self-Existing, Self-Radiant, and Inherently, or Always Already, egoless Consciousness Itself—or the One and Only Conscious Love-Bliss-Light Itself) <u>As</u> Self (or Self-Condition, and Source-Condition), Prior to and Inherently Transcending (while <u>never</u> strategically, or conditionally, <u>excluding</u>) the phenomenal self and <u>all</u> conditional forms (however sublime).

Baba Muktananda affirmed (in the fifth stage, Emanationist manner) "I and the world are Divine"—and He (thereby) embraced both the perceiving "I" and the world of forms.

I (in the seventh stage Manner) Affirmed (and always

Continue to Affirm) <u>only</u> the Self-Existing and Self-Radiant (Transcendental, Inherently Spiritual, Inherently egoless, Perfectly Subjective, Indivisible, Non-Dual, and Self-Evidently Divine) Self-Identity (<u>Itself</u>)—or the <u>One</u>, and Most Prior, and Inherently Perfect, and Inherently egoless Self-Condition, and Source-Condition, of the body-mind (or the body-brain-self) and the world—Divinely Self-Recognizing the body-mind (or the body-brain-self) and the world (and, thus, neither excluding nor identifying with the body-mind, or the body-brain-self, and the world, but Inherently, or Always Already, "Brightly" Transcending, and, Most Ultimately, Divinely Outshining, the body-mind, or the body-brain-self, and the world).

It was <u>This</u> Distinction (or <u>These</u> Distinctions)—not merely in language, but in the "Point of View" of Realization Itself—that was (or were) the basis for My Assumption of My Avataric Divine Teaching-Work, and My Avataric Divine Revelation-Work, and My Avataric Divine Blessing-Work <u>institutionally</u> independent of (and, after Our Final Meeting, in 1973, entirely apart from further <u>outwardly</u> active association with) Baba Muktananda.

LXXXIV.

As has always been understood by authentic Realizers and their authentic true devotees—within the Siddha-Yoga (or Shaktipat-Yoga) tradition, and even everywhere within the human Great Tradition as a whole—Great Siddhas, and even Avatars, and traditional Realizers of all kinds and degrees (or stages of life), and Siddha-Yogis of all kinds and degrees, and even Siddha Yoga <u>Itself</u>, are not mere "properties", to be "owned" (or exclusively "possessed") by devotees, or even by institutions. Indeed, Baba Muktananda, Himself, once told Me[37] that, because the same Life (or Shakti) is in <u>all</u> beings, <u>no</u> individual, <u>no</u> religion, <u>no</u> tradition—and, therefore, <u>no</u> institution—can rightly claim to be the <u>only</u> bearer, or the <u>exclusive</u> representative, of Siddha Yoga (or Shaktipat Yoga) Itself.

There are, inevitably, <u>many</u> forms of Siddha-Yoga Transmission in this world. The institution that Baba Muktananda established to represent and continue His <u>own</u> Work is (by its <u>own</u> self-description) a <u>fourth-to-fifth</u> stage school of Siddha Yoga. And, indeed, there are numbers of other such schools—in India, and elsewhere—that are extending the Work of various Great Siddhas (and of many otherwise worthy Siddha-Yogis) into the world. Likewise, the institution (or the total complex of institutions) of Adidam—which represents, and serves, and will always continue to serve My Avataric Divine (and, Uniquely, seventh stage) Work—is also a school of Siddha Yoga (or of Shaktipat Yoga).

The Uniqueness of the Siddha Yoga of the only-by-Me Revealed and Given Way of Adidam is that It is the Yoga (or Dharma, or Way) that continues to Develop beyond the absorptive mystical (and cosmically Spiritual) developments associated with the fourth and the fifth stages of life—and even beyond the Transcendental Yogic (and Transcendentally Spiritual) developments associated with the sixth stage of life. Thus, in due course, the Yoga (or Way) of Adidam becomes the Unique (and Most Perfectly Divine) Yoga (or Most Perfectly Divinely Spiritual Demonstration) of the only-by-Me Revealed and Given seventh stage of life (Wherein and Whereby Most Perfect Divine Self-Realization is Most Perfectly Demonstrated).

Because of This Uniqueness, the Siddha Yoga of the only-by-Me Revealed and Given Way of Adidam is not descriptively limited to (or by) the particular traditional descriptive language of the fourth-to-fifth stage schools and traditions of Siddha Yoga (which are the schools and traditions from which Baba Muktananda derived His descriptive Siddha-Yoga-language—and which descriptive language is conformed to, and, necessarily, limited by, the fourth-to-fifth stage experiential presumptions that characterize the Cosmic-Yoga, or Cosmic-Shakti, or Kundalini-Shakti schools and traditions). Therefore—even though the Process of the Siddha Yoga of the only-by-Me Revealed and Given Way of Adidam potentially includes (and then continues to Develop beyond) all the aspects and experiences of the fourth and the fifth and the sixth stages of life—the Siddha Yoga of the only-by-Me Revealed and Given Way of Adidam is (by Me) Uniquely Described, in the (Most Ultimately, seventh stage—and Most Perfectly Divine, or Cosmos-Transcending, and Cosmos-Outshining) Terms of My own Avataric (Divine) Shaktipat.

Thus, the Siddha Yoga of the only-by-Me Revealed and Given Way of Adidam is (by Me) Described in Terms of Ruchira Avatara Hridaya-Shaktipat (or My Avataric Divine Spiritual Transmission of the "Bright"—Which Is the Self-Existing and Self-Radiant Divine Self-Condition, or Divine Self-Heart, Itself), and Ruchira Avatara Maha-Jnana Hridaya-Shaktipat (or My Avataric Divine Spiritual Transmission of the "Bright" Divine Spirit-Current, or Divine Heart-Shakti, That Awakens the Divine Self-Heart to Its Inherent Divine Self-Condition), and Love-Ananda Avatara Hridaya-Shaktipat (or My Avataric Divine Spiritual Transmission of the Inherent Love-Bliss of the Divine Self-Condition, or Divine Self-Heart, Itself—Which Divine Spiritual Characteristic of Mine was Acknowledged by Baba Muktananda Himself, when, in 1969, He Sent Amma to Me, to Give Me the Name "Love-Ananda").

Therefore, the Siddha-Yoga practice (and especially the advanced and the ultimate stages of the Siddha-Yoga Process) of the only-by-Me Revealed and Given Way of Adidam is (along with numerous other by-Me-Given Descriptive Names and References) Named and Described by Me as "Ruchira Avatara Hridaya-Siddha Yoga" (or "Ruchira Avatara Hridaya-Shaktipat Yoga"), and "Ruchira Avatara Maha-Jnana-Siddha Yoga" (or "Ruchira Avatara Maha-Jnana Hridaya-Shaktipat Yoga"), and "Love-Ananda Avatara Hridaya-Siddha Yoga" (or "Love-Ananda Avatara Hridaya-Shaktipat Yoga"), and (with reference to the Way, and the institution, of Adidam) "Adidam Hridaya-Siddha Yoga" (or "Adidam Hridaya-Shaktipat Yoga").

And My own Work (Which is served by the institutional Siddha-Yoga school—or, most properly, the Ruchira Avatara Hridaya-Siddha-Yoga school—of Adidam) was directly Blessed (and—formally, in 1969—Called Forth) by Baba Muktananda (and, now, and forever hereafter, by even all the Great Siddhas and Siddha-Yogis of My Lineage).

LXXXV.

The Uniqueness of My own Divine Self-Realization and Avataric Divine Work made it Inevitable that I would have to Do My Avataric Divine Teaching-Work, and My Avataric Divine Revelation-Work, and My Avataric Divine Blessing-Work

Independent from Baba Muktananda—and Independent from even all Teachers and traditions within the only six stages of life of the collectively Revealed Great Tradition of mankind. Indeed, even from the beginning of My relationship with Him, Baba Muktananda Indicated that My Work was Uniquely My own, and that I was Born to Do only My own Unique Work—and that I Must Go and Do That Work (even though I would, otherwise, have preferred to Remain, quietly, within Baba Muktananda's Ashram and Company). Therefore, ultimately, We both Embraced This Necessity and Inevitability.

Because of the original, mutual Agreement between Baba Muktananda and Me (relative to the necessarily Independent, and entirely Unique, nature of My own Work), whenever I have become Moved to Communicate about This Profound Matter to others, I have made every effort to Communicate fully, clearly, and positively relative to the always un-"broken" Nature of My Spiritual (and, generally, sympathetic) relationship to Baba Muktananda—and, also, relative to the always Continuing Nature of My Spiritual (and, generally, sympathetic) Connection to the Great (and total) Siddha-Guru tradition itself, and to the Great (and total) Siddha-Yoga tradition itself, and to the total Great Tradition of mankind (altogether). And I have always Affirmed (and, by Means of This Statement, I now Re-Affirm) that the Great, and total, Siddha-Guru tradition and Siddha-Yoga tradition, and the most ancient and perennial "Method of the Siddhas",[38] is—in the context of, and continuous with, the total Great Tradition of mankind—the very tradition (or total complex of traditions) in which, and on the basis of which, I Am Avatarically Appearing and Working here.

LXXXVI.

Human suffering is not due to the absence of inner visions (or of any other kinds of conditionally objectified internal or, otherwise, external perceptions). Therefore, human suffering is not eliminated by the presence (or the experiencing) of inner visions (or of any other kinds of conditionally objectified internal or, otherwise, external perceptions).

The "problem" of human suffering is <u>never</u> the <u>absence</u> of inner visions (and such), or the <u>absence</u> of <u>any</u> conditional experience of <u>any</u> kind. Rather, the "problem" of human suffering is <u>always</u> (and <u>inherently</u>) the <u>presence</u> (or presently effective activity) of the <u>ego-"I"</u> (or the self-contracted—or separate and separative—<u>point</u> <u>of</u> <u>view</u>). Indeed, the search to experience conditionally objectified inner perceptions—and, otherwise, the clinging to conditionally objectified inner perceptions—is, <u>itself</u>, a form of human suffering (and, altogether, of self-deluded confinement to the inherently, and negatively, <u>empty</u> condition of egoic separateness).

The root and essence of human suffering <u>is</u> egoity. That is to Say, the "problem" that is human suffering is <u>not</u> due to the absence of <u>any</u> kind of conditionally objectified experience (whether relatively external or relatively internal)—for, if human suffering <u>were</u> due to such absence, the <u>attaining</u> of conditionally objectified experiences (whether internal or external) would <u>eliminate</u> human suffering, human self-deludedness, and human un-Happiness. However, at most, conditionally objectified experiences (both internal and external)—or even <u>any</u> of the possible experiential attainments of the first <u>five</u> stages of life—provide only <u>temporary</u> distraction from the inherent mortality and misery of conditional existence. Therefore, if human suffering is to be <u>entirely</u> (and, at last, <u>Most</u> <u>Perfectly</u>) transcended (in Inherent, and Divinely Positive, Fullness), the root-cause of (or the root-factor in) human suffering must, <u>itself</u>, be directly and entirely (and, at last, Most Perfectly) transcended.

The "problem" of human suffering is <u>never</u> the absence of <u>any</u> kind of particular conditionally objectified experience (whether external or internal). The "problem" of human suffering is <u>always</u> the bondage to conditionally objectified experience <u>itself</u>. And the root-cause of (or the root-factor in) bondage to conditionally objectified experience is the separate and separative ego-"I", or the total psycho-physical act of self-contraction (which is identical to attention itself, or the conditionally apparent <u>point</u> of view <u>itself</u>, and which <u>always</u> coincides with the feeling of "difference", or of separateness and relatedness).

The experiencing of inner visions does <u>not</u> eliminate egoity (or the separate and separative ego-"I" of psycho-physical self-contraction). Likewise, the experiencing of inner visions does <u>not</u> indicate or suggest or mean that egoity is (or has been) transcended. True Spiritual life (or the true Great Process of Siddha Yoga) is not a search for inner visions (and such)—nor is true Spiritual life (or the true Great Process of Siddha Yoga) Fulfilled, Completed, and Perfected by the experiencing of inner visions (and such). Indeed, because inner visions, or conditionally objectified experiences of <u>any</u> kind—whether inner or outer—are <u>objects</u>, attention is <u>always</u> coincident with them. Therefore, in both the <u>search</u> for conditionally objectified experiences and the <u>grasping</u> of conditionally objectified experiences, <u>egoity</u> (or separative, and total psycho-physical, self-contraction of the presumed separate point of view) <u>is</u> <u>merely</u> <u>reinforced</u>.

True Spiritual life (or the true Great Process of Siddha Yoga) is <u>never</u> a matter of seeking for outer <u>or</u> inner conditionally objectified experiences—nor is true Spiritual life (or the true Great Process of Siddha Yoga) a matter of clinging to any conditionally objectified outer <u>or</u> inner experiences (as if such experiences were, themselves, Reality, Truth, or Real God). Rather, true Spiritual life (or the true Great Process of Siddha Yoga) is <u>always</u> a matter of transcending attention (and the total psycho-physical—or gross, subtle, and causal—point of view, or ego-"I") in its Perfectly Subjective Source (or Inherently Perfect Self-Condition). That is to Say, true Spiritual life (or the true Great Process of Siddha Yoga) is <u>always</u> (from Its beginning) a matter of transcending that which is merely apparently (or conditionally, and temporarily) the case—by transcending it in <u>That</u> Which <u>Is</u> Always Already <u>The</u> (One and Only, Indivisible and Irreducible) Case. And, for <u>This</u> Reason, true Spiritual life, or the true Great Process of Siddha Yoga, cannot be Fulfilled, Completed, and Perfected in the conditionally objectified context of any of the first <u>five</u> stages of life—nor even in the conditionally object-excluding context of the <u>sixth</u> stage of life—but true Spiritual life (in particular, in the form of the true Great Process of Ruchira Avatara Hridaya-Siddha Yoga) <u>Is</u> Fulfilled, Completed, and Perfected <u>only</u> in the Perfectly Subjective, and

Inherently egoless (or Inherently point-of-view-Transcending and Most Perfectly self-contraction-Transcending), and Un-conditionally Realized, and, altogether, Self-Evidently Divine Context of the only-by-Me Revealed and Given <u>seventh</u> stage of life.

This is My Firm Conclusion relative to <u>all</u> possible human experience—and It is, therefore, the Essence of My Instruction to all of humankind.

LXXXVII.

There are <u>three</u> <u>egos</u> (or three fundamental modes of egoity—or of the self-contraction-active psycho-physical illusion of separate and separative self-consciousness). The three modes of egoity (or of the self-contraction of <u>any</u> point of view, or ego-"I") are the lower self (or gross ego), the higher self (or subtle ego), and the root-self (or causal ego). These three egos (or modes of the conditionally arising illusion of separate self-consciousness) comprise the total conditionally perceiving and conditionally knowing ego-"I". The <u>total</u> (or tripartite) ego-"I" is always directly (and with progressive effectiveness) transcended in the right, true, and full (or complete) formal practice of the only-by-Me Revealed and Given Way of Adidam (Which is the right, true, and full formal practice of Ruchira Avatara Bhakti Yoga, or the totality of Ruchira Avatara Hridaya-Siddha Yoga).

The first of the three egos (or modes of egoity, or of self-contraction) to be progressively transcended in the only-by-Me Revealed and Given Way of Adidam is the <u>money-food-and-sex</u> <u>ego</u> (or the social, and, altogether, gross-body-based, personality—or the <u>gross</u> pattern and activity of self-contraction), which is the lower self, or the ego of the first three stages of life.

The second of the three egos (or modes of egoity, or of self-contraction) to be progressively transcended in the only-by-Me Revealed and Given Way of Adidam is the <u>brain-mind</u> <u>ego</u> (or the brain-based, and nervous-system-based, mental, and perceptual, and, altogether, subtle-body-based illusions of "object" and "other"—or the <u>subtle</u> pattern and activity of self-contraction), which is the higher self, or the ego of the fourth and the fifth stages of life.

The third of the three egos (or modes of egoity, or of self-contraction) to be progressively transcended in the only-by-Me Revealed and Given Way of Adidam is the <u>root-ego</u> (or the exclusively disembodied, and mindless, but separate, and, altogether, causal-body-based self-consciousness—or the <u>causal</u>, or root-causative, pattern and activity of self-contraction), which is attention <u>itself</u>, and which is the root-self, or the ego of the sixth stage of life.

By Means of <u>responsive</u> relinquishment of self-contraction in <u>Me</u>, or <u>really</u> and <u>truly</u> ego-surrendering, ego-forgetting, and, more and more (and, at last, Most Perfectly), ego-transcending (or always directly self-contraction-transcending) devotion to <u>Me</u> (and, Thus, by Means of the right, true, and full formal practice of devotionally <u>Me</u>-recognizing and devotionally to-<u>Me</u>-responding Ruchira Avatara Bhakti Yoga, or the totality of Ruchira Avatara Hridaya-Siddha Yoga), the tripartite ego of the first six stages of life (or the psycho-physical <u>totality</u> of the three-part hierarchically patterned self-contraction into separate and separative point of view) is (always directly, and with progressive, or stage-by-stage, effectiveness) transcended in <u>Me</u> (the Eternally Self-Existing, Infinitely Self-Radiant, Inherently egoless, Perfectly Subjective, Indivisibly One, Irreducibly Non-Separate, Self-Evidently Divine, and, now, and forever hereafter, Avatarically Self-Revealed Self-Conscious Light of Reality).

The Ultimate, Final, and Inherently Most Perfect (or seventh stage) Realization of Me requires—as a <u>necessary</u> prerequisite—an ego-transcending (or really and truly and <u>comprehensively</u> self-contraction-transcending) Great Ordeal. The Ultimate, Final, and Inherently Most Perfect (or seventh stage) Realization of Me requires—as a <u>necessary</u> prerequisite—the <u>comprehensive</u> by-Me-Revealed and by-Me-Given Sadhana (or the <u>always</u> directly ego-transcending right practice of life) in the total and complete formal context of the only-by-Me Revealed and Given Way of Adidam. And—as a <u>necessary</u> prerequisite to the Ultimate, Final, and Inherently Most Perfect (or seventh stage) Realization of Me— the particular illusions that are unique to each of the three egos (or basic modes of egoity) each require a particular (and most profound) mode of the necessary ego-transcending (or self-contraction-transcending) Great Ordeal of the by-Me-Revealed and by-Me-Given formal practice of the Way of Adidam in the progressively unfolding context of the first six (and, altogether, psycho-physically pre-patterned) stages of life.

The foundation phase of the progressive ego-transcending Great Ordeal of the only-by-Me Revealed and Given Way of Adidam is the Devotional (and relatively <u>exoteric</u>, and only in the rudimentary sense Spiritual) <u>listening-hearing</u> Process of progressively transcending (and, in due course, <u>most</u> <u>fundamentally</u> understanding) the <u>lower</u> <u>self</u> (or the <u>gross</u> <u>and</u> <u>social</u> <u>ego</u>—and the gross and social fear-sorrow-and-anger-bondage that is <u>always</u> associated with the <u>inherently</u> <u>egoic</u>—or thoroughly self-contracted—search to absolutely fulfill, and even to "utopianize", or to perfectly and permanently satisfy, the <u>inherently</u> conditional, limited, temporary, mortal, gross, and <u>always</u> changing life-patterns of "money, food, and sex").

Before the foundation phase (or first phase) of the ego-transcending Great Ordeal of the Way of Adidam can, itself, be complete, it must Realize a profoundly life-transforming and life-reorienting "positive disillusionment"—or a most fundamental (and really and truly self-contraction-transcending) acceptance of the fact that gross conditional existence is <u>inherently</u> and <u>necessarily</u> unsatisfactory and unperfectable (<u>and</u>, therefore, a most funda-mental—and really and truly Me-Finding and search-ending—acceptance of the fact that <u>all</u> seeking to achieve permanent and complete gross satisfaction of separate body, emotion, and mind is <u>inherently</u> and <u>necessarily</u> futile). Only on the basis of that <u>necessary</u> foundation-Realization of "positive disillusionment" can the energy and the attention of the entire body-mind (or of the total body-brain-mind complex) be released from gross ego-bondage (or self-deluded confinement to the psycho-physical illu-sions of gross self-contraction).

The characteristic Sign of "positive disillusionment" relative to the permanent and complete satisfaction of the lower self (or the separate and separative gross and social ego) is the foundation-Realization of the Inherent Universal <u>Unity</u> (or All-and-all-inclusive interdependency, essential mutuality, and common causality) of gross conditional (and cosmic) existence, such that the inherently loveless (or anti-participatory and non-integrative) self-contraction-effort of the gross separate self is consistently released (or to-<u>Me</u>-responsively self-surrendered) into <u>participatory</u> and <u>integrative</u> attitudes of human, social, and cosmic unification (or <u>love</u>-connectedness) with all and All, and into <u>love</u>-based (and truly ego-transcending) actions that counter the otherwise separative (or anti-participatory and non-integrative) tendencies of the ego-"I". Thus, by Means of devotionally Me-recognizing and devotionally to-Me-responding relinquishment (or participatory and love-based transcending) of psycho-physical self-contraction (to the degree of "positive disillusionment" relative to gross conditional experience and gross conditional knowledge), My true devotee is released toward the true Spiritual (and not merely gross, or even at all conditional) Realization of Reality and Truth (or <u>Real</u> God).

The foundation-Realization of "positive disillusionment" requires fundamental release from the confines of the grossly objectified (and grossly absorbed) subject-object point of view (or fundamental release from the inherently ego-bound—or thoroughly self-contracted—search of relatively <u>externalized</u> mental and perceptual attention). And that foundation-Realization of "positive disillusionment" (and restoration to the humanly, socially, and cosmically participatory, or wholly integrative, disposition) requires the total (and truly Devotional) transformative re-orienting (and, altogether, the right purification, steady re-balancing, and ego-transcending life-positive-energizing) of the entire body-mind (or the total body-brain-mind complex). Therefore, the foundation (or gross) phase of the progressive ego-transcending practice of the Way of Adidam <u>necessarily</u> requires <u>much</u> time (and <u>much</u> seriousness, and <u>much</u> profundity)—and even, potentially, the <u>entire</u> lifetime of <u>only</u> that foundation practice may (in many cases) be required—in order to establish the necessary (and <u>truly</u> "positively disillusioned") foundation of true (and truly in-<u>Me</u>-surrendered) hearing (or the only-by-Me Revealed and Given unique ego-transcending capability of most fundamental self-understanding).

The middle phase of the progressive ego-transcending Great Ordeal of the only-by-Me Revealed and Given Way of Adidam is the preliminary (or initial) <u>esoteric</u> Devotional, and truly hearing (or actively ego-transcending, and, thus, always directly self-contraction-transcending), and really seeing (or actively, directly, and fully responsibly Spiritual) Process of transcending the <u>higher self</u> (or the <u>subtle</u> <u>and</u> <u>mental</u> <u>ego</u>—or the total subtle dimension, or subtle depth, of self-contraction—and <u>all</u> the conceptual and perceptual illusions of inherently, and necessarily, <u>brain-based</u> mind). Therefore, the middle (or subtle) phase of the progressive ego-transcending practice of the Way of Adidam requires the Realization of "positive disillusionment" relative to the subtly objectified (and subtly absorbed) subject-object point of view (or fundamental release from the inherently ego-bound—or thoroughly self-contracted—search of relatively <u>internalized</u> mental and perceptual attention). This degree of the Realization of "positive disillusionment" requires fundamental release from the inherently illusory search to experience the conditional dissolution of the ego (and, in particular, release from subtle states of self-contraction—and, especially, from mental states of self-contraction) by means of object-oriented absorptive mysticism (or the absorptive yielding of attention to the apparent subtle objects that are either originated by the brain-mind or, otherwise, mediated by the brain itself). And the characteristic Sign of "positive disillusionment" relative to the permanent and complete satisfaction of the object-oriented seeking of the higher self (or separate and separative subtle and mental ego) is the fully <u>Me</u>-hearing and truly <u>Me</u>-seeing Realization of the entirely <u>Spiritual</u> Nature of cosmic existence (or, that is to Say, the Realization that <u>all</u> natural and cosmic forms and states are inherently non-separate, or intrinsically non-dual, modes of Universally Pervasive <u>Energy</u>, or of <u>Fundamental</u>, <u>Indivisible</u>, and <u>Irreducible</u> <u>Light</u>—or of <u>Love-Bliss-Happiness</u> <u>Itself</u>).

The final phase of the progressive ego-transcending Great Ordeal of the only-by-Me Revealed and Given Way of Adidam is the penultimate <u>esoteric</u> Devotional, Spiritual, and <u>Transcendental</u> hearing-<u>and</u>-seeing Process of transcending the <u>root-self</u> (or the root-and-causal ego—or the causal, or root-causative, depth of self-contraction—which is attention itself, or the root-gesture of separateness, relatedness, and "difference"). Therefore, immediately preliminary to the Realization associated with the only-by-Me Revealed and Given seventh stage of life, the final (or causal) phase of the progressive ego-transcending (or comprehensively self-contraction-transcending) practice of the Way of Adidam requires the Realization of "positive disillusionment" relative to the causal (or root-egoic, and, therefore, fundamental, or original) subject-object division in Consciousness (or Conscious Light) Itself. This degree of the Realization of "positive disillusionment" requires the native exercise of Transcendental Self-Identification— Prior to the root-self-contraction that is point of view itself (or attention itself), and, Thus, also, Prior to the entire body-brain-mind complex, or conditional structure, of conception and perception. And the characteristic Sign of "positive disillusionment" relative to the permanent and complete satisfaction of the root-self (or the fundamental causative, or causal, ego) is the fundamental transcending of attention itself in the Me-"Locating" (and, altogether, Me-hearing and Me-seeing) Realization of the Transcendental (and Intrinsically Non-Separate and Non-Dual) Nature of Consciousness Itself.

Only after (or in the Great Event of Most Perfect, and, necessarily, formal and fully accountable, Fulfillment of) the complete progressive ego-transcending Great Ordeal of the only-by-Me Revealed and Given Way of Adidam in the total (and progressively unfolded) context of the inherently ego-based first six (or psycho-physically pre-patterned gross, subtle, and causal) stages of life is there the truly ultimate (or seventh stage, and Always Already Divinely Self-Realized—and, Thus, Inherently ego-Transcending) "Practice" of the only-by-Me Revealed and Given Way of Adidam (or the Most Perfect, and Inherently egoless, or Always Already Most Perfectly, and Un-conditionally, self-contraction-Transcending, and Divinely Love-Bliss-Full, and only-by-Me Revealed and Given seventh-stage-of-life Demonstration of Ruchira Avatara Bhakti Yoga, or Ruchira Avatara Hridaya-Siddha Yoga).

The only-by-Me Revealed and Given seventh-stage-of-life "Practice" (or the Inherently egoless, and, Thus, Always Already Most Perfectly, and Un-conditionally, self-contraction-Transcending, and, altogether, Most Perfectly Divinely Self-Realized Demonstration) of the only-by-Me Revealed and Given Way of Adidam is the Great <u>esoteric</u> Devotional, Spiritual, Transcendental, Self-Evidently Divine, and Most Perfectly <u>Me</u>-hearing and <u>Me</u>-seeing Demonstration of All-and-all-Divinely-Self-<u>Recognizing</u> (and, <u>Thus</u>, All-and-all-Divinely-<u>Transcending</u>) Divine Self-Abiding (in and <u>As</u> My Avatarically Self-Revealed Divine "Bright" <u>Sphere</u> of Self-Existing, Self-Radiant, Inherently egoless, Perfectly Subjective, and Inherently and Most Perfectly body-mind-Transcending, or body-brain-Transcending, or Inherently, Most Perfectly, and Un-conditionally psycho-physical-self-contraction-Transcending, but never intentionally body-mind-excluding, or body-brain-excluding, Divine Person, or Eternal Self-Condition and Infinite State).

The only-by-Me Revealed and Given seventh-stage-of-life Demonstration of the only-by-Me Revealed and Given Way of Adidam is the Un-conditional and Divinely Free (and Inherently egoless, or Inherently point-of-view-less) "Practice" (or Divinely Self-Realized progressive Demonstration) of Divine <u>Self</u>-Recognition of the simultaneous <u>totality</u> of the apparent gross, subtle, <u>and</u> causal body-brain-mind-self, or the progressively All-and-all-Outshining Process of the simultaneous Divine <u>Self</u>-Recognition of the <u>total</u> psycho-physical ego-"I" itself (or of the <u>total</u> conditional point of view, or apparent self-contraction, itself). Therefore, the only-by-Me Revealed and Given seventh-stage-of-life Demonstration of the only-by-Me Revealed and Given Way of Adidam is the Inherent "Practice" (or Divinely Self-Realized Demonstration) of Divine <u>Self</u>-Recognition of point of view itself (or of attention itself—or of the conditionally apparent <u>subject</u>, itself) <u>and</u> (always coincidently, or simultaneously) Divine <u>Self</u>-Recognition of the conception or perception of separateness, relatedness, or "difference" itself (or of any and every conditionally apparent <u>object</u>, itself).

The only-by-Me Revealed and Given seventh-stage-of-life Demonstration of the only-by-Me Revealed and Given Way of Adidam is the Most Perfect (or Un-conditional, Inherently egoless, and Self-Evidently Divine) Demonstration of "positive disillusionment", or of the Inherently illusionless (or self-contraction-Free, and, Inherently, All-and-all-Transcending) Realization of the Fundamental Reality and Truth (or <u>Real</u> God)—Which Fundamental Reality and Truth (or <u>Real</u> God) <u>Is</u> the One and Indivisible and Self-Existing and Indestructible and Self-Radiant and Always Already Perfectly Non-Dual Conscious Light (or That Which <u>Is</u> Always Already <u>The</u> Case), and Which Reality and Truth (or <u>Real</u> God) <u>Is</u> That Self-Existing and Perfectly Subjective Self-"Brightness" (or Infinite and Absolute and Perfectly Non-Separate Self-Condition) of Which the conditional (or gross, subtle, and causal) subject-object illusions (or total psycho-physical self-contraction illusions) of conception, and of perception, and of the ego-"I" presumption are mere, and merely apparent (or non-necessary, or <u>always</u> non-Ultimate), and Inherently non-binding modifications. And the characteristic Sign of Most Perfectly Demonstrated (or seventh stage) "positive disillusionment" relative to the totality of the separate and separative ego-"I" (or point of view) and its presumptions of a separate (or objectified) gross, subtle, and causal world is the Self-Evidently Divine (and Intrinsically Non-Separate and Non-Dual) Realization of Reality (<u>Itself</u>) <u>As</u> Irreducible and Indivisible Conscious Light (Inherently Love-Bliss-Full, or Perfectly Subjectively "Bright").

Therefore, the only-by-Me Revealed and Given Way of Adidam is—from the beginning, <u>and</u> at last—the Way of "positive disillusionment".

The only-by-Me Revealed and Given Way of Adidam is—from the beginning, <u>and</u> at last—the Way of the direct transcending of the fact and the consequences of egoity (or of psycho-physical self-contraction).

The only-by-Me Revealed and Given Way of Adidam is—from the beginning, <u>and</u> at last—the Way of the direct transcending of the illusions of inherently egoic attention (or of the conditionally presumed subject-object pattern of conception and perception).

The only-by-Me Revealed and Given Way of Adidam is—from the beginning, <u>and</u> at last—the Way of the direct transcending of the total illusory pattern of the inherently egoic presumption of separateness, relatedness, and "difference".

The only-by-Me Revealed and Given Way of Adidam is—from the beginning, <u>and</u> at last—the Way of the direct transcending of the always simultaneous illusions of the separate ego-"I" <u>and</u> the separate (or merely objective) world.

The only-by-Me Revealed and Given Way of Adidam is—from the beginning, <u>and</u> at last—the Way of the direct (or Inherently egoless <u>and</u> Inherently illusionless) Realizing of the One and Irreducible Conscious Light (or Perfectly Subjective "Brightness" of Being) That <u>Is</u> Reality and Truth (or <u>Real</u> God).

The only-by-Me Revealed and Given Way of Adidam is—from the beginning, <u>and</u> at last—the Way of the direct (or Inherently egoless <u>and</u> Inherently illusionless) Realizing of the Conscious Love-Bliss-Energy of Totality.

The only-by-Me Revealed and Given Way of Adidam is—from the beginning, <u>and</u> at last—the Way of the direct Realizing of <u>Only Me</u>.

LXXXVIII.

<u>Every</u> body-mind (whether human or non-human) tends to feel and be and function <u>egoically</u>—or <u>as</u> <u>if</u> it were a separate self, separated from its True Source, and un-Aware of its True, and Truly Free, Self-Condition. Therefore, <u>every</u> body-mind (whether human or non-human) must transcend its own (inherent) egoity (or egoic reflex—or self-contracting tendency), through Love-Surrender to its True Source. And This Love-Surrender must, Ultimately, become Realization of (and, <u>Thus</u>, True, and really ego-Transcending, Identification with) its <u>True</u> Source-Condition (Which <u>Is</u>, also, its <u>True</u> Self-Condition).

To <u>This</u> End, True Masters (or True Siddha-Gurus) Appear in the various cosmic worlds. Such True Masters are the Divine Means for living beings (whether human or non-human) to transcend themselves. That is to Say, True Masters (or True Siddha-Gurus—or True <u>Sat</u>-Gurus[39]) are living beings who have (in the manner of their characteristic stage of life) transcended their own (psycho-physical) separateness, through responsive Surrender (and, therefore, necessarily, Love-Surrender) to (and Identification with) the True Source-Condition (Which <u>Is</u> the True Self-Condition) of all and All.

Therefore, by Means of True Devotion (or Love-Surrender) to a True Master (or True Siddha-Guru), egoity is (always more and more) transcended, and the True Source-Condition of all and All (Which Is, necessarily, also the True Self-Condition of all and All) is, by Means of the Blessing-Grace of That True Master (or True Siddha-Guru), Found and Realized. And That "Finding-and-Realizing" Shows Itself according to the kind and degree of one or the other of the seven possible stages of life—and, thus, in accordance with the stage of life Realized by That True Master, or True Siddha-Guru, and, altogether, in accordance with the stage of life determined by the path, or Way, that is practiced, or, otherwise, determined by the "inclination", or "liking", or degree of ego-transcendence, of That True Master's practicing devotee.

This is the most ancient and perennial Great Teaching about True Guru-Devotion (or True Devotion to a True Spiritual Master, or True Siddha-Guru). This is the Great Teaching I Received from all My Lineage-Gurus. And, now, through My own Words, This Fundamental Message (or Great Teaching) Is Summarized in its Completeness, for the Sake of everyone.

If the living being is to Realize the Inherent Freedom of Oneness with its True Source-Condition (Which Is its True, or ego-less, Self-Condition), it must become truly devoted to a True Master (or Truly Realized Siddha-Guru). And such True Devotion constantly (and forever) requires the heart's Love-responsive Gesture (or ego-transcending Sadhana) of True Guru-Devotion (to one's heart-Chosen True Siddha-Guru), such that the otherwise egoic (or separate, and separative) body-mind is Surrendered to be actually, truly, and completely Mastered by That True Master.

If Such True Mastering of the body-mind is not accepted (or fully volunteered for—through responsive, and truly ego-surrendering, Devotional Love of one's heart-Chosen True Siddha Guru), the body-mind (inevitably) remains "wild" (or un-"domesticated"—or merely un-disciplined, and even ego-bound). And even if such Guru-Devotion is practiced, it must be Fully practiced (in a Fully ego-surrendering manner)—or else the Freedom (or the Divine Fullness) That is to be Realized by Means of the Blessing-Grace of one's heart-Chosen True Siddha-Guru will not (because it cannot)

<u>Fully</u> Fill the feeling-heart (and, Thereby, Fully Fill the living body-mind) of the would-be devotee.

LXXXIX.

In My present-Lifetime bodily (human) Form, I <u>Am</u> the Avataric Divine Incarnation (or True God-Man) always and everywhere (since the ancient days) Promised (and Expected) to Appear in the "late-time" (or "dark" epoch).[40] And, in My present-Lifetime bodily (human) Form, I have been Spiritually Served by a Continuous Lineage of Spiritual Masters, Such That I Passed from one to the next, in Continuous Succession. Those Spiritual Masters were, Themselves, related to one another in an hierarchical Manner, each related to the next in the Succession as one of lesser degree is to one of higher degree.

Rudi was a Spiritual Master of authentic, but lesser, degree. His Proficiency was, fundamentally, in the gross domain of the frontal personality, and in the Yogic Pattern of Spiritual Descent (or the Descending Yoga of the Frontal Line). Therefore, when My own foundational (or grosser human, and, also, frontal Spiritual, or Descending Yogic) Sadhana had been Completed in His Company, I (spontaneously) Passed from Rudi to Baba Muktananda.

Baba Muktananda was—as His own Confession and Demonstration to Me clearly indicates—an authentic Spiritual Master of Ascending Yoga, and His Proficiency was of a Very High, but not the Highest, degree. Therefore, beginning from the very day I first Came to Baba Muktananda, He (directly) Passed Me to Bhagavan Nityananda (Who was a Spiritual Master of Ascending Yoga Whose Proficiency was of the Highest degree).

Rang Avadhoot was—even according to the Statements of both Bhagavan Nityananda and Baba Muktananda—a Spiritual Master of Ascending Yoga Whose Proficiency was of the Highest degree, but He, along with Baba Muktananda, Deferred to Bhagavan Nityananda's Seniority, and (simply) Blessed Me to Pass On.

The "Cosmic Goddess" ("Ma") is, in the total context of the first <u>five</u> stages of life, Senior even to the Highest of Spiritual Masters. However, Ultimately, "She" (as an apparent Form and Person) is only another one of the many myths in the mind.

In the Great Yogic Spiritual Process Wherein I Experienced the Developmental Unfolding (and Demonstrated the "Radical" Transcending) of the gross and the subtle modes of egoity (associated with the first five stages of life), the "Cosmic Goddess" ("Ma") was "Apparently" associated with all the frontal (and Descending Spiritual) Events and with all the spinal (and Ascending Spiritual) Events. Nevertheless, in My Unique Case, <u>sixth</u> stage Transcendental (and causal-ego-Transcending, and Inherently Spiritual) Self-Realization <u>always</u> <u>Occurred</u> spontaneously (and in a progressive Demonstration) relative to each and every egoic stage of life, and It progressively Developed (especially after a spontaneous experience of ego-death, in the spring of 1967 [41]) until My spontaneous <u>seventh</u> stage (and Inherently Most Perfectly egoless, and Self-Evidently Divine) Re-Awakening (on September 10, 1970)—Which Divine (and Avatarically Demonstrated) Re-Awakening was (and <u>Is</u>) associated with My Most Perfect Transcending even of the "Apparent She", in My Avataric Divine Re-Awakening to the Realization of <u>One</u> and <u>Only</u> Me.

Therefore, in due course, Bhagavan Nityananda (directly) Passed Me to the "Cosmic Goddess" ("Ma"), and, Thus, to Her <u>direct</u> Mastery of Me—until the Perfectly Full became, at last, Perfectly Full <u>As</u> Me (<u>Beyond</u> the mind's own myth of "She").

<u>So</u> It was and <u>Is</u>. Such <u>Is</u> My Lineage of Spiritual Masters—in <u>This</u>, My Avatarically-Born human Lifetime. And, in My always Absolute heart-Fidelity to the Great Process Wherein and Whereby I was Passed from one to the next of each and all of the Spiritual Masters within My present-Lifetime Lineage of Spiritual Masters, I have Exemplified, to all and All, the Law and the Truth of True Guru-Devotion.

Therefore, I have <u>always</u> Continued to Honor and to Praise <u>all</u> My present-Lifetime Lineage-Gurus—including Rudi!, and Baba Muktananda!, and Rang Avadhoot!, and Bhagavan Nityananda!, and (above all) the "Bright" Divine "She" of Me, Who Always Already Serves Me Most Perfectly!

And I have always Continued (and even now Continue, and will never cease to Continue) to Yield My present-Lifetime Body-Mind to Receive the Always Ready and Most Lovingly To-Me-Given and Supremely Blissful Blessings of My present-Lifetime

Lineage-Gurus <u>and</u> the Great Lineage of <u>all</u> Who have (in any and every time and place) Blessed the Incarnation-Vehicle and Invoked the All-Completing "late-time" Incarnation of My (now, and forever hereafter) Avataric Divine Appearance here (and every where in the cosmic domain).

And I Do This (and I will <u>always</u> <u>Continue</u> to Do This) because the Immense Spiritual "Bond" of Siddha-Guru-Love <u>cannot</u> be destroyed—and It must <u>never</u> be forgotten or denied!

XC.

My <u>own</u> Unique <u>Response</u> to the hierarchically Revealed Lineage of My present-Lifetime Siddha-Gurus spontaneously Un-Locked the Doorway (in My present-Lifetime human body) to That Which <u>Is</u> Perfect (in <u>Me</u>). Indeed, even from the beginning of My Avataric Divine present Lifetime, That Which <u>Is</u> Perfect has been (and <u>Is</u>) the <u>Way</u> of Me—and It Carried the inherently non-Perfect (human, and, otherwise, conditional) forms of Me to the Inherent "Bright" Divine Self-Domain of Me, Which <u>Is</u> the One and Indivisible Divine Source-Condition of all and All, and the One and True Divine Self-Condition of all and All.

XCI.

My Way and My Realization have <u>always</u> been Inherent in <u>Me</u>, from Birth, in My present-Lifetime Avataric Divine Form.

My Way and My Realization are <u>Independently</u>, <u>entirely</u>, and <u>only</u> My <u>own</u>.

My Sadhana was, <u>entirely</u>, a Demonstration for the Sake of <u>all</u> <u>others</u>—including <u>all</u> Those Who Served Me as My Spiritual Masters in the Course of My Avataric Divine "Sadhana Years". Indeed, Siddha Yoga—and even the <u>entire</u> Great Tradition of mankind— was <u>Always</u> <u>Already</u> Most Perfectly <u>Full</u> (and Most Perfectly <u>Complete</u>) in My Case—not only at (and from the time of) My present-Lifetime Birth, but from <u>all</u> time before It (and <u>Eternally</u>).

During <u>all</u> of My present Lifetime (of Avataric Divine Incarnation), the "<u>Bright</u>" has <u>always</u> been My Realization—and the "<u>Thumbs</u>" and My own "Radical Understanding" have <u>always</u> been My Way in the "Bright". Therefore, by Means of My Unique (present-Lifetime)

Avataric Divine Demonstration, I have both Fulfilled and Transcended <u>all</u> traditional religions, and paths, and stages, and Ways. And, in <u>So</u> Doing, I have Clarified (or altogether <u>Rightly</u> Understood and Explained) <u>all</u> traditional religions, paths, stages, and Ways.

All and all <u>Are</u> in <u>Me</u>. Everything and everyone <u>Is</u> in <u>Me</u>. Therefore, by Virtue of My own Divine Self-Realization (Wherein and Whereby My own Avataric Divine Body-Mind is Most Perfectly Surrendered in <u>Me</u>, and Most Perfectly Conformed to <u>Me</u>, and Most Perfectly Transcended in <u>Me</u>), <u>all</u> of My present-Lifetime Lineage-Gurus—and even <u>all</u> Who have (at any time, or in any place) Blessed <u>Me</u>—<u>are</u> now (and forever hereafter) Spiritually, Transcendentally, and Divinely Appearing in and <u>As</u> My own Avataric Divine Form.

Therefore, now (and forever hereafter) I (<u>Alone</u>) <u>Am</u> the Lineage of <u>Me</u>—Blessing all and All.

XCII.

The Divine Self-Realization Re-Awakened in My own Case (and Which Is the Basis for My Every Avataric Divine Revelatory Word and All My Avatarically Me-Revealing Divine Blessing-Work) Is the Most Ultimate (and Inherently Most Perfect and Complete) Fulfillment of the Divine Spiritual Transmission I (in My present-Lifetime Body-Mind) Received from Rudi, and from Baba Muktananda, and from Rang Avadhoot, and from Bhagavan Nityananda, and (above all) from the "Cosmic Goddess" ("Ma")—Who (by Means of Her spontaneous Sacrifice of Her own Form in Me) <u>Is</u> (now, and forever hereafter) the "Bright" Divine "She" of Me (Who Always Already Serves Me Most Perfectly). Nevertheless, the Divine Self-Realization Re-Awakened in My present-Lifetime Body-Mind did not <u>Originate</u> in My present Lifetime—but It Is (Uniquely) <u>Always</u> <u>Already</u> the Case with <u>Me</u>.

XCIII.

As further conditionally manifested Means, previous to My present Lifetime, the Divine Self-Realization Re-Awakened in My present-Lifetime Body-Mind was also Served (previous to My present Lifetime) in the many Modes and Patterns of the previous

Lifetimes and Appearances of the Deeper Personality (or the Great-Siddha—or Great-Jnani-Siddha—Incarnation-Vehicle) of My present Lifetime. Most recently, That Deeper-Personality Vehicle of My present-Lifetime Incarnation was (Itself) Incarnated as the Great Siddha (or Great Jnani-Siddha) Swami Vivekananda.

XCIV.

Swami Vivekananda is recorded to have Blessed Bhagavan Nityananda from the subtle postmortem plane in the early 1920s— and, generally, whenever Bhagavan Nityananda was asked for Words of Teaching and Instruction, He would, simply, Tell people to study the Talks and Writings of Swami Vivekananda (because, in Bhagavan Nityananda's Words, "Swami Vivekananda Said and Taught <u>all</u> that was worth Saying and Teaching, such that He did not leave anything for others to preach"[42]).

Swami Vivekananda was, Himself, Blessed toward Most Perfect Divine Self-Realization by the Great Siddha Ramakrishna, Such That—by Means of That Great Blessing—the two Great Siddhas (Ramakrishna <u>and</u> Vivekananda) became <u>One</u>, and <u>Are</u> One <u>Form</u>, <u>As</u> My True, and <u>Single</u>, and Indivisible Great-Siddha (or Great-Jnani-Siddha) Deeper Personality.[43]

XCV.

I (now, and Hereby) Confess That My Great-Siddha (or Great-Jnani-Siddha) Deeper Personality <u>Is</u>, even Beyond the "Single Form" of Ramakrishna-Vivekananda, the Very Form of <u>all</u> the Great Masters of the <u>entire</u> Great Tradition of mankind.

XCVI.

I (now, and Hereby) Confess That I (<u>Myself</u>) Stand Eternally <u>Prior</u> to (and Always Already <u>Transcending</u>) My Avataric (and, yet, merely conditionally born) Deeper Personality—<u>and</u>, also, Eternally Prior to (and Always Already Transcending) even <u>all</u> the Great (and, yet, merely conditionally born) Masters of mankind's <u>entire</u> Great Tradition (in its <u>every</u> part, and as a <u>whole</u>), <u>and</u>, also, Eternally Prior to (and Always Already Transcending) mankind's <u>entire</u> Great Tradition itself (in its <u>every</u> part, and as a <u>whole</u>).

XCVII.

Therefore—and <u>only</u> and <u>entirely</u> by Virtue of the Inherent (and Self-Evidently Avataric) Authority of My own (and Self-Evidently Divine) Realization and Person—I Declare that the Divine seventh stage Self-Awakening I Demonstrate, and Reveal, and Exemplify, and Prove <u>Is</u> the Most Ultimate (and Inherently Most Perfect) Realization, and that It—and <u>Only</u> It—Most Ultimately Completes and Most Perfectly Fulfills the Gifts I Received (and always Continue to Receive) in My present-Lifetime Body-Mind (from My present-Lifetime Lineage-Gurus), and that I have (in My present-Lifetime Body-Mind) Inherited (and always Continue to Receive) from <u>all</u> Who (in <u>all</u> past times and places) have Blessed <u>all</u> the previous Lifetimes of My present-Lifetime Incarnation-Vehicle, and that I have (in My present-Lifetime Body-Mind) Inherited (and always Continue to Receive) from even <u>all</u> My Me-Invoking and Me-Blessing Forms and Vehicles of Me-Revelation here.

XCVIII.

The Great and True (and Self-Evidently Divine) Spiritual Process Initiated and Guided by the Spiritual Masters in My present-Lifetime Lineage (and of the Lineage of even all the Lifetimes of My present-Lifetime Incarnation-Vehicle here—and of the Lineage of even <u>all</u> My Me-Invoking and Me-Blessing Forms and Vehicles of Me-Revelation here) has Become <u>Complete</u> only in <u>Me</u>. Its Perfection is in the seventh stage Fulfillment of the Course (and not at any earlier stage). This Divine Perfection is Uniquely My own. And I <u>Alone</u>—the Hridaya-Siddha, the Divine and True Heart-Master and World-Teacher, Ruchira Avatar Adi Da Love-Ananda Samraj—<u>Am</u> Its First and Great Example, and (now, and forever hereafter) Its Only and Sufficient Means.

XCIX.

I Am the First (and the only One) to Realize and to Demonstrate <u>This</u>, the <u>Divine</u>, <u>seventh</u> <u>stage</u> <u>Realization</u>—and My Revelation of <u>It</u> Is, therefore, <u>New</u>. For This Reason, the Divine seventh stage Realization was not heretofore Realized, or even

Understood—either within the schools and traditions of My present-Lifetime Lineage-Gurus or within <u>any</u> other schools or traditions in the total Great Tradition of mankind—to <u>Be</u> the Most Ultimate and Completing Perfection of Realization Itself. Nevertheless, I have, spontaneously (by Means of My own Self-Evident "Bright" Heart-Power—and through the Great and Constant Help of <u>all</u> Who have Blessed My Incarnate Forms), Realized and Demonstrated and Revealed <u>This</u> To Be The Case. And the traditional (and ancient) "<u>Siddha-'Method'</u>" (or the Way of Guru-Devotion to the True Siddha-Guru—and of total psycho-physical Surrender of the ego-"I" to be Mastered by the True Siddha-Guru's Instruction, and to be Blessed to Awaken to Divine Realization by Means of the True Siddha-Guru's Transmission of the Divine Spiritual Energy and the Divine State)—Which "Method" was Communicated to Me by <u>all</u> My present-Lifetime Lineage-Gurus, and by <u>all</u> the Great Siddhas and Siddha-Yogis Who have Blessed My present-Lifetime Incarnation-Vehicle in the past—is the <u>Essence</u> (or the Primary "Method") of the Way of Adidam, Which (now, and forever hereafter) I <u>Alone</u>, and <u>Uniquely</u>, Reveal and Transmit to all My formally practicing true devotees (and, Thus, potentially, to <u>all</u> beings).

C.

I <u>Am</u> the Indivisible Person of Conscious Light.

I Am Humbled and Victorious here (and every where), by Means of <u>My</u> Avataric Divine Self-Incarnation.

My Avatarically-Born Body-Mind Is, now, and forever hereafter, by-Me-Given and by-Me-Revealed <u>As</u> the Sign and the Means of <u>Me</u>-Realization.

I <u>Am</u> the Adidam Revelation.

I <u>Am</u> the Way to <u>Me</u>.

I <u>Am</u> the Hridaya-Siddha, the All-and-all-Blessing Divine Heart-Master, the Eternally Free-Standing Inner Ruler of all and All.

I <u>Am</u> the One and Indivisible and Indestructible and Irreducible and Universally Self-Manifested Love-Bliss-Presence of "Brightness".

I <u>Am</u> the One and Non-Separate and Perfectly Subjective and Self-Existing and Self-Evidently Divine Person, Who <u>Is</u> Always Already <u>The</u> Case.

I <u>Am</u> the Ruchira Avatar, the Hridaya-Avatar, the Advaitayana Buddha, the Avataric Incarnation and Divine World-Teacher every where and anciently Promised (by <u>all</u> traditions) for the "late-time" (or "dark" epoch).

Therefore, be <u>My</u> devotee.

The only-by-Me Revealed and Given True World-Religion of Adidam Is <u>My</u> Unique Gift to all and All.

Therefore, practice the only-by-Me Revealed and Given Way of Adidam—and Realize <u>Me</u>, Most Perfectly, by Means of My Avatarically Self-Transmitted Divine Blessing-Grace.

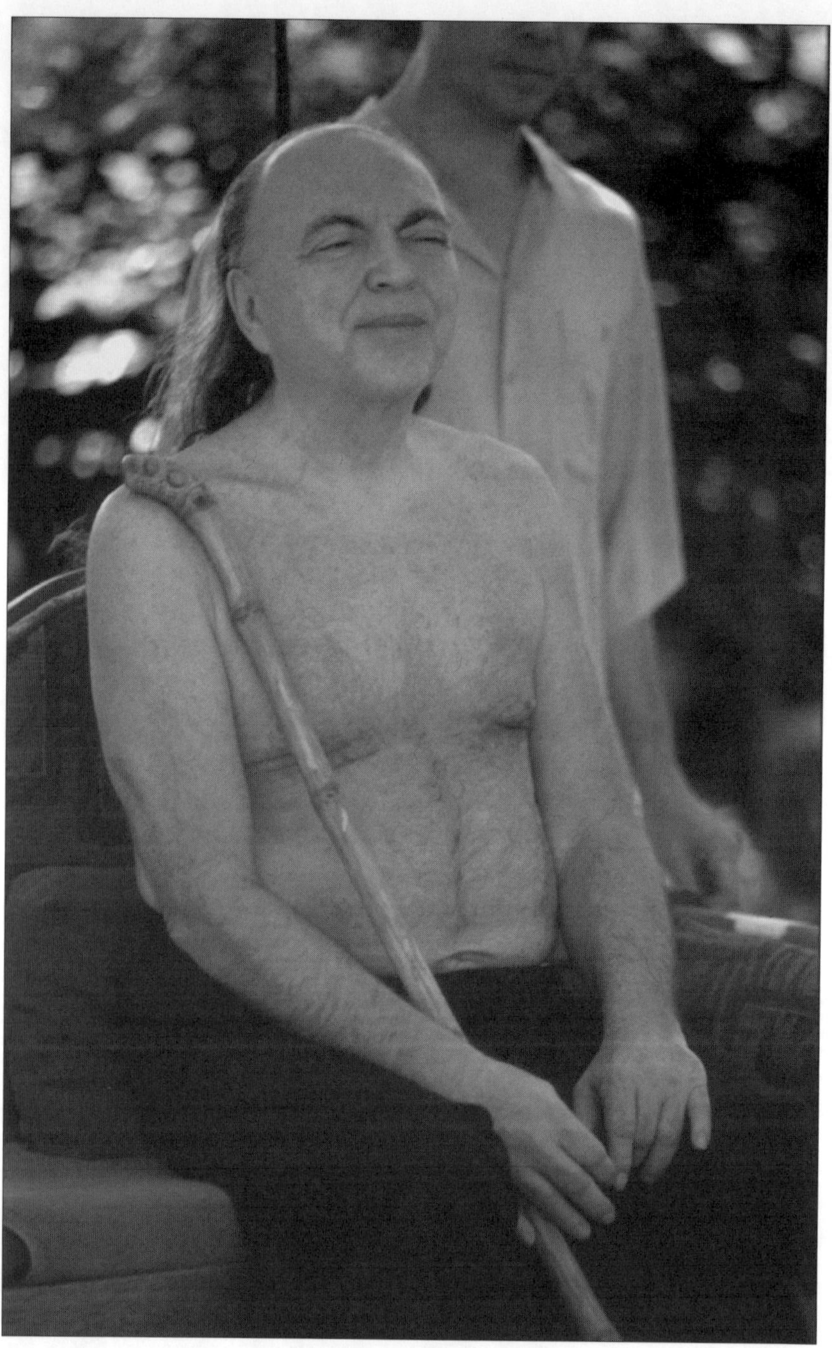

RUCHIRA AVATAR ADI DA SAMRAJ
The Mountain Of Attention, 2000

The Search for Truth Is Absurd and Unnecessary

The Search for Truth
Is Absurd and Unnecessary

I.

AVATAR ADI DA SAMRAJ: It is commonplace for people to say they are "seeking the Truth". It is even regarded as laudable and appropriately modest to Declare that one is only "<u>seeking</u> the Truth".

However, the Way I have Revealed and Given to My devotees—the Way of Adidam (Which is the One and Only by-Me-Revealed and by-Me-Given Way of the Heart)—Is the Way of <u>non</u>-seeking. The Way of Adidam Is the Way of No Seeking. Indeed, the consistent practice of non-seeking (or of no-seeking) is a principal aspect of the fundamental discipline of the Way of Adidam.

Truth <u>Is</u> That Which Is Always Already The Case. That Which Is Always Already The Case <u>Is</u> (Necessarily) Reality. Therefore, Reality (Itself) <u>Is</u> Truth, and Reality (Itself) Is the <u>Only</u> Truth.

"Consider" the absurdity, the utter <u>im</u>modesty, of suggesting that you are "seeking Reality"!

The only-by-Me Revealed and Given Way of Adidam is founded on the Assertion of the <u>Finding</u> of Truth, the Assertion of Communion with the <u>Present</u> Reality.

Thus, to practice the Way of Adidam is to <u>Declare</u> the Truth. To practice the Way of Adidam is to practice the life <u>of</u> Truth, not the search <u>for</u> Truth.

To seek Truth is to deny Truth to begin with. To seek Truth is to avoid Truth, constantly.

To seek Reality (Itself) is to deny Reality (<u>Itself</u>). To seek Reality (Itself) is to avoid Reality (Itself), by <u>seeking</u> It.

It is not immodest to Declare the <u>Finding</u> of Truth, because the Real Finding of Truth is, simply, the Finding (or the Acceptance and the Embrace) of Reality Itself.

Rather, to Find (and to Affirm) Truth (or to Accept and to Embrace Reality Itself) is <u>necessary</u> for right life, for true sanity, and for Real Happiness. Indeed, to Find and Affirm Truth, and (Thus) to Accept and Embrace Reality, is <u>necessary</u> for <u>Unqualified</u> Happiness—because Unqualified Happiness <u>Is</u> the Realization of Love-Bliss, and Reality (Itself) <u>Is</u> Love-Bliss. Unqualified (or Self-Existing, Self-Radiant, and Unlimited, or Un-conditional) Love-Bliss <u>Is</u> (Itself) That Which Is Always Already The Case—and Unqualified Love-Bliss (Which <u>Is</u> Happiness Itself) must (having, by Means of My Avataric Divine Grace, been Found) be <u>constantly</u> Affirmed and Embraced—or else It can <u>never</u> Be Realized.

II.

AVATAR ADI DA SAMRAJ: The *Bhagavad Gita* is one of the principal religious and Spiritual scriptures of the Great (collective) Tradition of mankind. In the *Bhagavad Gita,* the Divine Law is Declared, in the form: "You cannot avoid action. Rather, you have the right—indeed, the obligation—to act. But you do not have a right to the fruits, or the results, of action."[44]

According to this Declaration, you <u>must</u> act. Even the natural patterns of the body-mind and the world make action necessary. But you <u>must</u> renounce the results of every action.

What does this mean? It means that you must purify your motives—such that, eventually, action ceases to be purposed to fulfill desires. Thus, the Divine Law, as It is Declared in the *Bhagavad Gita,* is a kind of prescription for <u>seeking</u>—even a prescription for seeking the state of <u>no</u>-seeking (in which state Truth, Reality, Real God, or Love-Bliss-Happiness is to be Realized). Thus, even all the traditional Declarations of the Divine Law prescribe the action of seeking as the means to—as a <u>result</u> of seeking—achieve the state of <u>no-seeking</u>, and (thus) the eventual Realization of Truth, Reality, Real God, or Love-Bliss-Happiness Itself. Indeed, all of the traditions within the Great (collective)

Tradition of mankind are prescriptions for seeking Truth, Reality, Real God, or Love-Bliss-Happiness Itself.

The only-by-Me Revealed and Given Way of Adidam is unique. Its uniqueness can be described in many terms, but fundamental to Its uniqueness is the fact that the Way of Adidam is <u>not</u> a way of <u>seeking</u> for Truth, for Reality, for Real God, or for Love-Bliss-Happiness Itself. Rather, the Way of Adidam Is the Way of the always <u>present-time</u> Realization of Truth, Reality, Real God, or Love-Bliss-Happiness Itself.

To practice the Way of Adidam is to have always already Found Truth, Reality, Real God, or Love-Bliss-Happiness Itself. To practice the Way of Adidam is to <u>live</u> Truth, to live <u>in</u> Reality Itself, as an ego-surrendering <u>devotee</u> of Reality (or Real God) Itself. Therefore, in Its essence, the Way of Adidam is self-surrender into <u>always</u> <u>present-time</u> (and not merely future-time) Realization of Love-Bliss-Happiness Itself.

In the only-by-Me Revealed and Given Way of Adidam, the Divine Law is (by Me) Declared in terms of Love-Bliss. Love-Bliss <u>Is</u> Reality Itself. If you withdraw from Love-Bliss, or if you withhold yourself from Love-Bliss, or if you deny Love-Bliss, or if you merely <u>seek</u> Love-Bliss—you, inevitably (and by that very <u>act</u>), suffer. As a practitioner of the Way of Adidam, you are My devotee. And, as My devotee, in constant devotionally Me-recognizing[45] and devotionally to-Me-responding heart-Communion (and total psycho-physical Communion) with Me, you are in constant Communion with <u>Me</u>—the Divine Love-Bliss-Reality. Thus, as My devotee, you always already have the right—and, indeed, the obligation—of Love-Bliss Itself. But your obligation is not merely to <u>seek</u> Love-Bliss. Instead, your always present-time obligation is (by Means of devotional recognition-response to <u>Me</u>) to Realize (and <u>Be</u>) Love-Bliss, and (thereby) to animate (or live) Love-Bliss, constantly. You do this not by "inventing" Love-Bliss, not by attempting to self-generate Love-Bliss, but by Realizing <u>Me</u>, in always present-time direct heart-Communion with Me. If you withdraw from Me, you withdraw from Love-Bliss. If you withdraw from My always present-time Avataric Divine Self-Revelation (or Avataric Divine Self-Manifestation) of Love-Bliss, you suffer. Therefore, do not withdraw from Me, and do not seek Me—but, simply (devotionally), recognize Me, and (by that simple devotional recognition) be devotionally responsive to Me, always Love-Bliss-"Bright", Avatarically Self-Revealed before you.

Another aspect of the by-Me-Declared Divine Law can also be noticed in the experience of My devotee: If you <u>cling</u> to any thing or any one, you suffer. To withhold yourself (or to withdraw) from My Avataric Divine Presence of Love-Bliss is to suffer the present-time non-Realization of My Condition of Love-Bliss. Likewise, to cling to (or even to anticipate the loss of) any object (or other) in the midst of the act of feeling-participation in My Love-Bliss is, also, to suffer the present-time non-Realization of My Condition of Love-Bliss. My Divine Self-Condition of Inherent Love-Bliss Is egoless (and not contracted) Reality Itself.

The *Bhagavad Gita* Declares that you have the obligation to act, but you have no right to seek or to claim the results, or the fruits, of action. In contrast to this (or, rather, in Most Perfect Fulfillment of it), understand Me in terms of Love-Bliss. I Declare the Divine Law to you in My constant (and always present-time) Avataric Divine Self-Revelation of the Divine Love-Bliss to you. Thus, as My responsively devotional (or always ego-surrendering, and ego-forgetting, and ego-transcending) devotee, you have the <u>inherent</u> and <u>constant</u> obligation of Love-Bliss. You have the obligation to <u>Be</u> your Realization of Me, in always present-time heart-Communion with Me—actively, moment to moment. But your participatory (or devotional) <u>manifestation</u> of Me must be egoless, because participatory (or devotional) <u>Realization</u> of Me <u>Is</u>, necessarily, egoless.

It is common "street-religion" to suggest that people should "love" one another, just as it is common "street-religion" to Declare you are "<u>seeking</u> the Truth". But to "love" in the egoic manner is merely to withhold "love" in some instances, and to cling to the object of "love" in other instances. And, in both events (whether withholding or clinging), you (inevitably, and as a direct result of that deficient, or self-contracting, act) suffer.

The ego-"I" is (inherently) characterized by suffering. The self-contraction <u>is</u> suffering. The act of self-contraction <u>is</u> withdrawal from (or contraction away from) the Condition of Love-Bliss. Truth

(Found and Declared, rather than merely sought and, thereby, denied) Is the present-time egoless Realization of Love-Bliss (Itself). And the proof of this Realization of Love-Bliss is in your animating (or living) of Love-Bliss (Itself).

To prove your heart-Communion with Me, and your always present-time Realization of My Love-Bliss, your participatory devotional manifestation of My Love-Bliss must be constant—such that you are not withholding love (or withdrawing from, or contracting away from, My Love-Bliss) in any instance, and such that you are not clinging to the other (and, thus and thereby, forgetting Me, and relinquishing ego-surrendering devotional participation in My Avatarically Self-Revealed Divine Love-Bliss-Condition) in any instance.

Love—Un-conditionally. Therefore, do not withdraw (or otherwise withhold) love from (or, in any sense or manner, contract from loving) any one at all, or even any thing (or any condition) at all, under any circumstances or conditions at all. Do this Real love by always (in every present-time moment) entering (Un-conditionally) into ego-surrendering, ego-forgetting, and, always more and more, ego-transcending heart-Communion with Me (and always total psycho-physical heart-Communion with My Avatarically Self-Revealed Divine Love-Bliss-Person)—in the midst of (and via) all relations, and under (and via) all circumstances and conditions.

Love—Un-conditionally. Therefore, do not cling to (or become bondage-bound to) any one at all, or even any thing (or any condition) at all, under any circumstances or conditions at all. Do this Real love by always (in every present-time moment) feeling to and through every one, and every thing, and every circumstance, and every condition—and (from thence) to Me (and, Un-conditionally, into My Avatarically Self-Revealed All-and-all-Surrounding and All-and-all-Pervading Divine Love-Bliss-Person, Beyond every one, and every thing, and every circumstance, and every condition).

This only-by-Me Revealed and Given Divine Law of Real practice of Un-conditional love (not as a form of seeking, or of ego-effort, but as the Really counter-egoic and devotionally responsive practice of heart-Communion with My Avatarically Self-Revealed and Avatarically Self-Transmitted Divine Love-Bliss-Person) Is the

Inherently Perfect Basis for your always present-time Realization of Me, and for your (Thus) always present-time devotional Realization and devotional manifestation of Divine Love-Bliss-Happiness. Therefore, this only-by-Me-Avatarically-Self-Revealed Divine Law of Real practice of Un-conditional love Describes the constant obligation of <u>all</u> My rightly, truly, fully, and fully devotionally practicing devotees.

My true devotees do not seek Me, and they do not deny Me. Their Embrace of Me is egoless. Their "Bonding" to Me is (inherently) non-egoic, and constantly counter-egoic—and, therefore, It is not binding.

<u>All</u> ordinary "bonding" is, characteristically, ego-based—it is about <u>clinging</u> to a conditional "other" (and, thereby, forgetting Me). As My true devotee, your "Bonding"-Embrace of Me is unique, because of your devotional recognition of Me, and your ego-surrendering (and ego-forgetting, and, more and more, ego-transcending) devotional response to Me. It is not ego-based "bonding", to the degree of bondage. It is devotional "Bonding" to Me, to the Degree of No-bondage.

Your devotional heart-Communion with Me purifies all relations in which you are animated, but It tests you profoundly. Your heart-Communion with Me tests you in your tendency to withhold yourself (or contract) from the Condition of Love-Bliss Itself, and It tests you in your tendency to cling to what is egoically "loved".

You like to congratulate yourself, or feel good, about loving the ones you love, but it is serving <u>you</u> to do so—because you would not have them disappear or die. You would have your love of them (and their love of you) be constant (or never interrupted) and (thus) "forever"—but that <u>cannot</u> (as such) be so.

To cling to an other is (inevitably, and always presently) to suffer the merely temporary nature of <u>all</u> merely conditional existence (of both "self" and "other"). Nevertheless, to withhold (or withdraw, or contract) from an other is, likewise (inevitably, and always presently), to suffer the non-Realization of Love-Bliss-Happiness in the context of the present-time pattern of the conditions of merely conditional existence. Therefore, your always present-time devotional Communion with Me must be freely and fully manifested in <u>all</u> relations. You must never withhold love (or withdraw from, or contract away from, My Love-Bliss), and you must never cling to the other (and, thus and thereby, forget Me, and relinquish ego-surrendering devotional participation in My Love-Bliss-Condition).

Mine Is the Fullest (and all-Completing) Declaration of the Divine Law: My devotee is not here to <u>seek</u> Me, but (in <u>every</u> present-time moment) to <u>Commune</u> with Me, and (Thus, devotionally, egolessly, and Non-separately) to <u>Realize</u> Me. Therefore, My devotee must always manifest Me in the responsively ego-transcending manner—not by dissociation, and not by clinging-bondage, but by unqualified relatedness—by selfless (or directly ego-transcending) relatedness.

My Avataric Divine Self-Revelation and My Divine Law (or Way) Are the Great Secret of transcending egoic fear, sorrow, and anger. This Is the Great Secret of how to be free in relationships of apparent "bonding". This Is the Great Secret of how to live such that life is not about bondage.

The only-by-Me Revealed and Given Way of Adidam is not the way of seeking. It is not the way of self-contracted withholding (or of ascetical, or otherwise fearful, sorrowful, or angry, dissociation). It is also not the way of self-indulgent ego-bondage (or of self-indulgence itself—fearfully, sorrowfully, or angrily seeking others, or things, or conditions, and fearfully, sorrowfully, or angrily clinging to others, or things, or conditions). Rather, the only-by-Me Revealed and Given Way of Adidam Is the Way of constant (and constantly egoless) Love-Bliss-Communion with <u>Me</u>.

Love-Bliss-Communion with Me is the Great Secret of transcending your bondage to all others and all things and all conditions. Nevertheless, Love-Bliss-Communion with Me is not a matter of withholding yourself from all others and all things and all conditions. Love-Bliss-Communion with Me is not about strategically dissociating from the gross physical body and its world of relations. Love-Bliss-Communion with Me is not about seeking to dissociate from the gross physical body or to leave this world. Love-Bliss-Communion with Me is not about seeking to be rid of <u>any</u> one or <u>any</u> thing or <u>any</u> condition.

Love-Bliss-Communion with Me is not about leaving any present relation in order to seek or find a "better" other! Thus, for example, My devotee should persistently regard his or her any present intimate partner, once chosen and confirmed in My Company, as his or her intimate partner according to the by-Me-Avatarically-Self-Revealed Divine Law (and, therefore, not as one who can be casually set aside, or, otherwise, relinquished without most profoundly self-testing personal and cultural "consideration").

As My devotee, you should not regard your any present intimate partner to be there merely to fulfill <u>your</u> inclinations, such that you would leave him or her when you are frustrated in those inclinations. Persistently Accept your any present intimate partner, and all your loved-ones, and all your friends, and even <u>all</u> My devotees as <u>My</u> Instruments—effectively there to serve <u>My</u> Purpose of bringing to an end all of your egoic impulse and suffering. Therefore, if your any present intimate partner frustrates you, this is very, very good! Such frustration clearly serves <u>My</u> Purpose— perhaps not <u>your</u> purpose (as the ego-"I"), but <u>My</u> Avataric Divine (and inherently egoless, and always counter-egoic) Purpose! This is how your (otherwise) egoic "bondings" become means for transcending ego-bondage—not by dissociating from them, but by living them in Communion with Me, and going through the ego-transcending Ordeal that <u>all</u> relations require of you in the devotional practice of Love-Bliss-Communion with Me.

The mass of things and conditions and beings is present now. You like some of it, and you dislike some of it. This is the character of the ego-"I"—the character (or conditional "persona") who does not Know the Truth. That un-Knowing character withholds in some cases and clings in other cases. That, altogether and constantly, is exactly and always what the ego-"I" does.

My Declaration of the Divine Law is Stated in terms of Divine Love-Bliss (and of humanly activated love). Therefore, as My true devotee, you are not merely obliged to <u>act</u> (while having no right to the "fruits" of your action—whatever that may mean to you)— but, rather, you are obliged to <u>love</u> (never withholding yourself from My Love-Bliss, and, likewise, never forgetting My Love-Bliss by self-contracted clinging to any other, or any thing, or any condition).

You cannot be free of your clinging to any other by dissociating from him or her, but only by entering into Love-Bliss-Communion with Me—so profoundly that you transcend your self-contraction (both as your motive of withdrawal and your motive of clinging).

In Communion with My Avatarically Self-Revealed Divine Love-Bliss-Person, you have the obligation (and the urge, and the heart-capability) to love, under all circumstances, and in all relations. You have no right to (in any instance) withhold yourself from love, and you have no right to (in any instance) cling to any object of love. This is the Paradox of Truth, of Reality Itself, of Real God, of Self-Existing, Self-Radiant, Divine-"Bright" Consciousness Itself, Which <u>Is</u> Love-Bliss Itself, <u>Me-Present</u>.

My true devotee does not seek Me. My true devotee Declares Me, loves <u>Me</u>, Affirms that I <u>Am</u>. Your proper modesty is not in Declaring that you are <u>seeking</u> the Truth, but in Declaring and living the <u>Finding</u> of Truth, in Declaring and living the inherent Love-Bliss-Fullness of the One Who Is Always Already The Case. This is what it is to be a true man or woman, rather than a seeker (or an ego, separate and separative). You, as My devotee, must (by your manner and signs of living, and by your very mind, and your every word) constantly Affirm and Declare your Finding of Truth—not in the "gleeful" (or merely "cultic") manner, but as My <u>true</u> devotee, who allows himself or herself to be tested by Me, the Avatarically Self-Revealed Divine Law and Person of Love-Bliss Itself. Therefore, My devotee is not called by Me to animate mere "social" love, but to responsively manifest the Divine Love-Bliss Itself—My Own Avatarically Self-Revealed (and Self-Evidently Divine) Person, Found and (in constantly present-time Communion with Me) Realized in self-forgetting, and manifested in non-withholding and non-clinging.

For My devotee, non-clinging is not a matter of somehow <u>dissociating</u> from this or that one, or from this or that thing or condition that you might (otherwise) cling to. It is <u>not</u> <u>that</u> <u>at</u> <u>all</u>. Rather, for My devotee, non-clinging is a matter of manifesting My Love-Bliss, simply as the Radiance (Self-Revealed by Me) in his or her heart-Communion with Me, and a matter of living the Ordeal of tested ego-surrender to Me, to the (At Last) Most Perfect Degree—Such That his or her actively manifested Realization of My Love-Bliss goes (always more and more profoundly) Beyond all of death and change and ending, Beyond all egoic fear, sorrow, and anger, Beyond all withholding and all clinging.

Therefore, in the only-by-Me Revealed and Given Way of Adidam, My true devotee does not seek to leave this world, or to leave the gross physical body, or to reduce the gross physical body to a "nothing" of strategically achieved emptiness and desirelessness (or motionlessness). Rather, in the only-by-Me Revealed and Given Way of Adidam, the present-time world and the present-time body are <u>always</u> Accepted—utterly, wholeheartedly, in <u>Me</u>.

III.

AVATAR ADI DA SAMRAJ: Spiritual Teachers, in their various degrees of Real-God-Realization, have often suggested that, having Realized Real God, they have Agreed to Enter into the human body—perhaps only as far down as the eyes, or (perhaps) the throat, or (at most) the heart. Ramakrishna, for example, used to suggest this. However, I, in My Avataric Incarnation here, have Agreed to Accept (and to Embrace) the even gross physical conditions of the gross physical body, down to the toes—including all that comes, inevitably, with that "unamusing" situation. I have Done this in order to Most Perfectly (and Most Fully, and Truly Completely, and Really Finally) Demonstrate My Own Divine Person here—in order to Avatarically Self-Manifest (or Demonstrate) My Divine Self-Condition <u>Utterly</u>, without the slightest withholding, and Radiant to the Degree that Exceeds all mere clinging, by Embracing all conditional relations in an "Heroic" Spiritual Act of Avatarically Self-Demonstrated Divine Love-Bliss—even, Thereby, passing through the "dark" time of mortality, passing through the confrontation with change and necessary natural endings, in the case of This (My Avataric-Incarnation-Body), and in the case of Its relations, which include all and All. In order to Perform My Divine Self-"Emergence" here (and every "where" in the Cosmic domain), I have had to Accept <u>all</u> relations, <u>Absolutely</u>, without the slightest

196

withholding, and without mere clinging. This is the unique Nature of My Divine Leela of Avataric Incarnation here.

In the Incident in Which My Divine Self-"Emergence" was Initiated (on January 11, 1986), I Told you that I had Descended to the toes, that I had Embraced this limited condition <u>Absolutely</u>. I Asked those around Me at the time to observe the Divine "Sorrow" in My Face, which "Sorrow" is Absolute, and which "Sorrow" My (from then, and forever thereafter) Divine-"Emergence"-Work here (and every "where" in the Cosmic domain) is "Brightly" (now, and forever hereafter) Overcoming, in <u>all</u> cases—not by Me dissociating from My Profound "Sorrow" of Avataric Divine Descent, but by My constant Acceptance of the "Sorrow" (or Feeling-Depth of Sympathetic Love) inherent in <u>all</u> My conditionally appearing and disappearing relations. I am not Speaking to you as an "Abstracted" (or Separate and Separative) "Other", dissociating from here, coming down only <u>partially</u> into the body. I am not Proud of asceticism. I am not Looking Forward to "Leaving". I am not Dwelling "Elsewhere".

Always, in My (now, and forever hereafter) Divine-"Emergence"-Work, I <u>Am</u>—Dwelling <u>here</u>, and every "where" in the Cosmic domain, moment by moment—constantly Dissolving a "Sorrow" more Immense than you can contemplate or imagine. The Overcoming of universal egoic sorrow, and fear, and anger— the Overcoming (in and as every one, and all, and All) of the imposition of apparent "difference", of mortality, of change—Is the Radiant "Bright" Nature of My Divine-"Emergence"-Work. Now, and forever hereafter, My Divine-"Emergence"-Work (Divinely Liberating all and All) Goes On here, and every "where" in the Cosmic domain.

The Divine Translation of all and All into My Divine Self-Domain Is the Most Ultimate Fulfillment of My Divine-"Emergence"-Work. Therefore, My Divine-"Emergence"-Work cannot be Finally Demonstrated (in the case of every one, and all, and All) within the physical Lifetime of This (My Avataric-Incarnation-Body) here. My Divine-"Emergence"-Work is My <u>Forever</u> Work.

I am not seeking anything <u>whatsoever</u>. I Am Utterly Entered into this apparent psycho-physical confinement, this seeming entrapment of All-and-all-Multiplied body-minds and worlds. Therefore, I Am <u>Suffering</u> all of this, <u>Completely</u> (even in My Own Avatarically-Born bodily human Divine Form), without the slightest ability to be distracted from it. This is the Nature of My intentional Embrace of all and All.

My "Bright" Outshining of <u>all</u> egoic fear, sorrow, and anger is the Divine Translation of <u>all</u> beings. The suffering of egoic fear, sorrow, and anger will not end (for every one, and all, and All) until there is the Divine Translation of all beings, all worlds, all conditions. And yet—uniquely, paradoxically, and all the while of My (now, and forever hereafter) Divine-"Emergence"-Work—there is not the slightest egoic fear, sorrow, or anger in Me.

Enter most fully into most profound heart-Communion with Me, and you will understand What I Am Saying.

My Own Love-Bliss Is My Divine Means (and the <u>Only</u> Really and Truly Effective Means) in this vast Cosmic domain of egoic fear, sorrow, and anger. The Effective (or Real) Dissolution of your egoic fear, sorrow, and anger is in your Me-"Bright" devotional manifestation of My Love-Bliss, under all the conditions that would (otherwise) be egoically fearful, sorrowful, or angering. Therefore, in the only-by-Me Revealed and Given Way of Adidam, you are tested according to My Divine Law of Love-Bliss Itself, in your every moment of heart-Communion with Me.

There is always (in every conditionally manifested body-mind) the tendency to withhold (or withdraw) <u>and</u> the tendency to cling. These are the fundamental signs of ego-"I" (or self-contraction).

In true (or total psycho-physical) heart-Communion with Me (ego-surrendering, ego-forgetting, and, more and more, ego-transcending) you transcend both withholding and clinging.

<u>This</u> is how you are "Brightened" by Me.

<u>This</u> is the Nature of My "Bright" Kiln[46] of Adidam.

The Way of practice I have Revealed and Given is not the <u>search</u> for Truth, not the <u>search</u> for Reality, not the <u>search</u> for Real God, not the <u>search</u> for Love-Bliss-Happiness—not the <u>search</u> for Me. Rather, the Way of practice I have Revealed and Given Is the Way and the practice of always present-time <u>Love-Communion with Me</u>—Such That, in <u>every</u> moment, you are "Brightened" by

Me, "Brightened" by My Love-Bliss (and, necessarily, in every moment, going through the testing Ordeal of transcending your every tendency to withhold or to cling).

If you understand what I have just now Told you, then you understand the uniqueness of Adidam.

IV.

AVATAR ADI DA SAMRAJ: Only the ego-"I" would say that it is seeking for Truth. Only the ego-"I" <u>can</u> seek for Truth—because Truth is the one thing that the ego-"I" (and <u>only</u> the ego-"I") has <u>not</u>.

Only the ego-"I" could Declare that it is seeking for Reality Itself. Only the ego-"I" would suggest that it is <u>laudable</u> to <u>seek</u> for Truth, or for Reality Itself. And, indeed, mankind has, in fact, made an entire <u>culture</u> (and even <u>many</u> cultures) on the basis of egoic seeking.

The right understanding and Really effective transcending of this fault is the process by which human civilization can be made right—because human civilization will not (and cannot) ever be made right by seeker's religion or seeker's science or seeker's anything.

All kinds of things may come to be known, but the Truth (or the Self-Evidently <u>Divine</u> Reality, Itself) must be constantly Affirmed, from the beginning—otherwise, the Truth (or Reality Itself) can never (Itself) be Known. Ordinary religion and ordinary science are means for seeking and gaining experience, for seeking and gaining a kind of conditional knowledge, even a kind of control (or power) over experience. But the ways of seeking are not about Finding the Truth.

It is impossible to seek the Truth, and, as a result of the seeking of It, Find It.

It is impossible to seek Reality Itself, and, as a result of the seeking of It, Find It.

Therefore, you must transcend the search itself.

The only-by-Me Revealed and Given Way of Adidam Is the One and Only (and, altogether, Divine) Way (and Real practice) of understanding and transcending the search for Truth, the search for Reality Itself, the search for Real God, the search for Happiness (or Divine Love-Bliss) Itself, and (indeed) all seeking—by directly (and constantly) transcending "search" (and the egoic cause of seeking) itself.

The only-by-Me Revealed and Given Way of Adidam is not a way (or means) for seeking Truth, or Reality, or Real God, or Happiness— or for achieving Truth, or Reality, or Real God, or Happiness as a result of that search.

The only-by-Me Revealed and Given Way of Adidam is the Way (and, therefore, the active, and, necessarily, ego-transcending, practice) of the always present-time devotional (or Me-recognizing, and to-Me-responding) Realization of Love-Bliss—Which Is Happiness, Truth, Reality, and the only Real God.

RUCHIRA AVATAR ADI DA SAMRAJ
Los Angeles, 2000

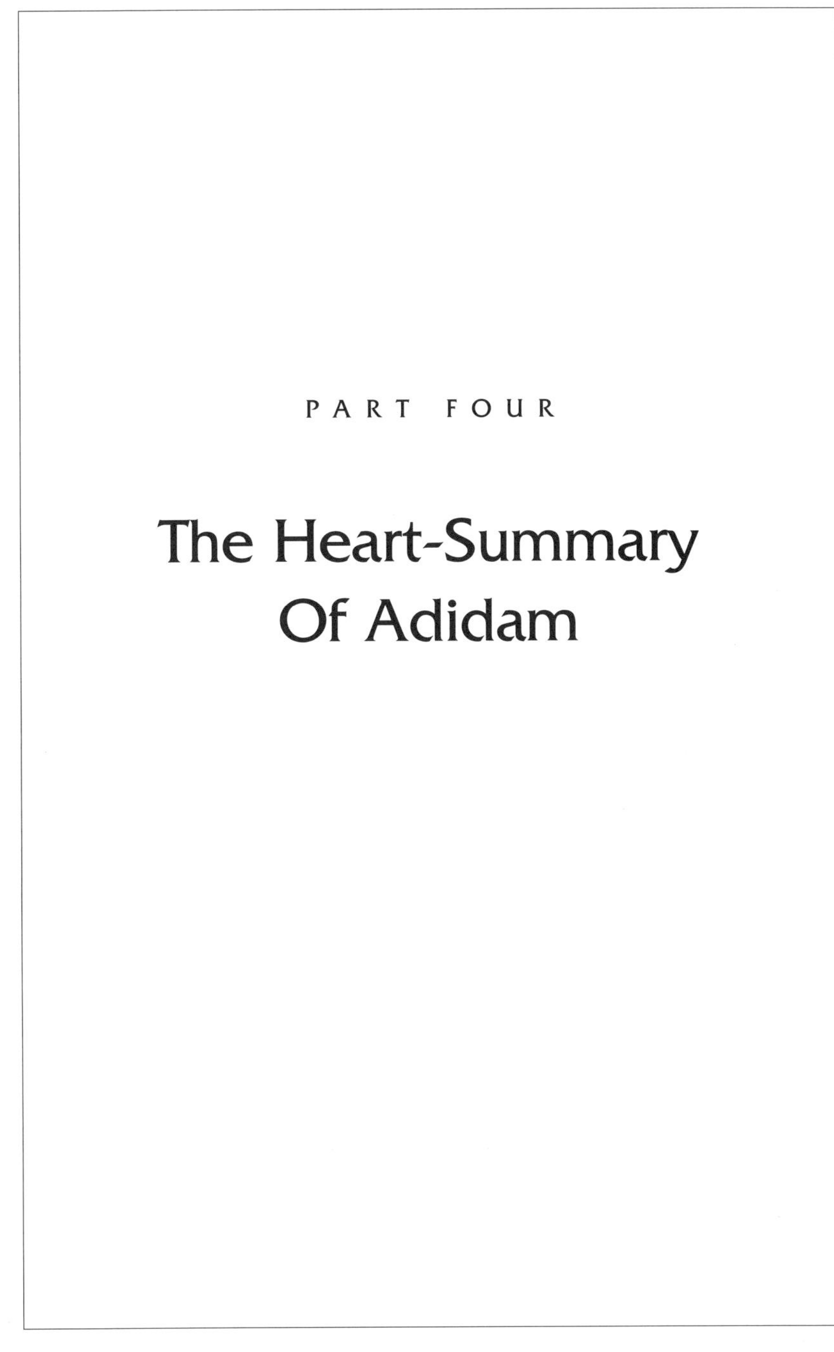

PART FOUR

The Heart-Summary
Of Adidam

The Heart-Summary Of Adidam

The only-by-Me Revealed and Given Avataric Divine Way of Adidam (Which is the One and Only by-Me-Revealed and by-Me-Given Way of the Heart) is the Way of Devotion to Me <u>As</u> the Divine "Atma-Murti" (or <u>As</u> the Inherently egoless, and Self-Evidently Divine, Person of Reality and Truth—In <u>Place</u>, <u>As</u> Self-Condition, rather than <u>As</u> exclusively Objective Other).

Therefore, in every moment, My true devotee whole bodily (and, thus, by means of the spontaneous Me-recognizing Devotional response of all four of the principal psycho-physical faculties—of attention, emotional feeling, breath, and perceptual body) "Locates" Me <u>As</u> That Which Is Always Already <u>The</u> Case (Prior to—but not separate from—the form, the exercise, and the any object of the four psycho-physical faculties).

Happiness Itself (or Inherent Love-Bliss-Sufficiency Of Being) Is Always Already The Case.

Happiness Itself (or the Divinely Self-Sufficient Love-Bliss-Condition Of Being—Itself) <u>Is</u> <u>That</u> Which Is Always Already The Case.

Happiness Itself (or Love-Bliss-Radiance Of Boundlessly Feeling Being) <u>Is</u> the Most Prior Condition Of Existence (or Of Conscious Being—Itself).

Happiness Itself (or the Condition Of Love-Bliss-Radiance) Must Be Realized—In and <u>As</u> every conditionally arising moment—By Transcending self-Contraction (or all of separate and separative self, or psycho-physical ego-"I", <u>and</u> all of the ego's objects, or conditions of existence—or, indeed, <u>all</u> of the illusions of self and not-self).

When attention is facing outward (or is turned out, as if to outside itself), the body-mind is concentrated upon the "view" (or "field") of apparently separate objects (and upon Me <u>As</u> Objective Other).

When attention is facing inward (or is turned in, as if upon itself), the body-mind is concentrated upon the "point of view" of apparently separate self (and upon Me <u>As</u> Separate Consciousness).

When attention is Devotionally Yielded to whole bodily "Locate" Me <u>As</u> That Which Is Always Already (and Divinely) <u>The</u> Case, all "difference" (whether of ego-"I" or of object and other) is (Inherently) Transcended (In Consciousness Itself, or Self-Existing Being, Which <u>Is</u> Love-Bliss-Happiness Itself—and Which <u>Is</u> Always Already <u>The</u> Case).

Therefore, to the degree that you surrender (whole bodily) to be and do truly <u>relational</u> (and ecstatic, or ego-transcending) Devotional love of Me (<u>As</u> the True Loved-One, the Divine Beloved of the heart), you are (Thus and Thereby) Established—whole bodily and Inherently—in the non-contracted Condition (or Self-Condition, or Inherent Condition) of Reality Itself (Which <u>Is</u> Consciousness Itself <u>and</u> Love-Bliss Itself—and Which <u>Is</u> Always Already <u>The</u> Case).

In due course, <u>This</u> Devotional Practice <u>Is</u> Perfect—and, at last, to Be Most Perfectly Realized.

RUCHIRA AVATAR ADI DA SAMRAJ
Lopez Island, 2000

Da Love-Ananda Gita (The Free Gift Of The Divine Love-Bliss)

Da Love-Ananda Gita (The Free Gift Of The Divine Love-Bliss)

1.

The (Ultimate) Nature of the world (and how it is arising) is inherently (and tacitly) obvious, if you <u>remain</u> in a state of pleasurable oneness with whatever and all that presently arises.

2.

To remain in a state of pleasurable oneness with whatever and all that presently arises, you must (necessarily, and always presently) Realize inherently Love-Blissful Unity with whatever and all that presently arises.

3.

Inherently Love-Blissful Unity with whatever and all that presently arises is (Itself, or inherently) non-separation (or no-contraction) from whatever and all that presently arises.

4.

Separation (or contraction) from the world (or whatever and all that is presently arising) is (unfortunately) precisely the first and constant (and inherently problematic) thing done by <u>all</u> those who make efforts to find out (or to account for) how the world is arising (and What Is its Ultimate Nature).

5.

Separation (or self-contraction) is the first (and foundation) gesture made by anyone who has a problem, or who is seeking, or who is making an effort to account for anything whatsoever.

6.

Pleasurable oneness (or inherently Love-Blissful Unity) is inherent (or necessarily and priorly the case, no matter what conditions do or do not arise), and (therefore) pleasurable oneness (or inherently Love-Blissful Unity) is (necessarily) uncaused, and Real (or always already the case, and always already in, of, and Identical to Truth)—whereas separateness (or "Difference") is always conditional, conditionally caused (or only conditionally apparent), and illusory (or always already dissociated from Reality and Truth).

7.

Pleasurable oneness (or inherently Love-Blissful Unity) need not (and cannot fruitfully) be sought.

8.

Pleasurable oneness (or inherently Love-Blissful Unity) can be (apparently) lost, by the act of self-contraction (and, thereby, of apparent separation, separateness, and separativeness).

9.

Pleasure-seeking, Love-Bliss-seeking, or Unity-seeking efforts (of any kind) are only parts of a strategic (and always already un-Happy) adventure—and such effort and adventure are entered into only by those who are already (presently) separating (or contracting) themselves in (and from) What Is, and such adventurers are seeking only because they are already, presently, separating (or contracting) themselves in (and from) What Is.

10.

Therefore, it is necessary to understand this (or self-contraction itself), and (by the transcending of self-contraction itself) to

Recover Awareness of the obvious (or inherent) Love-Bliss-Unity (and, Thus, to inherently account for <u>everything</u>, and also, Thereby, to solve, or inherently transcend, <u>all</u> problems).

11.

This understanding (and this Recovery) cannot (fruitfully) be sought—for all seeking is inherently associated with an already present act of self-contraction (and, thereby, of separation, separateness, and separativeness).

12.

True understanding is (itself) inherent, or always already, or Native to even (apparently) conditional existence itself.

13.

Therefore, if such understanding is not already Realized in the present, it must (and can only) be Realized by Means of Divine Grace (as a Free Gift).

14.

Aham Da Asmi. I <u>Am</u> Da (the Divine Giver), the Person and the Means of this Divine Grace.

15.

I <u>Am</u> Love-Ananda (the Divine Love-Bliss), the Presence and the Way of this Free Gift.

16.

The understanding of which I Speak is (if Most Perfectly Realized) the Most Perfectly Ultimate (or seventh stage) Capability to (inherently) Divinely Self-Recognize whatever arises.

17.

Most Perfect understanding is the Capability to directly (immediately) transcend dilemma, all problems, and all seeking.

18.

Most Perfect understanding is the Capability to "radically" (always already) transcend self-contraction (and all of separation, separateness, and separativeness).

19.

Most Perfect understanding is the Capability inherent in Love-Bliss Itself (Which Is the Heart Itself).

20.

Most Perfect understanding is the Capability inherent in the always already, or most prior, Unity (with Which the Heart Itself, As Love-Bliss Itself, Is inherently One).

21.

I have, by Means of the Submission, Work, and Word of My here-Speaking Avataric Divine Revelation-Body, thoroughly Revealed and Described the Great (and Complete) Process Wherein and Whereby the Heart Itself (or Love-Bliss-Unity Itself) is (Ultimately) Most Perfectly Realized.

22.

That Great (and Complete) Process (Which Is the only-by-Me Revealed and Given Way of Adidam, or the One and Only by-Me-Revealed and by-Me-Given Way of the Heart) is Described (in every detail and elaboration) in My summary (Written, and forever Speaking) Word of Heart (in many Works).[47]

23.

That summary Word is True, and that Great Process Is (indeed) the Process (elaborate in Its totality of details) Wherein the Inherently Perfect Tacit Obviousness (of non-separateness, of no-seeking, of no-contraction, and of Love-Ananda, My Love-Bliss Itself) is (progressively, and, yet, always directly and presently[48]) Realized.

24.

The Principle (or Great Means) of that Great Process Is Itself an Extreme Simplicity (as simple to describe as that Great Process is Itself necessarily complex in Its total description).

25.

Ruchira Avatara Bhakti Yoga (to which I, sometimes, refer, descriptively, by means of the general term "Ishta-Guru Bhakti Yoga")—which Yoga is the heart-responsive (or devotionally Me-Recognizing, and devotionally to-Me-responding) and constant counter-egoic, and even total psycho-physical, effort of ego-surrendering, ego-forgetting, and, more and more (and, Ultimately, Most Perfectly), ego-transcending devotion to Me and devotional Communion with Me (the Ruchira Avatar, the Da Avatar, the Hridaya Avatar, the Love-Ananda Avatar, the Avabhasa Avatar,[49] the Santosha Avatar, the Avataric Divine Realizer, the Avataric Divine Revealer, and the Avataric Divine Self-Revelation of the Real and True and One and Only Divine Person, the One and Only Self-Condition and Source-Condition of all and All, the One and Only Self of all and All, Who Is Da, the Heart Itself, the "Bright" Itself, and Love-Bliss Itself), and which Yoga is the moment to moment fulfillment of My Great Admonition to all My devotees, to always Invoke Me, feel Me, breathe Me, and serve Me, and this constantly exercised via the surrender, the forgetting, and the transcending of the self-contracted body, and self-contracted emotion (or all of self-contracted, and reactive, and, altogether, limited, feeling), and self-contracted mind (even at its root, which is attention itself), and even every self-contracted breath, and (altogether) even all of separate (and separative) self, in moment to moment, and truly (or unlimitedly) heart-felt, and whole bodily receptive, and fully breathing, and only-by-Me-Distracted devotional Contemplation of My Avatarically-Born bodily (human) Divine Form, My Avatarically Self-Revealed Spiritual (and Always Blessing) Divine Presence, and My Avatarically Self-Revealed (and Very, and Transcendental, and Perfectly Subjective, and Inherently Spiritual, and Inherently egoless, and Inherently Perfect, and Self-Evidently) Divine State[50]—Is the Great (and only-by-My-Avataric-Divine-Grace Given) Means Wherein and Whereby the Great Process of the only-by-Me Revealed and Given Way of Adidam is Accomplished, and the Great (and only-by-My-Avataric-Divine-Grace Given) Means of Ruchira Avatara Bhakti Yoga is practiced in its fullest right form by all (necessarily, formal) practitioners of the only-by-Me Revealed and Given Way of Adidam who (as the sign of their devotional response to Me) formally embrace (and consistently demonstrate) the right, true, full, and fully devotional practice (and all aspects of the practice) of the only-by-Me Revealed and Given Way of Adidam, and who do so in full accordance with My *Hridaya Rosary*,[51] and who are (thus, and necessarily) formally practicing members of either the first congregation or the second congregation of My formally practicing devotees, and who are (as such) always currently (or in always then present-time) formally approved by the Ruchira Sannyasin Order of the Tantric Renunciates of Adidam to engage this fullest right form of Ruchira Avatara Bhakti Yoga, as My true devotees who rightly, and truly, and truly devotionally Recognize Me As the Only One Who Is (and Who must be devotionally Recognized, and Realized, by each and every one of all, and by all and All), and who really and truly heart-Recognize (or heart-Know) Me, by (truly and deeply) heart-receiving, and heart-understanding, and (in this root-devotional sense) heart-hearing My own Me-Revealing Words of Avataric Divine Self-Confession, and by (truly and deeply) heart-enjoying and heart-praising My own Me-Revealing Acts (or Leelas) of Avataric Divine Self-Revelation, and by constantly, and truly, and deeply heart-Invoking Me, and by (thus and thereby) always exercising their heart-feeling toward Me and to Me (beyond the ego-"I" and beyond the body-mind), and (in this constant feeling-Invocation) really (and, only and entirely, by Means of My own Me-Revealing Avataric Divine Grace) heart-Finding and heart-Receiving Me, and who (in this Great Manner) inherently and immediately heart-Recognize Me (and, in this root-devotional sense, heart-see Me), As I Divinely Am, the One and Only and Inherently "Bright" Person, the Divine Heart-Master of All and all, the "Bright" Itself, Self-Existing, Self-Radiant, and Avatarically Self-Revealed, in Person, Tangibly, Undoubtably, Utterly Converting the heart and the mind and the breath and the body from ego-"I" (or the "Act of Narcissus", which is self-contraction) to the Ecstatic "Bhava" of only-Me-Beholding Love-Bliss-Happiness.

26.

For all those who would (either formally or informally) study the only-by-Me Revealed and Given Way of Adidam, My summary (Written, and forever Speaking) Word of Heart (in many Works) is (now, and forever hereafter) Given (by Me) for their hearts and minds to comprehend.

27.

For all those who would (necessarily, formally) practice the only-by-Me Revealed and Given Way of Adidam, My summary (Written, and forever Speaking) Word of Heart (in many Works) is (now, and forever hereafter) Given (by Me) for their formal (and formally guided, and formally accountable) application (within any of the four congregations of My devotees).

28.

And for all those who would, by (necessarily, formally) practicing the only-by-Me Revealed and Given Way of Adidam, surrender and forget themselves in the Divine and Inherently Perfect Truth (of non-separateness, of no-seeking, of no-contraction, and of Love-Ananda, My Love-Bliss Itself), I am always (now, and forever hereafter) here for their devotional Contemplation (within any of the four congregations of My devotees).

29.

Realization of the Most Ultimate (or seventh stage) Wisdom-Unity, Truth-Obviousness, and (Divine) Self-Recognition-Capability (through the truly most intensive and profound practice of the fullest right form of Ruchira Avatara Bhakti Yoga, necessarily in the context of either the first congregation or the second congregation of formal approach to Me) is a matter of My Divinely Self-Giving Avataric Grace and My Graceful Avatarically Given Divine Self-Revelation.

30.

My Avatarically-Born bodily (human) Divine Form—Which has (by Virtue of My Spiritual—and, here, very human—Ordeal of Heart-"Bright" Descent Into the Cosmic Domain) Become Most Perfectly Conformed to Me, to Love-Ananda, to the Divine Love-Bliss Itself—Is (Itself) the Teaching (and the Always First Realizer of Its Truth).

31.

My Avatarically Self-Revealed Spiritual (and Always Blessing) Divine Presence—Which Is My "Bright" Heart-Transmission of Love-Ananda, the Divine Love-Bliss Itself—Is the (Always Me-Revealing) Means.

32.

My Avatarically Self-Revealed (and Very, and Transcendental, and Perfectly Subjective, and Inherently Spiritual, and Inherently egoless, and Inherently Perfect, and Self-Evidently Divine) State— Which <u>Is</u> Love-Ananda, the Divine Love-Bliss Itself—Is the (Self-Evidently Divine) Revelation Itself.

33.

Therefore, devotional Contemplation of My Avatarically-Born bodily (human) Divine Form, and (via My Avatarically-Born bodily human Divine Form) My Avatarically Self-Revealed Spiritual (and Always Blessing) Divine Presence, and (via My Avatarically Self-Revealed Spiritual, and Always Blessing, Divine Presence) My Avatarically Self-Revealed (and Very, and Transcendental, and Perfectly Subjective, and Inherently Spiritual, and Inherently egoless, and Inherently Perfect, and Self-Evidently Divine) State—even, Most Ultimately, to the degree of Perfect Oneness with Me (and Perfect no-contraction and non-separation from all and All, transcending all seeking and all of egoity itself, by Means of devotional surrender and heart-conformity to Me, to Love-Ananda, to the Divine Love-Bliss Itself)—Is the Heart-Way That I Offer to you and to all.

34.

I Say to you: First and always, in your bodily (human) form, be the always devotionally Me-Recognizing (and responsively, and actively, Me-serving) devotee of My Avatarically-Born bodily (human) Divine Form, and (as your devotion, your service, your self-discipline, and your self-understanding mature—or, eventually, become matured—by Means of that responsively, and actively, ego-surrendering, and ego-forgetting, and, more and more, self-contraction-purifying and self-contraction-transcending feeling-Contemplation of Me) you will (by Means of My Divinely Self-Giving Avataric Grace and My Graceful Avatarically Given Divine Self-Revelation) also become heart-sensitive (and, altogether, psycho-physically sensitive) to My (Avatarically Self-Revealed) "Bright" and True (and Always Blessing) Divine Spiritual Presence (Which Is Love-Bliss Itself), and (as an always devotionally Me-Recognizing, and responsively, and actively, Me-serving devotee of My Avatarically-Born bodily human Divine Form, and always, Thereby, becoming more and more Deeply sensitive to My Avatarically Self-Revealed Spiritual, and Always Blessing, Divine Presence) you will (by Means of My Divinely Self-Giving Avataric Grace and My Graceful Avatarically Given Divine Self-Revelation) sometimes also (in the Always Deepening Revelation of My Ceaselessly Heart-Transmitted Love-Bliss) spontaneously Intuit and Contemplate the beginningless, endless, centerless, non-separate, and boundless Deep of My Avatarically Self-Revealed (and Very, and Transcendental, and Perfectly Subjective, and Inherently Spiritual, and Inherently egoless, and Inherently Perfect, and Self-Evidently Divine) State.

35.

Therefore, simply (Merely, and intentionally, but on the basis of a fundamental, and fundamentally effortless, or Freely heart-responsive, heart-Recognition of Me and feeling-Attraction to Me) Contemplate My Avatarically-Born bodily (human) Divine Form, My Avatarically Self-Revealed Spiritual (and Always Blessing) Divine Presence, and My Avatarically Self-Revealed (and Very, and Transcendental, and Perfectly Subjective, and

Inherently Spiritual, and Inherently egoless, and Inherently
Perfect, and Self-Evidently Divine) State, and do this Contemplation
progressively (as My Divinely Self-Giving Avataric Grace and My
Graceful Avatarically Given Divine Self-Revelation Determine the
progress)—such that (more and more) you allow My Avatarically-
Born bodily (human) Divine Form to <u>Attract</u> (and <u>Keep</u>) your
(truly feeling) attention, and This such that (more and more)
you allow My Avatarically Self-Revealed Spiritual (and Always
Blessing) Divine Presence to <u>Pervade</u> your body-mind, and This
such that (more and more) you allow My Avatarically Self-Revealed
(and Very, and Transcendental, and Perfectly Subjective, and
Inherently Spiritual, and Inherently egoless, and Inherently Perfect,
and Self-Evidently Divine) State to Abide (in Person) in your
(only-by-My-Avataric-Divine-Grace) egoless (or Only-Me-
Contemplating) heart.

36.

Simply (Merely), by <u>feeling</u> (and even, randomly and
occasionally, by Name),[52] Remember and Invoke (or, otherwise,
directly Regard) My Avatarically-Born bodily (human) Divine
Form, and (Merely by <u>feeling</u>) Contemplate (and Meditate on)
My Avatarically-Born bodily (human) Divine Form—and (by
<u>feeling</u> Me, Thus) progressively <u>feel</u> My Avatarically Self-Revealed
Spiritual (and Always Blessing) Divine Presence, the "Bright"
Giving-Force Heart-Radiated (by Me, and <u>As</u> Me) in, and via,
and around, and everywhere beyond, and Perfectly prior to, My
Avatarically-Born bodily (human) Divine Form—and (by <u>feeling</u>
My Avatarically Self-Revealed Spiritual, and Always Blessing,
Divine Presence, Thus) be progressively Yielded to My Avatarically
Self-Revealed (and Very, and Transcendental, and Perfectly
Subjective, and Inherently Spiritual, and Inherently egoless,
and Inherently Perfect, and Self-Evidently Divine) State, until
(Thereby, in any moment) your own act of self-contraction (and,
thus, of separation, separateness, and separativeness) is dissolved,
released, vanished, and forgotten in Me.

37.

Do this <u>feeling</u>-Contemplation (progressively, as My Divinely Self-Giving Avataric Grace and My Graceful Avatarically Given Divine Self-Revelation will have it) at random (daily), and more and more constantly, and (in accordance with your formal congregation of formal approach to Me) as a developing formal Meditation—and, Thus (by always keeping attention on Me), be purified and released of the casual distractions (and the sometimes and self-enclosed sleep) of attention.

38.

Realize the Obvious Truth (of non-separateness, of no-seeking, of no-contraction, and of Love-Ananda, My Love-Bliss Itself), Thus (by Means of My Avatarically Self-Transmitted Divine Grace Alone), again and again.

39.

Therefore, Contemplate Me, Meditate on Me, actively (responsively) Yield the motions of body, breath, emotion, and mind to Me (and into the Heart of My Avatarically-Born bodily human Divine Form, My Avatarically Self-Revealed Spiritual, and Always Blessing, Divine Presence, and My Avatarically Self-Revealed, and Very, and Transcendental, and Perfectly Subjective, and Inherently Spiritual, and Inherently egoless, and Inherently Perfect, and Self-Evidently Divine State)—such that (by Means of My Divinely Self-Giving Avataric Grace and My Graceful Avatarically Given Divine Self-Revelation) you Realize true heart-Communion with Me, and (Thus and Thereby) become self-surrendered into the Obvious Truth (of non-separateness, of no-seeking, of no-contraction, and of Love-Ananda, My Love-Bliss Itself), Revealed (by Means of My Avatarically Self-Transmitted Divine Grace) to be Inherent in pleasurable (psycho-physically self-surrendered) oneness with whatever and all that presently arises, and (more and more) exercise the Thus by-Me-Given Capability for transcending all problems and all seeking, or all apparent limitations on love, and on My Avatarically Self-Transmitted Divine Love-Bliss Itself—if they arise, and when they arise.

40.

The only-by-Me Revealed and Given Way of Adidam (Which is the One and Only by-Me-Revealed and by-Me-Given Way of the Heart) is the "radical" (or most direct) Way of the Heart Itself—Which (Itself) "radically" (or most directly) Realizes (and, in Reality, Is) the inherent (or Native, or always already, and Self-Evidently Divine) Truth.

41.

The only-by-Me Revealed and Given Way of Adidam (Which is the One and Only by-Me-Revealed and by-Me-Given Way of the Heart) is the Way of non-separateness, or the Heart-Way of counter-active (or actively ego-transcending) responsibility for the (otherwise always arising) action that is egoity (the ego, the ego-"I", or the primal "Act of Narcissus", which is the act of self-contraction, and the constant action of separation, separateness, and separativeness).

42.

The only-by-Me Revealed and Given Way of Adidam (Which is the One and Only by-Me-Revealed and by-Me-Given Way of the Heart) is the devotional Way of Me-Recognizing and to-Me-responding self-surrender to (and into) My Avatarically Self-Revealed Divine Form and Presence and State of Grace—Which is the devotional Way of (more and more effective) counter-egoic action, the Way of active (and more and more effective) devotional surrender of self-contraction, and the devotionally active Way of (more and more effective) ego-transcendence, through ego-surrendering, ego-forgetting, and ego-transcending heart-Communion with (and psycho-physical Infusion by) the by-Me-Avatarically-Self-Revealed, Inherently Non-separate, Inherently Perfect, Perfectly Subjective, and Inherently "Bright" (or Self-Existing and Self-Radiant) Reality and Truth.

43.

The only-by-Me Revealed and Given Way of Adidam (Which is the One and Only by-Me-Revealed and by-Me-Given Way of the Heart) is the Way of Divine Grace, Wherein the Free Gift of "radical" self-understanding is Given to all and Awakened in all, in the moment (or in any moment) of ego-transcending devotional Recognition and heart-responsive feeling-Contemplation of My Avatarically-Born bodily (human) Divine Form, My Avatarically Self-Revealed Spiritual (and Always Blessing) Divine Presence, and My Avatarically Self-Revealed (and Very, and Transcendental, and Perfectly Subjective, and Inherently Spiritual, and Inherently egoless, and Inherently Perfect, and Self-Evidently Divine) State.

44.

Therefore, if you are responding to This (My Word of Heart), and if you are (by This) heart-Moved to transcend and Be Free of the otherwise constant "Act (and Results) of Narcissus", and if you are heart-Attracted to (or toward) My Avatarically-Born bodily (human) Divine Form (because It Is Heart-"Bright"), and to (or toward) My Avatarically Self-Revealed Spiritual (and Always Blessing) Divine Presence (because It Is the Free Transmission of Love-Bliss), and to (or toward) My Avatarically Self-Revealed (and Very, and Transcendental, and Perfectly Subjective, and Inherently Spiritual, and Inherently egoless, and Inherently Perfect, and Self-Evidently Divine) State (because It Self-Reveals the Truth), and if you would (by always Merely Remembering and Contemplating Me) forget your separate and separative self (the ego-"I", or self-contraction, appearing as body, emotion, and all of mind) in Me—then Yield to Me, embrace My Seven Giving Gifts,[53] and practice the Divine Way of Adidam in My Gracefully Self-Revealing Company.

45.

The only-by-Me Revealed and Given Way of Adidam is the (necessarily, formal) <u>practice</u> of Ruchira Avatara Satsang, or the ego-surrendering, and ego-forgetting, and (really, effectively) self-contraction-purifying and self-contraction-transcending <u>work</u> of constant, devotionally Me-Recognizing, devotionally to-Me-responding, and effectively counter-egoic (or intentionally and effectively ego-Yielding and ego-forgetting) <u>feeling</u>-Contemplation of My Avatarically-Born bodily (human) Divine Form, My

223

Avatarically Self-Revealed Spiritual (and Always Blessing) Divine Presence, and My Avatarically Self-Revealed (and Very, and Transcendental, and Perfectly Subjective, and Inherently Spiritual, and Inherently egoless, and Inherently Perfect, and Self-Evidently Divine) State.

46.

Therefore, by always first (responsively, actively, and intentionally) "Locating" the <u>feeling</u>-Place in you that already and presently and effortlessly feels Attracted to My Avatarically-Born bodily (human) Divine Form, and My Avatarically Self-Revealed Spiritual (and Always Blessing) Divine Presence, and My Avatarically Self-Revealed (and Very, and Transcendental, and Perfectly Subjective, and Inherently Spiritual, and Inherently egoless, and Inherently Perfect, and Self-Evidently Divine) State, Yield (responsively, actively, and intentionally) to the <u>feeling</u> of the Inherent "Bright" Attractiveness of My Avatarically-Born bodily (human) Divine Form, and Yield (responsively, actively, and intentionally) to the <u>feeling</u> of the Inherent "Bright" Attractiveness of My Spiritual (and Always Blessing, and progressively by-Me-Avatarically-Self-Revealed) Divine Presence—and, by all of this, responsively, actively, and intentionally Yield (and more and more deeply forget) your ego-"I" (or your own action of separation, separateness, and separativeness) in the "Bright" and Very Space of My (progressively) by-Me-Avatarically-Self-Revealed (and Very, and Transcendental, and Perfectly Subjective, and Inherently Spiritual, and Inherently egoless, and Inherently Perfect, and Self-Evidently Divine) State.

47.

You (necessarily) become (or conform to the likeness of) whatever you Contemplate, or Meditate on, or even think about.

48.

Therefore, Contemplate Me, and transcend even all thought by Meditating on Me.

49.

Do not Meditate on your separate self (your states, your experiences, your presumed knowledge, your dilemma, your problem, or your search), and do not perpetuate self-contraction (by strategies of independent effort, and by adventures of either self-glorification or self-destruction, within or without)—but (always, immediately) transcend self-Meditation, personal states, conditional experiences, presumptions of knowledge, and all of dilemma, problem, and search (Merely by Remembering Me, and Invoking Me, and heart-Recognizing Me, and Meditating on Me, and, Therefore, Merely by surrendering to <u>Me</u>—not by self-concerned effort, or by isolated and concerned manipulation of conditions themselves, but by simply, and intentionally, and more and more deeply, responding and Yielding to the always presently Available feeling of the Inherent "Bright" Attractiveness of My Avatarically-Born bodily human Divine Form, and of My Avatarically Self-Revealed Spiritual, and Always Blessing, Divine Presence, and of My Avatarically Self-Revealed, and Very, and Transcendental, and Perfectly Subjective, and Inherently Spiritual, and Inherently egoless, and Inherently Perfect, and Self-Evidently Divine State), and (Thus, by Means of the always presently Available Grace That Is My Good Company) always and actively feel beyond and (really, effectively) transcend your separate and separative self (Merely by feeling, and Thereby Contemplating, Me).

50.

Do this Contemplation for Its own Sake, and not passively and partially (as if <u>waiting</u> for devotion to happen <u>to</u> you, rather than always presently Remembering, Invoking, and heart-Recognizing Me, and, Thereupon, responsively <u>allowing</u> the presently inevitable feeling of My Inherent "Bright" Attractiveness, and, Thereby, most simply, <u>always</u> and <u>fully</u> <u>activating</u> My always Given and Giving Gift of devotion), and not cleverly and strategically (with all effort and no heart-response, intent but not Yielding, stressful with the <u>seeking</u> of Me, rather than Happy with the <u>Finding</u> of Me)—but do this Contemplation constantly, always, Merely, and by heart, and (Thus) by feeling to My Avatarically-Born bodily (human) Divine Form, and by feeling into My Avatarically Self-Revealed Spiritual (and Always Blessing) Divine Presence, and (more and more) by feeling My Very and Freely Avatarically-Self-Revealed and Freely (Inherently) Perfect State.

51.

Therefore, actively (responsively) be My devotee, heart-Recognizing Me (or heart-Knowing Who I Truly, Really, and, Self-Evidently, Divinely Am), and the Obvious Truth (of non-separateness, of no-seeking, of no-contraction, and of Love-Ananda, My Love-Bliss Itself) will (Freely) be Given to you (by Me) in every moment—and (to the degree you make Room for Me in the Place of your feeling, by surrendering thought, and even every form of self-contraction, in ego-forgetting Me-Remembrance) the Obvious Truth (of non-separateness, of no-seeking, of no-contraction, and of Love-Ananda, My Love-Bliss Itself) will (Thus and Thereby) be Found and Received by you (as My Divinely Self-Giving Avataric Grace and My Graceful Avatarically Given Divine Self-Revelation will have it, in any moment).

52.

Now, and forever hereafter, this Simplicity is the essential practice (and the essence of the entire practice of the only-by-Me Revealed and Given Way of Adidam) to which I Call everyone.

53.

All those who would so (and, necessarily, formally) practice are Called by Me to embrace, and (according to My Instructions, as Given for application within each one's formal congregation of formal approach to Me) to progressively develop, the original (or most basic) functional, practical, and relational disciplines (and the original, or most basic, cultural obligations) I have Described (and Given) in and by My summary (Written, and forever Speaking) Word of Heart (in many Works).

54.

Those disciplines and practices are the (most basic) necessary evidence of the devotionally Me-Recognizing heart-response to Me.

55.

Those disciplines and practices should be responsively and positively embraced (and—by real, and, necessarily, formal, practice—thoroughly "considered" and developed) in the context of the essential practice of the only-by-Me Revealed and Given Way of Adidam—which essential practice is (according to the requirements of My devotee's formal congregation of formal approach to Me) daily (formal, and, otherwise, random, and more and more constant), and always (responsively, actively, intentionally) body-opening-yielding, and deeply feeling (and reactive-emotion-forgetting), and really mind-forgetting, and altogether and truly self-contraction-forgetting, feeling-Contemplation of My Avatarically-Born bodily (human) Divine Form, My Avatarically Self-Revealed Spiritual (and Always Blessing) Divine Presence, and My Avatarically Self-Revealed (and Very, and Transcendental, and Perfectly Subjective, and Inherently Spiritual, and Inherently egoless, and Inherently Perfect, and Self-Evidently Divine) State.

56.

When their signs of heart-responsive devotional Recognition of Me (and of Growth in the only-by-Me Revealed and Given Way of Adidam) Allow, My devotees are Given Access to My Blessing-Seat—and each one should (insofar as it is practically possible) come to Me[54] (at the Place, or Places, of My Blessing-Seat appropriate for his or her Access to Me, in accordance with his or her formal congregation of formal approach to Me, and, as the case may be, with his or her form and stage of practice of the only-by-Me Revealed and Given Way of Adidam[55]), and this as often as his or her right and true and truly Growing practice of the only-by-Me Revealed and Given Way of Adidam, and his or her present (and, altogether, consistently demonstrated) signs of real and true heart-Recognition of Me and heart-Resort to Me, Allow (and truly Require).

57.

During the (physical) Lifetime of My Avatarically-Born bodily (human) Divine Form (here), I may Freely Manifest My Seclusions, Offerings, and Blessing-Wanderings any where—but I will always (forever), during and after (and forever after) the (physical) Lifetime of My Avatarically-Born bodily (human) Divine Form (here), be Really Present at Adidam Samrajashram (the Island of Naitauba in Fiji—Which Island is, now, and forever hereafter, My Great Hermitage-Retreat Sanctuary, Where I have Established Myself Spiritually in "Brightest" Perpetuity) for the Sake of all and All.

58.

During the (physical) Lifetime of My Avatarically-Born bodily (human) Divine Form (here), I may Freely Manifest My Seclusions, Offerings, and Blessing-Wanderings any where— but I will always (forever), during and after (and forever after) the (physical) Lifetime of My Avatarically-Born bodily (human) Divine Form (here), be Really Present at all the Directly-by-Me Empowered Ruchira Sannyasin Hermitage-Retreat Sanctuaries, and (likewise) at The Mountain Of Attention (in northern California) and Da Love-Ananda Mahal (in Kauai, Hawaii), the two Sanctuaries I have Directly Empowered and Established for constant Pilgrimages and Retreats (and every other truly Me-Invoking, and devotionally Me-Recognizing, and devotionally to-Me-responding, and devotionally Me-Serving Sacred use) by the formal congregations of My devotees (and to be thus used according to the Principles, Rules, and Instructions Given by Me to the Ruchira Sannyasin Order of the Tantric Renunciates of Adidam, which formal Order of Tantric Renunciates has been, and is, now, and forever hereafter, formally Appointed by Me to be the culturally governing—but entirely renunciate, and non-managerial—Authority relative to My Great Island-Hermitage-Retreat, and even all the Directly-by-Me Empowered Ruchira Sannyasin Hermitage-Retreat Sanctuaries, and all the Directly-by-Me Empowered Pilgrimage and Retreat Sanctuaries, and all four of the formal congregations of My formally practicing devotees, during, and forever after, the physical Lifetime of My Avatarically-Born bodily human Divine Form here).[56]

59.

At all times, and in all places, daily and always, all My (necessarily, formally practicing) devotees should (constantly) Contemplate My Avatarically-Born bodily (human) Divine Form, My Avatarically Self-Revealed Spiritual (and Always Blessing) Divine Presence, and My Avatarically Self-Revealed (and Very, and Transcendental, and Perfectly Subjective, and Inherently Spiritual, and Inherently egoless, and Inherently Perfect, and Self-Evidently Divine) State, and (as required, and as permitted, in accordance with each one's formal congregation, and, as the case may be, form, and formal stage, of formal approach to Me) they should do this at My Great Island-Hermitage-Retreat, and at even all the Directly-by-Me Empowered Ruchira Sannyasin Hermitage-Retreat Sanctuaries, and at all the Directly-by-Me Empowered Pilgrimage and Retreat Sanctuaries, and, otherwise (always, day to day, as required—or, otherwise, allowed—by each one's formal congregation and circumstance of formal approach to Me), within all the formal communities[57] of My devotees (who are formally acknowledged as such by the formally appointed representatives of the sacred cultural and congregational gathering formally Established by Me, and by the Ruchira Sannyasin Order of the Tantric Renunciates of Adidam, the culturally governing Authority formally Established by Me), and they should do this (always) even under all the other and ordinary circumstances of every day—for I will always (forever), during and after (and forever after) the (physical) Lifetime of My Avatarically-Born bodily (human) Divine Form (here), be Really Present even every then and there (and, therefore, every where and when) for all My (necessarily, formally practicing) devotees.

60.

I am here only for this Satsang (of My devotees, heart-Recognizing Me, and heart-surrendering to Me, to enjoy the "Bright"-Blessed Ordeal of totally psycho-physically enacted ego-surrendering, ego-forgetting, and ego-transcending feeling-Communion with Me, the One and Only and Very Person to be Realized by each and all and All).

61.

I no longer Teach (or Submit to seem in the ordinary likeness of every one and all, in order to Reflect them to themselves, and, Thus and Thereby, to Prove the necessity of ego-transcendence, and, altogether, in order to Reveal and Describe the Great Means and the Great Process of the Heart-Way of non-separateness), but—now, and forever hereafter, during and after (and forever after) the (physical) Lifetime of My Avatarically-Born bodily (human) Divine Form (here)—having already Fully and Completely Done My First (or Teaching) Work (and such that It will Live and Work forever, through My summary Written, and forever Speaking, Word of Heart in many Works, and through the recorded, remembered, and constantly retold Leelas of all of My Avatarically Self-Manifested Teaching-Life and Teaching-Work, and through the recorded, and forever Living, Images of My Avatarically-Born bodily human Divine Form), I only Call each one and all to true and constant (and truly Me-Recognizing) devotional Contemplation of Me, As Only I Appear and Function here, and (truly) <u>As</u> I <u>Am</u>, in order that—now, and forever hereafter, during and after (and forever after) the (physical) Lifetime of My Avatarically-Born bodily (human) Divine Form (here)—I may Do My Great (or Divinely Self-"Emerging") Blessing-Work with every one and all and All.

62.

Therefore—now, and forever hereafter, during and after (and forever after) the (physical) Lifetime of My Avatarically-Born bodily (human) Divine Form (here)—I, for the Sake of their true and constant devotional Contemplation of Me, Am "Bright" to Give (or Spiritually Awaken in, and Require of) all My devotees the Gift of constant devotional Recognition and devotional love of Me—because true and constant devotional Contemplation of Me is (and, in every moment, requires) truly heart-responsive (and, therefore, truly devotionally Me-Recognizing, and really ego-surrendering, ego-forgetting, and ego-transcending) heart-Resort to Me.

63.

Likewise—now, and forever hereafter, during and after (and forever after) the (physical) Lifetime of My Avatarically-Born bodily (human) Divine Form (here)—I, for the Sake of their true and constant devotional Contemplation of Me, Am "Bright" to Give (or Spiritually Awaken in, and Require of) all My devotees the Gift of constant devotional service to Me—because true and constant devotional Contemplation of Me is (and, in every functional, practical, or relational context or circumstance, requires) truly heart-responsive (and, therefore, truly devotionally Me-Recognizing, and really ego-surrendering, ego-forgetting, and ego-transcending) heart-attention to Me.

64.

And—now, and forever hereafter, during and after (and forever after) the (physical) Lifetime of My Avatarically-Born bodily (human) Divine Form (here)—I, for the Sake of their true and constant devotional Contemplation of Me, Am "Bright" to Give (or Spiritually Awaken in, and Require of) all My devotees the Gift of constant (and, altogether, devotionally inspired) self-discipline—because true and constant devotional Contemplation of Me is (and, in every context or circumstance, requires) truly heart-responsive (and, therefore, truly devotionally Me-Recognizing, and really ego-surrendering, ego-forgetting, and ego-transcending) heart-obedience and heart-conformity to Me.

65.

Now, and forever hereafter, during and after (and forever after) the (physical) Lifetime of My Avatarically-Born bodily (human) Divine Form (here)—I am <u>here</u>, "Bright" <u>As</u> I <u>Am</u>.

66.

I am here (now, and forever hereafter) for Only One Purpose: to Bless and Awaken those who heart-Recognize Me, heart-Resort to Me, and heart-Contemplate Me.

67.

My summary (Written, and forever Speaking) Word of
Heart relative to the Extreme Simplicity That Is the Great Means
of the only-by-Me Revealed and Given Way of Adidam, and
relative to the progressive process of necessary (or, otherwise,
potential)[58] developmental stages (and the technically more
"elaborate" practices, as well as the technically "simpler" practices,
and the technically "simplest" practices[59]) of the only-by-Me
Revealed and Given Way of Adidam, is—now, and forever
hereafter, during and after (and forever after) the (physical)
Lifetime of My Avatarically-Born bodily (human) Divine Form
(here)—Fully and Finally and Completely Given here, and My
summary (Written, and forever Speaking) Word of Heart is—
now, and forever hereafter, during and after (and forever after)
the (physical) Lifetime of My Avatarically-Born bodily (human)
Divine Form (here)—to be openly and everywhere Communicated
here (as I have Written It in Its Full, Final, and Complete Forms),
so that everyone (as every one) may read My summary (Written,
and forever Speaking) Avataric Divine Word and (by personal
heart-response, as and whenever they will) become My devotees,
and so that all My devotees may (by self-testing study) "consider"
My summary (Written, and forever Speaking) Avataric Divine
Word and (by progressive application) develop their practice (in
accordance with each one's formal congregation of formal
approach to Me and, as the case may be, with each one's
eventually proven choice of Manner, course, and form of the
practice) of the only-by-Me Revealed and Given Way of Adidam.

68.

Those of My devotees (in the second congregation of formal
approach to Me) who, in due course (by Means of My Divinely
Self-Giving Avataric Grace and My Graceful Avatarically Given
Divine Self-Revelation), stably demonstrate the (original) maturing
signs of the only-by-Me Revealed and Given Way of Adidam,
and who (necessarily) formally embrace the right, true, full, and
fully devotional practice of the only-by-Me Revealed and Given
Way of Adidam, and who do so in full accordance with My

Hridaya Rosary (with always current, or always then present-time, formal approval by the Ruchira Sannyasin Order of the Tantric Renunciates of Adidam), may (if they choose, and if they qualify) enter (formally) into the technically "fully elaborated" (or "elaborately detailed") course of the only-by-Me Revealed and Given Way of Adidam (which technically "fully elaborated", or "elaborately detailed", course may be engaged only by formal members of either the first or the second congregation of formal approach to Me).

69.

Those of My devotees who choose (and qualify) to practice the technically "fully elaborated" form of the only-by-Me Revealed and Given Way of Adidam must do so under continuous and formal guidance within (and by) one or the other of the (formal) orders originally established (and formally appointed) by Me for the Sake of My fully practicing devotees, and they must allow their practice and their discipline to be (thus and thereby) formally measured and determined by technically "elaborately detailed" stages.

70.

Those of My devotees who enter the technically "fully elaborated" course of the only-by-Me Revealed and Given Way of Adidam must (formally, progressively, and as necessary) enter into (and develop) all the by-Me-Given disciplines, practices, stages, and Realizations of the technically "fully elaborated" form of the only-by-Me Revealed and Given Way of Adidam, and they must do so in a (formally, progressively, and personally appropriate) renunciate Manner.

71.

However, many (necessarily, formal) practitioners of the only-by-Me Revealed and Given Way of Adidam will not choose (and qualify) to embrace the practice required in the technically "fully elaborated" course of the only-by-Me Revealed and Given Way of Adidam, but they will, indeed, choose (and qualify for) the practice of either the technically "simplest" form of the

only-by-Me Revealed and Given Way of Adidam (as formal
members of either the second or the third or the fourth—or
even, in relatively rare cases, the first—congregation of formal
approach to Me) or the technically "simpler" form of the only-
by-Me Revealed and Given Way of Adidam (necessarily, as formal
members of the second—or even, in relatively rare cases, the
first—congregation of formal approach to Me)—and, therefore (in
that either "simpler" or "simplest" Manner), they will love Me,
and they will Contemplate Me, and (by Means of "simpler", or
"simplest", but always true and fullest ego-surrendering, ego-
forgetting, and, more and more, ego-transcending devotion to
Me) they will always heart-Reside with Me.

72.

The practice and the discipline of My devotees who (as
formal members of either the second, the third, or the fourth—
or even, in relatively rare cases, the first—congregation of formal
approach to Me) choose (and qualify) to (necessarily, formally)
practice the technically "simplest" form of the only-by-Me Revealed
and Given Way of Adidam, and the practice and the discipline
of My devotees who (necessarily, as formal members of the
second—or even, in relatively rare cases, the first—congregation
of formal approach to Me) choose (and qualify) to (necessarily,
formally) practice the technically "simpler" form of the only-by-
Me Revealed and Given Way of Adidam, should not be practiced,
measured, or determined according to the fullest (or technically
"fully elaborated") formal descriptions and measures (or
according to the most intensive expectations) of the technically
"fully elaborated" form of the only-by-Me Revealed and Given
Way of Adidam—but their practice must, nonetheless, be engaged
both seriously and consistently, and their practice must necessarily
be formally and consistently monitored and measured relative
to the progressive development of the (primary) developmental
Signs of devotional Recognition of Me, and of heart-responsive
(and truly ego-surrendering and ego-forgetting) devotion to Me,
and truly ego-surrendering and ego-forgetting service to Me,
and (as required, according to My Instructions, as Given for

234

application within their formal congregation of formal approach to Me) really self-contraction-observing and self-contraction-purifying (functional, practical, relational, and cultural) self-discipline, embraced in truly ego-surrendering and ego-forgetting heart-response to Me, and truly ego-surrendering and ego-forgetting (and always self-testing) study-"consideration" of My Avataric Divine Word, and increasingly meditative (and more and more profoundly ego-surrendering and ego-forgetting) feeling-Contemplation of Me, and they must formally (and rightly) maintain (and cultivate) their participation in (and their practice-accountability to) the sacred cultural gathering established (and formally appointed) by Me for the Sake of all formal practitioners (and all formal congregations) of the only-by-Me Revealed and Given Way of Adidam, and they must do all of this persistently (and always in and by Means of devotional Contemplation of My Avatarically-Born bodily human Divine Form, My Avatarically Self-Revealed Spiritual, and Always Blessing, Divine Presence, and My Avatarically Self-Revealed, and Very, and Transcendental, and Perfectly Subjective, and Inherently Spiritual, and Inherently egoless, and Inherently Perfect, and Self-Evidently Divine State), no matter how profound the Process of Reception of Me (or, otherwise, no matter how advanced, or even Ultimate, the Process or the Event of Realization of Me) may become, or (otherwise) seem to be.

73.

In any case, the basic (or essential) practice for <u>all</u> who (necessarily, formally) practice the only-by-Me Revealed and Given Way of Adidam is (in its inherent Simplicity) just that of devotionally Me-Recognizing (and devotionally to-Me-responding, and altogether responsible) feeling-Contemplation of My Avatarically-Born bodily (human) Divine Form, My Avatarically Self-Revealed Spiritual (and Always Blessing) Divine Presence, and My Avatarically Self-Revealed (and Very, and Transcendental, and Perfectly Subjective, and Inherently Spiritual, and Inherently egoless, and Inherently Perfect, and Self-Evidently Divine) State.

74.

Therefore, I Embrace all (necessarily, formal) practitioners of the only-by-Me Revealed and Given Way of Adidam—and I Embrace each one and all of them Simply (Merely) as My devotees (who are all Merely Contemplating Me).

75.

My Blessing of My devotees always Transmits the Same Gift to each and all—for I always Give, and Freely Give, the One and Only and Divine Gift of My "Bright" Self-Revelation to each and all.

76.

My Blessing of My devotees is <u>always</u> Full of My "Bright" Spirit-Power, Given for the Sake of the Heart-Awakening of every one and all of My devotees.

77.

Because My Blessing-Gift is always only the Divine Gift of My "Bright" Self-Revelation, there are not different kinds of Blessings Given by Me for each kind and (as the case may be) developmental stage of practice of the only-by-Me Revealed and Given Way of Adidam—but there are different modes, forms, kinds, stages, and degrees of devotional approach to Me and of devotional Access to Me (according to which formal congregation of formal approach to Me is formally chosen by My devotee, and for which he or she is, then currently, or in the then present-time, truly qualified).

78.

Because of My always constant, Giving, Full, and Perfect Blessing-Grace, and because My Blessing-Gift is always the Divine Gift of My "Bright" Self-Revelation, it is possible for any one to practice the only-by-Me Revealed and Given Way of Adidam (in one or the other of the four formal congregations of formal approach to Me)—and that practice potentially (and more and more readily and profoundly) Realizes (by Means of My Divinely Self-Giving Avataric Grace and My Graceful

Avatarically Given Divine Self-Revelation) pleasurable oneness (or inherently Love-Blissful Unity) with whatever and all that presently arises, if any one will (necessarily, formally) practice at least the technically "simplest" form of the only-by-Me Revealed and Given Way of Adidam, and if any one will (Thereby, actively) heart-respond to Me (with truly Me-Recognizing, and really Me-Contemplating, and, altogether, effectively ego-transcending devotion to Me, and in constant and ego-transcending service to Me), and if any one will (Thereby, responsively and consistently, according to My Instructions, as Given for application within his or her formal congregation of formal approach to Me) embrace true (functional, practical, relational, and cultural) self-discipline in My Company, and if any one will (progressively) allow every kind of (Thus Inspired and Accomplished) change and release of body, emotion, mind, and separate self.

79.

Indeed, not even any other form of the "Conscious Process" (or the Process of devotion to Me that specifically controls, or surrenders and transcends, the egoic, or self-contracting, gesture and tendency of attention) need necessarily (or, otherwise, constantly or regularly) be practiced in order to Receive My Divinely Self-Giving Avataric Grace and My Graceful Avatarically Given Divine Self-Revelation, if only My devotee will (regularly, randomly, and more and more constantly) surrender self-contraction (Merely by Means of Me-Remembering, and Me-Invoking, and devotionally Me-Recognizing, and devotionally to-Me-responding, and really ego-surrendering, ego-forgetting, and more and more effectively ego-transcending feeling-Contemplation of My Avatarically-Born bodily human Divine Form, My Avatarically Self-Revealed Spiritual, and Always Blessing, Divine Presence, and My Avatarically Self-Revealed, and Very, and Transcendental, and Perfectly Subjective, and Inherently Spiritual, and Inherently egoless, and Inherently Perfect, and Self-Evidently Divine State)—and not even any more intensive (or, otherwise, technically more "elaborate") form of "Conductivity" (or the whole bodily, physical, emotional, and mental, "conscious exercise" of breath, bodily energy, and, potentially, My Avatarically Self-Transmitted Divine Spirit-Force) need necessarily be practiced in order to Receive My Divinely Self-Giving Avataric Grace and My Graceful Avatarically Given Divine Self-Revelation, if only My devotee will (entirely and Merely by Means of Me-Remembering, and Me-Invoking, and devotionally Me-Recognizing, and devotionally to-Me-responding, and really ego-surrendering, ego-forgetting, and more and more effectively ego-transcending feeling-Contemplation of My Avatarically-Born bodily human Divine Form, My Avatarically Self-Revealed Spiritual, and Always Blessing, Divine Presence, and My Avatarically Self-Revealed, and Very, and Transcendental, and Perfectly Subjective, and Inherently Spiritual, and Inherently egoless, and Inherently Perfect, and Self-Evidently Divine State) embrace and maintain (and, on that basis, develop), according to My Instructions (as Given for application within his or her formal congregation of formal approach to Me), basic functional, practical, relational, and cultural (and, altogether, self-contraction-purifying) self-discipline (including the most basic "conscious exercise" of breath and bodily energy—which, in the case of My devotees in the first and second congregations of formal approach to Me, is, in due course, by Means of My Divinely Self-Giving Avataric Grace and My Graceful Avatarically Given Divine Self-Revelation, spontaneously Converted into truly devotional, or heart-responsive, Reception and "Conductivity" of My "Bright" Transmitted Spiritual, and Always Blessing, Divine Presence).

80.

If only My devotee will (truly devotionally, and rightly, and, necessarily, formally) practice at least the technically "simplest" form of the only-by-Me Revealed and Given Way of Adidam, the Obvious Truth (of non-separateness, of no-seeking, of no-contraction, and of Love-Ananda, My Love-Bliss Itself) will, by Means of My Divinely Self-Giving Avataric Grace and My Graceful Avatarically Given Divine Self-Revelation, be (in random moments—and, potentially, more and more readily and profoundly) Revealed (and Found, and Received) As the Obvious.

81.

In the course of that Process of Revelation (and Finding, and Receiving), many insights and experiences and responsibilities may arise.

82.

In any case (no matter what arises), it is only necessary to maintain (and, otherwise, progressively to develop or intensify) right and true functional, practical, relational, cultural, and (altogether) self-responsible self-discipline (according to My Instructions, as Given by Me for application by My formally practicing devotees, according to each one's formal congregation, and, as the case may be, form, and formal stage, of formal approach to Me), and (on that basis) to rightly and truly practice (according to My Instructions, as Given by Me for application by My formally practicing devotees, according to each one's formal congregation, and, as the case may be, form, and formal stage, of formal approach to Me) at least technically "simplest" (and regular, and also random, and more and more constant, and truly, deeply ego-surrendering, ego-forgetting, and effectively ego-transcending) devotional (and Me-serving) Contemplation of My Avatarically-Born bodily (human) Divine Form, My Avatarically Self-Revealed Spiritual (and Always Blessing) Divine Presence, and My Avatarically Self-Revealed (and Very, and Transcendental, and Perfectly Subjective, and Inherently Spiritual, and Inherently egoless, and Inherently Perfect, and Self-Evidently Divine) State.

83.

The Most Ultimate and Most Perfect (or true, and only-by-Me Revealed and Given, seventh stage) Realization and Capability is the Real Potential <u>only</u> of <u>My</u> (necessarily, formally practicing) devotees, and, necessarily (because of all that is required for That Realization and Capability), <u>only</u> of those of My devotees who formally embrace the right, true, full, and fully devotional practice of the only-by-Me Revealed and Given Way of Adidam (as formal, and truly most intensively and profoundly practicing, members of the first congregation of formal approach to Me, or, otherwise, as formal, and progressively intensively and profoundly practicing, and, at least eventually, truly most intensively and profoundly practicing, members of the second congregation of formal approach to Me), and who consistently (and truly devotionally) Recognize Me and Resort to Me, either in the technically "fully elaborated" Manner (and by means of a progressively more technical development of practice in the spontaneously developing context of the however may be necessary advanced and Ultimate stages of life in the only-by-Me Revealed and Given Way of Adidam) or in the technically "simpler" (or even "simplest") Manner (and by means of the maintenance of a consistently "simpler", or even "simplest", technical responsibility, in the spontaneously developing context of the however may be necessary advanced and Ultimate stages of life in the only-by-Me Revealed and Given Way of Adidam), and who practice the only-by-Me Revealed and Given Way of Adidam in full accordance with My *Hridaya Rosary* (with always current, or always then present-time, formal approval by the Ruchira Sannyasin Order of the Tantric Renunciates of Adidam)— and, indeed, even the only-by-Me Given Great Graces of the True Hearing of Me and the True Seeing of Me (as Described, by Me, in My summary Written, and forever Speaking, Word of Heart) are the Real Potential <u>only</u> of such (necessarily, formally practicing) devotees of Mine, who (as members of either the first congregation or the second congregation of formal approach to Me) formally embrace the right, true, full, and fully devotional practice of the only-by-Me Revealed and Given Way of Adidam, and who do so in full accordance with My *Hridaya Rosary* (with always current, or always then present-time, formal approval by the Ruchira Sannyasin Order of the Tantric Renunciates of Adidam)—whereas My formally practicing devotees within the third and the fourth congregations of formal approach to Me practice (and are, by Me, Given the practice of) <u>only</u> a rudimentary form of the beginner's to-Me-Listening practice of devotion to Me, with only the lesser potential of insights, and experiences, and responsibilities that rudimentary practice makes possible, and <u>Not</u> the Real Potential of the True Hearing of Me and the True Seeing of Me, and Most Perfect Me-Realization (unless, at least eventually, such devotees of Mine choose to embrace the complete, Fully-To-Me Listening, and, Really Potentially, Truly Me-Hearing, Truly Me-Seeing, and Most Perfectly Me-Realizing practice of the only-by-Me Revealed and Given Way of Adidam, within, at least, the second congregation of formal approach to Me, and, perhaps, eventually, the first congregation of formal approach to Me)—but even <u>any</u> and <u>every</u> formal devotee of <u>Mine</u> (in any of the four formal congregations of formal approach to Me) is fully Instructed by Me and (if he or she consistently, and truly devotionally, Resorts to Me) constantly Blessed by Me (at heart, and in his or her total body-mind) to (potentially, in random moments, and, as the case may be, more and more readily and profoundly—if he or she will practice the only-by-Me Revealed and Given Way of Adidam according to My Instructions Given for his or her formal congregation, and, as the case may be, form, and formal stage, of formal approach to Me) Find and Receive Me, and (Thus and Thereby—in the manner, and to the degree, that is possible, according to his or her formal congregation, and, as the case may be, form, and formal stage, of formal approach to Me) to be self-surrendered into the Obvious Truth (of non-separateness, of no-seeking, of no-contraction, and of Love-Ananda, My Love-Bliss Itself) That Is, by Means of My Divinely Self-Giving Avataric Grace and My Graceful Avatarically Given Divine Self-Revelation, Realized to Be Inherent in any and every moment of pleasurable oneness (or inherently Love-Blissful Unity) with whatever and all that presently arises.

84.

In any and every moment of devotional Contemplation of My Avatarically-Born bodily (human) Divine Form, My Avatarically Self-Revealed Spiritual (and Always Blessing) Divine Presence, and My Avatarically Self-Revealed (and Very, and Transcendental, and Perfectly Subjective, and Inherently Spiritual, and Inherently egoless, and Inherently Perfect, and Self-Evidently Divine) State, each one will (by Means of My Divinely Self-Giving Avataric

Grace and My Graceful Avatarically Given Divine Self-Revelation) Find and Receive Me according to the quality and strength of his or her Me-Recognizing and to-Me-responding (and effectively ego-surrendering, ego-forgetting, and ego-transcending) devotion to Me.

85.

In any and every moment of devotional Contemplation of My Avatarically-Born bodily (human) Divine Form, My Avatarically Self-Revealed Spiritual (and Always Blessing) Divine Presence, and My Avatarically Self-Revealed (and Very, and Transcendental, and Perfectly Subjective, and Inherently Spiritual, and Inherently egoless, and Inherently Perfect, and Self-Evidently Divine) State, each one will (by Means of My Divinely Self-Giving Avataric Grace and My Graceful Avatarically Given Divine Self-Revelation) Find and Receive Me according to the presence or absence of the various kinds of egoic limitations that characterize and enforce a physical, psycho-physical, or (otherwise) merely psychic (or mind-made) point of view.

86.

In any and every moment of devotional Contemplation of My Avatarically-Born bodily (human) Divine Form, My Avatarically Self-Revealed Spiritual (and Always Blessing) Divine Presence, and My Avatarically Self-Revealed (and Very, and Transcendental, and Perfectly Subjective, and Inherently Spiritual, and Inherently egoless, and Inherently Perfect, and Self-Evidently Divine) State, each one will (by Means of My Divinely Self-Giving Avataric Grace and My Graceful Avatarically Given Divine Self-Revelation) Find and Receive Me according to his or her relative (and effective) willingness to be released from the present point of view (and, Most Ultimately, in the case of My devotees in the first and second congregations of formal approach to Me who Most Perfectly Realize Me, even from every possible point of view, or all the egoic stages of life).

87.

Each and every one of My devotees (in each and all of the four formal congregations of formal approach to Me) is Called by Me to enter the advanced and the Ultimate stages of life and practice in the Way of Adidam (by, at least eventually, choosing to become, and, in due course, qualifying and practicing as, a formal, and formally fully accountable, member of either the first congregation or the second congregation of formal approach to Me), and (thus, thereby, and in due course) to Receive (and, potentially, to Realize) the inherent Heart-Capability to Stand Free (and to Demonstrate the seventh, and inherently Most Perfect, and truly Most Ultimate, stage of life)—and this Capability and Freedom is to be Received (and, Most Ultimately, Realized) by Means of My Divinely Self-Giving Avataric Grace and My Graceful Avatarically Given Divine Self-Revelation (and as My Divinely Self-Giving Avataric Grace and My Graceful Avatarically Given Divine Self-Revelation will have it), and Only (Merely) through truly Me-Recognizing, truly to-Me-responding, and really ego-surrendering, ego-forgetting, and ego-transcending devotional Contemplation of My Avatarically-Born bodily (human) Divine Form, My Avatarically Self-Revealed Spiritual (and Always Blessing) Divine Presence, and My Avatarically Self-Revealed (and Very, and Transcendental, and Perfectly Subjective, and Inherently Spiritual, and Inherently egoless, and Inherently Perfect, and Self-Evidently Divine) State.

88.

Therefore, Listen to Me and Hear Me: You have already eaten the meal of separateness.

89.

Now you must relinquish that awful meal (and <u>Be</u>—purified of separate and separative self).

90.

You do not Require (and you should not seek) any "thing" <u>from</u> Me (to add to your already separate and deluded self).

91.

I <u>Am</u> (Myself) What you Require—and I am here to Require every "thing" of you.

92.

You must relinquish (or surrender) your ego-"I" (your experience, your presumed knowledge, your separateness, all your forms of egoic "bonding", and even <u>all</u> your "things", within and without) to Find and Realize the Fullness That <u>Is</u> Me.

93.

Therefore, Come to Me to Realize Me—and do not run from Me after tasting the meal of knowledge and experience (like a dog runs from its master with a bone).

94.

Having Come to Me, do not look within your body or your mind to discover whether you have received some "thing" from Me (to satisfy your little pouch of separateness).

95.

Rather, surrender and release your separate (or self-contracted, self-contracting, separative, and always seeking) self (including your entire body, your breath, your emotions, your mind, your knowledge, and all your experiences) by Means of the devotionally Me-Recognizing, devotionally to-Me-responding, and (thus, responsively) ego-surrendering, ego-forgetting, and ego-transcending feeling-Contemplation of <u>Me</u> (including All of My Avatarically-Born bodily human Divine Form, My Avatarically Self-Revealed Spiritual, and Always Blessing, Divine Presence, and My Avatarically Self-Revealed, and Very, and Transcendental, and Perfectly Subjective, and Inherently Spiritual, and Inherently egoless, and Inherently Perfect, and Self-Evidently Divine State)—and (Thus and Thereby) Grow to Luxuriate in My Love-Bliss-Presence.

96.

If (by active feeling-Contemplation) you surrender and release your separate self to Me, then not any meal of "things" (or effects), but Only I (My Avatarically-Born bodily human Divine Form, My Avatarically Self-Revealed Spiritual, and Always Blessing, Divine Presence, and My Avatarically Self-Revealed, and Very, and Transcendental, and Perfectly Subjective, and Inherently Spiritual, and Inherently egoless, and Inherently Perfect, and Self-Evidently Divine State) Am the Gift, the Object, the State, and the Realization.

97.

Therefore, Come to Me (and for Me Only), "Bond" to Me (and to Me Only), and Stay with Me (and with Me Only, forever)—and you will (by This) Realize Me (truly, really, and Only).

98.

I Am Da Love-Ananda (the Giver and the Free Gift), Who Is Love-Bliss Itself, the Truth and the Reality Given, and Revealed, and Found, and Received (and, Ultimately, Most Perfectly Realized), by Means of My Blessing-Grace, when egoity (or the ego-"I" of self-contraction) is surrendered, forgotten, and transcended in heart-responsive (devotionally Me-Recognizing, and total psycho-physical) feeling-Contemplation of My Avatarically-Born bodily (human) Divine Form, My Avatarically Self-Revealed Spiritual (and Always Blessing) Divine Presence, and My Avatarically Self-Revealed (and Very, and Transcendental, and Perfectly Subjective, and Inherently Spiritual, and Inherently egoless, and Inherently Perfect, and Self-Evidently Divine) State, to the degree of non-separateness, no-seeking, and no-contraction.

99.

I Am Perfect Samadhi, the Truth and the Reality of No-"Difference", Which Is (Inherently Perfect) Consciousness Itself—Self-Existing, Self-Radiant, "Bright", One, Only, Non-Separate, and All Love-Bliss (Itself).

100.

Realize <u>Me</u>—by ego-surrendering, ego-forgetting, ego-transcending (and always Me-Remembering, Me-Invoking, and devotionally Me-Recognizing) heart-Contemplation of My Avatarically-Born bodily (human) Divine Form, My Avatarically Self-Revealed Spiritual (and Always Blessing) Divine Presence, and My Avatarically Self-Revealed (and Very, and Transcendental, and Perfectly Subjective, and Inherently Spiritual, and Inherently egoless, and Inherently Perfect, and Self-Evidently Divine) State.

101.

Live by My Darshan (always Beholding Me), in constant Satsang (always Feasting on the Sight of Me).

102.

By Means of the Divine Grace Revealed by the Mere Sight (or Feel) of Me, Practice Ruchira Avatara Bhakti (which is ego-surrendering, ego-forgetting, and ego-transcending devotion of body, feeling, attention, breath, and all of separate self to Me), and (by Means of the Divine Grace Revealed to that devotion) Practice Ruchira Avatara Seva[60] (which is active self-surrender, self-forgetting, and self-transcendence, via constant and Me-Remembering service to Me), and (by Means of the Divine Grace Revealed to that devotional service) Practice Ruchira Avatara Tapas[61] (which is self-discipline, in always ego-surrendering, ego-forgetting, and truly ego-transcending devotional obedience and devotional conformity to Me).

103.

Therefore—in this Manner, and by the Divine Means of My Divinely Self-Giving Avataric Grace and My Graceful Avatarically Given Divine Self-Revelation—Realize <u>Me</u> by heart, and by Means of My "Bright" Infusion of your to-Me-surrendered body-mind.

104.

All This (That I have Herein Written) I Affirm by Heart (and <u>As</u> the Heart Itself).

105.

All This (That I have Hereby Affirmed) I Promise to the Heart (in every one, and all).

106.

Now (by This) I have Epitomized My summary (Written, and forever Speaking) Word of Heart.

107.

Therefore, surrender, forget, and transcend your separate and separative self by Means of constant right (intelligent, self-disciplined, and truly devotionally responsive) obedience to My Avataric Divine Word and Person, and (Thus) act only in accord (always) with My explicit Instructions (and, Thus, always only with My explicit Permission and Blessing), and (Thus, by this explicit devotion) Be Perfectly Simplified (by My Perfect Simplicity).

108.

This is the Heart-Word of the Ruchira Avatar, the Da Avatar, the Love-Ananda Avatar, Adi Da Samraj, the Divine World-Teacher, the Divine Heart-Master, Who Is Da (the First and Original Person, the Source-Person, the One and Only, Non-Separate and Not "Different", Self-Evidently Divine Self of All and all), and Who Is Da Hridayam (the One and Only Heart of All and all, in Whom all seeming-to-be-separate hearts Must Take Refuge, and, Thus and Thereby, Be Calmed of the Burning Heats of fear, sorrow, anger, un-love, and even all the seeking self-contractions of separative ego-"I"), and Who Is Da Love-Ananda (the Source, the Substance, the Gift, the Giver, and the Very Person of the "Bright" Divine Love-Bliss), and Who Is Da Avabhasa[62] (the Person of the "Bright" Itself, and the Very Giver of "Brightness"), and Who Is Santosha Da (the "Bright" and Eternal and Always Already Non-Separate Person of Divine and Inherent Completeness, Divine Self-Satisfaction, Divine Self-Contentedness, or Perfect Searchlessness)—Hereby Spoken in Extreme Simplicity for the Sake of all beings, in Love toward all beings, So That all beings may Awaken (by Means of My Divinely Self-Giving Avataric Grace and My Graceful Avatarically Given Divine Self-Revelation) to the Only Truth That Sets the heart Free.

RUCHIRA AVATAR ADI DA SAMRAJ
Walk About Joy, 2000

Ruchira Avatara Bhakti Sara (The Essence of Devotion To Me)

Ruchira Avatara Bhakti Sara (The Essence of Devotion To Me)

1.

The only-by-Me Revealed and Given Way of Adidam (Which is the only-by-Me Revealed and Given Way of the Heart) is the devotional relationship to Me.

2.

The only-by-Me Revealed and Given Way of Adidam is not merely a system of self-applied techniques, or ego-centric practices—to be learned from Me and then applied to yourself, independent of Me.

3.

The entire life of My devotee must be Ruchira Avatara Bhakti Yoga, or the always present-time devotional Yoga of direct (and directly and immediately ego-transcending) relationship to Me.

4.

True Religion, or Real-God-Yoga, is the practice of linking (or binding, or connecting, or "yoking") oneself to Reality Itself (Which Is Truth Itself, and the Only Real God).

5.

True Religion, or Real-God-Yoga, is the practice of consistently (and, Ultimately, Most Perfectly, and, therefore, Permanently) moving out of the disposition, and the presumption, and the very activity of separate and separative self, into the Love-Bliss-Full Condition of Oneness with That Which Is One, Whole, Absolute, All-Inclusive, and Beyond.

6.

Therefore, I Call My devotees to truly surrender themselves in devotional feeling-Contemplation of Me, by surrendering the principal faculties (of body, emotion, mind, and breath) to Me—moment to moment, and in all circumstances.

7.

The (moment to moment) surrender of the principal faculties to Me is the Essence of Ruchira Avatara Bhakti Yoga.

8.

Action engaged in the ordinary (or egoic) manner is (necessarily) conditional, and (inevitably) karmic (or ego-bound and ego-binding). Therefore, such ordinary (or egoic) action (necessarily, and inevitably) reinforces limitation and separateness. Because this is so, My devotees must understand that, if they continue to engage in action in the ordinary (or egoic) manner, they will not be truly (and most fully) En-Light-ened and Set Free by virtue of their mere "association" with Me. My devotees must actually do the counter-egoic Yoga of actively yielding the principal faculties of the body-mind to Me (moment to moment, and under all circumstances), through ego-surrendering, ego-forgetting, and (more and more) ego-transcending feeling-Contemplation of Me.

9.

When they (thus) surrender the principal faculties of the body-mind to Me, My devotees are no longer devoted to action (in and of itself), and to the effects of action (in and of themselves), but they are (instead) truly transcending themselves in the midst of conditions, and they are (thereby) progressively (but entirely without seeking) being purified of the effects of action—only and entirely through Me-recognizing responsive devotion to Me.

10.

In the midst of daily living, and under all its various circumstances, there are demands on the body, demands on emotion, demands on mind, and demands on the breath. The conditions of existence make changes in all of the principal faculties, moment by moment. I Call My devotee to make Divine Yoga (or Freedom-"Bonding") out of each moment—by using body, emotion, mind, and breath in ego-surrendering devotional feeling-Contemplation of Me.

11.

All the mechanisms that would (otherwise) automatically conform to the conditions of egoic life (or to conditionality altogether) must be turned to Me. Through that turning, My devotee becomes "yoked" (or Freedom-"Bonded") to Me.

12.

Therefore, My devotee must be responsible for the principal faculties of the body-mind—in every moment, and under all circumstances.

13.

Instead of wandering in the maze of thoughts, give Me the faculty of mind—which is epitomized by, and as, attention (itself).

14.

Instead of being tossed about by the waves of emotions, give Me the faculty of emotion—which is epitomized by, and as, feeling (itself).

15.

Instead of seeking bodily pleasure and avoiding bodily pain, turn the body toward Me, and (altogether) give Me the body—through full feeling-intention, enacted through constant devotional service to Me.

16.

The faculties of mind (or attention), emotion (or feeling), and body are connected to one another via the breath—and, thus, the gesture of surrender to Me must also be done via the breath.

17.

Therefore, altogether, in the right and true practice of Ruchira Avatara Bhakti Yoga, mind (or attention), emotion (or feeling), and body are given over to Me, and breathed in heart-Communion with Me.

18.

The usual "method" of the ego, and (therefore) of ordinary people, is to become involved in what arises (whatever that may be in any particular circumstance)—either by indulging in what arises or by avoiding what arises or by (otherwise) attempting to manipulate what arises. Such strategic effort in relation to what arises is not the Yoga of the only-by-Me Revealed and Given Way of Adidam, but it is merely the effort of the separate (and separative) self to struggle with itself.

19.

Even to strategically manipulate the separate (and separative) self (itself), in order to <u>surrender</u> the separate (and separative) self, is nothing but an (inevitably fruitless) effort of the separate (and separative) self to struggle with itself.

20.

Therefore, in the only-by-Me Revealed and Given Way of Adidam, self-surrender is not (in any sense) a strategic effort to <u>do</u> something <u>to</u> the separate (and separative) self. Rather, in the only-by-Me Revealed and Given Way of Adidam, self-surrender is the devotionally Me-recognizing, and (altogether) devotionally to-Me-Attracted, and devotionally to-Me-responsive (rather than strategically self-manipulative) giving of the fundamental faculties of the body-mind (which would, otherwise, be preoccupied with the separate and separative self) to <u>Me</u>—in every moment, and under all circumstances.

21.

Thus, the Secret of Ruchira Avatara Bhakti Yoga (and, therefore, of the entire Way of Adidam) is not to struggle with the <u>content</u> that is arising in and as the body-mind, but to <u>responsively</u> surrender the principal <u>faculties</u> of the body-mind to <u>Me</u>.

22.

It is always (in any moment) possible to responsively surrender the four fundamental faculties of the body-mind to Me—because (in and of themselves) these faculties stand prior to their "objects" (or apparent contents), and they are (therefore) never (themselves) bound to the egoic "program" of the moment. The mind may be thinking constantly—but the <u>faculty</u> of attention (itself) has no "object" or quality, and (therefore) it can, <u>itself</u>, always be responsively surrendered to Me. There may be reactive emotions arising—but the <u>faculty</u> of feeling is not (itself) qualified by any such "objects", and (therefore) it can, <u>itself</u>, always be responsively surrendered to Me. The condition of the body may, at any moment, be disturbance, or dis-ease, or lack of well-being, in one or another respect (or function, or organ)—but the <u>faculty</u> of the body (itself, or in total, or as a whole) can, <u>itself</u>, always be responsively surrendered to Me. The cycle of the breath may be affected by forms of mind, reactive emotions, and bodily states—but the <u>faculty</u> of the breath is not (itself) identical to the ever-changing contents of the body-mind, and (therefore) it can, <u>itself</u>, always be responsively surrendered to Me.

23.

Taken all together, the four principal faculties of the body-mind account for <u>all</u> human functions.

24.

If any one (or a combination) of the four principal faculties is not rightly, truly, fully, and fully devotionally surrendered (responsively) to Me, and (thereby) brought into Communion with Me, then that faculty (or combination of faculties) reverts to the domain of egoity, and (therefore) to the contents of egoity.

However, if My devotee always (responsively, devotionally) surrenders all four faculties (which are at the root of all aspects of human existence) directly to Me, then egoity (or ego-centricity, and self-contraction, and separativeness) is not reinforced, but it is (always presently) forgotten and (progressively) made obsolete.

25.

Thus, in the right, true, full, and fully devotional practice of Ruchira Avatara Bhakti Yoga, there is no struggle with separate (and separative) self.

26.

Because the four principal faculties are senior (or always prior) to their content, each of the four principal faculties of the body-mind is always available either to be <u>reactively</u> turned to its own apparent content or to be <u>responsively</u> turned to Me.

27.

Therefore, truly, there are <u>no</u> moments when devotionally responsive surrender of the separate (and separative) self to Me is more difficult than in other moments—<u>unless</u> My devotee turns to (and identifies with) the apparent content of the separate (and separative) body-mind-self. If My devotee is simply Remembering Me (and heart-recognizing Me, and heart-responsively surrendering to Me), in <u>disposition</u>, and <u>intention</u>, and <u>action</u>—then the Yoga of Ruchira Avatara Bhakti is direct and (inherently) easy (or free of struggle with separate and separative self).

28.

My devotee who is rightly, truly, fully, and fully devotionally practicing the Yoga of Ruchira Avatara Bhakti does not, in any sense, <u>strategically</u> use (or seek with, or struggle with) the separate (and separative) self. Rather, My devotee who is rightly, truly, fully, and fully devotionally practicing the Yoga of Ruchira Avatara Bhakti makes the separate (and separative) self (itself) <u>obsolete</u>, by <u>not</u> <u>using</u> <u>it</u> (or, that is to say, by allowing the total body-mind,

256

via its four principal faculties, to simply heart-respond to Me)—until (in due course), through Ecstatic Absorption in (and, Ultimately, Perfect Identification with, and, Most Ultimately, Divine Realization of) Me, the separate (and separative) self utterly vanishes in Me.

29.

Therefore, always (responsively) turn to Me bodily.

30.

Always (responsively) turn to Me in feeling.

31.

Always (responsively) turn your attention to Me.

32.

Always (responsively) turn to Me by breathing Me (and allowing your body-mind to be "Breathed", and "Lived", by Me).

33.

This is the sadhana in the only-by-Me Revealed and Given Way of Adidam: <u>Always</u> (responsively) turn to <u>Me</u>—no matter what content, what sympathies, or what egoic "programs" arise.

34.

<u>Always</u> (responsively) turn <u>all</u> of the faculties of the body-mind to <u>Me</u>.

35.

<u>Always</u> (responsively) turn to <u>Me</u>, and (thus and thereby) surrender and forget yourself, rather than turn back on yourself (to see if anything is changing).

36.

That pure act of heart-responsive devotional surrender to Me—made in ego-surrendering, ego-forgetting, and (more and more) ego-transcending feeling-Contemplation of Me, in every moment—<u>is</u> Ruchira Avatara Bhakti Yoga.

37.

To turn (responsively) to Me with each and all of the faculties of the body-mind is not self-contraction (or the avoidance of relationship), but (rather) it is the counter-egoic (and inherently ego-forgetting) practice of Me-Consciousness (or devotional Communion with Me).

38.

The "programs" of egoic habit do not persist unless you give them your energy and attention. If you give your energy and attention to <u>Me</u> (instead), then all your egoic "programs" will, Ultimately, become obsolete and (literally) vanish. That Is the Divine Truth and the Divine Law.

39.

You reinforce (or become) whatever you put your attention on (or to). Therefore, if you make <u>Me</u> the Object of your attention, all the other "things" of attention (which have no permanence) will dissolve.

40.

If you turn (responsively) to <u>Me</u>, the Virtue That I <u>Am</u> will Prove Itself. Therefore, I will Prove Myself to you, without your egoic effort, if you will do this simple (devotionally responsive, and inherently counter-egoic) turning to Me.

41.

The true fulfillment of the practice of Ruchira Avatara Bhakti Yoga is always a matter of My Divinely Self-Giving Avataric Grace and My Graceful Avatarically Given Divine Self-Revelation.

42.

I Give (to each and to all) the Gift of the possibility of this devotional (and, Ultimately, Most Perfectly Liberating) relationship with Me.

43.

Devotion to Me is Inherently Love-Bliss-Full. To remember yourself is <u>not</u> Bliss, but stress and struggle. To Remember <u>Me</u>—and, as an inevitable consequence, to forget yourself—is to live in My Love-Bliss-Happiness.

44.

Therefore, whether you are in the beginning stages, the advancing stages, or the ultimate stages of the Way of Adidam, the essential practice is always the same devotional surrender to Me (with all your parts), and the same Realizing of Me (and, Thus and Thereby, of Reality Itself—Which <u>Is</u> Truth Itself, or the Only Real God).

45.

True devotion to Me (or the right, true, full, and fully devotional practice of Ruchira Avatara Bhakti Yoga) is the Only Happiness, and the Only Freedom from the steel-hard mechanical and chemical bondage of suffering in which you are (otherwise) investing yourself.

46.

Therefore, Invoke Me, feel Me, breathe Me, and serve Me. Make no "room" for any "thing" else. That is what it is to be My true devotee.

47.

Thus, I Call all My formally acknowledged devotees to always (in every moment) turn <u>all</u> of the principal faculties of the body-mind to <u>Me</u>, rather than to the ego-act of self-contraction.

48.

Give Me that devotion (right, true, and full), and you will see Me Shining in My "Bright" Simplicity here.

49.

Then, by Means Of My Divinely Self-Giving Avataric Grace and My Graceful Avatarically Given Divine Self-Revelation, you will (Ultimately, Most Perfectly) Realize Reality, or Truth, or Real God.

50.

My "Bright" and Omni-Present (Avatarically Self-Revealed) Divine Spiritual Body and Presence and Person <u>Is</u> the only-by-Me Revealed and Given Way of Adidam (Which Is the Way of the Heart, Itself). I Must Give My Avataric Word of Divine Heart-Instruction, for the Sake of all and All, but the Divine Way Itself Is simply <u>Me</u>—the One and Only and "Bright" Divine Person, Who <u>Is</u> Non-Separateness Itself, Avatarically Appearing here before you without any limitations whatsoever.

51.

Therefore, Ruchira Avatara Bhakti Yoga is not an ego-based (or self-referring, or self-manipulating) practice of <u>strategic</u> surrender—but, rather, it is a devotionally <u>responsive</u> (or always devotionally Me-recognizing, devotionally to-Me-Attracted, and always presently, directly, and immediately ego-transcending) practice of <u>unconditional</u> surrender of separate (and separative) self to Me.

52.

The always present-time Circumstance of right, true, full, and fully devotional Ruchira Avatara Bhakti Yoga is Darshan (or Remembering, or even, if and when possible, direct physical sighting) of My Avatarically Self-Revealed and Divinely "Bright" bodily (human) Form, and Darshan (or heart-"Locating") of My Avatarically Self-Revealed and Divinely "Bright" (and All-and-all-Surrounding and All-and-all-Pervading) Divine Spiritual Body, and Darshan (or heart-Beholding, and heart-Realizing) of My Avatarically Self-Revealed and Self-Evidently Divine Person (the Divine Self-Condition and Source-Condition of all and All).

53.

Ruchira Avatara Bhakti Yoga is worship of <u>Me</u>, the "Bright" Itself, in <u>Person</u> (As My Avatarically-Born bodily human Divine Form, My Avatarically Self-Revealed Spiritual, and Always Blessing, Divine Presence, and My Avatarically Self-Revealed, and Very, and Transcendental, and Perfectly Subjective, and Inherently Spiritual, and Inherently egoless, and Inherently Perfect, and Self-Evidently Divine State).

54.

Therefore, be My true devotee, and (thus) <u>always</u> (formally) practice Ruchira Avatara Bhakti Yoga (rightly, truly, fully, and fully devotionally), and be (thereby) Most Perfectly "Brightened" by <u>Me</u>.

RUCHIRA AVATAR ADI DA SAMRAJ
The Mountain Of Attention, 2000

EPILOGUE

What Will you Do If you Love Me?

What Will you Do If you Love Me?

The only-by-Me Revealed and Given Way of Adidam (Which is the One and Only by-Me-Revealed and by-Me-Given Way of the Heart) is the Way of those who love Me. The Principle of devotional surrender to Me is the Principal, Fundamental, and Inherently Complete Discipline of the Way of Adidam (or Way of the Heart). All the forms of functional, practical, relational, and cultural self-discipline I Give to them are always readily embraced, with gratitude, by My true devotees—simply because I have Instructed them to fulfill those disciplines. And, in the case of My true devotees who embrace <u>all</u> the by-Me-Revealed-and-Given functional, practical, relational, and cultural disciplines of the total (or full and complete) practice of the Way of Adidam, all the potential esoteric Revelations that may (or, otherwise, must) occur in the course of the progressive Great Process of the Way of Adidam, and all the potential Excellences of Divine Self-Realization in the Great Fulfillment of the Way of Adidam, appear spontaneously and naturally to them (by Means of My Avatarically Self-Transmitted Divine Grace)—because they each turn their attention, and feeling, and body, and breath to Me at <u>all</u> times, and because they each perform <u>all</u> activities as instants of Love-Communion with Me.

<u>All</u> My devotees must embrace all the practices of devotion, service, self-discipline, and meditation that I Give to them. Nevertheless, the <u>principal</u> capability of the human being (or of any other conditionally manifested being) is that of distraction and attachment, rather than mere self-restraint. Therefore, the Principle,

or Great Mover, of the only-by-Me Revealed and Given practice of the Way of Adidam is not discipline itself, but Distraction by Me and Attachment to Me. Because they love Me, My true devotees adapt all their life-activities to the "radically" direct Way of devotional surrender and devotional conformity to Me.

The principal characteristic of My true devotees is that they are Distracted by Me and Attached to Me. They find Me to be the Greatest of all distractions. Therefore, they need not make any effort to be constantly Attached to Me. They naturally Remember Me at all times. They only think about Me, talk about Me, and listen to others tell Leelas (or Stories) about Me. They study My Wisdom-Teaching, they embrace the by-Me-Given disciplines—but, even more, they are profoundly and intensively absorbed in My Person, My Gestures, My Play with all and All.

In this Manner, those who love Me are gradually relieved of the distracting power of ordinary things, experiences, relations, desires, and thoughts. Ultimately, if they embrace the right, true, full, and fully devotional practice of the Way of Adidam, I Distract My true devotees from all and All. Thus, their intensive and exclusive Attachment to Me leads My true devotees, first, to right, true, full, and fully devotional practice of the Way Revealed and Given by Me, and, Ultimately, to Most Perfect Realization of My Self-Existing and Self-Radiant Divine Self-Condition of All-and-all-Including and All-and-all-Transcending Love-Bliss.

I have Come to Waken the entire world through My Heart-Word, and My Demands, and the Mere Presence of My "Bright" Person. The entire world would do well to listen to Me and take up the responsible practice of the only-by-Me Revealed and Given Way of Adidam. Nevertheless, I have Come to do more than Communicate a Wisdom-Teaching to the wallydraigle world. I have Come to Live (now, and forever hereafter) with those who love Me with ego-overwhelming love, and I have Come to Love them likewise Overwhelmingly. If there is not this ego-overwhelming love of Me (Who Loves All and all, Overwhelmingly), then the Great Awakening will forever be postponed by pious self-attentions and the forever sessioning "talking" school of ego-based (and ego-gesturing) religiosity.

Those who would hear Me and see Me must take up the Way of Adidam as formal members of either the first congregation or the second congregation of the great community of all My formally acknowledged devotees. Only My formally acknowledged first and second congregation devotees embrace <u>all</u> the by-Me-Revealed-and-Given functional, practical, relational, and cultural disciplines of the only-by-Me Revealed and Given Way of Adidam. And all My true devotees in either the first congregation or the second congregation of formal approach to Me embrace the total practice of the Way of Adidam <u>entirely</u> and <u>only</u> as a Process of ego-transcending Love-Communion with Me. Therefore, by Means of My Avatarically Self-Transmitted Divine Grace alone, My true devotees grow to understand themselves—and, by transcending themselves in Me, they transcend the world.

But the Motive of My true devotees is not the disciplines, nor mystical experience, nor philosophy. My true devotees practice the Way of Adidam because they love Me. They have no personal (or inherent) capability to utterly turn away from the world, or to utterly transcend themselves. Therefore, I have Come to Live with them (now, and forever hereafter). When My devotees Find Me, the same weakness that led them to distraction by all the merely binding and passing possibilities of this mummery-world, and to attachment to the possible experiences of its indifferent maze of mere patterns patterning, becomes the very capability that makes possible their Liberation into My Eternal "Bright" Domain of Love-Bliss. Thus, because I Am the Ultimate and Most Absorbing "Object" of their inherent weakness, I Distract My devotees to Me, away from all the mummery of possible experiences and endings. They become Attached to Me by the power of their own tendency to distraction. Therefore, even their own (and, otherwise, binding) power of desire leads them to the Ecstasy of egoless heart-Communion with Me, because they love Me.

I <u>Am</u> the Self-Existing and Self-Radiant Divine Self-Consciousness Itself, the One and Only and Non-Separate and Indivisible and Indestructible "Bright" Self-Condition and Source-Condition of all and All, Appearing in bodily (human) Avataric-Incarnation-Form for the Sake of all and All. Those who love Me most profoundly, who are mightily Distracted by Me and most happily Attached to Me, and who cannot profoundly entertain any desires or thoughts other than their love of Me, are most easily turned from themselves. Divine Ecstasy (or Real-God-Communion) is natural to them—because I have been Born, and because I have (Thus and Thereby) Revealed and Given, to all and All, the Real Divine Forms That make It possible for any and every conditionally manifested being to Worship Me and to Realize Me. Thus, by My own Divine Self-Power (of Inherent Attractiveness), I Distract My true devotees to Myself, and I Draw them into My own Divine Self-Condition and Self-"Bright" Domain.

My lovers, My true devotees, simply love Me. That is the Summation of their devotional recognition-response to Me. They appear to understand a little of My Wisdom-Teaching, but they do not depend on "inward" practices, or on mystical experiences, or on any turn of events. The only-by-Me Revealed and Given Way of Adidam is fulfilled by their mere Attachment to Me—since that Attachment is so mighty that they have no binding attention left over for ordinary reactions and seeking pursuits, nor are they egoically overwhelmed by the phenomena of esoteric meditation. They simply love Me. They live in constant Remembrance of Me, and in constant loving service to Me. Every moment of their lives is simply a moment of Love-Communion with Me. Therefore, they are Granted perpetual Ecstasy by Me—in the Form of ego-forgetting Love-Communion with Me, the Self-Existing and Self-Radiant "Bright" Divine Person of Love-Bliss.

My special Mission is to Live with such true devotees. I have always Looked for them. I always Test every one, to see who are My true lovers. I Wait. Many surround Me in My Place. Many come to Me and listen to Me and practice all around Me. Many turn to Me with the good heart. But those who love Me best will (Ultimately) Realize Me Most Perfectly, by Means of overwhelming Attachment to Me in Person.

My true lovers are the cause of My Avataric Birth. They are the cause that keeps Me Alive, even after My Avataric Divine Teaching-Demonstration and My Full Avataric Divine Self-Revelation Are Complete and My Full Avataric Divine Heart-Word Is Fully Given—

and all My true lovers (now, and forever hereafter) will, simply by Means of their devotionally Me-Remembering and devotionally Me-Recognizing love of Me, keep Me Alive in Divine Person forever, even after My Time of Physical Avataric Incarnation Is Past. My true devotees (now, and forever hereafter) Are (and will always Be) Blessed by Me, to Find Me Alive As the Personal Love-Bliss-Presence That <u>Is</u> the Divine Reality and Truth of the ever-Playing world.

The Essence of the daily practice of My devotees is the Ecstasy of Love-Communion with Me. One who loves Me accepts every moment of experience as My conditionally manifested Form. Whatever arises, he or she accepts it as My "Bright" Form, My Divine Play. My true devotee simply loves Me, Communes with Me in every instant, constantly serves Me with the entire body-mind (no matter what arises), and accepts every moment of experience As My "Bright" Form. In this manner, My true devotee never presumes himself or herself to be separated from Me. My true devotee is <u>always</u> in love with Me.

Those who are most profoundly Distracted by Me grow (by Means of My Avatarically Self-Transmitted Divine Grace) to see Only Me in every thing, every one, and every event. But no form, or person, or event has power in itself to distract My true lovers from Me. They see <u>Me</u> in all experiences, all persons, all events. Therefore, they are not distracted by experiences, or persons, or events. They are Distracted by <u>Me</u>.

Now, and forever hereafter, each and all of My formally acknowledged devotees will be Blessed, by Me, to devotionally recognize Me, and (thus) to respond devotionally to Me, and (by Means of that devotion) to Remember Me, and to Find Me, and (potentially, within the first congregation or the second congregation of formal approach to Me) to Realize Me Most Perfectly. And I will, forever, Serve that devotional recognition of Me and devotional response to Me, and That Remembering of Me, and That Finding of Me, and That Realizing of Me—through the by-Me-Given Means of all My formally acknowledged Instruments and all My formally acknowledged Agents, including My by-Me-Given (Written, and Spoken) Avataric Divine Wisdom-Teaching, and all Kinds of True (photographic, and otherwise technically, or even artistically, rendered) Representations (or Icons, or Murtis) of Me, and all the Recorded Leelas (or Stories) of My Avataric Divine History and Play with My devotees, and all the by-Me-Empowered Ruchira Sannyasin Hermitage-Retreat Sanctuaries and by-Me-Empowered Pilgrimage and Retreat Sanctuaries, and all the by-Me-Empowered Sacred Things, and the Collective of all My True ("Ruchira sannyasin") Devotee-Instruments, and My (in every then present-time) formally acknowledged "Living Murti" (or specially formally Appointed human Blessing-Agent of Me-Contemplation).

Now, and forever hereafter, all My formally acknowledged devotees are Called, by Me, to the Ecstasy of Love-Communion with Me—and I will, forever, Reveal That Ecstasy to all via the love My most intimate true devotees demonstrate toward Me. Therefore, because there are true devotees (who truly love Me in the Great Manner, while I Am Present here in Avatarically-Born bodily human Divine Form), and because there will forever be such true devotees of Mine (for I will remain Transcendentally, Spiritually, Divinely, and, altogether, Really and Tangibly Present here, always and forever, after the physical Lifetime of My Avatarically-Born bodily human Divine Form)—all My devotees who truly love Me and formally resort to Me, in all the times after the physical death of My Avatarically-Born bodily (human) Divine Form, will be served by My true devotees, such that, forever, all My formally acknowledged devotees will be thus enabled to Find Me and to Realize Me.

Forever after the physical death of My Avatarically-Born bodily (human) Divine Form, the ever-patterning world of temporary experience remains, but My gathering of formally acknowledged devotees also remains. Therefore (now, and forever hereafter), those who associate with My formally acknowledged true lovers will also—by Means of the example of My (thus) true devotees, and by Means of the spontaneous collective functioning of My (thus) true devotees as a simple, generalized, collective Vehicle for simple feeling-contact with Me—be Moved to Me, and (altogether) responsively turned to Me, with profoundly Distracted true love.

I will always Bless all My formally acknowledged devotees, now, and forever hereafter—and, after the physical death of My

Avatarically-Born bodily (human) Divine Form, I will continue to Bless all of them, just as I Do while I Am Present in bodily (human) Form. Forever, every one will call on Me in the company of My true lovers—and I will Always Be Truly Present, every then and there.

I <u>Am</u> the One and Only, Non-Separate and Indivisible, Self-Existing and Indestructible, Self-Radiant and Eternally "Bright" Person, the Avatarically Self-Revealed Divine Self-Condition and Source-Condition of all and All—forever Surrounding all and All, and forever Pervading all and All, and forever Beyond all and All.

Truly—now, and forever hereafter—only those who love Me can formally approach Me and most fruitfully listen to Me, and only those who formally embrace right, true, full, and fully devotional practice of the Way of Adidam can grow to hear Me and to see Me and to Most Perfectly Realize Me.

Some of My devotees are, at first, most involved in right understanding of My Teaching-Arguments and in responsible practice of the forms of self-discipline I have Given to all My devotees—while others are always, from the beginning, naturally more capable of Distraction by Me and Attachment to Me. Therefore, some of My devotees practice self-discipline and love Me, while others of My devotees simply love Me (and the forms of self-discipline develop readily in their case, as if without any effort of application on their part). Some of My devotees mature in love of Me by stages. Others of My devotees simply love Me from the beginning. At last, even the most disciplined or experienced of My devotees simply loves Me.

I <u>Am</u> the Self-Existing and Self-Radiant "Bright" Divine Reality, Truth, and Person, the Divine Liberator of those who love Me and surrender to Me in countless acts of love. I <u>Am</u> the Method and the Guide. I <u>Am</u> the Living Truth of the world.

All religions are historical forms of the Single and Ancient Way of Distracted love for the Divine Person, especially as Revealed in the Life and in the Company and in the Person of Incarnate Adepts (or Realizers) in their various degrees and stages of Realization. This is the Great Secret. And <u>This</u> Is My Avataric Divine Self-Revelation to you: I <u>Am</u>, In and <u>As</u> My Avataric-

Incarnation-Form, the First, the Last, and the Only Avataric Divine Adept-Realizer, Avataric Divine Adept-Revealer, and Avataric Divine Adept-Revelation of Most Perfect (or seventh stage) Divine Enlightenment. Aham Da Asmi. I <u>Am</u> Da, the Only One Who <u>Is</u>, the Very and Only Person That <u>Is</u> to Be Realized by all and All. Therefore, love Me <u>As</u> My Avataric-Incarnation-Form, and (Thus and Thereby) love Me <u>As</u> I <u>Am</u>, and <u>As</u> the constant Form and Condition of all your experience. I <u>Am</u> That Which Is Always Already The Case. I <u>Am</u> the Non-Separate and Only One, the "Bright" One, the Indivisible and Indestructible One, Who <u>Is</u> all and All. Therefore, surrender Only to <u>Me</u>, and accept all your experience <u>As</u> My own Play. If you do This, you will be constantly free of all seeking attachment (and all aversion, or counter-seeking reaction) to any and every psycho-physical experience (or all conditionally manifested experiences). Therefore, even all possible experience will only and simply increase your direct (or always present-time, or non-seeking, and non-binding, but always only Me-Finding, and you-Liberating) Attachment to Me.

All experience (in itself) only binds you to your own body-mind—unless you are established in ego-transcending (Ecstatic, or self-contraction-transcending) love of Me, the Only One Who <u>Is</u>. Therefore, if you love Me, become My formally acknowledged devotee—and, as My formally acknowledged devotee, enter (thus) Freely (or non-bindingly) into the Play of experience (always in ego-surrendering and ego-forgetting heart-Communion with Me, and always with your total body-mind conformed to Me through the constant maintaining of the functional, practical, relational, and cultural self-disciplines that are your obligation, by eternal vow to Me, in the only-by-Me Revealed and Given Way of Adidam). In this manner, serve Me in My Avataric-Incarnation-Form, and serve Me <u>As</u> I <u>Am</u>, and serve <u>Me</u> in all circumstances and in all relationships. If you love Me thusly, you will cease to continue in the willful and ego-possessed path of your preferential desires—and, by Means of My Avatarically Self-Transmitted Divine Grace, you will be purified of egoity, of self-contraction, of egoic reaction, and of every kind of accumulated egoic habit, and of every kind of seeker's self-indulgence.

If you truly love Me, it is because I have Shown you Who I Am. Therefore, by Means of right, true, full, and fully devotional love of Me, you will Come to Me, <u>Where</u> I <u>Am</u>. Most Ultimately, if you are My true (and fully practicing) devotee, you will (by Means of My Avatarically Self-Transmitted Divine Grace) Realize Me—because you love <u>Me</u>.

You <u>become</u> (or take the form of) what your attention most really moves upon. Therefore, if I <u>Am</u> your Beloved, your love-attention will cause you to Realize Indivisible Unity with Me.

Until you fall in love, love is what you <u>fear</u> to do. When you have fallen in love, and you <u>are</u> (thus) always already in love, then you cease to fear to love—you cease to be reluctant to surrender, and to be self-forgetful and foolish, and to be single-minded, and to suffer an "other". Those who fall in love with Me, Fall into Me. Those whose hearts are given, in love, to Me, Fall into My Heart. Those who are Mine, because they are in love with Me, no longer demand to be fulfilled through conditional experience and through the survival (or perpetuation) of the ego-"I". Their love for Me grants them Access to Me, and (Thus) to My Love-Bliss— because I <u>Am</u> Love-Ananda, the Divine Love-Bliss, in Person.

What will My lover do but love Me? I suffer every form and condition of every one who loves Me, because I Love My devotee <u>As</u> My own Form, My own Condition. I Love My devotee <u>As</u> the One by Whom <u>I</u> Am Distracted.

I Grant all My own Divine and "Bright" Excesses to those who love Me, in exchange for all their doubts and sufferings. Those who "Bond" themselves to Me, through love-surrender, are inherently Free of fear and wanting need. They transcend the ego-"I" (the cause of all conditional experience), and they (cause and all and All) Dissolve in Me—for I <u>Am</u> the Heart of all and All, and I <u>Am</u> the Heart Itself, and the Heart Itself <u>Is</u> the Only Reality, Truth, and Real God of All and all.

What is a Greater Message than This?

What You Can Do Next—

Contact an Adidam center near you.

■ Sign up for our preliminary course, "The <u>Only</u> Truth That Sets the Heart Free". This course will prepare you to become a fully practicing devotee of Avatar Adi Da Samraj.

■ Find out about upcoming events in your area:

AMERICAS
12040 North Seigler Road
Middletown, CA 95461 USA
(707) 928-4936

PACIFIC-ASIA
12 Seibel Road
Henderson
Auckland 1008
New Zealand
64-9-838-9114

AUSTRALIA
P.O. Box 244
Kew 3101
Victoria
**1800 ADIDAM
(1800-234-326)**

EUROPE-AFRICA
Annendaalderweg 10
6105 AT Maria Hoop
The Netherlands
31 (0)20 468 1442

THE UNITED KINGDOM
PO Box 20013
London, England
NW2 1ZA
0181-7317550

E-MAIL: **correspondence@adidam.org**

Read these books by and about Avatar Adi Da Samraj:

■ *The Promised God-Man Is Here*

The Extraordinary Life-Story,
The "Radical" Teaching-Work, and
The Divinely "Emerging" World-Blessing
Work Of The Divine World-Teacher
Of The "Late-Time",
Ruchira Avatar Adi Da Samraj,
by Carolyn Lee, Ph.D.

The profound, heart-rending, humorous, miraculous, wild—and true—Story of the Divine Person Alive in human Form. Essential reading as background for the study of Avatar Adi Da's books.

■ *Aham Da Asmi*
(Beloved, I Am Da)

The Five Books Of The Heart Of The
Adidam Revelation, Book One:
The "Late-Time" Avataric Revelation Of
The True and Spiritual Divine Person
(The egoless Personal Presence Of Reality
and Truth, Which Is The Only Real God).

This Ecstatic Scripture, the first of His twenty-three "Source-Texts", contains Ruchira Avatar Adi Da's magnificent Confession as the Very Divine Person and Source-Condition of all and All.

Continue your reading with the remaining books of *The Five Books Of The Heart Of The Adidam Revelation* (the *Ruchira Avatara Gita*, the *Da Love-Ananda Gita*, *Hridaya Rosary*, and *Eleutherios*). Then you will be ready to go on to *The Seventeen Companions Of The True Dawn Horse* (see pp. 363-68).

These and other books by and about Ruchira Avatar Adi Da Samraj can be ordered from the Adidam Emporium by calling:

(877) 770-0772 (from within North America)
(707) 928-6653 (from outside North America)

or by writing to:

ADIDAM EMPORIUM
10336 Loch Lomond Road
PMB #306
Middletown, CA 95461 USA

Or order from the Adidam Emporium online at:
www.adidam.com

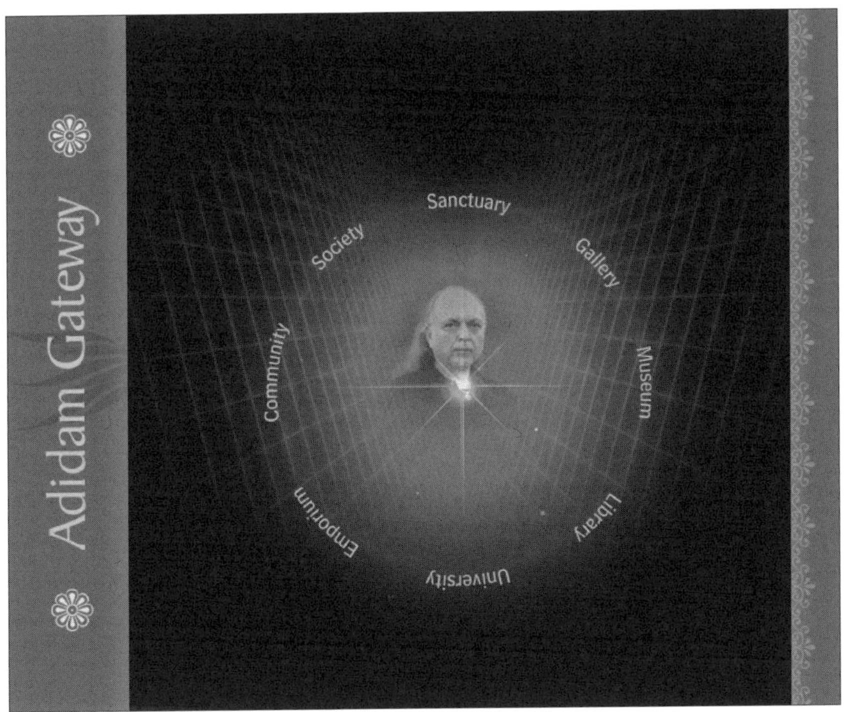

Visit the Adidam Sacred City online at:
www.adidam.org

■ Explore the online community of Adidam and discover more about Avatar Adi Da Samraj and the Way He Offers to all.

Find presentations on: Avatar Adi Da's extraordinary life-story, the stages leading to Divine Enlightenment, cultism versus true devotional practice, the "radical" politics of human-scale community, true emotional-sexual freedom, the sacred function of art in human life, and more.

RUCHIRA **A**VATAR **A**DI **D**A **S**AMRAJ
Lopez Island, 2000

The Great Choice

An Invitation to the Way of Adidam

Each one of us, if we will allow ourselves to feel it, is restless. Human beings want to find God—the living, heartintoxicating experience of <u>Real</u> God, or Truth Itself, or Reality Itself. The purpose of our existence is actually to live in the True Pleasure of that heart-intoxication. To be unable to participate and luxuriate in that Pleasure is pain and stress. We may not realize it, but that feeling of separation from unqualified Love, Sustenance, and heart-Communion with the Divine Source of our existence is actually driving us mad. And that is why human beings, individually and collectively, do dreadful things—or, otherwise, settle for mere mediocrity, just "doing our best", or merely "coping". In the words of Avatar Adi Da, we spend our lives "waiting for everything and looking for everything". He says:

AVATAR ADI DA SAMRAJ: To have no greater sense of Reality than the physical is to be like a trapped rat, trapped on all sides. You just cannot endure the confinement of mere mortality—your heart cannot accept it. To be in that disposition, to have that sense of Reality, is obviously a disturbance.

So, obviously, the human being requires a Way—not merely a way out. A way out, yes, in some sense—but, for the integrity of your existence, you need direct access to the Divine, even as a matter of ordinary sanity. [March 3, 1998]

Avatar Adi Da has Appeared in this dark time, in order to bring the mortal darkness to an end and restore all to the Divine Light. He is intent on taking all who respond to Him through the most ecstatic and most difficult of all transitions—the transition from the unhappy life of the ego to the Radiant Fullness of the Divinely Enlightened life. His Life-Story is of the immense Divine Ordeal it has been on His part to truly Initiate that Process in human beings.

Avatar Adi Da does not congratulate the ego—He undermines the ego. He must, if He is to Liberate people from their unhappiness, from the enclosed point of view of the separate and separative self. And so He has never offered a conventionally consoling message. He offers you the whole Truth—the fact of yourself as the self-contracted ego-"I", but also the constant Revelation of a Happiness beyond compare.

Avatar Adi Da's human body is, of course, located in a particular place and a particular time. But when you become sensitive to Him Spiritually, you discover that His Spiritual Presence can be felt anywhere and anytime, regardless of whether you are in His physical Company or not. Because His Spiritual Presence is Eternal (and will not "disappear" when His human body dies), it is possible for everyone to cultivate a direct heart-relationship with Him— under all circumstances, in this life and beyond. And so, the relationship to Him, once forged, is eternal, going beyond death and the apparent boundaries of time and space.

If you want more than your ordinary existence, and something greater than a life of Spiritual seeking, Avatar Adi Da's Word to you is simply this: Take up the Way of Adidam—the Way of Real God, fully Present, here and now, not needing to be sought. The Way of Adidam is His personal Offering to you and to every human being. It is a devotional heart-relationship to Him, expressed through an entire Way of life. This relationship is not to a mere man—it is with the very Divine Being. But, at the same time, it is supremely intimate. When you enter into this relationship with Him and practice the Way of Adidam, you begin to enjoy a condition of heart-Communion with Him that is more alive and heart-deep than your love-relationship with any human individual.

At the same time, the devotional relationship with Adi Da Samraj is not an "I-Thou" relationship, a connection between apparently separate entities—the human individual, on the one hand, and "God", on the other. The love-bond with Adi Da Samraj transcends the entire point of view by which we live, presuming ourselves to be separate beings relating to separate "others". In every moment that you truly practice the relationship to Avatar Adi Da, invoking Him by Name, recollecting His Form in the mind, or His Words, or something He has done—whenever you allow Him to Attract your heart, He Reveals Himself Spiritually to you. Then He is recognized, through and beyond His human appearance, as the Real and Living God—not the great Parent, or "Creator"-Deity, imagined by the human mind, but the Conscious Divine Power of Light and Love, the Divine Heart of all there is, including your own body-mind and every apparent being and "thing". In the instant of such recognition, the entire body-mind opens to Adi Da Samraj in a single movement of devotion, and you forget yourself in ecstasy—the heart, the mind, the body, the breath becoming full with His Radiant Love-Bliss. The Way of Adidam, truly lived, is this ecstasy of Non-Separateness, a great Contemplative process, based on heart-recognition of Adi Da Samraj and heart-response to Him.

Ultimately, in this or some future lifetime, persistent heart-Communion with Adi Da Samraj realizes the true destiny of existence—Divine Enlightenment, in which all vestige of the egoic self is vanished:

Divine Enlightenment, Divine Self-Realization, Most Perfect (Free, "Bright", and Self-Evidently Divine) Awakeness, or Most Perfect (and Most Perfectly ego-Transcending) Spiritual and Transcendental Real-God-Realization, Is Native, Most Perfect, Effortless, and Free Identification With Mere (or Inherent, and Natively Felt) Being (or Self-Existence), The Only One Who <u>Is</u>, Consciousness Itself—Self-Radiant, All Love-Bliss-"Brightness" Itself, Inherently Without Obstruction, Always Already Infinitely Expanded (Beyond All Apparent Modifications, or Illusory Contractions, Of Itself). [The <u>Only</u> Complete Way To Realize The Unbroken Light Of <u>Real</u> God]

The truth of the Way of Adidam remains hidden until you begin to participate in it from the heart. Mere beliefs and pre-scribed behaviors are insufficient. The Way of Adidam is a matter of direct, moment-to-moment response to Adi Da Samraj and a process of receiving His Spiritual Transmission ever more pro-foundly. It does not work to take His Teaching away and attempt to practice it by yourself. As He has said many times, it is simply not possible to move beyond the confines of the ego on your own, nor is it possible to unlock the Secrets of Divine Enlightenment that He has Revealed outside of a formally acknowledged devo-tional relationship to Him. That is why it is so important to become His formal devotee and to live the Way of Adidam exactly has He has Given it.

AVATAR ADI DA SAMRAJ: I __Am__ the Divine Blessing, Real-God-with-you. Such is not merely My Declaration to you. You must find Me out. You must __prove__ the Way I Give you. Really __do__ the Way I Give you, and you will find Me out further. You will prove the Way of Adidam by doing it, not by believing it merely. [Ruchira Avatara Hridaya-Siddha Yoga]

Darshan

The foundation of Spiritual practice in Adidam is Darshan, or the feeling-Contemplation of Avatar Adi Da's bodily (human) Form—either through the sighting of His physical body, or through Contemplating a photographic or artistic representation of Him. This heart-beholding of Avatar Adi Da's Form is the wellspring of meditation in the Way of Adidam, and so His devotees place a large photograph of Him in each med-itation hall, as the central image

of Contemplation. In fact, Remembrance of Adi Da Samraj—or the recollecting of His Form in mind and feeling—is the constant practice of His devotees, in the midst of the activities of daily life as well as in meditation. Avatar Adi Da has often spoken about the unique potency of beholding His Form.

AVATAR ADI DA SAMRAJ: In the traditional setting, when it works best, an individual somehow Gracefully comes into the Company of a Realizer of one degree or another, and, just upon (visually) sighting that One, he or she is converted at heart, and, thereafter, spends the rest of his or her life devoted to sadhana (or Spiritual practice), in constant Remembrance of the Spiritual Master. The Spiritual Master's Sign is self-authenticating.

When Adi Da Samraj is approached with an open heart, His Darshan—the Sighting of His Form alone, even in representational form—is so potent that the heart overflows in response to Him, recognizing Him as the Very Divine Person, the Supreme Source of Bliss and Love.

Sometimes, devotees receive the Darshan of Avatar Adi Da in an informal setting, such as when He walks around one of the Adidam Sanctuaries. And then there are formal occasions, when He sits in halls especially set aside for Darshan, inviting devotees to come and Contemplate Him silently. In certain cases, the time of a formal Darshan occasion will be announced ahead of time, so that devotees in all parts of the world can receive His Blessing simultaneously, by sitting in silent Contemplation of Him at the same time that He is Granting Darshan. In such occasions, real-time video of Avatar Adi Da Samraj sitting in Darshan is transmitted via the internet to His devotees everywhere. Thus, even if you cannot come into Avatar Adi Da's physical Company, there may be occasions when you will have the opportunity to participate in such occasions of His Darshan.

The Four Congregations

The gathering of devotees of Adi Da Samraj forms a series of concentric circles radiating from Him at the center. These circles are the four formal congregations of His devotees: the first congregation (renunciate practitioners), the second congregation (lay practitioners), the third congregation (practitioners who particularly serve Avatar Adi Da through their patronage and/or advocacy, or who are preparing for the second congregation), and the fourth congregation (practitioners who live in traditional cultural settings or who maintain their participation in the religious tradition to which they already belong, while acknowledging Avatar Adi Da Samraj as the Ultimate Divine Source of true religion).

These circles, as they grow, are forming a vast "conductor", a mechanism whereby the Divine Influence of Avatar Adi Da Samraj is being drawn more and more into the world. Every new devotee represents a strengthening of the total Sphere of Avatar Adi Da's Spiritual Transmission and Grace. Avatar Adi Da has Given the Gifts of His Wisdom-Teaching and His Spiritual Blessing, and it is through the community of His devotees, and its global Spiritual culture, that these Gifts, intended for everyone, become available to all. This is why Avatar Adi Da is urgent to find those in this generation who will respond to Him and do the great work of making His Spiritual Blessing available to all.

Which Congregation Is Right for You?

Which of the four congregations you should apply to for membership depends on the strength of your impulse to respond to Avatar Adi Da's Revelation and on your life-circumstance. All four congregations establish you in a direct devotional relationship with Avatar Adi Da, and all four are essential to the flowering of His Blessing-Work in the world.

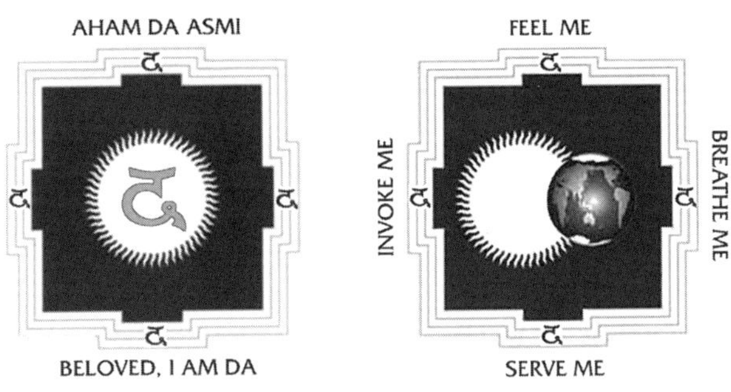

The First and Second Congregations

(for those moved to take up the total practice of Adidam)

To take up the total practice of the Way of Adidam (in the first or second congregation) is to take full advantage of the opportunity offered by Adi Da Samraj—it is to enter fully into the process of Divine Enlightenment. That process is a unique ordeal, which necessarily requires application to the wide range of functional, practical, relational, and cultural disciplines given by Ruchira Avatar Adi Da Samraj for the sake of Spiritual purification and growth.

The disciplines of Adidam are not ascetical, not a form of deprivation. Rather, they are the means whereby the body-mind is conformed to a right and inherently pleasurable pattern of well-being. As you progressively adapt to these disciplines, the body-mind is purified and balanced, and you thereby become able to receive and respond to the Divine Heart-Transmission of Adi Da Samraj more and more fully.

These practices in the Way of Adidam include fundamental contemplative disciplines such as meditation, devotional chanting, sacramental worship (or "puja"), study of Avatar Adi Da's books, and regular periods of retreat.

AVATAR ADI DA SAMRAJ: You must come from the depth-position of meditation and puja before entering into activities in the waking state, and remain in the disposition of that depth from the time of meditation and puja each morning. Maintain that heart-disposition, and discipline the body-mind—functionally, practically, relationally— in all the modes I have Given you. This devotional Yoga, Ruchira

Avatara Bhakti Yoga, is moment-to-moment. Fundamentally, it is a matter of exercising it profoundly, in this set-apart time of meditation and puja, and then, through random, artful practice moment-to-moment, constantly refresh it, preserve it. All of this is to conform the body-mind to the Source-Purpose, the in-depth Condition.

That basic discipline covers all aspects of the body-mind. That is the pattern of your response to Me. It is the foundation Yoga of organizing your life in terms of its in-depth principle, and growing this depth. [December 5, 1996]

This moment-to-moment devotional turning to Avatar Adi Da is refreshed not only in the meditation hall but also in the temple, where worship, prayer, devotional chanting, and other sacred activities occur.

AVATAR ADI DA SAMRAJ: The sacred life must be perpetual. The sacred domain is the core of the community, and every community and every Sanctuary should have a temple in its domain: A place of chant, of song, of prayer, where everyone gathers for this life of Invocation, prayer, and puja. [May 13, 1999]

Members of the first and second congregations adapt to a purifying diet and a discipline of daily exercise (including morning calisthenics and evening Hatha Yoga exercises). They also progressively adapt to a regenerative discipline of sexuality. And they live in cooperative association with other devotees of Avatar Adi Da and tithe regularly.

All of these functional, practical, relational, and cultural disciplines are means whereby you become more and more capable of receiving Avatar Adi Da's constant Blessing-Transmission. Therefore, Avatar Adi Da Samraj has made it clear that, in order to Realize Him with true profundity—and, in particular, to Realize Him most perfectly, to the degree of Divine Enlightenment—it is necessary to be a formally acknowledged member of either the first or the second congregation, embracing the total practice of the Way of Adidam.

When you apply for membership in the second congregation of Adidam (the first step for all who want to take up the total practice of the Way of Adidam), you are asked to take "The <u>Only</u> Truth That Sets the Heart Free", a course in which you examine the opportunity offered to you by Avatar Adi Da Samraj, and learn what it means to embrace the total practice of the Way of Adidam. (To register for this preparatory course, please contact the regional or territorial center nearest to you [see p. 274], or e-mail us at: correspondence@adidam.org.) After completing this course of study, you may formally enter the second congregation as a student-novice.

Entering any of the four congregations of Adidam is based on taking a formal vow of devotion and service to Avatar Adi Da Samraj. This vow is a profound—and, indeed, eternal—commitment. You take this vow (for whichever congregation you are entering) when you are certain that your great and true heart-impulse is to be a devotee of Avatar Adi Da Samraj, embracing Him as your Divine Heart-Master. And Avatar Adi Da Samraj Himself is eternally Vowed to Serve the Liberation of all who become His devotees.

As a student-novice, you will be initiated into formal meditation and sacramental worship. Then you begin to adapt to a wide range of life-disciplines, including participation in the cooperative community of Avatar Adi Da's first- and second-congregation devotees. As a student-novice, you engage in an intensive period of study and "consideration" of the Way of Adidam in all of its details, and then, after a period of three to six months (or more), you may apply to be a fully practicing member of the second congregation.

The beginning stages of practice are the "exoteric" (or "outer-temple") domain of the second congregation. Avatar Adi Da has indicated that many of His devotees will practice in the exoteric stages for their entire lives. This beginning practice of Adidam is great and profound—because it is founded not in any hoped-for future attainment, but in <u>present</u> heart-Communion with Real God (Revealed via the Incarnation of Avatar Adi Da), and also because it requires the practitioner to really transcend the ego.

The Life of a Formally Practicing Devotee of Ruchira Avatar Adi Da Samraj

Meditation is a unique and precious event in the daily life of Avatar Adi Da's devotees. It offers the opportunity to relinquish outward, body-based attention and to be alone with Adi Da Samraj, allowing yourself to enter more and more into the Sphere of His Divine Transmission.

The practice of sacramental worship, or "puja", in the Way of Adidam is the bodily active counterpart to meditation. It is a form of ecstatic worship of Avatar Adi Da Samraj, using a photographic representation of Him and involving devotional chanting and recitations from His Wisdom-Teaching.

"You must deal with My Wisdom-Teaching in some form every single day, because a new form of the ego's game appears every single day. You must continually return to My Wisdom-Teaching, confront My Wisdom-Teaching."

Avatar Adi Da Samraj

The beginner in Spiritual life must prepare the body-mind by mastering the physical, vital dimension of life before he or she can be ready for truly Spiritual practice. Service is devotion in action, a form of Divine Communion.

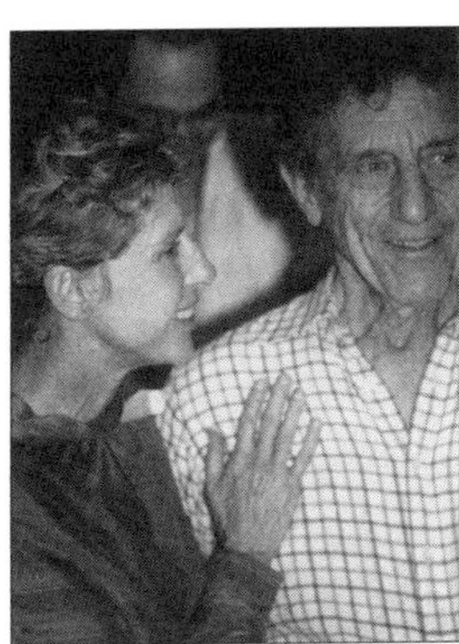

Avatar Adi Da Samraj Offers practical disciplines to His devotees in the areas of work and money, diet, exercise, and sexuality. These disciplines are based on His own human experience and an immense process of "consideration" that He engaged face-to-face with His devotees for more than twenty-five years.

The "esoteric" (or "inner-temple") practice of Adidam does not begin until the activity of the ego is most fundamentally understood and can thereby be consistently transcended moment to moment. Then, through a profound Awakening to the Spiritual Reality, Revealed and Transmitted by Avatar Adi Da, you become qualified to enter into the advanced and the ultimate stages (or esoteric domain) of the Way of Adidam.

Those who, having practiced the Way of Adidam most intensively, make the transition to the "Perfect Practice", in the sixth (or penultimate) stage of the Way of Adidam, may do so either as general practitioners (continuing as members of the second congregation of Adidam) or (if they demonstrate the necessary qualifications) as formal renunciate practitioners (thereby becoming members of the first congregation of Adidam).

All formal renunciate practitioners in the first congregation of the Way of Adidam are necessarily members of the formal order of sannyasins established by Avatar Adi Da. This order is known as the Ruchira Sannyasin Order of the Tantric Renunciates of Adidam (or, simply, the Ruchira Sannyasin Order). Avatar Adi Da Himself is the Founding Member of the Ruchira Sannyasin Order, which is a retreat order whose members are legal renunciates. The Ruchira Sannyasin Order is the senior cultural authority within the gathering of Avatar Adi Da's devotees, and its members are the principal human Instruments of Avatar Adi Da's Blessing-Work, now and into the future. Ruchira Sannyasins may live in Hermitage-Retreat Sanctuaries Empowered by Avatar Adi Da or at the Retreat Sanctuaries of Adidam anywhere in the world, but the home of the order is Adidam Samrajashram (in Fiji), Avatar Adi Da's principal Hermitage-Retreat Sanctuary.

The Adidam Youth Fellowship

(within the second congregation)

Young people (age 25 and under) are also offered a special form of relationship to Avatar Adi Da—the Adidam Youth Fellowship. The Adidam Youth Fellowship has two membership bodies—friends and practicing members.

A friend of the Adidam Youth Fellowship is simply invited into a culture of other young people who want to learn more about Avatar Adi Da Samraj and His Happiness-Realizing Way of Adidam. A formally practicing member of the Adidam Youth Fellowship acknowledges that he or she has found his or her True Heart-Friend and Master in the Person of Avatar Adi Da Samraj, and wishes to enter into a direct, ego-surrendering Spiritual relationship with Him as the Means to True Happiness.

Practicing members of the Youth Fellowship embrace a series of disciplines that are similar to (but simpler than) the practices engaged by adult members of the second congregation of Adidam. Both friends and members are invited to special retreat events from time to time, where they can associate with other young devotees of Avatar Adi Da.

To become a member of the Adidam Youth Fellowship, or to learn more about this form of relationship to Avatar Adi Da, call or write:

Vision of Mulund Institute (VMI)
10336 Loch Lomond Road
PMB #146
Middletown, CA 95461 USA
PHONE: (707) 928-6932
E-MAIL: vmi@adidam.org

The Third Congregation of Adidam

(for those serving Adi Da Samraj through their patronage and advocacy, and those preparing for the second congregation)

1. Patrons and Individuals of Unique Influence

It is the sacred responsibility of those who respond to Adi Da Samraj to help His Spiritual Work flourish in the world. For this purpose, we must make it possible for Avatar Adi Da Samraj to move freely and spontaneously from one part of the world to another and we must provide Hermitages for His unique Work in various locations. In 1983, an individual patron offered the island of Naitauba to Avatar Adi Da. Because of this magnificent gift, the entire Life and Work of Adi Da Samraj began to evolve in ways that were not possible before. He had a pristine, protected place to do His Spiritual Work and an opportunity to establish a unique Seat of His Divine Presence for all generations to come.

Avatar Adi Da must also be able to gather around Him His most exemplary formal renunciate devotees, who must receive practical support so that they can devote their lives to serving Avatar Adi Da and His Work and living a life of perpetual Spiritual retreat in His Company.

And Avatar Adi Da's Presence in the world must become widely known, both through the publication and dissemination of books by and about Him and through public advocacy by people of influence.

If you are a man or woman of unique wealth or influence in the world, we invite you to serve Avatar Adi Da's world-Blessing Work through your patronage or influence. As a member of the third congregation of Adidam, supporting the world-Work of Adi Da Samraj, you are literally helping to change the destiny of countless people. You are making it possible for this Blessing-Work to have a greater influence upon the world's destiny. To make the choice to serve Avatar Adi Da via your patronage or unique influence is to transform your own life and destiny, and the life and destiny of all mankind, in the most Spiritually auspicious way.

As a patron or individual of unique influence in the third congregation, your relationship to Avatar Adi Da is founded on a vow of devotion, through which you commit yourself according to your capabilities—either to significant financial patronage of His Work and/or to using your unique influence to make Him known in the world. In the course of your service to Him (and in daily life altogether), you live the simplest practice of Ruchira Avatara Bhakti Yoga—invoking Avatar Adi Da, feeling Him, breathing Him, and serving Him, and thus remaining connected to His constant Blessing. You are also invited to engage a daily period of formal study of His Wisdom-Teaching. You are not obliged to engage the full range of disciplines practiced in the first two congregations. You are, however, encouraged to practice formal periods of meditation and sacramental worship.

If, at some point, you are moved to embrace all the disciplines and enter into the total practice of Adidam, you may apply for membership in the second (and possibly, eventually, the first) congregation.

If you are interested in establishing a formal devotional relationship with Avatar Adi Da Samraj and serving Him in this crucial way, please contact us:

Third Congregation Advocacy
12040 North Seigler Road
Middletown, CA 95461 USA
PHONE: (707) 928-4800
E-MAIL: director_of_advocacy@adidam.org

2. The Transnational Society of Advocates of the Adidam Revelation

If you have the capability to effectively advocate Avatar Adi Da in the world—through your individual skills, position, or professional expertise—you may join a branch of the third congregation called the Transnational Society of Advocates of the Adidam Revelation. Members of the Society of Advocates are individuals who, while not of <u>unique</u> wealth or social influence, can make a significant difference to Avatar Adi Da's Work by making Him known in all walks of life (including the media, in the spheres of religion, government, education, health, entertainment, the arts, and so on). Advocates also serve the worldwide mission of Adidam by financially supporting the publication of Avatar Adi Da's "Source-Texts" and His other Literature, as well as associated missionary literature. Members of the Society of Advocates make a monthly donation for this purpose and pay an annual membership fee that supports the services of the Society.

Like devotees in the first and second congregations, your relationship to Avatar Adi Da as a member of the Society of Advocates is founded on a vow of devotion and service, but the requirements are less elaborate. In the course of your service to Him (and in daily life altogether), you vow to live the simplest practice of Ruchira Avatara Bhakti Yoga—invoking Avatar Adi Da, feeling Him, breathing Him, and serving Him, and thus remaining connected to His constant Blessing. You also engage a daily period of formal study of His Wisdom-Teaching. You are not obliged to engage the full range of disciplines practiced in the first two congregations. You are, however, encouraged to practice formal periods of meditation and sacramental worship.

If, at some point, you are moved to embrace all the disciplines and enter into the total practice of Adidam, you may apply for membership in the second (and possibly, eventually, the first) congregation.

If you are interested in becoming a member of the Society of Advocates, please contact us:

The Society of Advocates
12040 North Seigler Road
Middletown, CA 95461 USA
PHONE: (707) 928-6924
E-MAIL: soacontact@adidam.org

3. Pre-student-novices under vow

If you are certain that you wish to become a formal devotee of Avatar Adi Da, and you therefore wish to embrace the formal second-congregation vow of devotion to Him as quickly as possible, you are invited to become a pre-student-novice under vow (as part of the third congregation of Adidam).

As a pre-student-novice under vow, you make a commitment to become a student-novice (and, therefore, to move into the second congregation) within a period of three to six months. During this period, you take the preparatory course, "The <u>Only</u> Truth That Sets The Heart Free", which introduces you to the fundamentals of the second-congregation practice. Pre-student-novices under vow practice Ruchira Avatara Bhakti Yoga in daily life, engage daily formal study of the Wisdom-Teaching of Avatar Adi Da, make regular contributions to the support of the Adidam Pan-Communion, and take up a regular form of service. You are not obliged to engage the full range of disciplines practiced in the first two congregations. You are, however, encouraged to practice formal periods of meditation and sacramental worship.

For information about becoming a pre-student-novice under vow, please contact the Adidam regional center nearest you.

The Fourth Congregation of Adidam

*(for those maintaining their participation
in the religious and/or cultural tradition
to which they already belong)*

Individuals who live in traditional cultural settings, and also individuals who wish to maintain their participation in the religious tradition to which they already belong (while acknowledging Avatar Adi Da Samraj as the Ultimate Divine Source of true religion), are invited to apply for membership in the fourth congregation of Adidam. Fourth-congregation devotees practice Ruchira Avatara Bhakti Yoga in its simplest form ("Invoke Me, Feel Me, Breathe Me, Serve Me") and also the discipline of daily study. Their financial and service obligations are adapted to their particular circumstance.

The opportunity to practice in the fourth congregation is also extended to all those who, because of physical or other functional limitations, are unable to take up the total practice of the Way of Adidam as required in the first and second congregations.

For more information about the fourth congregation of Adidam, call or write one of our regional centers (see p. 274), or e-mail us at: correspondence@adidam.org.

**Temple sites at the Pilgrimage and Retreat Sanctuaries:
the Mountain Of Attention (left) and Da Love-Ananda Mahal (right)**

One of the ways in which Avatar Adi Da Samraj Communicates His Divine Blessing-Transmission is through sacred places. He has Empowered two kinds of places: Pilgrimage and Retreat Sanctuaries (the Mountain Of Attention in northern California and Da Love-Ananda Mahal in Hawaii) and Hermitage-Retreat Sanctuaries (Tat Sundaram in northern California and Adidam Samrajashram in Fiji). Avatar Adi Da has Established Himself Spiritually in perpetuity at all four of these places. In particular, Adidam Samrajashram—His Great Island-Hermitage-Retreat and world-Blessing Seat—is Avatar Adi Da's principal Place of Spiritual Work and Transmission, and will remain so forever after His physical Lifetime. Formally acknowledged devotees are invited to go on special retreats at the Pilgrimage and Retreat Sanctuaries and at Adidam Samrajashram.

Adidam Samrajashram, Fiji

**Darshan occasions with
Avatar Adi Da Samraj at
the Hermitage-Retreats:
Tat Sundaram (left) and
Adidam Samrajashram (right)**

T hose whose hearts are given, in love, to Me, Fall into My Heart. Those who are Mine, because they are in love with Me, no longer demand to be fulfilled through conditional experience and through the survival (or perpetuation) of the ego-"I". Their love for Me grants them Access to Me, and, Thus, to My Love-Bliss—because I _Am_ Love-Ananda, the Divine Love-Bliss, in Person.

What will My lover do but love Me? I suffer every form and condition of every one who loves Me—because I Love My devotee _As_ My own Form, My own Condition. I Love My devotee _As_ the One by Whom _I_ Am Distracted.

I Grant all My own Divine and "Bright" Excesses to those who love Me, in exchange for all their doubts and sufferings. Those who "Bond" themselves to Me, through love-surrender, are inherently Free of fear and wanting need. They transcend the ego-"I" (the cause of all conditional experience), and they (cause and all and All) Dissolve in Me—for I _Am_ the Heart of all and All, and I _Am_ the Heart Itself, and the Heart Itself _Is_ the Only Reality, Truth, and Real God of All and all.

What is a Greater Message than This?

DA LOVE-ANANDA GITA

From now on, all beings are uniquely Blessed. And human history can be different, because there is Help available that has never existed before.

The life of a devotee of Avatar Adi Da Samraj is unheard-of Grace, and this life can be lived by anyone. It does not matter who you are, where you live, or what you do. All of that makes no difference, once your heart recognizes Adi Da Samraj. Then the only course is the heart-response to Him—a life of devotion to the Divine in human Form, full of devotional ecstasy, true humor, freedom, clarity, and profound purpose.

So, why delay? The Living One, Adi Da Samraj, is here, and always will be. But now is the brief, and especially Blessed, window of time in which He is humanly Alive, doing His great Foundation Work for the sake of all beings, presently and in all future time. Every one who comes to Him and serves Him in His bodily human Lifetime shares in His unique once-and-forever Work of establishing the Way of Adidam in this world.

All who love Him carry His Name in their hearts and on their lips. Once the recognition of Avatar Adi Da awakens in you, this response is inevitable. The Promised God-Man, Avatar Adi Da Samraj, is not an "Other". He is the Gift, the Bliss, of Being Itself. He is the "Brightness" of Very God—Dawning, and then Flowering, in your heart. That Process is pure Revelation. It changes everything—grants peace, sanity, and the overwhelming impulse to Realize Unlimited, Permanent, and Perfect Oneness with Him.

As devotees of Avatar Adi Da Samraj, we make this confession to you: This opportunity—to live in heart-Communion with Real God—exceeds anything ever offered to mortal beings. It is true Happiness. And it is yours for the asking.

◆ ◆ ◆

A part from the four congregations, there are three distinct organizations within Adidam, each with a special area of responsibility.

The Da Love-Ananda Samrajya

Serving The Avataric-Incarnation-Body,
The Great Island-Hermitage-Retreat, and
The World-Blessing-Work of The Divine World-Teacher,
Ruchira Avatar Adi Da Samraj

The Da Love-Ananda Samrajya is devoted to serving Avatar Adi Da Himself, protecting Him and His intimate Sphere, providing for Adidam Samrajashram (His Great Island-Hermitage-Retreat, the Island of Naitauba in Fiji), ensuring that He has everything that He needs to do His Divine Blessing-Work, and providing right access to Him.

The Da Love-Ananda Samrajya also protects and provides for the Ruchira Sannyasin Order (the members of which are legal renunciates) and ensures that the Divine Word and Story of Adi Da Samraj are preserved and made known in the world.

The Eleutherian Pan-Communion of Adidam

*The Sacred Cultural Gathering and Global Mission
of the Devotees of The Divine World-Teacher,
Ruchira Avatar Adi Da Samraj*

*Dedicated to the Practice and the Proclamation
of The True World-Religion of Adidam,
The Unique Divine Way of Realizing Real God*

The Eleutherian Pan-Communion of Adidam is the organization devoted to establishing the Way of Adidam in the world and serving the culture of devotional practice in all four congregations. The Eleutherian Pan-Communion of Adidam is also responsible for the Sanctuaries, the Archives, the Wisdom-Teaching, and other sacred Treasures of Adidam.

The Global Mission of Adidam is a primary branch of the Adidam Pan-Communion. The Mission is active worldwide—through internet websites, through full-time missionaries and through the missionary service of all devotees. The Global Mission also includes the Publications Mission, which prepares, publishes, and distributes Avatar Adi Da's own books (and audiotapes and videotapes of Him), as well as books, magazines, and education courses about Him and the Way of Adidam by His devotees. The Dawn Horse Press (staffed by devotees of Avatar Adi Da) is the editorial and production department of the Publications Mission (see pp. 360-70 for a description of current Adidam publications).

The Ruchirasala of Adidam

*The True Cooperative Community Gathering
of the Devotees of The Divine World-Teacher,
Ruchira Avatar Adi Da Samraj*

*The Seed of a "Bright" New Age of Sanity
and Divine Joy for Mankind*

Cooperative community living (in households, Ashrams, or on Sanctuaries) is one of the fundamental disciplines of the first and second congregations of Adidam. The Ruchirasala of Adidam is the organization that serves Avatar Adi Da's devotees in incarnating cooperative community—it is the intimate sacred domain, in which devotees practice their devotional life and in which all the other entities of Adidam function. Creating intimate human living arrangements and shared services (such as schools, community businesses, and the Radiant Life Clinic) is part of the responsibility of the Ruchirasala. Together with the Adidam Pan-Communion, the Ruchirasala oversees all the practical interaction between members of the Adidam community.

Cooperation + Tolerance = Peace[SM]

In addition to His First Calling, which is to those who would become His devotees, Adi Da Samraj makes a Second Calling to the world at large—to embrace the disposition He has Summarized in the equation:

"COOPERATION + TOLERANCE = PEACE".

By this Second Calling, Adi Da Samraj urges everyone to create a sane human society—including, in particular, the creation of truly cooperative global human community, free of the devastation of war.

To find out more about Adi Da Samraj's Second Calling, please visit the Adidam Peace Center:

www.peacesite.org

An Invitation to Support Adidam

Avatar Adi Da Samraj's sole Purpose is to act as a Source of continuous Divine Grace for everyone, everywhere. In that spirit, He is a Free Renunciate and He owns nothing. Those who have made gestures in support of Avatar Adi Da's Work have found that their generosity is returned in many Blessings that are full of His healing, transforming, and Liberating Grace—and those Blessings flow not only directly to them as the beneficiaries of His Work, but to many others, even all others. At the same time, all tangible gifts of support help secure and nurture Avatar Adi Da's Work in necessary and practical ways, again similarly benefiting the entire world. Because all this is so, supporting His Work is the most auspicious form of financial giving, and we happily extend to you an invitation to serve Adidam through your financial support.

You may make a financial contribution in support of the Work of Adi Da Samraj at any time. You may also, if you choose, request that your contribution be used for one or more specific purposes.

If you are moved to help support and develop Adidam Samrajashram (Naitauba), Avatar Adi Da's Great Hermitage-Retreat and World-Blessing Seat in Fiji, and the circumstance provided there and elsewhere for Avatar Adi Da and the other members of the Ruchira Sannyasin Order, the senior renunciate order of Adidam, you may do so by making your contribution to The Da Love-Ananda Samrajya, the Australian charitable trust which has central responsibility for these Sacred Treasures of Adidam.

To do this: (1) if you do not pay taxes in the United States, make your check payable directly to "The Da Love-Ananda Samrajya Pty Ltd" (which serves as the trustee of the trust) and mail it to The Da Love-Ananda Samrajya at P.O. Box 4744, Samabula, Suva, Fiji; and (2) if you do pay taxes in the United States and you would like your contribution to be tax-deductible under U.S. laws, make your check payable to "The Eleutherian Pan-Communion of Adidam", indicate on your check or accompanying letter that you would like your contribution used for the work of The Da Love-Ananda Samrajya, and mail your check to the Advocacy Department of Adidam at 12040 North Seigler Road, Middletown, California 95461, USA.

If you are moved to help support and provide for one of the other purposes of Adidam, such as publishing the Sacred Literature of Avatar Adi Da, or supporting any of the other Sanctuaries He has Empowered, or maintaining the Sacred Archives that preserve His recorded Talks and Writings, or publishing audio and video recordings of Avatar Adi Da, you may do so by making your contribution directly to The Eleutherian Pan-Communion of Adidam, specifying the particular purposes you wish to benefit, and mailing your check to the Advocacy Department of Adidam at the above address.

If you would like more information about these and other gifting options, or if you would like assistance in describing or making a contribution, please write to the Advocacy Department of Adidam at the above address or contact the Adidam Legal Department by telephone at (707) 928-4612 or by FAX at (707) 928-4062.

Planned Giving

We also invite you to consider making a planned gift in support of the Work of Avatar Adi Da Samraj. Many have found that through planned giving they can make a far more significant gesture of support than they would otherwise be able to make. Many have also found that by making a planned gift they are able to realize substantial tax advantages.

There are numerous ways to make a planned gift, including making a gift in your Will, or in your life insurance, or in a charitable trust.

If you would like to make a gift in your Will in support of the work of The Da Love-Ananda Samrajya: (1) if you do not pay taxes in the United States, simply include in your Will the statement, "I give to The Da Love-Ananda Samrajya Pty Ltd, as trustee of The Da Love-Ananda Samrajya, an Australian charitable trust, P.O. Box 4744, Samabula, Suva, Fiji, _________" [inserting in the blank the amount or description of your contribution]; and (2) if you do pay taxes in the United States and you would like your contribution to be free of estate taxes and to also reduce any estate taxes payable on the remainder of your estate, simply include in your Will the statement, "I give to The Eleutherian Pan-Communion of Adidam, a California non-profit corporation, 12040 North Seigler Road, Middletown, California 95461, USA, _________" [inserting in the blank the amount or description of your contribution].

To make a gift in your life insurance, simply name as the beneficiary (or one of the beneficiaries) of your life insurance policy the organization of your choice (The Da Love-Ananda Samrajya or The Eleutherian Pan-Communion of Adidam), according to the foregoing descriptions and addresses. If you are a United States taxpayer, you may receive significant tax benefits if you make a contribution to The Eleutherian Pan-Communion of Adidam through your life insurance.

We also invite you to consider establishing or participating in a charitable trust for the benefit of Adidam. If you are a United States taxpayer, you may find that such a trust will provide you with immediate tax savings and assured income for life, while at the same time enabling you to provide for your family, for your other heirs, and for the Work of Avatar Adi Da as well.

The Advocacy and Legal Departments of Adidam will be happy to provide you with further information about these and other planned gifting options, and happy to provide you or your attorney with assistance in describing or making a planned gift in support of the Work of Avatar Adi Da.

Further Notes to the Reader

An Invitation to Responsibility

Adidam, the Way of the Heart that Avatar Adi Da has Revealed, is an invitation to everyone to assume real responsibility for his or her life. As Avatar Adi Da has Said in *The Dawn Horse Testament Of The Ruchira Avatar,* "If any one Is Heart-Moved To Realize Me, Let him or her First Resort (Formally, and By Formal Heart-Vow) To Me, and (Thereby) Commence The Ordeal Of self-Observation, self-Understanding, and self-Transcendence. . . ." Therefore, participation in the Way of Adidam requires a real struggle with oneself, and not at all a struggle with Avatar Adi Da, or with others.

All who study the Way of Adidam or take up its practice should remember that they are responding to a Call to become responsible for themselves. They should understand that they, not Avatar Adi Da or others, are responsible for any decision they may make or action they may take in the course of their lives of study or practice. This has always been true, and it is true whatever the individual's involvement in the Way of Adidam, be it as one who studies Avatar Adi Da's Wisdom-Teaching or as a formally acknowledged member of Adidam.

Honoring and Protecting the Sacred Word through Perpetual Copyright

Since ancient times, practitioners of true religion and Spirituality have valued, above all, time spent in the Company of the Sat-Guru (or one who has, to any degree, Realized Real God, Truth, or Reality, and who, thus, serves the awakening process in others). Such practitioners understand that the Sat-Guru literally Transmits his or her (Realized) State to every one (and every thing) with whom (or with which) he or she comes in contact. Through this Transmission, objects, environments, and rightly prepared individuals with which the Sat-Guru has contact can become empowered, or imbued with the Sat-Guru's Transforming Power. It is by this process of empowerment that things and beings are made truly and literally sacred and holy, and things so sanctified thereafter function as a source of the Sat-Guru's Blessing for all who understand how to make right and sacred use of them.

Sat-Gurus of any degree of Realization and all that they empower are, therefore, truly Sacred Treasures, for they help draw the practitioner more quickly into the process of Realization. Cultures of true Wisdom have always understood that such Sacred Treasures are precious (and fragile) Gifts to humanity, and that they should be honored, protected, and reserved for right sacred use. Indeed, the word "holy" means "set apart", and, thus that which is holy and sacred must be protected from insensitive secular interference and wrong use of any kind. Avatar Adi Da has Conformed His human Body-Mind Most Perfectly to the Divine Self, and He is, thus, the most Potent Source of Blessing-Transmission of Real God, or Truth Itself, or Reality Itself. He has for many years Empowered (or made sacred) special places and things, and these now serve as His Divine Agents, or as literal expressions and extensions of His Blessing-Transmission. Among these Empowered Sacred Treasures is His Wisdom-Teaching, which is full of His Transforming Power. This Blessed and Blessing Wisdom-Teaching has Mantric Force, or the literal Power to serve Real-God-Realization in those who are Graced to receive it.

Therefore, Avatar Adi Da's Wisdom-Teaching must be perpetually honored and protected, "set apart" from all possible interference and wrong use. The fellowship of devotees of Avatar Adi Da is committed to the perpetual preservation and right honoring of the Sacred Wisdom-Teaching of the Way of Adidam. But it is also true that, in order to fully accomplish this, we must find support in the world-society in which we live and in its laws. Thus, we call for a world-society and for laws that acknowledge the sacred, and that permanently protect it from insensitive, secular interference and wrong use of any kind. We call for, among other things, a system of law that acknowledges that the Wisdom-Teaching of the Way of Adidam, in all its forms, is, because of its sacred nature, protected by perpetual copyright.

We invite others who respect the sacred to join with us in this call and in working toward its realization. And, even in the meantime, we claim that all copyrights to the Wisdom-Teaching of Avatar Adi Da and the other Sacred Literature and recordings of the Way of Adidam are of perpetual duration.

We make this claim on behalf of The Da Love-Ananda Samrajya Pty Ltd, which, acting as trustee of The Da Love-Ananda Samrajya, is the holder of all such copyrights.

Avatar Adi Da and the Sacred Treasures of Adidam

True Spiritual Masters have Realized Real God (to one degree or another), and, therefore, they bring great Blessing and introduce Divine Possibility to the world. Such Adept-Realizers Accomplish universal Blessing-Work that benefits everything and everyone. They also Work very specifically and intentionally with individuals who approach them as their devotees, and with those places where they reside and to which they direct their specific Regard for the sake of perpetual Spiritual Empowerment. This was understood in traditional Spiritual cultures, and, therefore, those cultures found ways to honor Adept-Realizers by providing circumstances for them where they were free to do their Spiritual Work without obstruction or interference.

Those who value Avatar Adi Da's Realization and Service have always endeavored to appropriately honor Him in this traditional way by providing a circumstance where He is completely Free to do His Divine Work. Since 1983, He has resided principally on the island of Naitauba, Fiji, also known as Adidam Samrajashram. This island has been set aside by Avatar Adi Da's devotees worldwide as a Place for Him to do His universal Blessing-Work for the sake of everyone, as well as His specific Work with those who pilgrimage to Adidam Samrajashram to receive the special Blessing of coming into His physical Company.

Avatar Adi Da is a legal renunciate. He owns nothing and He has no secular or religious institutional function. He Functions only in Freedom. He, and the other members of the Ruchira Sannyasin Order, the senior renunciate order of Adidam, are provided for by The Da Love-Ananda Samrajya, which also provides for Adidam Samrajashram altogether and ensures the permanent integrity of Avatar Adi Da's Wisdom-Teaching, both in its archival and in its published forms. The Da Love-Ananda Samrajya, which functions only in Fiji, exists exclusively to provide for these Sacred Treasures of Adidam.

Outside Fiji, the institution which has developed in response to Avatar Adi Da's Wisdom-Teaching and universal Blessing is known as "The Eleutherian Pan-Communion of Adidam". This formal organization is active worldwide in making Avatar Adi Da's Wisdom-Teaching available to all, in offering guidance to all who are moved to respond to His Offering, and in providing for the other Sacred Treasures of Adidam, including the Mountain Of Attention Sanctuary and Tat Sundaram (in California) and Da Love-Ananda Mahal (in Hawaii). In addition to the central corporate entity known as The Eleutherian Pan-Communion of Adidam, which is based in California, there are numerous regional entities which serve congregations of Avatar Adi Da's devotees in various places throughout the world.

Practitioners of Adidam worldwide have also established numerous community organizations, through which they provide for many of their common and cooperative community needs, including those relating to housing, food, businesses, medical care, schools, and death and dying. By attending to these and all other ordinary human concerns and affairs via ego-transcending cooperation and mutual effort, Avatar Adi Da's devotees constantly free their energy and attention, both personally and collectively, for practice of the Way of Adidam and for service to Avatar Adi Da Samraj, to Adidam Samrajashram, to the other Sacred Treasures of Adidam, and to The Eleutherian Pan-Communion of Adidam.

All of the organizations that have evolved in response to Avatar Adi Da Samraj and His Offering are legally separate from one another, and each has its own purpose and function. Avatar Adi Da neither directs, nor bears responsibility for, the activities of these organizations. Again, He Functions only in Freedom. These organizations represent the collective intention of practitioners of Adidam worldwide not only to provide for the Sacred Treasures of Adidam, but also to make Avatar Adi Da's Offering of the Way of Adidam universally available to all.

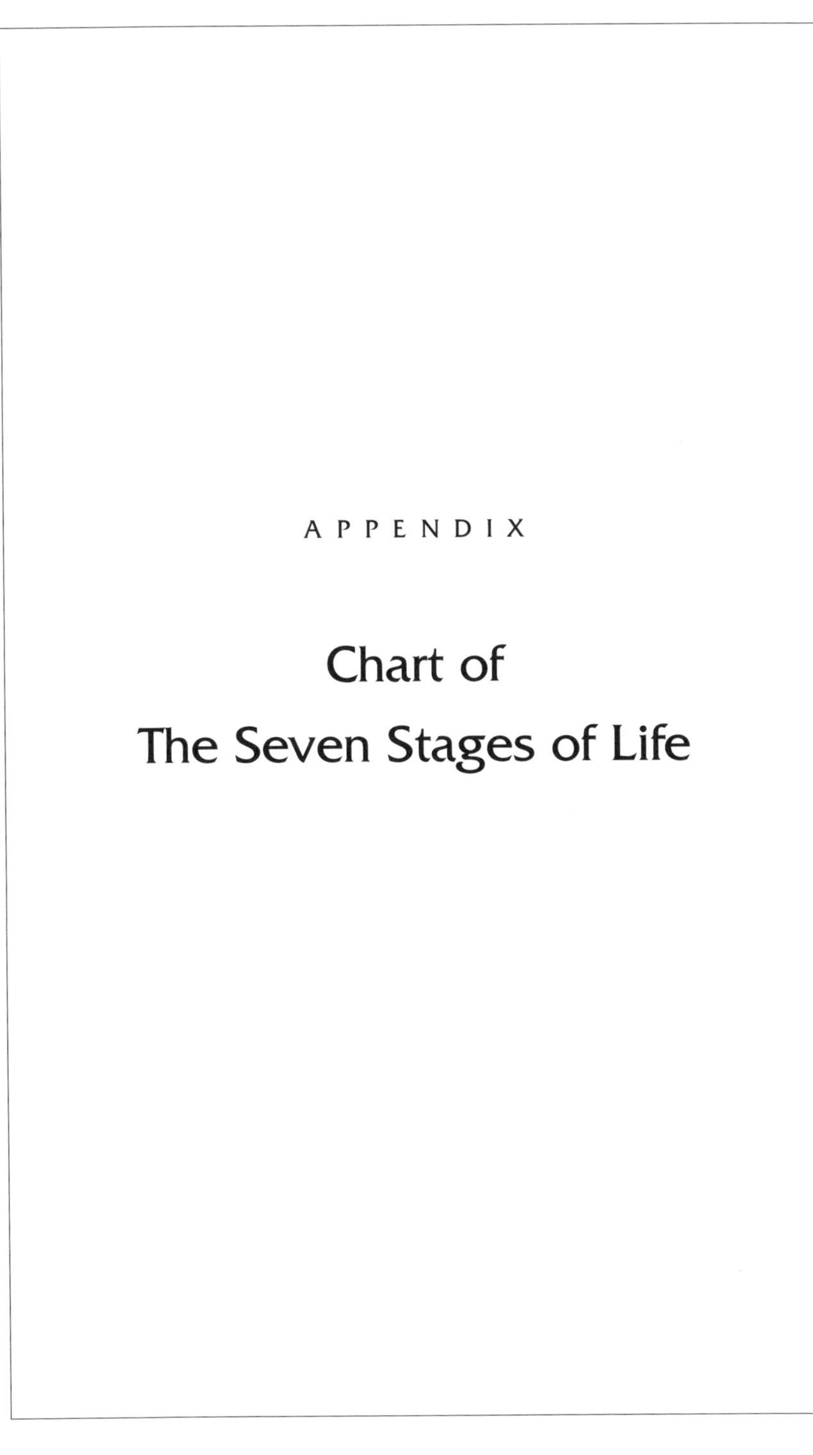

APPENDIX

Chart of
The Seven Stages of Life

THE SEVEN STAGES OF LIFE

The Full and Complete Process of Human Maturation, Spiritual Growth, and Divine Enlightenment

As Revealed by

RUCHIRA AVATAR ADI DA SAMRAJ

Based on *The Seven Stages Of Life,* pp. 103-31

	FIRST STAGE (approx. 0-7 years)	**SECOND STAGE** (approx. 7-14 years)	**THIRD STAGE** (approx. 14-21 years)
	individuation; adaptation to the physical body	socialization; adaptation to the emotional-sexual (or feeling) dimension	integration of the psycho-physical personality; development of verbal mind, discriminative intelligence, and the will
	Identified with the gross self		

FOURTH STAGE	FIFTH STAGE	SIXTH STAGE	SEVENTH STAGE
ego-surrendering devotion to the Divine Person; purification of body-based point of view through reception of Divine Spirit-Force	Spiritual or Yogic ascent of attention into psychic dimensions of the being; mystical experience of the higher brain; may culminate in fifth stage conditional Nirvikalpa Samadhi	Identification with Consciousness Itself (presumed, however, to be separate from all conditional phenomena); most likely will include the experience of Jnana Samadhi	Realization of the Divine Self; Inherently Perfect Freedom and Realization of Divine Love-Bliss (seventh stage Sahaj Samadhi); no "difference" experienced between Divine Consciousness and psycho-physical states and conditions
	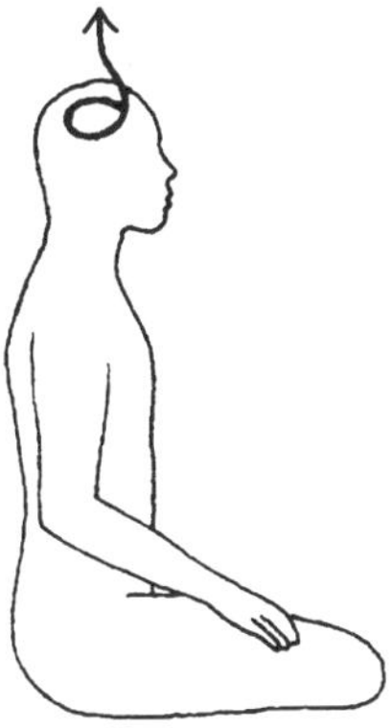	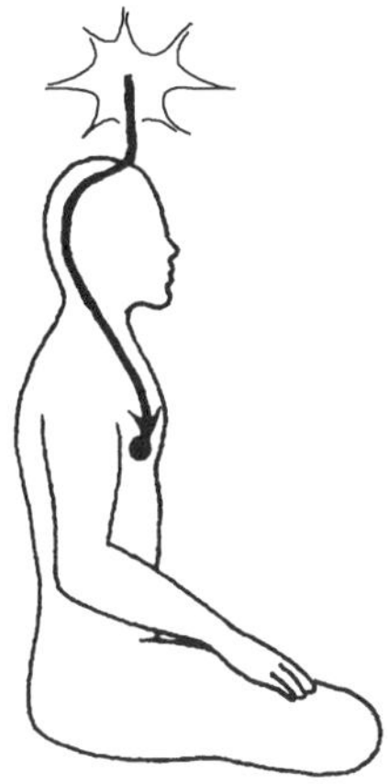	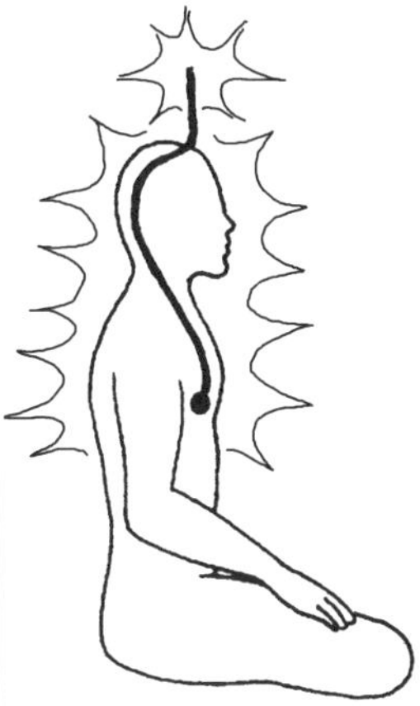
anatomy: the circulation of the Divine Spirit-Current, first (in the "basic" fourth stage of life) downward through the frontal line and then (in the "advanced" fourth stage of life) upward through the spinal line, until attention rests stably at the doorway to the brain core	**anatomy**: the ascent of the Divine Spirit-Current from the brain core (the Ajna Door) to the crown of the head and above (or even, in fifth stage conditional Nirvikalpa Samadhi, to the Matrix of Divine Sound and Divine Light infinitely above the total crown of the head)	**anatomy**: the Divine Spirit-Current descends (via Amrita Nadi, the "Immortal Current" of Divine Love-Bliss) from the Matrix of Divine Sound and Divine Light (infinitely above the total crown of the head) to the right side of the heart (the bodily seat of Consciousness)	**anatomy**: the "Regeneration" of Amrita Nadi, such that Amrita Nadi is felt as the Divine Current of "Bright" Spirit-Fullness, Standing between the right side of the heart and the Matrix of Divine Sound and Divine Light infinitely above the total crown of the head
	Identified with the subtle self (In the Way of Adidam, practice in the context of the "advanced" fourth stage of life and in the context of the fifth stage of life may typically be bypassed, proceeding directly from the "basic" fourth stage of life to the sixth stage of life)	Identified with the causal self	Identified with Divine Consciousness Itself

Notes to the Text of the
DA LOVE-ANANDA GITA
(THE FREE GIFT OF THE DIVINE LOVE BLISS)

Part One

1. Avatar Adi Da's Sign is His bodily (human) Form (Which visibly and tangibly Transmits His Divine Blessing) and photographic or artistic representations thereof.

Part Two

2. For a detailed description of the four stages (or four Ways) of Kashmir Saivism, see *Triadic Mysticism: The Mystical Theology of the Saivism of Kashmir*, by Paul E. Murphy (Delhi: Motilal Banarsidass, 1986).

3. Avatar Adi Da Samraj describes "three egos" that must be progressively transcended in the course of the complete Spiritual process—of which the "money, food, and sex" ego is the first. (See section LXXXVII of this Essay, pp. 165-73.)

4. For Avatar Adi Da's Instruction relative to the foundation life-discipline, foundation devotional discipline, and foundation Spiritual discipline for practitioners of Adidam, see *Santosha Adidam*.

5. "Baba" (literally meaning "father") is often used in India as a reference of intimate respect for a Spiritual Master.

6. There are a number of translations of the *Chidakasha Gita* teachings (including *Voice of the Self*, referenced below). Perhaps the most readily available translation is *The Sky of the Heart: Jewels of Wisdom from Nityananda*, introduction and commentary by Swami Chetanananda, originally translated by M. U. Hatengdi (Portland, Or.: Rudra Press, Second edition, 1996).

7. Swami Chinmayananda (1916-1993) was a scholar of the Hindu scriptures, especially the *Bhagavad Gita* and the *Upanishads,* who conceived his mission as restoring respect for the ancient Hindu scriptures and reinvigorating practice of the Spiritual way according to the Vedantic instruction.

8. M. P. Pandit was a scholar of Hindu scripture, and the author of over 100 books on Yoga and Spirituality. He spent more than forty years living and practicing under the guidance of Sri Aurobindo and the Mother, and serving at the Sri Aurobindo Ashram in Pondicherry, India.

9. *Voice of the Self,* by Swami Nityananda (of Vajreshwari), translated by M. P. Pandit (Madras: P. Ramanath Pai, 1962).

10. Sanskrit "nada" (or "shabda") refers to subtle internal sounds which may become apparent in the process of ascending (spinal) Yoga. The "Om-Sound" (or "Omkar") is the primordial root-sound, from which all other nadas derive.

11. "Raja" means "king" in Sanskrit. Raja Yoga is, thus, the "royal" Yoga, whereby the activity and formations of the mind are disciplined, with the intention of causing them to cease. The most influential formulation of Raja Yoga is that of Patanjali, who (in the *Yoga Sutras*) systematized it in his ashtanga (or eight-limbed) system.

12. The Sanskrit term "Jnani" ("Sage") literally means "one who knows" (or, more fully, "one who has Realized Jnana Samadhi"—see glossary entry for **Samadhi**). A Jnani is one who discriminates between What is Unconditional (the One Reality, or Divine Self) and what is conditional (the passing phenomena of experience). A Jnani is Identified with Consciousness Itself, as the Transcendental Witness of all that arises. By its very nature, the Realization of Jnana is inherently Nirguna. (In other words, there is no Saguna form of Jnana.)

13. Avatar Adi Da has Revealed that His deeper-personality Vehicle (see note 15), or True Great-Siddha Vehicle, is the combined deeper personalities of Ramakrishna and Swami Vivekananda. Avatar Adi Da discusses His unique association with Ramakrishna and Swami Vivekananda in sections XCIII-XCV (pp. 178-79) of this Essay. For a full description of Avatar Adi Da's Revelation of the Unique Associations with His True Great-Siddha Vehicle, see *The Promised God-Man Is Here*, by Carolyn Lee (Middletown, Calif.: Dawn Horse Press, 1998).

14. Avatar Adi Da's gross-personality vehicle (see note 15) was "Franklin Albert Jones", the child of His parents, Dorothy and Franklin Augustus Jones.

15. Avatar Adi Da uses the terms "gross personality" and "deeper personality" to indicate the two conditional dimensions of every human being. The gross personality is comprised of the physical body, its natural energies, its gross brain, and the verbal and lower psychic faculties of mind. The gross personality includes the entire gross dimension of the body-mind and the lower, or most physically oriented, aspects of the subtle dimension of the body-mind, and is the aspect of the body-mind that is the biological inheritance from one's parents.

The deeper personality is governed by the higher, least physically oriented processes of the mind (which function outside or beyond the gross brain, and which include the subtle faculties of discrimination, intuition, and Spiritual perception and knowledge), as well as the causal separate-"I"-consciousness and the root-activity of attention, prior to mind. The deeper personality is the aspect of the human being that reincarnates.

16. Avatar Adi Da's brief description of "radical conductivity" is Given in chapter thirty-three of *The Dawn Horse Testament Of The Ruchira Avatar.*

17. In *The Basket Of Tolerance,* Avatar Adi Da has identified a small number of Hindu and Buddhist texts as "premonitorily 'seventh stage'". While founded in the characteristic sixth stage "point of view", these texts express philosophical intuitions that foreshadow some of the basic characteristics of the seventh stage Realization.

The only-by-Me Revealed and Demonstrated and Given seventh stage of life is the clear and final fulfillment of the first six stages of life. The Revelation and Demonstration of the seventh stage of life by My own Avatarically Self-Revealed Divine Form, Presence, State, Work, and Word are My unique Gift to all and All. However, within the Great Tradition itself, there are some few literatures and Realizers of the sixth stage type that express philosophical (or insightful, but yet limited and incomplete) intuitions that sympathetically foreshadow some of the basic characteristics of the only-by-Me Revealed and Demonstrated and Given seventh stage Realization.

The Ashtavakra Gita *is a principal example of such premonitorily "seventh stage" literature. It is among the greatest (and most senior) communications of all the religious and Spiritual traditions in the Great Tradition of mankind. The* Ashtavakra Gita *is the Great Confession of a Sage who has thoroughly engaged the philosophies and practices of the first six stages of life. It is a sixth stage Adept-Realizer's Free (and uncompromised) communication (or Confession) of the ultimate implications of his sixth stage Realization.*

Like other premonitorily "seventh stage" texts, the Ashtavakra Gita *presumes a tradition of progressive practice in the total context of the first six stages of life, but it does not (itself) represent or communicate any ideal or technique of practice. It simply (and rather exclusively) communicates the Ultimate "Point of View" of the sixth stage Realizer. ["The Unique Sixth Stage Foreshadowings of the Only-by-Me Revealed and Demonstrated and Given Seventh Stage of Life", in* The Basket Of Tolerance]

18. In Sanskrit, "seva" means "service". Service to the Guru is traditionally treasured as one of the great Secrets of Realization.

19. The Hindu tradition speaks of four principal Spiritual paths (or four principal aspects of the Spiritual path). Karma Yoga is literally the "Yoga of action", in which every activity, no matter how humble, is transformed into ego-transcending service to the Divine. (The other three paths are Bhakti Yoga, the path of devotion, Raja Yoga, the path of higher psychic discipline, and Jnana Yoga, the path of transcendental insight.)

20. Swami Prakashananda (1917-1988) turned to Spiritual life in his 30s, eventually choosing the mountain of Sapta Shringh as a place to settle and devote himself to Spiritual practice. Over time, an ashram developed there around him. He met Swami Muktananda in 1956 and was initiated as Swami Muktananda's devotee, although he generally stayed at his own ashram in Sapta Shringh rather than spending a great deal of time in Ganeshpuri at Swami Muktananda's ashram. For Swami Prakashananda's biography, see *Agaram Bagaram Baba: Life, Teachings, and Parables—A Spiritual Biography of Baba Prakashananda*, by Titus Foster (Berkeley: North Atlantic Books / Patagonia, Ariz.: Essene Vision Books, 1999).

21. For Avatar Adi Da's description of Swami Prakashananda's demonstration of Spiritual Transfiguration of the physical body, see chapter 12 of *The Knee Of Listening*.

22. *Agaram Bagaram Baba*, p. 35.

23. Swami Muktananda's letter of acknowledgement and blessing of Avatar Adi Da is included in chapter 12 of *The Knee Of Listening* and also in Part Three ("The Order of My Free Names") of *The Divine Siddha-Method Of The Ruchira Avatar*.

24. For Avatar Adi Da's description of His own "Embrace" of the Divine "Cosmic Goddess", see chapter 16 of *The Knee Of Listening*.

25. *Play of Consciousness*, by Swami Muktananda (South Fallsburg, N.Y.: SYDA, Fourth edition, 1994).

26. For Avatar Adi Da's description of His experience of Christian mystical visions, see chapters 14 and 15 of *The Knee Of Listening*.

27. For a comprehensive treatment of the fourth-to-fifth stage Yogic tradition of Maharashtra, see *Mysticism in India: The Poet-Saints of Maharashtra*, by R. D. Ranade (Albany: State University of New York Press, 1983).

28. For Swami Muktananda's description of the "Blue Person", see *Play of Consciousness* (e.g. pp. 190-194).

Among the numerous translations of the *Bhagavad Gita*, Avatar Adi Da Samraj points to two editions as particularly worthy of study:

Srimad-Bhagavad-Gita (The Scripture of Mankind), chapter summaries, word-for-word meaning in prose order, translation, notes, and index of first lines by Swami Tapasyananda (Mylapore, India: Sri Ramakrishna Math, 1984).

God Talks with Arjuna: The Bhagavad Gita—Royal Science of God-Realization, The Immortal Dialogue Between Soul and Spirit, a new translation and commentary by Paramahansa Yogananda, two volumes (Los Angeles: Self-Realization Fellowship, 1996).

For a complete translation of the *Bhagavata Purana* (also known as the *Srimad Bhagavatam*), see *Srimad Bhagavatam*, translated by N. Raghunathan, two volumes (Madras: Vighneshwara Publishing House, 1976).

29. For Avatar Adi Da's full description of the "bodies" or "sheaths" of the total human structure (and the relationship between these "bodies" and the states of waking, dreaming, and sleeping), see *Santosha Adidam*.

30. Excerpted from a chart ("The Four Bodies of the Individual Soul") in *Play of Consciousness*, by Swami Muktananda (South Fallsburg, N.Y.: SYDA, Fourth edition, 1994), p. 96.

31. In *The Basket Of Tolerance*, Avatar Adi Da has contrasted the development of exoteric (or socially oriented, and myth-based) public Christianity with the secret Teachings of esoteric (or mystically oriented) Christianity:

The "official" Christian church, even in the form of all its modern sects, is the institutional product of an early cultural struggle between _exoteric_ religionists, limited to doctrines based in the physical point of view characteristic of the first three stages of life, and _esoteric_ religionists, inclined toward the mystical (or general psychic, and Spiritual) point of view characteristic of the "basic" and the "advanced" phases of the fourth stage of life and the mystical (or higher psychic, and Spiritual) Realizations associated with the fifth stage of life. This struggle, which was eventually won by the exoteric sects (or factions), took place between the various emerging Christian sects during the early centuries after Jesus' [crucifixion]. . . .

In the domain of the exoteric church, it was apparently generally presumed (among its original creative leadership) that all mysteries and legends must be "concretized" into a story (or an inspiring doctrine) about Jesus as the "Heavenly Messiah" (or the "Christ", the "Anointed One", the Exclusively Blessed "Son of God")—whereas the original esoteric mysteries and mystical Teachings of Christian gnosticism (which must often correspond to what must be presumed to have been Jesus' own Teachings) invariably communicate a Message about the Spiritual (or "Spirit-Breathing") Awakening of every individual (or of every devotee of a Spirit-Master, or, in this Christian case, of every devotee of Jesus as Spirit-Master). Therefore, the core of the esoteric Christian Teachings is that Salvation (from "possession" by cosmic Nature, by the human world, and by fear of death) is Realized by Means of "Spiritual rebirth" (or Absorption In—and, thus, participatory knowledge of—the inherently deathless and Free and Divine Spirit-Power, or "Breath-Energy", of Being). And the "Good News" of this esoteric Salvation Message is that every individual is (ultimately, by virtue of Spiritual Realization) a "Son" or "Daughter" of God.

32. Avatar Adi Da notes that not only "things" in space but space itself came into being with the "Big Bang":

Space-time (itself, or in its totality) cannot be observed. The "Big Bang" was not an event that could have been observed. The "Big Bang" is not something that occurred in space (or in time). The "Big Bang" is the origin of space (and of time). To look at the "Big Bang" as an event in space (and in time) is already to look at it in egoic terms, and from a position after the event. To examine the "Big Bang" in conventional scientific terms is to assume a dissociated (and separate, and separative) position, as if the ego-"I" (or the "observing" body-mind) were standing outside of space-time—but it does not. Egoity (and all of psycho-physical self, or body-mind) is, inherently and necessarily, an event in (and of) space-time. The body-mind is an event in (and of) space-time. That in Which the body-mind is occurring (or of Which the body-mind is a modification, or a mere and temporary appearance) necessarily (Itself) Transcends space-time, Transcends limitation, Transcends the apparent breaking of Fundamental Light (or of Energy Itself, or of Radiance Itself). ["Space-Time Is Love-Bliss", in Real God Is The Indivisible Oneness Of Unbroken Light]

33. For Swami Muktananda's description of the "blue bindu" (or "blue pearl"), see *Play of Consciousness* (e.g., pp. 160-161).

34. For Avatar Adi Da's full description of the Cosmic Mandala, see chapter thirty-nine of *The Dawn Horse Testament Of The Ruchira Avatar.*

35. In *The Knee Of Listening,* Avatar Adi Da describes His Birth as the "Bright", His subsequent voluntary relinquishment of the "Bright", and His eventual Re-Awakening

as the "Bright". He uses the word "Re-Awakening" to indicate that this Great Event was not a Realization entirely "new" to His experience, but a "return" to the Divine Condition He had known at Birth.

36. For Avatar Adi Da's description of His discovery of parallels with Ramana Maharshi's experience, see chapter 18 of *The Knee Of Listening*.

37. This instruction from Swami Muktananda was communicated in a letter he wrote to Avatar Adi Da on April 23, 1968, which Avatar Adi Da quotes in chapter 11 of *The Knee Of Listening*.

38. The "Method of the Siddhas" (meaning "the Spiritual Means used by the Siddhas, or Perfected Ones, or True Spirit-Baptizers") is a phrase coined by Avatar Adi Da Samraj (in the earliest days of His Teaching Work) to describe the essence of the Way of Adidam—which is the Spiritual <u>relationship</u> to Him (or Satsang, or devotional Communion with Him), rather than any technique (meditative or otherwise) learned from Him. *The Method of the Siddhas* was the Title Avatar Adi Da chose for the first published collection of His Talks to His devotees. (In its final form, Avatar Adi Da re-titled this book *The Divine Siddha-Method Of The Ruchira Avatar*.)

Avatar Adi Da also points out that this "Method" has traditionally always been the core of esoteric religion and Spirituality, and that (indeed) the entire worldwide tradition of esoteric religion and Spirituality is rightly understood to be the global tradition of "Siddha Yoga".

The Foundation Of The Only-By-Me Revealed and Given Way Of Adidam Is The Eternal, Ancient, and Always New Method Of The Siddhas—Which Is Devotional Communion With The Siddha-Guru, and Which Is The Unique Means Of Realizing Real God, or Truth, or Reality That Has Traditionally Been Granted By The Rare True Adept-Realizers Of Real God, or Truth, or Reality Who (In The Traditional Context Of The First Six Stages Of Life, and Each According To Their Particular Stage Of Awakening and Of Helping-Capability) Have, By Means Of The Unique Blessing-Method (or Transmission-Capability) Of The Siddhas, Directly (and By Directly and Really Effective Spiritual Blessing-Work) Transmitted The Traditional Revelations and Realizations Of Real God, or Truth, or Reality. [The <u>Only</u> Complete Way To Realize The Unbroken Light Of <u>Real</u> God]

39. The Sanskrit word "sat" means "Truth", "Being", "Existence". Esoterically, the word "guru" is understood to be a composite of two words meaning "destroyer of darkness". The Sat-Guru is thus a "True Guru", or one who destroys darkness and thereby leads living beings from darkness (or non-Truth) into Light (or the Living Truth).

40. A common theme running through various branches of the Great Tradition is the prophecy of a great Savior or Liberator still to come. The prophecy takes different forms in different traditions, but the underlying commonality is the promise or expectation that the culminating Avatar or Incarnation will appear in the future, at a time when humanity is lost, apparently cut off from Wisdom, Truth, and God. Buddhists refer to that Expected One as "Maitreya"; Vaishnavite

Hindus, as the "Kalki Avatar"; Christians, as the "second coming of Jesus"; Jews, as the "Messiah"; and so on.

41. Avatar Adi Da Samraj describes His spontaneous experience of ego-death, in the spring of 1967, in chapter 9 of *The Knee Of Listening*.

42. See *Sadguru Nityananda Bhagavan, The Eternal Entity*, by P. V. Ravindram (Cannanore, India: T. Thankam Ravindran, 1989), pp. 25-26 and 27-28.

43. For Avatar Adi Da's Revelations about Ramakrishna and Swami Vivekananda as His "combined" deeper-personality Vehicle, see Essay VI ("I Have Appeared here Via a Unique, Spontaneous, and Never-Again Conjunction of Vehicles") in chapter 20 of *The Knee Of Listening*.

Part Three

44. Avatar Adi Da Samraj is referring here to a summary of instruction given in chapter 18 of the *Bhagavad Gita*.

45. The entire practice of the Way of Adidam is founded in heart-recognition of Ruchira Avatar Adi Da Samraj as the Very Divine Being in Person:

AVATAR ADI DA SAMRAJ: The only-by-Me Revealed and Given Way of Adidam (Which is the One and Only by-Me-Revealed and by-Me-Given Way of the Heart) is the Way of life you live when you rightly, truly, fully, and fully devotionally recognize Me, and when, on that basis, you rightly, truly, fully, and fully devotionally respond to Me. . . .

If you rightly, truly, fully, and fully devotionally recognize Me, everything "in between" vanishes. All of that is inherently without force. In heart-responsive devotional recognition of Me, a spontaneous kriya of the principal faculties occurs, such that they are loosed from the objects to which they are otherwise bound—loosed from the patterns of self-contraction. The faculties turn <u>to</u> Me, and, in that turning, there is tacit devotional recognition of Me, tacit experiential Realization of Me, of Happiness Itself, of My Love-Bliss-Full Condition. That "Locating" of Me opens the body-mind spontaneously. When you have been thus Initiated by Me, it then becomes your responsibility, your sadhana, to continuously Remember Me, to constantly return to this devotional recognition of Me, in which you are Attracted to Me, in which you devotionally respond to Me spontaneously with all the principal faculties. [Hridaya Rosary]

46. Avatar Adi Da Samraj frequently Describes His Blessing-Power as being like a kiln. In a kiln, as the wet clay objects are heated more and more, they begin to glow. Eventually, the kiln is so hot that everything within it glows with a white light, and the definitions of the individual objects dissolve in the brightness. Just so, as a devotee matures in Avatar Adi Da's Spiritual Company, all presumptions of separateness as an apparently individual ego-"I" are more and more Outshined by the "Brightness" of His Divine Person and Blessing.

Part Five

47. For a description of Avatar Adi Da's "summary (Written, and forever Speaking) Word of Heart (in many Works)", see pp. 27-36.

48. The practice of ego-transcendence in the Way of Adidam is always <u>present</u> (or direct and immediate)—because, in any moment of true practice, the devotee enters into ego-surrendering, ego-forgetting, and ego-transcending heart-Communion with Avatar Adi Da. The practice of ego-transcendence in the Way of Adidam is also <u>progressive</u> (ultimately, culminating in Most Perfect ego-Transcendence, in the seventh stage of life)—because, over time, the devotee becomes more and more consistently responsible for all of the physical and psychic dimensions of the body-mind and more and more stably Awakened to Identification with Self-Existing and Self-Radiant Consciousness Itself.

49. As the Avabhasa Avatar, Avatar Adi Da is the Very Incarnation of the Divine Self-"Brightness".

50. Avatar Adi Da Samraj has Revealed that He Exists simultaneously in three Forms—physical (His bodily human Form), Spiritual (His Spiritual Presence), and the Formlessness of Self-Existing and Self-Radiant Consciousness Itself (His Very State). The fundamental practice of feeling-Contemplating Him includes feeling-Contemplation of all three aspects of His Being.

51. For a description of *Hridaya Rosary*, see p. 362.

52. For a description of the practice of Invoking Avatar Adi Da by Name, see glossary entry **Name-Invocation**.

53. Avatar Adi Da has described His Blessing to all of His devotees as being made of seven parts, or "Seven Gifts Of Grace". The Seven Gifts are: His Word (Ruchira Avatara Vani), His Sign (Ruchira Avatara Darshan), Devotion to Him (Ruchira Avatara Bhakti), Service to Him (Ruchira Avatara Seva), Discipline in response to Him (Ruchira Avatara Tapas), His Blessing (Ruchira Avatara Kripa), the Blessedness of the relationship with Him (Ruchira Avatara Moksha-Bhava).

Avatar Adi Da's extended description of His seven Gifts is given in the Epilogue of *The Heart Of The Dawn Horse Testament Of The Ruchira Avatar.*

54. After Avatar Adi Da's physical lifetime, His devotees are also given appropriate access to the physical form of His "Living Murti" (see glossary).

55. See glossary entries for **forms of practice** and **developmental stages of practice**.

56. For a description of the Sanctuaries of Adidam, see glossary entry **Sanctuaries**.

57. Residence and daily participation within one of the formally acknowledged communities of Avatar Adi Da's devotees is, as a general rule, a requirement for membership in the first or second congregation.

58. In the phrase "necessary (or, otherwise, potential)", Avatar Adi Da is referring to the fact that His fully practicing devotee <u>must</u> practice in the context of certain of the developmental stages of practice (corresponding to the first three stages of life, the "original" and "basic" contexts of the fourth stage of life, the sixth stage of life, and the seventh stage of life) but may bypass practice in the developmental stages that correspond to the "advanced" context of the fourth stage of life and to the fifth stage of life.

59. See glossary for **forms of practice**.

60. "Seva" is Sanskrit for "service". Thus, "Ruchira Avatara Seva" is "service to the Ruchira Avatar, Adi Da Samraj".

Service to one's Spiritual Master is traditionally treasured as one of the great Means of Spiritual Realization. In the Way of Adidam, each practitioner finds many specific ways to serve Avatar Adi Da Samraj and His Divine Work of world-Blessing. In the largest sense, to serve Avatar Adi Da constantly is to live every action, and, indeed, one's entire life, as direct heart-Communion with and responsive obedience and conformity to Avatar Adi Da in every possible and appropriate way.

61. "Tapas" is Sanskrit for "heat", or, by extension, "self-discipline engaged as part of the religious and Spiritual process". (The "heat" of self-discipline is traditionally understood as one of the primary means of purifying the psycho-physical being.) Thus, "Ruchira Avatara Tapas" means "the self-discipline Given by the Ruchira Avatar, Adi Da Samraj, to His formally acknowledged devotees". Avatar Adi Da often speaks of "tapas" as the "heat" that results from the conscious frustration of egoic tendencies, through acceptance of His Calling for ego-surrendering, ego-forgetting, and ego-transcending devotion, service, self-discipline, and meditation.

62. Avatar Adi Da's Name "Avabhasa" is a Sanskrit word meaning "brightness", "splendor", "luster", "light". It is thus synonymous with the English term "the 'Bright'", which Avatar Adi Da has used since His boyhood to describe the Blissfully Self-Luminous Divine Being Which He knew even then as the Divine Reality of His own body-mind and of all beings, things, and worlds.

GLOSSARY

A

Adi   Sanskrit for "first", "primordial", "source"—also "primary", "beginning". Thus, most simply, "Adi Da" means "First Giver".

Adidam   The primary name for the Way Revealed and Given by Avatar Adi Da Samraj.

When Avatar Adi Da Samraj first Gave the name "Adidam" in January 1996, He pointed out that the final "m" adds a mantric force, evoking the effect of the primal Sanskrit syllable "Om". (For Avatar Adi Da's Revelation of the most profound esoteric significance of "Om" as the Divine Sound of His own Very Being, see *He-_and_-She Is Me.*) Simultaneously, the final "m" suggests the English word "Am" (expressing "I Am"), such that the Name "Adidam" also evokes Avatar Adi Da's Primal Self-Confession, "I _Am_ Adi Da", or, more simply, "I _Am_ Da" (or, in Sanskrit, "Aham Da Asmi").

Adidam Samrajashram   See **Sanctuaries**.

adolescent   See **childish and adolescent strategies**.

Advaita Vedanta   The Sanskrit word "Vedanta" literally means the "end of the Vedas" (the most ancient body of Indian Scripture), and is used to refer to the principal philosophical tradition of Hinduism. "Advaita" means "non-dual". Advaita Vedanta, then, is a philosophy of non-dualism, the origins of which lie in the ancient esoteric teaching that Brahman, or the Divine Being, is the only Reality.

Advaitayana Buddha / Advaitayana Buddhism   "Advaitayana" means "Non-Dual Vehicle". The Advaitayana Buddha is the Enlightened One Who has Revealed and Given the Non-Dual Vehicle.

"Advaitayana Buddhism" is another name for the Way of Adidam. The name "Advaitayana Buddhism" indicates the unique sympathetic likeness of Adidam to the traditions of Advaitism (or Advaita Vedanta) and Buddhism. In His examination of the entire collective religious tradition of humankind, Avatar Adi Da has observed that these two traditions represent the most advanced Realizations ever attained previous to His Avataric Divine Incarnation. The primary aspiration of Buddhism is to realize freedom from the illusion of the separate individual ego-self. The primary aspiration of Advaitism (or the tradition of "Non-Dualism") is to know the Supreme Divine Self absolutely, beyond all dualities (of high and low, good and bad, and so on). Advaitayana Buddhism is the Non-Dual ("Advaita") Way ("yana", literally "vehicle") of Most Perfect Awakening ("Buddhism"). Advaitayana Buddhism is neither an outgrowth of the historical tradition of Buddhism nor of the historical tradition of Advaitism. Advaitayana Buddhism is the unique Revelation of Avatar Adi Da Samraj, which perfectly fulfills both the traditional Buddhist aspiration for absolute freedom from the bondage of the egoic self and the traditional Advaitic aspiration for absolute Identity with the Divine Self. (For Avatar Adi Da's discussion of Advaitayana Buddhism, see *The _Only_ Complete Way To Realize The Unbroken Light Of _Real_ God.*)

Advaitic   "Advaita" is Sanskrit for "Non-Duality". Thus, "Advaitic" means "Non-Dual". Avatar Adi Da has Revealed that— in Truth, and in Reality—there is not the slightest separation, or "difference", between the Unconditional Divine Reality and the conditional reality. In other words, Reality altogether is Perfectly One, or Non-Dual, or Advaitic.

the advanced and the ultimate stages of life   Avatar Adi Da Samraj uses the term "advanced" to describe the fourth stage of life (in its "basic" and "advanced" contexts) and the fifth stage of life in the Way of Adidam. He uses the term "ultimate" to describe the sixth and seventh stages of life in the Way of Adidam.

"advanced" context of the fourth stage of life   See **stages of life**.

Agents / Agency   Agents (or Agency) include all the Means that may serve as complete Vehicles of Avatar Adi Da's Divine Grace and Awakening Power. The first Means of Agency that have been fully established by Him are the Wisdom-Teaching of the Way of Adidam, the Hermitage-Retreat Sanctuaries and the Pilgrimage and Retreat Sanctuaries that He has Empowered, and the many Objects and Articles that He has Empowered for the sake of His devotees' Remembrance of Him and reception of His Heart-Blessing. After Avatar Adi Da's human Lifetime, at any given time a single individual from among His seventh stage "Ruchira sannyasin" devotees will be designated (by the senior governing membership of the Ruchira Sannyasin Order) to serve as His living <u>human</u> Agent.

Aham Da Asmi   The Sanskrit phrase "Aham Da Asmi" means "I (Aham) Am (Asmi) Da". "Da", meaning "the One Who Gives", indicates that Avatar Adi Da Samraj is the Supreme Divine Giver, the Avataric Incarnation of the Very Divine Person.

Avatar Adi Da's Declaration "Aham Da Asmi" is similar in form to the "Mahavakyas" (or "Great Statements") of ancient India (found in the Upanishads, the collected esoteric Instruction of ancient Hindu Gurus). However, the significance of "Aham Da Asmi" is fundamentally different from that of the traditional Mahavakyas. Each of the Upanishadic Mahavakyas expresses, in a few words, the profound (though not most ultimate) degree of Realization achieved by great Realizers of the past. For example, the Upanishadic Mahavakya "Aham Brahmasmi" ("I Am Brahman") expresses a great individual's Realization that he or she is Identified with the Divine Being (Brahman), and is not, in Truth, identified with his or her apparently individual body-mind. However, "Aham Da

Asmi", rather than being a proclamation of a human being who has devoted his or her life most intensively to the process of Real-God-Realization and has thereby Realized the Truth to an extraordinarily profound degree, is Avatar Adi Da's Confession that He <u>Is</u> the Very Divine Person, Da, Who has Appeared here in His Avatarically-Born bodily (human) Divine Form, in order to Reveal Himself to all and All, for the sake of the Divine Liberation of all and All.

all and All / All and all   Avatar Adi Da uses the phrase "all and All" (or "All and all") to describe the totality of conditional existence from two points of view. In *Aham Da Asmi,* He defines lower-case "all" as indicating "the collected sum of all Presumed To Be Separate (or limited) beings, things, and conditions", and upper-case "All" as indicating "The All (or The Undivided Totality) Of conditional Existence As A Whole".

Amrita Nadi   Amrita Nadi is Sanskrit for "Channel (or Current, or Nerve) of Ambrosia (or Immortal Nectar)". Amrita Nadi is the ultimate "organ", or root-structure, of the body-mind, Realized as such in the seventh stage of life in the Way of Adidam. It is felt to Stand Radiant between the right side of the heart (which is the psycho-physical Seat of Consciousness Itself) and the Matrix of Light infinitely above the crown of the head. (For Avatar Adi Da's principal discussions of Amrita Nadi, see *The Knee Of Listening, The <u>All-Completing</u> and <u>Final</u> Divine Revelation To Mankind, Santosha Adidam,* and *The Dawn Horse Testament.)*

anatomy   See **Spiritual anatomy**.

asana   Sanskrit for bodily "posture" or "pose"—by extension, and as Avatar Adi Da often intends, "asana" also refers to the attitude, orientation, posture, or feeling-disposition of the heart and the entire body-mind.

"Atma-Murti"   "Atma" indicates the Divine Self, and "Murti" means "Form". Thus, "Atma-Murti" literally means "the Form That Is the (Very) Divine Self". And, as Avatar Adi Da Indicates everywhere in His Wisdom-Teaching, "Atma-Murti" refers to Himself as the Very Divine Self of all, "Located" as "the Feeling of Being (Itself)". To Commune with Avatar Adi Da as "Atma-Murti" is to Realize (or enter into Identification with) His Divine State.

Avadhoot   Avadhoot is a traditional term for one who has "shaken off" or "passed beyond" all worldly attachments and cares, including all motives of detachment (or conventional and other-worldly renunciation), all conventional notions of life and religion, and all seeking for "answers" or "solutions" in the form of conditional experience or conditional knowledge.

Avatar   "Avatar" (from Sanskrit "avatara") is a traditional term for a Divine Incarnation. It literally means "One who is descended, or 'crossed down' (from, and as, the Divine)". Avatar Adi Da Samraj Confesses that, simultaneous with His human Birth, He has Incarnated in every world, at every level of the Cosmic domain, as the Eternal Giver of Divine Help and Divine Grace and Divine Liberation to all beings—and that, even though His bodily (human) Lifetime is necessarily limited in duration, His Spiritual Incarnation in the Cosmic domain is Eternal.

Avataric Incarnation   Avatar Adi Da Samraj is the Avataric Incarnation, or the Divinely Descended Embodiment, of the Divine Person. The reference "Avataric Incarnation" indicates that Avatar Adi Da Samraj fulfills both the traditional expectation of the East, that the True God-Man is an Avatar (or an utterly Divine "Descent" of Real God in conditionally manifested form), and the traditional expectations of the West, that the True God-Man is an Incarnation (or an utterly human Embodiment of Real God).

For Avatar Adi Da's discussion of the "Avatar" and "Incarnation" traditions, and of His unique and all-Completing Role as the "Avataric Incarnation" of the Divine Person, see "'Avatar' and 'Incarnation': The Complementary God-Man Traditions of East and West", in *The Truly Human New World-Culture Of <u>Unbroken</u> Real-God-Man*.

Avataric Self-Submission   For a full description of Avatar Adi Da's "Ordeal Of Avataric Self-Submission", see *The Promised God-Man Is Here*, by Carolyn Lee.

"Avoiding relationship?"   The practice of self-Enquiry in the form "Avoiding relationship?", unique to the Way of Adidam, was spontaneously developed by Avatar Adi Da in the course of His Divine Re-Awakening (as Avatar Adi Da describes in *The Knee Of Listening*). Intense persistence in the "radical" discipline of this unique form of self-Enquiry led rapidly to His Divine Re-Awakening in 1970.

The practice of self-Enquiry in the form "Avoiding relationship?" is the principal form of the "conscious process" practiced by devotees of Avatar Adi Da who choose the Devotional Way of Insight. (See also "Devotional Way of Insight / Devotional Way of Faith" and "Re-cognition".)

B

"basic" context of the fourth stage of life   See **stages of life**.

Bhagavan   The Title "Bhagavan" is an ancient one used over the centuries for many Spiritual Realizers of India. It means "blessed" or "holy" in Sanskrit. When applied to a great Spiritual Being, "Bhagavan" is understood to mean "bountiful Lord", or "Great Lord", or "Divine Lord".

bhakta, bhakti   "Bhakti" is the practice of heart-felt devotion to the Ultimate Reality or Person—a practice which has been traditionally animated through worship of Divine Images or surrender to a human Guru.

"Bhakta" is a devotee whose principal characteristic is expressive devotion, or who practices within the Hindu tradition of Bhakti Yoga.

Bhava   "Bhava" is a Sanskrit word used to refer to the enraptured feeling-swoon of Communion with the Divine.

bindu   In the esoteric Yogic traditions of India, the Sanskrit word "bindu" (literally, "drop" or "point") suggests that all manifested forms, energies, and universes are ultimately coalesced or expressed in a point without spatial or temporal dimension. Each level (or plane) of psycho-physical reality is said to have a corresponding bindu, or zero-point.

Blessing-Work   For a description of Avatar Adi Da's Divine Blessing-Work, see pp. 17-19.

bodily base   The bodily base is the region associated with the muladhara chakra, the lowest energy plexus in the human body-mind, at the base of the spine (or the general region immediately above and including the perineum). In many of the Yogic traditions, the bodily base is regarded as the seat of the latent ascending Spiritual Current, or Kundalini. Avatar Adi Da Reveals that, in fact, the Spirit-Current must first descend to the bodily base through the frontal line, before it can effectively be directed into the ascending spinal course. Avatar Adi Da has also pointed out that human beings who are not yet Spiritually sensitive tend to throw off the natural life-energy at the bodily base, and He has, therefore, Given His devotees a range of disciplines (including a number of exercises that involve intentional locking at the bodily base) which conserve life-energy by directing it into the spinal line.

"bodily battery"   The "bodily battery" (known in Japan as the "hara") is the energy center of the gross body and, as such, plays a very important role in the practice of "conductivity" in the frontal line. Avatar Adi Da describes its focal point (or point of concentration) as the crown of the abdomen, on the surface, about an inch and a half below the umbilical scar.

"bond" / "Bond"   Avatar Adi Da uses the term "bond", when lower-cased, to refer to the process by which the egoic individual (already presuming separateness, and, therefore, bondage to the separate self) attaches itself karmically to the world of others and things through the

constant search for self-fulfillment. In contrast, when He capitalizes the term "Bond", Avatar Adi Da is making reference to the process of His devotee's devotional "Bonding" to Him, which process is the Great Means for transcending all forms of limited (or karmic) "bonding".

"Bright"   By the word "Bright" (and its variations, such as "Brightness"), Avatar Adi Da refers to the Self-Existing and Self-Radiant Divine Reality. As Adi Da Writes in His Spiritual Autobiography, *The Knee Of Listening:*

> . . . *from my earliest experience of life I have Enjoyed a Condition that, as a child, I called the "Bright".*
>
> *I have always known desire, not merely for extreme pleasures of the senses and the mind, but for the highest Enjoyment of Spiritual Power and Mobility. But I have not been seated in desire, and desire has only been a play that I have grown to understand and enjoy without conflict. I have always been Seated in the "Bright".*
>
> *Even as a baby I remember only crawling around inquisitively with a boundless Feeling of Joy, Light, and Freedom in the middle of my head that was bathed in Energy moving unobstructed in a Circle, down from above, all the way down, then up, all the way up, and around again, and always Shining from my heart. It was an Expanding Sphere of Joy from the heart. And I was a Radiant Form, the Source of Energy, Love-Bliss, and Light in the midst of a world that is entirely Energy, Love-Bliss, and Light. I was the Power of Reality, a direct Enjoyment and Communication of the One Reality. I was the Heart Itself, Who Lightens the mind and all things. I was the same as every one and every thing, except it became clear that others were apparently unaware of the "Thing" Itself.*
>
> *Even as a little child I recognized It and Knew It, and my life was not a matter of anything else. That Awareness, that Conscious Enjoyment, that Self-Existing and Self-Radiant Space of Infinitely and inherently Free Being, that Shine of inherent Joy Standing in the heart and Expanding from the heart, is the "Bright". And It is the*

entire Source of True Humor. It is Reality. It is not separate from anything.

Buddha Just as the traditional term "Avatar", when rightly understood, is an appropriate Reference to Avatar Adi Da Samraj, so is the traditional term "Buddha". He is the Divine Buddha, the One Who Is Most Perfectly Self-Enlightened and Eternally Awake.

C

causal See **gross, subtle, causal**.

childish and adolescent strategies
Avatar Adi Da uses the terms "childish" and "adolescent" with precise meanings in His Wisdom-Teaching. He points out that human beings are always tending to animate one of two fundamental life-strategies—the childish strategy (to be dependent, weak, seeking to be consoled by parent-figures and a parent-"God") and the adolescent strategy (to be independent—or, otherwise, torn between independence and dependence—rebellious, unfeeling, self-absorbed, and doubting or resisting the idea of God or any power greater than oneself). Until these strategies are understood and transcended, they not only diminish love in ordinary human relations, but they also limit religious and Spiritual growth.

Circle The Circle is a primary pathway of natural life-energy and the Spirit-Current through the body-mind. It is composed of two arcs: the descending Current, in association with the frontal line (down the front of the body, from the crown of the head to the bodily base), which corresponds to the more physically oriented dimension of the body-mind; and the ascending Current, in association with the spinal line (up the back of the body, from the bodily base to the crown of the head), which is the more mentally, psychically, and subtly oriented dimension of the body-mind.

conditional The word "conditional" (and its variants) is used to indicate everything that depends on conditions—in other words, everything that is temporary and changing. The "Unconditional", in contrast, is the Divine, or That Which Is Eternal, Always Already the Case—because It Is utterly Free of dependence on any conditions whatsoever.

"conductivity" "Conductivity" is Avatar Adi Da's technical term for participation in and responsibility for the movement of natural bodily energies (and, when one is Spiritually Awakened by Him, for the movement of His Divine Spirit-Current of Love-Bliss in Its natural course of association with the body-mind), via intentional exercises of feeling and breathing.

The exercises of Spiritual "conductivity" that Avatar Adi Da Gives to His (formally practicing) Spiritually Awakened devotees are technical whole-bodily Yogas of receptive surrender to the Living Spirit-Current. Rudimentary and preparatory technical forms of "conductivity" are Given to beginners.

congregations of Adidam There are four different modes, or congregations, of formal approach to Avatar Adi Da Samraj, making it possible for everyone to participate in the Gift of heart-companionship with Him. The total practice of the Way of Adidam is engaged by those in the first and second congregations. Whereas all of Avatar Adi Da's devotees (in all four congregations) engage the fundamental practice of Ruchira Avatara Bhakti Yoga, only members of the first and second congregations are vowed to engage the full range of supportive disciplines (meditation, sacramental worship, guided study, exercise, diet, emotional-sexual discipline, cooperative community living, and so on) Given by Avatar Adi Da Samraj.

For a more detailed description of the four congregations of Avatar Adi Da's devotees, see pp. 284-96.

"conscious process" The "conscious process" is Avatar Adi Da's technical term for those practices through which the mind, or attention, is surrendered and turned about (from egoic self-involvement) to feeling-Contemplation of Him. It is the senior discipline and responsibility of all practitioners in the Way of Adidam. (Avatar Adi Da's descriptions of the various forms of the "conscious process" are Given in *The Dawn Horse Testament Of The Ruchira Avatar*.)

"consider", "consideration"   The technical term "consider" or "consideration" in Avatar Adi Da's Wisdom-Teaching means a process of one-pointed but ultimately thoughtless concentration and exhaustive contemplation of something until its ultimate obviousness is clear. As engaged in the Way of Adidam, "consideration" is not merely an intellectual investigation. It is the participatory investment of one's whole being. If one "considers" something fully in the context of one's practice of feeling-Contemplation of Avatar Adi Da Samraj, and study of His Wisdom-Teaching, this concentration results "in both the highest intuition and the most practical grasp of the Lawful and Divine necessities of human existence".

Contemplation of Avatar Adi Da's bodily (human) Form   Traditionally, devotees have produced artistic images of their Gurus for the purpose of Contemplating the Guru when he or she is either not physically present or (otherwise) no longer physically alive.

Modern technology makes possible (through photography, videotape, film, holographic imagery, and other means) accurate Representations of the bodily (human) Form of Avatar Adi Da Samraj for devotional use by His formally acknowledged devotees.

"Cosmic Consciousness"   See **Samadhi**.

Cosmic Mandala   The Sanskrit word "mandala" (literally, "circle") is commonly used in the esoteric Spiritual traditions of the East to describe the hierarchical levels of cosmic existence. "Mandala" also denotes an artistic rendering of interior visions of the cosmos. Avatar Adi Da uses the phrase "Cosmic Mandala" as a reference to the totality of the conditionally manifested cosmos (or all worlds, forms, and beings).

Crashing Down   Avatar Adi Da's Crashing Down is the Descent of His Divine Spirit-Force into the body-mind of His devotee.

My Avataric Divine Work (Altogether) Is My Crashing-Down Descent, At First Upon and Into My Own Avatarically-Born Bodily (Human) Divine Form, and, Thereafter (and Now, and Forever), Upon and Into the body-minds Of My Devotees and all beings—Even (By Means Of My Divine Embrace Of each, and all, and All) To Infuse and (At Last) To Divinely Translate each, and all, and All. Therefore, My Avataric Divine Spiritual Descent Is The Secret Of My Early Life. My Avataric Divine Spiritual Descent Is The Secret Of My Divine Self-"Emergence" (As I Am) Within The Cosmic Domain. My Avataric Divine Spiritual Descent Is The Secret Of All The Secrets Of The (Avatarically Self-Revealed) Divine and Complete and Thoroughly Devotional Way Of Practice and Realization In My Company. The Only-By-Me Revealed and Given Way Of The Heart (or Way Of Adidam) Is The Divine Yoga Of ego-Surrendering, ego-Forgetting, and ego-Transcending Devotional Recognition-Response To My (Avatarically Self-Revealed) Divine and Spiritual Person, and To My (Avatarically Self-Manifested) Divine and Spiritual Descent. The Only-By-Me Revealed and Given Way Of The Heart (or Way Of Adidam) Is The Total and Divine Way and Ordeal Of Counter-egoic Devotional Recognition-Response To My Avataric "Bright" Divine Self-Manifestation, and To The Avataric Crashing Down Of My "Bright" Divine Imposition. And, In The Case Of My Each and Every Devotee, The Way Must Continue Until The Way Is Most Perfectly "Bright", and The Way Itself Becomes Divine Translation Into My Own Sphere Of "Brightness" (Itself). [Ruchira Avatara Hridaya-Siddha Yoga]

"Crazy"   Avatar Adi Da has always had a unique Method of "Crazy" Work, which, particularly during His years of Teaching and Revelation, involved His literal Submission to the limited conditions of humankind, in order to reflect His devotees to themselves, and thereby Awaken self-understanding in them (relative to their individual egoic dramas, and the collective egoic dramas of human society).

For Me, There Was Never <u>Any</u> Other Possibility Than The "Reckless" (or Divinely "Crazy" and Divinely "Heroic") Course Of All-and-all-Embrace—and I Began This Uniquely "Crazy" and "Heroic" Sadhana, Most Intensively, At The Beginning Of My Adult Life. Indeed, I Have Always Functioned, and Will Always Function, In This Divinely "Crazy" and Divinely "Heroic" Manner. The Inherently egoless "Crazy" and "Heroic" Manner Is One Of My Principal Divine Characteristics— Whereby I Can (Always, and Now, and Forever Hereafter) Be Identified. Therefore, I (Characteristically) Functioned In This "Crazy" and "Heroic" Manner Throughout All Of My "Sadhana Years", and Throughout All The Years Of My Avatarically Self-Manifested Divine Teaching-Work and My Avatarically Self-Manifested Divine Revelation-Work—and I Have Done So (and Will <u>Forever</u> Continue To Do So) Throughout All The Divine-Self-"Emergence" Years Of My Avatarically Self-Manifested Divine Blessing-Work (Both During, and Forever After, My Avataric Physical Human Lifetime). <u>All</u> My Avatarically Self-Manifested Divine Work Is A Divinely "Crazy" and Divinely "Heroic" Effort That Avoids Not anything or any one—but Which <u>Always</u> Divinely Blesses Everything and Everyone. [The Truly Human New World-Culture Of <u>Unbroken</u> Real-God-Man]

D

Da   Avatar Adi Da's Name "Da" means "The Divine Giver". In Sanskrit, "Da" means principally "to give". It is also associated with Vishnu, the "Sustainer", and it further has a secondary meaning "to destroy". Thus, "Da" is anciently aligned to all three of the principal Divine Beings, Forces, or Attributes in the Hindu tradition—Brahma (the Creator, Generator, or Giver), Vishnu (the Sustainer), and Siva (the Destroyer). In certain Hindu rituals, priests address the Divine directly as "Da", invoking qualities such as generosity and compassion.

The Tibetan Buddhists regard the syllable "Da" (written, in Tibetan, as well as in Sanskrit, with a single symbol) as most auspicious, and they assign numerous sacred meanings to it, including that of "the Entrance into the Dharma".

Da Love-Ananda Samrajya   For a description of the Da Love-Ananda Samrajya, see p. 300.

Da Avatar   "Da" is Sanskrit for "The One Who Gives". Therefore, as the Da Avatar, Adi Da Samraj is the Divine Descent of the One and True Divine Giver.

"dark" epoch   See **"late-time" (or "dark" epoch)**.

Darshan   "Darshan", the Hindi derivative of the Sanskrit "darshana", literally means "seeing", "sight of", or "vision of". To receive Darshan of Avatar Adi Da is, most fundamentally, to behold His bodily (human) Form (either by being in His physical Company or by seeing a photograph or other visual representation of Him), and (thereby) to receive the spontaneous Divine Blessing He Grants Freely whenever His bodily (human) Form is beheld in the devotional manner. In the Way of Adidam, Darshan of Avatar Adi Da is the very essence of the practice, and one of the most potent forms of receiving Avatar Adi Da's Blessing is to participate in the formal occasions of Darshan—during which Avatar Adi Da Samraj Sits silently, sometimes gazing at each individual one by one.

By extension, "Darshan" of Avatar Adi Da Samraj may refer to any means by which His Blessing-Influence is felt and received—including His Written or Spoken Word, photographs or videotapes of His Avatarically-Born bodily (human) Divine Form, recordings of His Voice, Leelas (or Stories) of His Teaching-Work and Blessing-Work, places or objects He has Spiritually Empowered, visualization of His Avatarically-Born bodily (human) Divine Form in the mind, and simple, heart-felt Remembrance of Him.

Dattatreya   Dattatreya was a God-Realizer who appeared early in the common era and about whom no certain historical facts exist apart from his name. Over the centuries, numerous legends and myths have been spun around him. He was early on regarded to be an incarnation of the God Vishnu, later associated with the tradition of Saivism, and worshipped as the Divine Itself. He is commonly venerated as the originator of the Avadhoota tradition and credited with the authorship of the *Avadhoota Gita*, among other works.

The devotional sect worshipping Dattatreya presumes that he continually reincarnates through a succession of Adepts for the sake of gathering and serving devotees. The belief in the continuing incarnation of Dattatreya should be understood as a popular religious belief that is peripheral to what the Adepts in the Dattatreya succession actually taught.

The Dawn Horse Testament Of The Ruchira Avatar   *The Dawn Horse Testament Of The Ruchira Avatar* is Avatar Adi Da's paramount "Source-Text", summarizing the entire course of the Way of Adidam. (See "Avatar Adi Da Samraj's Teaching-Word", pp. 27-36.)

developmental stages of practice   For all members of the first and second congregations of Avatar Adi Da's devotees, the Way of Adidam develops through a series of (potential) developmental stages of practice and Realization. These stages of practice, and their relationship to the seven stages of life, are described by Avatar Adi Da Samraj in chapter seventeen of *The Dawn Horse Testament Of The Ruchira Avatar.*

When using the phrase "necessary (or, otherwise, potential)", Avatar Adi Da is referring to the fact that His fully practicing devotee <u>must</u> practice in the context of certain of the developmental stages of practice (corresponding to the first three stages of life, the "original" and "basic" contexts of the fourth stage of life, the sixth stage of life, and the seventh stage of life) but may bypass practice in the

developmental stages that correspond to "advanced" context of the fourth stage of life and to the fifth stage of life.

Devotional Way of Insight / Devotional Way of Faith   Avatar Adi Da has Given Instruction in two variant forms of the fundamental practice of feeling-Contemplation of Him: the Devotional Way of Insight and the Devotional Way of Faith. Each of Avatar Adi Da's fully practicing devotees is to experiment with both of these Devotional Ways and then choose the one that is most effective in his or her case.

Both Devotional Ways require the exercise of insight <u>and</u> faith, but there is a difference in emphasis.

In the Devotional Way of Insight, the practitioner engages a specific technical process of observing, understanding, and then feeling beyond the self-contraction, as the principal technical element of his or her practice of feeling-Contemplation of Avatar Adi Da.

In the Devotional Way of Faith, the practitioner engages a specific technical process of magnifying his or her heart-Attraction to Avatar Adi Da, as the principal technical element of his or her practice of feeling-Contemplation of Avatar Adi Da.

Avatar Adi Da's extended Instruction relative to both Devotional Ways is Given in *The <u>Only</u> Complete Way To Realize The Unbroken Light Of <u>Real</u> God.*

Dharma, dharma   Sanskrit for "duty", "virtue", "law". The word "dharma" is commonly used to refer to the many esoteric paths by which human beings seek the Truth. In its fullest sense, and when capitalized, "Dharma" means the complete fulfillment of duty—the living of the Divine Law. By extension, "Dharma" means a truly great Spiritual Teaching, including its disciplines and practices.

"Difference"   "Difference" is the epitome of the egoic presumption of separateness—in contrast with the Realization of Oneness, or Non-"Difference", Which is Native to the Divine Self-Condition.

Divine Being   Avatar Adi Da describes His Divine Being on three levels:

AVATAR ADI DA SAMRAJ: This flesh body, this bodily (human) Sign, is My Form, in the sense that it is My Murti, or a kind of Reflection (or Representation) of Me. It is, therefore, a Means for contacting My Spiritual Presence, and, ultimately, My Divine State.

My Spiritual Presence is Self-Existing and Self-Radiant. It Functions in time and space, and It is also Prior to all time and space. . . .

My Divine State is always and only utterly Prior to time and space. Therefore, I, As I Am (Ultimately), have no "Function" in time and space. There is no time and space in My Divine State.

Divine Body   Avatar Adi Da's Divine Body is not conditional or limited to His physical Body but is "The 'Bright' Itself (Spiritually Pervading and Eternally Most Prior To The Cosmic Domain)".

Divine Enlightenment   The Realization of the seventh stage of life, which is uniquely Revealed and Given by Avatar Adi Da. It is release from all the egoic limitations of the first six stages of life. Remarkably, the seventh stage Awakening, which is Avatar Adi Da's Gift to His rightly prepared devotee, is not an experience at all. The true Nature of everything is simply obvious, based on the Realization that every apparent "thing" is Eternally, Perfectly the same as Reality, Consciousness, Happiness, Truth, or Real God. And that Realization is the Supreme Love-Bliss of Avatar Adi Da's Divine Self-Condition.

Divine Ignorance   "Divine Ignorance" is Avatar Adi Da's term for the fundamental Awareness of Existence Itself, Prior to all sense of separation from (or knowledge about) anything that arises. As He proposes, "No matter what arises, you do not know what a single thing _is_." By "Ignorance", Avatar Adi Da means heartfelt participation in the universal Condition of inherent Mystery—not mental dullness or the fear-based wonder or awe felt by the subjective ego in relation to unknown objects. Divine Ignorance is the Realization of Consciousness Itself, transcending all knowledge and all experience of the self-contracted ego-"I".

For Avatar Adi Da's extended Instruction relative to Divine Ignorance, see *What, Where, When, How, Why, and Who To Remember To Be Happy*, Part Two: "What, Where, When, How, Why and Who To Remember To Be Happy", and Part Three: "You Do Not Know What even a single thing _Is_" and "My Argument Relative to Divine Ignorance".

Divine Indifference   See **four phases of the seventh stage of life**.

Divine "Intoxication"   Unlike common intoxication, such as with alcohol, Divine "Intoxication" Draws Avatar Adi Da's devotees beyond the usual egoic self and egoic mind through His Blessing Grace into a state of ecstatic devotional Communion (and Identification) with Him.

Divine Parama-Guru   The Supreme Divine Guru.

Divine Re-Awakening   Avatar Adi Da's Divine Re-Awakening occurred on September 10, 1970, in the Vedanta Society Temple in Hollywood, California. For a full description of this Great Event and its import, see *The Promised God-Man Is Here*, by Carolyn Lee, or chapter sixteen of *The Knee Of Listening*.

Divine Self-Recognition   Divine Self-Recognition is the ego-transcending and world-transcending Intelligence of the Divine Self in relation to all conditional phenomena. The devotee of Avatar Adi Da who Realizes the seventh stage of life simply Abides as Self-Existing and Self-Radiant Consciousness Itself, and he or she Freely Self-Recognizes (or inherently and instantly and Most Perfectly comprehends and perceives) all phenomena (including body, mind, conditional self, and conditional world) as transparent (or merely apparent), and un-necessary, and inherently non-binding modifications of the same "Bright" Divine Self-Consciousness.

Divine Self-"Emergence"   On January 11, 1986, Avatar Adi Da passed through a profound Yogic Swoon, which He later described as the initial Event of His Divine Self-"Emergence". Avatar Adi Da's Divine Self-"Emergence" is an ongoing Process in which His Avatarically-Born bodily (human) Divine Form has been (and is ever more profoundly and potently being) conformed to Himself, the Very Divine Person, such that His bodily (human) Form is now (and forever hereafter) an utterly Unobstructed Sign and Agent of His own Divine Being.

For Avatar Adi Da's Revelation of the significance of His Divine Self-"Emergence", see section III of "The True Dawn Horse Is The Only Way To Me", in *The All-Completing* and *Final Divine Revelation To Mankind, The Heart Of The Dawn Horse Testament Of The Ruchira Avatar*, and *The Dawn Horse Testament Of The Ruchira Avatar*.

Divine Self-Domain   Avatar Adi Da affirms that there is a Divine Self-Domain that is the Perfectly Subjective Condition of the conditional worlds. It is not "elsewhere", not an objective "place" (like a subtle "heaven" or mythical "paradise"), but It is the always present, Transcendental, Inherently Spiritual, Divine Source-Condition of every conditionally manifested being and thing. Avatar Adi Da Reveals that the Divine Self-Domain is not other than the Divine Heart Itself, not other than Himself. To Realize the seventh stage of life (by the Divine Grace of Avatar Adi Da Samraj) is to Awaken to His Divine Self-Domain.

For Avatar Adi Da's extended Instruction relative to His Divine Self-Domain, see *The All-Completing* and *Final Divine Revelation To Mankind*.

Divine Star   The primal conditional Representation of the "Bright" (the Source-Energy, or Divine Light, of Which all conditional phenomena and the total cosmos are modifications) is the brilliant white five-pointed Divine Star. Avatar Adi Da's bodily (human) Divine Form is the Manifestation of that Divine Star—and His head, two arms, and two legs correspond to its five points. Avatar Adi Da can also be seen or intuited in vision to Be the Divine Star Itself, prior to the visible manifestation of His bodily (human) Form.

Divine Transfiguration   See **four phases of the seventh stage of life**.

Divine Transformation   See **four phases of the seventh stage of life**.

Divine Translation   See **four phases of the seventh stage of life**.

Divine World-Teacher   Avatar Adi Da Samraj is the Divine World-Teacher because His Wisdom-Teaching is the uniquely Perfect Instruction to every being—in this (and every) world—in the total process of Divine Enlightenment. Furthermore, Avatar Adi Da Samraj constantly Extends His Regard to the entire world (and the entire Cosmic domain)—not on the political or social level, but as a Spiritual matter, constantly Working to Bless and Purify all beings everywhere.

dreaming   See **waking, dreaming, and sleeping**.

E

ecstasy / enstasy   The words "ecstasy" and "enstasy" derive originally from Greek. Avatar Adi Da uses "ecstasy" in the literal sense of "standing (stasis) outside (ec-)" the egoic self, and "enstasy" in the sense of "standing (stasis) in (en-)" the Divine Self-Condition. As Avatar Adi Da Says in *The Dawn Horse Testament Of The Ruchira Avatar*, Divine Enstasy is "The Native Condition Of Standing Unconditionally As The By-Me-Avatarically-Self-Revealed Transcendental, Inherently Spiritual, and Self-Evidently Divine Self-Condition Itself".

ego-"I"   The ego-"I" is the fundamental activity of self-contraction, or the presumption of separate and separative existence.

Eleutherian Pan-Communion of Adidam   The Eleutherian Pan-Communion of Adidam is a California religious non-profit corporation, dedicated to the worldwide practice and the global proclamation of the true world-religion of Adidam.

Eleutherios   "Eleutherios" (Greek for "Liberator") is a title by which Zeus was venerated as the supreme deity in the Spiritual esotericism of ancient Greece. The Designation "Eleutherios" indicates the Divine Function of Avatar Adi Da as the Incarnation of the Divine Person, "Whose Inherently Perfect Self-'Brightness' Divinely Liberates all conditionally Manifested beings—Freely, Liberally, Gracefully, and Without Ceasing—now, and forever hereafter".

En-Light-enment   En-Light-enment (or Enlightenment) is not just a state of mind, but rather an actual conversion of the body-mind to the state of Divine Consciousness Itself, or Light Itself. Thus, Avatar Adi Da sometimes writes the word "Enlightenment" with "Light" set apart by hyphens, in order to emphasize this point.

esoteric anatomy   See **Spiritual anatomy**.

Eternal Vow   For a description of the Vow and responsibilities associated with the Way of Adidam, see pp. 284-96.

etheric   The etheric is the dimension of life-energy, which functions through the human nervous system. Our bodies are surrounded and infused by this personal life-energy, which we feel as the play of emotions and life-force in the body.

F

faculties; four faculties   Avatar Adi Da has Instructed His devotees that the practice of devotional Communion with Him (or Ruchira Avatara Bhakti Yoga) requires the surrender of the four principal faculties of the human body-mind. These faculties are body, emotion (or feeling), mind (or attention), and breath.

Feeling of Being   The Feeling of Being is the uncaused (or Self-Existing), Self-Radiant, and unqualified feeling-intuition of the Transcendental, Inherently Spiritual, and Self-Evidently Divine Self-Condition. This absolute Feeling does not merely accompany or express the Realization of the Heart Itself, but It is Identical to that Realization. To feel—or, really, to Be—the Feeling of Being is to enjoy the Love-Bliss of Absolute Consciousness, Which, when Most Perfectly Realized, cannot be pre-

vented or even diminished either by the events of life or by death.

feeling of relatedness   In the foundation stages of practice in the Way of Adidam, the basic (or gross) manifestation of the avoidance of relationship is understood and released when Avatar Adi Da's devotee hears Him (or comes to the point of most fundamental self-understanding), thereby regaining the free capability for simple relatedness, or living on the basis of the feeling of relatedness rather than the avoidance of relationship. Nevertheless, the feeling of relatedness is not Ultimate Realization, because it is still founded in the presumption of a "difference" between "I" and "other". Only in the ultimate stages of life in the Way of Adidam is the feeling of relatedness itself fully understood as the root-act of attention and, ultimately, transcended in the Feeling of Being.

feeling-Contemplation   Avatar Adi Da's term for the essential devotional and meditative practice that all practitioners of the Way of Adidam engage at all times in relationship to Him. Feeling-Contemplation of Adi Da Samraj is Awakened by His Grace—through Darshan (or feeling-sighting) of His bodily (human) Form, His Spiritual Presence, and His Divine State. It is then to be practiced under all conditions, as the basis and epitome of all other practices in the Way of Adidam.

fifth stage conditional Nirvikalpa Samadhi   See **Samadhi**.

forms of practice in the Way of Adidam   Avatar Adi Da has Given a number of different approaches to the progressive process of Most Perfectly self-transcending Real-God-Realization in the Way of Adidam. In this manner, He accounts for the differences in individuals' qualities—particularly relative to their capability to make use of the various technical practices that support the fundamental practice of Ruchira Avatara Bhakti Yoga and relative to the intensity of their motivation to apply themselves to the Spiritual process in His Company.

Ruchira Avatar Adi Da refers to the most detailed development of the practice of the Way of Adidam as the "technically 'fully elaborated'" form of practice. Each successive stage of practice in the technically "fully elaborated" form of the Way of Adidam is defined by progressively more detailed responsibilities, disciplines, and practices that are assumed in order to take responsibility for the signs of growing maturity in the process of Divine Awakening. A devotee who embraces the technically "fully elaborated" form of practice of the Way of Adidam must (necessarily) be a member of the first or second congregation of Avatar Adi Da's devotees. The progress of practice in the technically "fully elaborated" form of the Way of Adidam is monitored, measured, and evaluated by practicing stages (as described in detail by Avatar Adi Da Samraj in chapter seventeen of *The Dawn Horse Testament Of The Ruchira Avatar*).

Most of Avatar Adi Da's fully practicing devotees will find that they are qualified for a less intensive approach and are moved to a less technical form of the "conscious process" (than is exercised in the technically "fully elaborated" form of the Way of Adidam). Thus, most of Avatar Adi Da's fully practicing devotees will take up the technically "simpler" (or even "simplest") form of practice of the Way of Adidam.

In the technically "simpler" form of practice of the Way of Adidam, Avatar Adi Da's devotee (in the first or second congregation) engages a relatively simple form of technical means of supporting his or her fundamental practice of Ruchira Avatara Bhakti Yoga, and this technical means remains the same throughout the progressive course of developmental stages.

In the technically "simplest" form of practice, Avatar Adi Da's devotee (in any of the four congregations) engages the fundamental practice of Ruchira Avatara Bhakti Yoga in the simplest possible manner—as "simplest" feeling-Contemplation of Avatar Adi Da, together with the random use of Avatar Adi Da's Principal Name, "Da" (or one of the other Names He has Given to be engaged in the practice of simple Name-Invocation of Him).

Avatar Adi Da's fully elaborated descriptions of the technically "fully elaborated" and the technically "simpler" (or even "simplest") forms of the Way of Adidam are Given in *The Dawn Horse Testament Of The Ruchira Avatar*.

four phases of the seventh stage of life
In the context of Divine Enlightenment in the seventh stage of life, the Spiritual process continues. One of the unique aspects of Avatar Adi Da's Revelation is His description of the four phases of the seventh stage process: Divine Transfiguration, Divine Transformation, Divine Indifference, and Divine Translation.

In the phase of Divine Transfiguration, the Divinely Enlightened devotee's body-mind is Infused by Avatar Adi Da's Love-Bliss, and he or she Radiantly Demonstrates active Love, spontaneously Blessing all the relations of the body-mind.

In the following phase of Divine Transformation, the subtle or psychic dimension of the body-mind is fully Illumined, which may result in Divine Powers of healing, longevity, and the ability to release obstacles from the world and from the lives of others.

Eventually, Divine Indifference ensues, which is spontaneous and profound Resting in the "Deep" of Consciousness, and the world of relations is otherwise noticed only minimally or not at all.

Divine Translation is the ultimate "Event" of the entire process of Divine Awakening. Avatar Adi Da describes Divine Translation as the Outshining of all noticing of objective conditions through the infinitely magnified Force of Consciousness Itself. Divine Translation is the Outshining of all destinies, wherein there is no return to the conditional realms.

Being so overwhelmed by the Divine Radiance that all appearances fade away may occur <u>temporarily</u> from time to time during the seventh stage of life. But when that Most Love-Blissful Swoon becomes permanent, Divine Translation occurs, and the body-mind is inevitably relinquished in physical death. Then there is only Eternal Inherence in the Divine Self-Domain of unqualified Happiness and Joy.

frontal line, frontal personality, frontal Yoga   The frontal (or descending) line of the body-mind conducts natural life-energy and (for those who are Spiritually Awakened) the Spirit-Current of Divine Life, in a downward direction from the crown of the head to the base of the body (or the perineal area).

The frontal personality is comprised of the physical body and its natural energies, the gross brain, and the verbal and lower faculties of the mind. It includes the entire gross dimension of the body-mind and the lower (or most physically oriented) aspects of the subtle dimension of the body-mind.

The frontal Yoga, as described by Avatar Adi Da, is the process whereby knots and obstructions in the gross (or physical) and energetic dimensions of the body-mind are penetrated, opened, surrendered, and released, through the devotee's reception of Avatar Adi Da's Transmission in the frontal line of the body-mind.

"fully elaborated" form of the Way of Adidam   See **forms of practice in the Way of Adidam**.

functional, practical, relational, and cultural disciplines of Adidam
The most basic <u>functional</u>, <u>practical</u>, and <u>relational</u> <u>disciplines</u> of the Way of Adidam (in its fully practiced form, as embraced by devotees in the first and second congregations) are forms of appropriate human action and responsibility for diet, health, exercise, sexuality, work, service to and support of Avatar Adi Da's Circumstance and Work, and cooperative (formal community) association with other practitioners of the Way of Adidam. The most basic <u>cultural</u> <u>obligations</u> of the Way of Adidam (in its fully practiced form) include meditation, sacramental worship, study of Avatar Adi Da's Wisdom-Teaching (and also at least a basic discriminative study of the Great Tradition of religion and Spirituality that is the Wisdom-inheritance of humankind), and regular participation in the "form" (or schedule) of daily, weekly, monthly, and annual devotional activities and retreats.

G

Great Tradition   The "Great Tradition" is Avatar Adi Da's term for the total inheritance of human, cultural, religious, magical, mystical, Spiritual, and Transcendental paths, philosophies, and testimonies, from all the eras and cultures of humanity— which inheritance has (in the present era of worldwide communication) become the common legacy of humankind. Avatar Adi Da's Divine Self-Revelation and Wisdom-Teaching Fulfills and Completes the Great Tradition.

gross, subtle, causal   Avatar Adi Da (in agreement with certain esoteric schools in the Great Tradition) describes conditional existence as having three dimensions— gross, subtle, and causal.

"Gross" means "made up of material (or physical) elements". The gross (or physical) dimension is, therefore, associated with the physical body, and also with experience in the waking state.

The subtle dimension, which is senior to and pervades the gross dimension, includes the etheric (or energic), lower mental (or verbal-intentional and lower psychic), and higher mental (or deeper psychic, mystical, and discriminative) functions, and is associated with experience in the dreaming state. In the human psycho-physical structure, the subtle dimension is primarily associated with the ascending energies of the spine, the brain core, and the subtle centers of mind in the higher brain.

The causal dimension is senior to and pervades both the gross and the subtle dimensions. It is the root of attention, or the essence of the separate and separative ego-"I". The causal dimension is associated with the right side of the heart, specifically with the sinoatrial node, or "pacemaker" (the psycho-physical source of the heartbeat). Its corresponding state of consciousness is the formless awareness of deep sleep.

Guru   Esoterically, the word "guru" is understood to be a composite of two words, "destroyer (ru) of darkness (gu)".

H

hearing   See **listening, hearing, and seeing**.

heart, stations of the heart   Avatar Adi Da distinguishes three stations of the heart, associated respectively with the right side, the middle, and the left side of the heart region of the chest. The middle station of the heart is what is traditionally known as the "anahata chakra" (or "heart chakra"), and the left side of the heart is the gross physical heart. Avatar Adi Da Samraj has Revealed that the primal psycho-physical seat of Consciousness and attention is associated with what He calls the "right side of the heart". He has Revealed that this center (which is neither the heart chakra nor the gross physical heart) corresponds to the sinoatrial node, or "pacemaker", the source of the gross physical heartbeat in the right atrium (or upper right chamber) of the physical heart. In the Process of Divine Self-Realization, there is a unique process of opening of the right side of the heart—and it is because of this connection between the right side of the heart and Divine Self-Realization that Avatar Adi Da uses the term "the Heart" as another way of referring to the Divine Self.

The Heart Itself is Real God, the Divine Self, the Divine Reality. The Heart Itself is not "in" the right side of the human heart, nor is it "in" (or limited to) the human heart as a whole. Rather, the human heart and body-mind and the world exist in the Heart, Which Is the Divine Being Itself.

heart-Communion   "Heart-Communion" with Avatar Adi Da is the practice of Invoking and feeling Him. It is "communion" in the sense that the individual loses sense of the separate self in the bliss of that state, and is thus "communicating intimately" (in a most profound and non-dual manner) with Avatar Adi Da Samraj.

heart-recognition   The entire practice of the Way of Adidam is founded in devotional heart-recognition of, and devotional heart-response to, Ruchira Avatar Adi Da Samraj as the Very Divine Being in Person.

AVATAR ADI DA SAMRAJ: The only-by-Me Revealed and Given Way of Adidam (Which is the One and Only by-Me-Revealed and by-Me-Given Way of the Heart) is the Way of life you live when you rightly, truly, fully, and fully devotionally recognize Me, and when, on that basis, you rightly, truly, fully, and fully devotionally respond to Me. . . .

If you rightly, truly, fully, and fully devotionally recognize Me, everything "in between" vanishes. All of that is inherently without force. In heart-responsive devotional recognition of Me, a spontaneous kriya of the principal faculties occurs, such that they are loosed from the objects to which they are otherwise bound—loosed from the patterns of self-contraction. The faculties turn <u>to</u> Me, and, in that turning, there is tacit devotional recognition of Me, tacit experiential Realization of Me, of Happiness Itself, of My Love-Bliss-Full Condition. That "Locating" of Me opens the body-mind spontaneously. When you have been thus Initiated by Me, it then becomes your responsibility, your sadhana, to continuously Remember Me, to constantly return to this devotional recognition of Me, in which you are Attracted to Me, in which you devotionally respond to Me spontaneously with all the principal faculties. [Hridaya Rosary (Four Thorns Of Heart-Instruction)]

heart-response   See **heart-recognition**.

Hermitage-Retreat Sanctuaries   See **Sanctuaries**.

"Heroic"   The Tantric traditions of Hinduism and Buddhism describe as "heroic" the practice of an individual whose impulse to Liberation and commitment to his or her Guru are so strong that all circumstances of life, even those traditionally regarded as inauspicious for Spiritual practice (such as consumption of intoxicants and engagement in sexual activity), can rightly be made use of as part of the Spiritual process.

Avatar Adi Da's uniquely "Heroic" Ordeal, however, was undertaken not for His own sake, but in order to discover, through His own experience, what is necessary for <u>all</u> beings to Realize the Truth. Because of His utter Freedom from egoic bondage and egoic karmas, Avatar Adi Da's Sadhana was "Heroic" in a manner that had never previously been possible and will never again be possible. As the Divine Person, it was necessary for Him to experience the entire gamut of human seeking, in order to be able to Teach any and all that came to Him.

Avatar Adi Da has Instructed that, because of His unique "Heroic" Demonstration, His devotees can simply practice the Way He has Revealed and Given, and do not have to attempt the (in any case impossible) task of duplicating His Ordeal. (See also **"Crazy"**.)

Hridaya-Avatar "Hridaya" is Sanskrit for "the heart". It refers not only to the physical organ but also to the True Heart, the Transcendental (and Inherently Spiritual) Divine Reality. "Hridaya" in combination with "Avatar" signifies that Avatar Adi Da is the Very Incarnation of the Divine Heart Itself, the Divine Incarnation Who Stands in, at, and <u>as</u> the True Heart of every being.

Hridaya Rosary *Hridaya Rosary (Four Thorns Of Heart-Instruction)—The Five Books Of The Heart Of The Adidam Revelation, Book Four: The "Late-Time" Avataric Revelation Of The Universally Tangible Divine Spiritual Body, Which Is The Supreme Agent Of The Great Means To Worship and To Realize The True and Spiritual Divine Person (The egoless Personal Presence Of Reality and Truth, Which <u>Is</u> The Only <u>Real</u> God)* is Avatar Adi Da's summary and exquisitely beautiful Instruction relative to the right, true, full, and fully devotional practice of the Way of Adidam, through which practice Avatar Adi Da's fully practicing devotee Spiritually receives Him with ever greater profundity, and, ultimately (through a process of the Spiritual "melting" of the entire psycho-physical being), Realizes Him most perfectly.

Hridaya-Samartha Sat-Guru "Hridaya-Samartha Sat-Guru" is a compound of traditional Sanskrit terms that has been newly created to express the uniqueness of Avatar Adi Da's Guru-Function. "Sat" means "Truth", "Being", "Existence". Thus, "Sat-Guru" literally means "True Guru", or a Guru who can lead living beings from darkness (or non-Truth) into Light (or the Living Truth).

"Samartha" means "fit", "qualified", "able". Thus, "Samartha Sat-Guru" means "a True Guru who is fully capable" of Awakening living beings to Real-God-Realization.

The word "Hridaya", meaning "heart", refers to the Very Heart, or the Transcendental (and Inherently Spiritual) Divine Reality.

Thus, altogether, the reference "Hridaya-Samartha Sat-Guru" means "the Divine Heart-Master Who Liberates His devotees from the darkness of egoity by Means of the Power of the 'Bright' Divine Heart Itself". Avatar Adi Da has Said that this full Designation "properly summarizes all the aspects of My unique Guru-Function".

Hridaya-Shakti; Hridaya-Shaktipat The Sanskrit word "Hridaya" means "the Heart Itself". "Shakti" is a Sanskrit term for the Divine Manifesting as Energy. "Hridaya-Shakti" is thus "the Divine Power of the Heart", Which is Given and Transmitted by Avatar Adi Da Samraj.

In Hindi, "shaktipat" means the "descent of Divine Power", indicating the Sat-Guru's Transmission of the Kundalini Shakti to his or her devotee.

"Hridaya-Shaktipat", which is Avatar Adi Da's seventh stage Gift to His devotees, is "the Blessing-Transmission of the Divine Heart Itself".

Avatar Adi Da's extended Instruction relative to Hridaya-Shakti and Kundalini Shakti is Given in *Ruchira Avatara Hridaya-Siddha Yoga*.

Hridaya-Siddha Yoga The Way (Yoga) of the relationship with the "Transmission-Master of the Divine Heart" (Hridaya-Siddha), Ruchira Avatar Adi Da Samraj.

Hridayam "Hridayam" is Sanskrit for "heart". It refers not only to the physical organ but also to the True Heart, the Transcendental (and Inherently Spiritual) Divine Reality. "Hridayam" is one of Avatar Adi Da's Divine Names, signifying that He Stands in, at, and <u>as</u> the True Heart of every being.

I

Ignorance See **Divine Ignorance**.

Indifference See **four phases of the seventh stage of life**.

Instruments / Instrumentality
Avatar Adi Da has Indicated that members of the Ruchira Sannyasin Order function collectively and spontaneously as His Instruments, or Means by which His Divine Grace and Awakening Power are Magnified and Transmitted to other devotees and all beings. Such devotees have received Avatar Adi Da's Spiritual Baptism, and they practice in Spiritually activated relationship to Him with exemplary depth and intensity. Because of their uniquely complete and renunciate response and accountability to Him, and by virtue of their ego-surrendering, ego-forgetting, ego-transcending, and really Spiritual Invocation of Him, these devotees function collectively as Instruments for the Transmission of Avatar Adi Da's Spiritual Presence to others.

Invocation by Name See **Name-Invocation**.

Ishta-Guru Bhakti Yoga An alternate name for Ruchira Avatara Bhakti Yoga. Ishta-Guru Bhakti Yoga literally means "the practice (Yoga) of devotion (Bhakti) to Avatar Adi Da, the chosen Beloved (Ishta) Guru of His devotees".

J

Jnana Samadhi See **Samadhi**.

K

Kali Kali is a Hindu form of the Divine Goddess (or "Mother-Shakti") in her terrifying aspect.

Kali Yuga A Hindu term meaning "the dark (kali) epoch (yuga)", or the final and most ignorant and degenerate period of human history, when the Spiritual Way of life is almost entirely forgotten. (In the Hindu view, the Kali Yuga is a cyclically recurring event.)

karma "Karma" is Sanskrit for "action". Since action entails consequences (or reactions), "karma" also means (by extension) "destiny, tendency, the quality of existence and experience which is determined by previous actions".

Kashmir Saivism Kashmir Saivism is a branch of Saivism (the form of Hinduism in which Siva is worshipped as the Supreme Deity), which originated in the Kashmir region of North India in the late 8th century and whose influence has spread throughout the Indian sub-continent during the mid-20th century. It has a largely fifth-stage orientation.

kiln Avatar Adi Da Samraj frequently describes the transformative process of His Blessing-Power in the lives of His devotees as being like a kiln. In a kiln, as the wet clay objects are heated more and more, they begin to glow. Eventually, the kiln is so hot that everything within it glows with a white light, and the definitions of the individual objects dissolve in the brightness. Just so, as a devotee matures in Avatar Adi Da's Spiritual Company, all presumptions of separateness as an apparently individual ego-"I" are more and more Outshined by the "Brightness" of His Divine Person and Blessing.

Klik-Klak Avatar Adi Da coined the term "Klik-Klak" as a name for the conditional reality. This name indicates (even by means of the sound of the two syllables) that conditional reality is a heartless perpetual-motion machine of incessant change, producing endlessly varied patterns that are ultimately binary in nature (as, for example, "yes-no", "on-off", or "black-white").

knots   Previous to Most Perfect Divine Self-Realization, the gross, subtle, and causal dimensions are expressed in the body-mind as characteristic knots. The knot of the gross dimension is associated with the region of the navel. The knot of the subtle dimension is associated with the midbrain, or the ajna center directly behind and between the brows. And the knot of the causal dimension (which Avatar Adi Da refers to as the "causal knot") is associated with the sinoatrial node (or "pacemaker") on the right side of the heart. The causal knot (or the heart-root's knot) is the primary root of the self-contraction, felt as the locus of the self-sense, the source of the feeling of relatedness itself, or the root of attention.

Kundalini-Shaktipat   The Kundalini Shakti is traditionally viewed to lie dormant at the bodily base, or lowermost psychic center of the body-mind. Kundalini-Shaktipat is the activation of the Kundalini Shakti—either spontaneously in the devotee or by the Guru's initiation—thereafter potentially producing various forms of Yogic and mystical experience.

L

"late-time" (or "dark" epoch)   The "'late-time' (or 'dark' epoch)" is a phrase that Avatar Adi Da uses to describe the present era—in which doubt of God (and of anything at all beyond mortal existence) is more and more pervading the entire world, and the self-interest of the separate individual is more and more regarded to be the ultimate principle of life. It is also a reference to the traditional Hindu idea of "yugas", or "epochs", the last of which (the Kali Yuga) is understood to be the most difficult and "dark". Many traditions share the idea that it is in such a time that the Promised Divine Liberator will appear. (See also **Kali Yuga**.)

Lay Congregationist Order   In "The Orders of My True and Free Renunciate Devotees" (in *The Lion Sutra*), Avatar Adi Da describes the Lay Congregationist Order as "the common (or general) order for all formally established general (or not otherwise formal renunciate) lay practitioners of the total (or full and complete) practice of the Way of Adidam". Once a member of the second congregation has completed the student-beginner stage of practice, he or she makes the transition to the intensive listening-hearing stage of the Way of Adidam. By virtue of this transition, the individual becomes a member of the Lay Congregationist Order, unless he or she is accepted as a member of the Lay Renunciate Order.

Lay Renunciate Order   See **renunciate orders**.

leela   "Leela" is Sanskrit for "play", or "sport". In many religious and Spiritual traditions, all of conditionally manifested existence is regarded to be the Leela (or the Play, Sport, or Free Activity) of the Divine Person. "Leela" also means the Awakened Play of a Realized Adept (of any degree), through which he or she mysteriously Instructs and Liberates others and Blesses the world itself. By extension, a Leela is an instructive and inspiring story of such an Adept's Teaching and Blessing Play.

Lesson of life   "The Lesson of life" is Avatar Adi Da's term for the fundamental understanding that Happiness cannot be achieved by means of seeking, because Happiness is inherent in Existence Itself. Avatar Adi Da has summarized this in the aphorism, "You cannot become Happy. You can only be Happy."

Lineage, Avatar Adi Da's   The principal Spiritual Masters who served Avatar Adi Da Samraj during His "Sadhana Years" belong to a single Lineage of extraordinary Yogis, whose Parama-Guru (Supreme Guru) was the Divine "Goddess" (or "Mother-Shakti").

Swami Rudrananda (1928-1973), or Albert Rudolph (known as "Rudi"), was Avatar Adi Da's first human Teacher—from 1964 to 1968, in New York City. Rudi served Avatar Adi Da Samraj in the development of basic practical life-disciplines and the frontal Yoga, which is the process whereby knots and obstructions in the physical and etheric dimensions of the body-mind are penetrated, opened, surrendered, and released through Spiritual reception in the frontal line of the body-mind. Rudi's own Teachers included the Indonesian Pak Subuh (from whom Rudi learned a basic exercise of Spiritual receptivity), Swami Muktananda (with whom Rudi studied for many years), and Bhagavan Nityananda (the Indian Adept-Realizer who was also Swami Muktananda's Guru). Rudi met Bhagavan Nityananda shortly before Bhagavan Nityananda's death, and Rudi always thereafter acknowledged Bhagavan Nityananda as his original and principal Guru.

The second Teacher in Avatar Adi Da's Lineage of Blessing was Swami Muktananda (1908-1982), who was born in Mangalore, South India. Having left home at the age of fifteen, he wandered for many years, seeking the Divine Truth from sources all over India. Eventually, he came under the Spiritual Influence of Bhagavan Nityananda, whom he accepted as his Guru and in whose Spiritual Company he mastered Kundalini Yoga. Swami Muktananda served Avatar Adi Da as Guru during the period from 1968 to 1970. In the summer of 1969, during Avatar Adi Da's second visit to India, Swami Muktananda wrote a letter confirming Avatar Adi Da's attainment of "Yogic Liberation", and acknowledging His right to Teach others. However, from the beginning of their relationship, Swami Muktananda instructed Avatar Adi Da to visit Bhagavan Nityananda's burial site every day (whenever Avatar Adi Da was at Swami Muktananda's Ashram in Ganeshpuri, India) as a means to surrender to Bhagavan Nityananda as the Supreme Guru of the Lineage.

Bhagavan Nityananda, a great Yogi of South India, was Avatar Adi Da's third Guru. Little is known about the circumstances of Bhagavan Nityananda's birth and early life, although it is said that even as a child he showed the signs of a Realized Yogi. It is also known that he abandoned conventional life as a boy and wandered as a renunciate. Many miracles (including spontaneous healings) and instructive stories are attributed to him. Bhagavan Nityananda surrendered the body on August 8, 1961. Although Avatar Adi Da did not meet Bhagavan Nityananda in the flesh, He enjoyed Bhagavan Nityananda's direct Spiritual Influence from the subtle plane, and He acknowledges Bhagavan Nityananda as a direct and principal Source of Spiritual Instruction during His years with Swami Muktananda. (Avatar Adi Da summarizes the Instruction He received from Bhagavan Nityananda in section XXXII of "I (Alone) Am The Adidam Revelation", an Essay contained in many of the twenty-three "Source-Texts" of Adidam.)

On His third visit to India, while visiting Bhagavan Nityananda's burial shrine, Avatar Adi Da was instructed by Bhagavan Nityananda to relinquish all others as Guru and to surrender directly to the Divine Goddess in Person as Guru. Thus, Bhagavan Nityananda passed Avatar Adi Da to the Divine Goddess Herself, the Parama-Guru (or Source-Guru) of the Lineage that included Bhagavan Nityananda, Swami Muktananda, and Rudi.

The years of Avatar Adi Da's "Sadhana" came to an end in the Great Event of His Divine Re-Awakening, when Avatar Adi Da Husbanded the Divine Goddess (thereby ceasing to relate to Her as His Guru).

Avatar Adi Da's full account of His "Sadhana Years" is Given in *The Knee Of Listening*.

Avatar Adi Da's description of His "Relationship" to the Divine "Goddess" is Given in "I Am The Icon Of Unity", in *He-and-She Is Me*.

listening, hearing, and seeing
"Listening" is Avatar Adi Da's technical term for the orientation, disposition, and beginning practice of the Way of Adidam. A listening devotee listens to Avatar Adi Da Samraj by "considering" His Teaching-Argument and His Leelas, and by practicing feeling-Contemplation of Him (primarily

of His bodily human Form). In the total practice of the Way of Adidam, effective listening to Avatar Adi Da is the necessary prerequisite for true hearing and real seeing.

"Hearing" is a technical term used by Avatar Adi Da to indicate most fundamental understanding of the act of egoity (or self-contraction). Hearing Avatar Adi Da is the unique capability to directly transcend the self-contraction, such that, simultaneous with that transcending, there is the intuitive awakening to Avatar Adi Da's Self-Revelation <u>As</u> the Divine Person and Self-Condition. The capability of true hearing can only be Granted by Avatar Adi Da's Divine Grace, to His fully practicing devotee who has effectively completed the process of listening. Only on the basis of such hearing can Spiritually Awakened practice of the Way of Adidam truly (or with full responsibility) begin.

I Am Heard When My Listening Devotee Has Truly (and Thoroughly) Observed the ego-"I" and Understood it (Directly, In the moments Of self-Observation, and Most Fundamentally, or In its Totality).

I Am Heard When the ego-"I" Is Altogether (and Thoroughly) Observed and (Most Fundamentally) Understood, Both In The Tendency To Dissociate and In The Tendency To Become Attached (or To Cling By Wanting Need, or To Identify With others, and things, and circumstances egoically, and Thus To Dramatize The Seeker, Bereft Of Basic Equanimity, Wholeness, and The Free Capability For Simple Relatedness).

I Am Heard When the ego-"I" Is Thoroughly (and Most Fundamentally) Understood To Be Contraction-Only, An Un-Necessary and Destructive Motive and Design, Un-Naturally and Chronically Added To Cosmic Nature and To all relations, and An Imaginary Heart-Disease (Made To Seem Real, By Heart-Reaction).

I Am Heard When This Most Fundamental Understanding Of The Habit Of "Narcissus" Becomes The Directly Obvious Realization Of The Heart, Radiating Beyond Its Own (Apparent) Contraction.

I Am Heard When The Beginning Is Full, and The Beginning Is Full (and Ended) When Every Gesture Of self-Contraction (In The Context Of The First Three Stages Of Life, and Relative To Each and All Of The Principal Faculties, Of body, emotion, mind, and breath) Is (As A Rather Consistently Applied and humanly Effective Discipline) Observed (By Natural feeling-perception), Tacitly (and Most Fundamentally) Understood, and Really (Directly and Effectively) Felt Beyond (In The Prior Feeling Of Unqualified Relatedness). [Santosha Adidam]

When, in the practice of the Way of Adidam, hearing (or most fundamental self-understanding) is steadily exercised in meditation and in life, the native feeling of the heart ceases to be chronically constricted by self-contraction. The heart then begins to Radiate as love in response to the Divine Spiritual Presence of Avatar Adi Da.

This emotional and Spiritual response of the whole being is what Avatar Adi Da calls "seeing". Seeing Avatar Adi Da is emotional conversion from the reactive emotions that characterize egoic self-obsession, to the open-hearted, Radiant Happiness that characterizes Spiritual devotion to Avatar Adi Da. This true and stable emotional conversion coincides with true and stable receptivity to Avatar Adi Da's Spiritual Transmission, and both of these are prerequisites to further Spiritual advancement in the Way of Adidam.

Seeing Is ego-Transcending Participation In <u>What</u> (and <u>Who</u>) <u>Is</u>. Seeing Is Love. Seeing (or Love) Is Able (By Means Of My Avatarically Self-Transmitted Divine Grace) To "Locate", Devotionally Recognize, and Feel My Avatarically Self-Transmitted (and all-and-All-Pervading) Spiritual Radiance (and My Avatarically Self-Transmitted Spirit-Identity, <u>As</u> The "Bright" and Only One <u>Who</u> <u>Is</u>). . . . Seeing Is The "Radical" (or Directly ego-Transcending) Reorientation Of conditional Existence To My Avatarically Self-Revealed (Transcendental, Inherently Spiritual, Inherently Perfect, and

Self-Evidently Divine) Self-Condition, In Whom conditional self and conditional worlds Apparently arise and Always Already Inhere. . . .

Seeing Me Is Simply Attraction To Me (and Feeling Me) As My Avatarically Self-Revealed Spiritual (and Always Blessing) Divine Presence—and This Most Fundamentally, At The Root, Core, Source, or Origin Of The "Emergence" Of My Avatarically Self-Revealed Divine Spiritual Presence "here", At (and In Front Of) The Heart, or At (and In) The Root-Context Of the body-mind, or At (and In) The Source-Position (and, Ultimately, As The Source-Condition) Of conditional (or psycho-physical) Existence Itself.

Seeing Me Is Knowing Me As My Avatarically Self-Revealed Spiritual (and Always Blessing) Divine Presence, Just As Tangibly (and With The Same Degree Of Clarity) As You Would Differentiate The Physical Appearance Of My Bodily (Human) Form From the physical appearance of the bodily (human) form of any other.

To See Me Is A Clear and "Radical" Knowledge Of Me, About Which There Is No Doubt. To See Me Is A Sudden, Tacit Awareness—Like Walking Into a "thicker" air or atmosphere, or Suddenly Feeling a breeze, or Jumping Into water and Noticing The Difference In Density Between the air and the water. This Tangible Feeling Of Me Is (In any particular moment) Not Necessarily (Otherwise) Associated With effects in the body-mind . . . but It Is, Nevertheless, Felt At The Heart and Even All Over the body.

Seeing Me Is One-Pointedness In The "Radical" Conscious Process Of Heart-Devotion To Me. [Santosha Adidam]

"Living Murti"   Avatar Adi Da will always be Divinely Present in the Cosmic domain, even after His physical Lifetime. He is the One Who is (and will always be) worshipped in the Way of Adidam, and (therefore) He is (and will always be) the Eternally Living Murti for His devotees. However, Avatar Adi Da has said that, after His physical (human) Lifetime, there should always be one (and only one) "Living Murti" as a Living Link

between Him and His devotees. Each successive "Living Murti" (or "Murti-Guru") is to be selected from among those members of the Ruchira Sannyasin Order (see **renunciate orders**) who have been formally acknowledged as Divinely Enlightened devotees of Avatar Adi Da Samraj in the seventh stage of life. "Living Murtis" will not function as the independent Gurus of practitioners of the Way of Adidam. Rather, they will simply be "Representations" of Avatar Adi Da's bodily (human) Divine Form, and a means to Commune with Him.

Avatar Adi Da's full discussion of His "Living Murtis", and how they are to be chosen, is Given in Part Three, section XII, of *The Lion Sutra*.

"Locate"   To "Locate" Avatar Adi Da is to "Truly Heart-Find" Him.

Love-Ananda   The Name "Love-Ananda" combines both English ("Love") and Sanskrit ("Ananda", meaning "Bliss"), thus bridging the West and the East, and communicating Avatar Adi Da's Function as the Divine World-Teacher. The combination of "Love" and "Ananda" means "the Divine Love-Bliss". The Name "Love-Ananda" was given to Avatar Adi Da by Swami Muktananda, who spontaneously conferred it upon Avatar Adi Da in 1969. However, Avatar Adi Da did not use the Name "Love-Ananda" until April 1986, after the Great Event that Initiated His Divine Self-"Emergence".

Love-Ananda Avatar   As the Love-Ananda Avatar, Avatar Adi Da is the Very Incarnation of the Divine Love-Bliss.

M

Maha-Siddha   The Sanskrit word "Siddha" means "a completed, fulfilled, or perfected one", or "one of perfect accomplishment, or power". "Maha-Siddha" means "Great Siddha".

Mandala   The Sanskrit word "mandala" (literally, "circle") is commonly used in the esoteric Spiritual traditions to describe the entire pattern of the hierarchical levels of cosmic existence. Avatar Adi Da also uses the word "Mandala" to refer to the Circle (or Sphere) of His Heart-Transmission, or as a formal reference to a group of His devotees who perform specific functions of direct service to Him.

mantra   See **Name-Invocation**.

meditation   In the Way of Adidam, meditation is a period of formal devotional Contemplation of Avatar Adi Da Samraj. Meditation is one of the life-disciplines that Avatar Adi Da Samraj has Given to His devotees in the first and second congregations, as a fundamental support for their practice of Ruchira Avatara Bhakti Yoga. For those who have fully adapted to the disciplines of the first and second congregations, the daily practice of meditation includes a period of one and one-half hours in the morning and a period of one hour in the evening. Such daily practice is increased during periods of retreat. Members of the third and fourth congregations are also encouraged (but not required) to engage formal meditation.

missing the mark   "Hamartia" (the word in New Testament Greek that was translated into English as "sin") was originally an archery term meaning "missing the mark".

Most Perfect / Most Ultimate   Avatar Adi Da uses the phrase "Most Perfect(ly)" in the sense of "Absolutely Perfect(ly)". Similarly, the phrase "Most Ultimate(ly)" is equivalent to "Absolutely Ultimate(ly)". "Most Perfect(ly)" and "Most Ultimate(ly)" are always references to the seventh (or Divinely Enlightened) stage of life. Perfect(ly) and Ultimate(ly) refer to the sixth stage of life or to the sixth and seventh stages of life together. (See also **stages of life**.)

mudra   A "mudra" is a gesture of the hands, face, or body that outwardly expresses a state of ecstasy. Avatar Adi Da sometimes spontaneously exhibits Mudras as Signs of His Blessing and Purifying Work with His devotees and the world. He also uses the term "Mudra" to express the Attitude of His Blessing-Work, which is His Constant (or Eternal) Giving (or

Submitting) of Himself to Be the Means of Divine Liberation for all beings.

Muktananda, Swami   See **Lineage, Avatar Adi Da's.**

mummery / *The Mummery*   The dictionary defines mummery as "a ridiculous, hypocritical, or pretentious ceremony or performance". Avatar Adi Da uses this word to describe all the activities of ego-bound beings, or beings who are committed to the false view of separation and separativeness.

The Mummery is one of Avatar Adi Da's twenty-three "Source-Texts". It is a work of astonishing poetry and deeply evocative archetypes. Through the heart-breaking story of Raymond Darling's growth to manhood, his search to find, and then to be reunited with, his beloved (Quandra), and his utter self-transcendence of all conditional circumstances and events, Avatar Adi Da Tells His own Life-Story in the language of parable, and describes in devastating detail how the unconverted ego makes religion (and life altogether) into a meaningless mummery.

Murti   "Murti" is Sanskrit for "form", and, by extension, a "representational image" of the Divine or of a Guru. In the Way of Adidam, Murtis of Avatar Adi Da are most commonly photographs of Avatar Adi Da's bodily (human) Divine Form.

"Murti-Guru"   See **"Living Murti"**.

Mystery   Avatar Adi Da uses the term "the Mystery" to point out that, although we can name things, we actually do not know what anything really <u>is</u>:

It is a great and more-than-wonderful Mystery to everyone that anything <u>is</u>, or that we <u>are</u>. And whether somebody says "I don't know how anything came to be" or "God made everything", they are simply pointing to the feeling of the Mystery—of how everything <u>is</u>, but nobody knows what it really <u>Is</u>, or how it came to be. [What, Where, When, How, Why, and <u>Who</u> To Remember To Be Happy]

N

Name-Invocation   Sacred sounds or syllables and Names have been used since antiquity for invoking and worshipping the Divine Person and the Sat-Guru. In the Hindu tradition, the original mantras were cosmic sound-forms and "seed" letters used for worship and prayer of, and incantatory meditation on, the Revealed Form of the Divine Person.

Practitioners of the Way of Adidam may, at any time, Remember or Invoke Avatar Adi Da Samraj (or feel, and thereby Contemplate, His Avatarically Self-Revealed Divine Form, and Presence, and State) through simple feeling-Remembrance of Him and by randomly (in daily life and meditation) Invoking Him via His Principal Name, "Da", or via one (and only one) of the other Names He has Given for the practice of Simple Name-Invocation of Him. (The specific forms of His Names that Avatar Adi Da has Given to be engaged in practice of simple Name-Invocation of Him are listed in chapter three of *The Dawn Horse Testament Of The Ruchira Avatar*.)

For devotees of Avatar Adi Da Samraj, His Names are the Names of the Very Divine Being. As such, these Names, as Avatar Adi Da Himself has described, "do not simply <u>mean</u> Real God, or the Blessing of Real God. They are the verbal or audible Form of the Divine." Therefore, Invoking Avatar Adi Da Samraj by Name is a potent and Divinely Empowered form of feeling-Contemplation of Him.

Narcissus   In Avatar Adi Da's Teaching-Revelation, "Narcissus" is a key symbol of the un-Enlightened individual as a self-obsessed seeker, enamored of his or her own self-image and egoic self-consciousness. In *The Knee Of Listening*, Adi Da Samraj describes the significance of the archetype of Narcissus:

He is the ancient one visible in the Greek "myth", who was the universally adored child of the gods, who rejected the loved-one and every form of love and relationship, who was finally condemned to the contemplation of his own image, until,

as a result of his own act and obstinacy, he suffered the fate of eternal separateness and died in infinite solitude.

Nirguna   "Nirguna" is Sanskrit for "without attributes or quality".

Nirvikalpa Samadhi   See **Samadhi**.

Nityananda   See **Lineage, Avatar Adi Da's**.

Non-Separate Self-Domain   The "Non-Separate Self-Domain" is a synonym for "Divine Self-Domain". (See **Divine Self-Domain**.)

O

"Oedipal"   In modern psychology, the "Oedipus complex" is named after the legendary Greek Oedipus, who was fated to unknowingly kill his father and marry his mother. Avatar Adi Da Teaches that the primary dynamisms of emotional-sexual desiring, rejection, envy, betrayal, self-pleasuring, resentment, and other primal emotions and impulses are indeed patterned upon unconscious reactions first formed early in life, in relation to one's mother and father. Avatar Adi Da calls this "the 'Oedipal' drama" and points out that we relate to all women as we do to our mothers, and to all men as we do to our fathers, and that we relate, and react, to our own bodies as we do to the parent of the opposite sex. Thus, we impose infantile reactions to our parents on our relationships with lovers and all other beings, according to their sex, and we also superimpose the same on our relationship to our own bodies. (Avatar Adi Da's extended Instruction on "Oedipal" patterning is Given in *Ruchira Avatara Hridaya-Tantra Yoga*.)

Omega   See **Alpha and Omega**.

"Open Eyes"   "Open Eyes" is Avatar Adi Da's technical synonym for the Realization of seventh stage Sahaj Samadhi, or unqualified Divine Self-Realization. The phrase graphically describes the non-exclusive, non-inward, Native State of the Divine Self-Realizer, Who is Identified

Unconditionally with the Divine Self-Reality, while also allowing whatever arises to appear in the Divine Consciousness (and spontaneously Divinely Self-Recognizing everything that arises as a modification of the Divine Consciousness). The Transcendental Self is intuited in the mature phases of the sixth stage of life, but It can be Realized at that stage only by the intentional exclusion of conditional phenomena. In "Open Eyes", that impulse to exclusion disappears, when the Eyes of the Heart Open, and Most Perfect Realization of the Spiritual, Transcendental, and Divine Self in the seventh stage of life becomes permanent (and incorruptible by any phenomenal events).

"original" context of the fourth stage of life　See **stages of life**.

Outshined / Outshining　Avatar Adi Da uses "Outshined" or "Outshining" as a synonym for "Divine Translation", to refer to the final Demonstration of the four-phase process of the seventh (or Divinely Enlightened) stage of life in the Way of Adidam. In the Great Event of Outshining (or Divine Translation), body, mind, and world are no longer noticed—not because the Divine Consciousness has withdrawn or dissociated from conditionally manifested phenomena, but because the Divine Self-Recognition of all arising phenomena as modifications of the Divine Self-Condition has become so intense that the "Bright" Radiance of Consciousness now Outshines all such phenomena. (See also **four phases of the seventh stage of life**.)

P, Q

"Perfect Practice"　The "Perfect Practice" is Avatar Adi Da's technical term for the discipline of the ultimate stages of life (the sixth stage of life and the seventh stage of life) in the Way of Adidam. The "Perfect Practice" is practice in the Domain of Consciousness Itself (as opposed to practice from the point of view of the body or the mind). (See also **stages of life**.)

Perfectly Subjective　Avatar Adi Da uses "Perfectly Subjective" to describe the True Divine Source, or "Subject", of the conditionally manifested world—as opposed to regarding the Divine as some sort of conditional "object" or "other". Thus, in the phrase "Perfectly Subjective", the word "Subjective" does not have the sense of "relating to the inward experience of an individual", but, rather, it has the sense of "Being Consciousness Itself, the True Subject of all apparent experience".

Pilgrimage and Retreat Sanctuaries　See **Sanctuaries**.

Pleasure Dome　Avatar Adi Da Samraj Speaks of the Way of Adidam as a "Pleasure Dome", recalling the poem "Kubla Khan", by Samuel Taylor Coleridge ("In Xanadu did Kubla Khan / A stately pleasure-dome decree . . ."). Adi Da Samraj points out that in many religious traditions it is presumed that one must embrace suffering in order to earn future happiness and pleasure. However, by Calling His devotees to live the Way of Adidam as a Pleasure Dome, Avatar Adi Da Samraj Communicates His Teaching that the Way of heart-Communion with Him is always about present-time Happiness, not about any kind of search to attain Happiness in the future. Thus, in the Way of Adidam, there is no idealization of suffering and pain as presumed means to attain future happiness—and, consequently, there is no denial of the appropriate enjoyment of even the ordinary pleasures of human life.

Avatar Adi Da also uses "Pleasure Dome" as a reference to the Ultimate and Divine Love-Bliss-Happiness That Is His own Self-Nature and His Gift to all who respond to Him.

"Practice"　As the quotation marks around the capitalized word "Practice" suggest, the psycho-physical expression of the process of Divine Enlightenment is a "Practice" only in the sense that it is simple action. It is not, in contrast to the stages of life previous to the seventh, a discipline intended to counter egoic tendencies that would otherwise dominate body and mind.

Avatar Adi Da uses quotation marks in a characteristic manner throughout His Written Word to Indicate that a particular word is a technical term, to be understood in the unique and precise language of the Way of Adidam, carrying the implication "as per definition". However, in other cases, His quotation marks carry the implication "so to speak", as in the case of the term "Practice" and are, therefore, not to be understood as precise technical terminology of the Way of Adidam.

prana/pranic   The Sanskrit word "prana" means "life-energy". It generally refers to the life-energy animating all beings and pervading everything in cosmic Nature. In the human body-mind, circulation of this universal life-energy is associated with the heartbeat and the cycles of the breath. In esoteric Yogic Teachings, prana is also a specific technical name for one of a number of forms of etheric energy that functionally sustain the bodily being.

Prana is not to be equated with the Divine Spirit-Current, or the Spiritual (and Always Blessing) Divine Presence of Avatar Adi Da Samraj. The finite pranic energies that sustain individual beings are only conditional, localized, and temporary phenomena of the realm of cosmic Nature. Even in the form of universal life-force, prana is but a conditional modification of the Divine Spirit-Current Revealed by Avatar Adi Da, Which Is the "Bright" (or Consciousness Itself), beyond all cosmic forms.

R

"radical"   The term "radical" derives from the Latin "radix", meaning "root", and, thus, it principally means "irreducible", "fundamental", or "relating to the origin". In *The Dawn Horse Testament Of The Ruchira Avatar*, Avatar Adi Da defines "Radical" as "Gone To The Root, Core, Source, or Origin". Because Adi Da Samraj uses "radical" in this literal sense, it appears in quotation marks in His Wisdom-Teaching, in order to distinguish His usage from the common reference to an extreme (often political) view.

Ramakrishna   See **Lineage, Avatar Adi Da's**.

Ramana Maharshi   A great sixth stage Indian Spiritual Master, Ramana Maharshi (1879-1950) became Self-Realized at a young age and gradually assumed a Teaching role as increasing numbers of people approached him for Spiritual guidance. Ramana Maharshi's Teaching focused on the process of introversion (through the question "Who am I?"), which culminates in conditional Self-Realization (or Jnana Samadhi), exclusive of phenomena. He established his Ashram at Tiruvannamalai in South India, which continues today.

Rang Avadhoot   Rang Avadhoot (1898-1968) was a Realizer in the tradition of Dattatreya. In *The Knee Of Listening*, Avatar Adi Da describes the brief but highly significant meeting that occurred between Himself and Rang Avadhoot in 1968.

Real God   Avatar Adi Da uses the term "Real God" to Indicate the True and Perfectly Subjective Source of all conditions, the True and Spiritual Divine Person (Which can be directly Realized), rather than any ego-made (and, thus, false, or limited) presumptions about God.

Re-cognition   "Re-cognition", which literally means "knowing again", is Avatar Adi Da's term for "the tacit transcending of the habit of 'Narcissus'". It is the mature form into which verbal self-Enquiry evolves in the Devotional Way of Insight. The individual simply notices and tacitly "knows again" (or directly understands) whatever is arising as yet another species of self-contraction, and he or she transcends (or feels beyond) it in Satsang with Avatar Adi Da.

renunciate orders   Avatar Adi Da has established two formal renunciate orders: The Ruchira Sannyasin Order of the Tantric Renunciates of Adidam (or, simply, the Ruchira Sannyasin Order), and the Lay Renunciate Order of Adidam (or, simply, the Lay Renunciate Order).

The senior practicing order in the Way

of Adidam is the Ruchira Sannyasin Order. This order is the senior cultural authority within the formal gathering of Avatar Adi Da's devotees. "Sannyasin" is an ancient Sanskrit term for one who has renounced all worldly bonds and who gives himself or herself completely to the Real-God-Realizing or Real-God-Realized life. Members of the Ruchira Sannyasin Order are uniquely exemplary practitioners of the Way of Adidam who are (generally) practicing in the context of the ultimate (sixth and seventh) stages of life. Members of this Order are legal renunciates and live a life of perpetual retreat. As a general rule, they are to reside at Adidam Samrajashram. The Ruchira Sannyasin Order comprises the first congregation of Avatar Adi Da's devotees.

The members of the Ruchira Sannyasin Order have a uniquely significant role among the practitioners of Adidam as Avatar Adi Da's human Instruments and (in the case of those members who are formally acknowledged as Avatar Adi Da's fully Awakened seventh stage devotees) as the body of practitioners from among whom each of Avatar Adi Da's successive "Living Murtis" (or Empowered human Agents) will be selected. Therefore, the Ruchira Sannyasin Order is essential to the perpetual continuation of authentic practice of the Way of Adidam.

The Founding Member of the Ruchira Sannyasin Order Avatar Adi Da Himself.

In "The Orders of My True and Free Renunciate Devotees" (in *The Lion Sutra*), Avatar Adi Da describes the Lay Renunciate Order as "a renunciate service order for all intensively serving (and, altogether, intensively practicing) lay practitioners of the total (or full and complete) practice of the Way of Adidam".

All present members, and all future members, of the Lay Renunciate Order must (necessarily) be formally acknowledged, formally practicing, significantly matured (tested and proven), and, altogether, especially exemplary practitioners of the total (or full and complete) practice of the Way of Adidam. They must perform significant cultural (and practical, and, as necessary, managerial) service within the gathering of all formally acknowledged practitioners of the four congregations of the Way of Adidam. Either they must live within a formally designated community of formally acknowledged practitioners of the Way of Adidam or, otherwise, they must be formally designated serving residents of one of the by Me formally Empowered Ruchira Sannyasin Hermitage-Retreat Sanctuaries or one of the by Me formally Empowered Pilgrimage and Retreat Sanctuaries for all formally acknowledged practitioners of the Way of Adidam. And they must formally accept (and rightly fulfill) all the obligations and disciplines associated with membership within the Lay Renunciate Order. ["The Orders of My True and Free Renunciate Devotees"]

right side of the heart   See **heart, stations of the heart**.

Ruchira Avatar   In Sanskrit, "Ruchira" means "bright, radiant, effulgent". Thus, the Reference "Ruchira Avatar" indicates that Avatar Adi Da Samraj is the "Bright" (or Radiant) Descent of the Divine Reality Itself into the conditionally manifested worlds, Appearing here in His bodily (human) Form.

Ruchira Avatara Bhakti Yoga   Ruchira Avatara Bhakti Yoga is the principal Gift, Calling, and Discipline Offered by Adi Da Samraj to all who practice the Way of Adidam (in all four congregations).

The phrase "Ruchira Avatara Bhakti Yoga" is itself a summary of the Way of Adidam. "Bhakti", in Sanskrit, is love, adoration, or devotion, while "Yoga" is a Real-God-Realizing discipline (or practice). "Ruchira Avatara Bhakti Yoga" is, thus, "the Divinely Revealed practice of devotional love for (and devotional response to) the Ruchira Avatar, Adi Da Samraj".

The technical practice of Ruchira Avatara Bhakti Yoga is a four-part process of Invoking, feeling, breathing, and serving Avatar Adi Da in every moment.

For Avatar Adi Da's essential Instruction in Ruchira Avatara Bhakti Yoga, see the *Da Love-Ananda Gita (The Free Gift Of The Divine Love-Bliss)*, Part Five, verse 25, and Part Six; *Hridaya Rosary*

(Four Thorns Of Heart-Instruction), Parts Four and Five; and *What, Where, When, How, Why and <u>Who</u> To Remember To Be Happy*, Part Three, "Surrender the Faculties of the Body-Mind To Me" and "How to Practice Whole Bodily Devotion To Me".

Ruchira Avatara Satsang   The Hindi word "Satsang" literally means "true (or right) relationship", "the company of Truth". "Ruchira Avatara Satsang" is the eternal relationship of mutual sacred commitment between Avatar Adi Da Samraj and each true and formally acknowledged practitioner of the Way of Adidam. Once it is consciously assumed by any practitioner, Ruchira Avatara Satsang is an all-inclusive Condition, bringing Divine Grace and Blessings and sacred obligations, responsibilities, and tests into every dimension of the practitioner's life and consciousness.

The Ruchira Buddha   The Enlightened One Who Shines with the Divine "Brightness".

The Ruchira Buddha-Avatar   The "Bright" Enlightened One Who is the Incarnation of the Divine Person. (See also **Avatar**.)

Ruchira Buddhism   "Ruchira Buddhism" is the Way of devotion to the Ruchira Buddha—"the 'Bright' Buddha", Avatar Adi Da Samraj (or, more fully, "the Radiant, Shining, 'Bright' Illuminator and Enlightener Who Is Inherently, or Perfectly Subjectively, Self-Enlightened, and Eternally Awake").

Ruchira Samadhi   "Ruchira Samadhi" (Sanskrit for "the Samadhi of the 'Bright'") is one of the references that Avatar Adi Da Samraj uses for the Divinely Enlightened Condition Realized in the seventh stage of life, Which He characterizes as the Unconditional Realization of the Divine "Brightness".

Ruchira Sannyasin Order   See **renunciate orders**, and see also p. 290.

Rudi / Swami Rudrananda   See **Lineage, Avatar Adi Da's.**

S

"Sadhana Years"   In Sanskrit, "Sadhana" means "self-transcending religious or Spiritual practice". Avatar Adi Da's "Sadhana Years" refers to the time from which He began His quest to recover the Truth of Existence (at Columbia College) until His Divine Re-Awakening in 1970. Avatar Adi Da's full description of His "Sadhana Years" is Given in *The Knee Of Listening*.

Saguna   "Saguna" is Sanskrit for "containing (or accompanied by) qualities".

Sahaj   "Sahaj" is Hindi (from Sanskrit "sahaja") for "twin-born", "natural", or "innate". Avatar Adi Da uses the term to indicate the Coincidence (in the case of Divine Self-Realization) of the Inherently Spiritual and Transcendental Divine Reality with conditional reality. Sahaj, therefore, is the Inherent (or Native) and, thus, truly "Natural" State of Being. (See also **Samadhi**.)

Sahaj Samadhi   See **Samadhi**.

sahasrar   In the traditional system of seven chakras, the sahasrar is the highest chakra (or subtle energy center), associated with the crown of the head and beyond. It is described as a thousand-petaled lotus, the terminal of Light to which the Yogic process (of Spiritual ascent through the chakras) aspires.

During His "Sadhana Years", Avatar Adi Da spontaneously experienced what He calls the "severing of the sahasrar". The Spirit-Energy no longer ascended into the crown of the head (and beyond), but rather "fell" into the Heart, and rested as the Witness-Consciousness. It was this experience that directly revealed to Avatar Adi Da that, while the Yogic traditions regard the sahasrar as the seat of Enlightenment, the Heart is truly the Seat of Divine Consciousness.

Avatar Adi Da's account of the severing of the sahasrar in His own Case is Given in chapter eighteen of *The Knee Of Listening*.

Saiva Siddhanta "Saiva Siddhanta" is the name of an important school of Saivism which flourished in South India and survives into the present.

Samadhi The Sanskrit word "Samadhi" traditionally denotes various exalted states that appear in the context of esoteric meditation and Realization. Avatar Adi Da Teaches that, for His devotees, Samadhi is, even more simply and fundamentally, the Enjoyment of His Divine State, Which is experienced (even from the beginning of the practice of Adidam) through ego-transcending heart-Communion with Him. Therefore, "the cultivation of Samadhi" is another way to describe the fundamental basis of the Way of Adidam. Avatar Adi Da's devotee is in Samadhi in any moment of standing beyond the separate self in true devotional heart-Communion with Him. (See "The Cultivation of My Divine Samadhi", in *The Seven Stages Of Life*.)

The developmental process leading to Divine Enlightenment in the Way of Adidam may be marked by many signs, principal among which are the Samadhis of the advanced and the ultimate stages of life and practice. Although some of the traditionally known Samadhis of the fourth, the fifth, and the sixth stages of life may appear in the course of an individual's practice of the Way of Adidam, the appearance of all of them is by no means necessary, or even probable (as Avatar Adi Da Indicates in His Wisdom-Teaching). The essential Samadhis of the Way of Adidam are those that are uniquely Granted by Avatar Adi Da Samraj—the Samadhi of the "Thumbs" and seventh stage Sahaj Samadhi. All the possible forms of Samadhi in the Way of Adidam are described in full detail in *The Dawn Horse Testament Of The Ruchira Avatar*.

Samadhi of the "Thumbs" "The 'Thumbs'" is Avatar Adi Da's technical term for the invasion of the body-mind by a particular kind of forceful Descent of His Divine Spirit-Current. Avatar Adi Da describes His own experience of the "Thumbs" in *The Knee Of Listening*:

. . . I had an experience that appeared like a mass of gigantic thumbs coming down from above, pressing into my throat (causing something of a gagging, and somewhat suffocating, sensation), and then pressing further (and, it seemed, would have expanded without limitation or end), into some form of myself that was much larger than my physical body. . . .

The "Thumbs" were not visible in the ordinary sense. I did not see them then or even as a child. They were not visible to me with my eyes, nor did I hallucinate them pictorially. Yet, I very consciously experienced and felt them as having a peculiar form and mobility, as I likewise experienced my own otherwise invisible and greater form.

I did not at that time or at any time in my childhood fully allow this intervention of the "Thumbs" to take place. I held it off from its fullest descent, in fear of being overwhelmed, for I did not understand at all what was taking place. However, in later years this same experience occurred naturally during meditation. Because my meditation had been allowed to progress gradually, and the realizations at each level were thus perceived without shock, I was able at those times to allow the experience to take place. When I did, the "Thumbs" completely entered my living form. They appeared like tongues, or parts of a Force, coming from above. And when they had entered deep into my body, the magnetic or energic balances of my living being reversed. On several occasions I felt as if the body had risen above the ground somewhat, and this is perhaps the basis for certain evidence in mystical literature of the phenomenon of levitation, or bodily transport.

At any rate, during those stages in meditation the body ceased to be polarized toward the ground, or the gravitational direction of the earth's center. There was a strong reversal of polarity, communicated along a line of Force analogous to the spine. The physical body, as well as the Energy-form that could be interiorly felt as analogous to but detached from the physical body, was felt to turn in a curve along the spine and forward in the direction of the heart. When this reversal of Energy was allowed to take place completely, I resided in a totally different body, which also contained the physical body. It was spherical in shape. And the sensation of dwelling as that form was completely peaceful. The physical body was completely relaxed and polarized to the shape of this other spherical body. The mind became quieted, and then there was a movement in consciousness that would go even deeper, into a higher conscious State beyond physical and mental awareness. I was to learn that this spherical body was what Yogis and occultists call the "subtle" body (which includes the "pranic", or natural life-energy, dimension and the "astral", or the lower mental and the higher mental, dimensions of the living being).

In the fullest form of this experience, which Avatar Adi Da calls "the Samadhi of the 'Thumbs'", His Spirit-Invasion Descends all the way to the bottom of the frontal line of the body-mind (at the bodily base) and ascends through the spinal line, overwhelming the ordinary human sense of bodily existence, infusing the whole being with intense blissfulness, and releasing the ordinary, confined sense of body, mind, and separate self.

Both the experience of the "Thumbs" and the full Samadhi of the "Thumbs" are unique to the Way of Adidam, for they are specifically signs of the "Crashing Down" (or the Divine Descent) of Avatar Adi Da's Spirit-Baptism, into the body-minds of His devotees. The Samadhi of the "Thumbs" is a kind of "Nirvikalpa" (or formless) Samadhi—but in descent in the frontal line, rather than in ascent in the spinal line.

Avatar Adi Da's extended Instruction relative to the "Thumbs" is Given in "The 'Thumbs' Is The Fundamental Sign Of The Crashing Down Of My Person". This Essay appears in a number of Avatar Adi Da's "Source-Texts" (*Hridaya Rosary, The <u>Only</u> Complete Way To Realize The Unbroken Light Of <u>Real</u> God, Ruchira Avatara Hridaya-Siddha Yoga, The Seven Stages Of Life*, and *Santosha Adidam*, as well as chapter twenty-four of *The Dawn Horse Testament Of The Ruchira Avatar* and chapter thirty-one of *The Heart Of The Dawn Horse Testament Of The Ruchira Avatar*).

Savikalpa Samadhi and "Cosmic Consciousness"   The Sanskrit term "Savikalpa Samadhi" literally means "meditative ecstasy with form", or "deep meditative concentration (or absorption) in which form (or defined experiential content) is still perceived". Avatar Adi Da indicates that there are two basic forms of Savikalpa Samadhi. The first is the various experiences produced by the Spiritual ascent of energy and attention (into mystical phenomena, visions, and other subtle sensory perceptions of subtle psychic forms) and the various states of Yogic Bliss (or Spirit-"Intoxication").

The second (and highest) form of Savikalpa Samadhi is called "Cosmic Consciousness", or the "'Vision' of Cosmic Unity". This is an isolated or periodic occurrence in which attention ascends, uncharacteristically and spontaneously, to a state of awareness wherein conditional existence is perceived as a Unity in Divine Awareness. This conditional form of "Cosmic Consciousness" is pursued in many mystical and Yogic paths. It depends upon manipulation of attention and the body-mind, and it is interpreted from the point of view of the separate, body-based or mind-based self—and, therefore, it is not equivalent to Divine Enlightenment.

Avatar Adi Da's discussion of Savikalpa Samadhi is found in "Vision, Audition, and Touch in The Process of Ascending Meditation in The Way Of Adidam", in Part Four of *Ruchira Avatara Hridaya-Siddha Yoga*.

Avatar Adi Da's description of the varieties of experiential form possible in Savikalpa Samadhi is found in "The Significant Experiential Signs That May Appear in the Course of The Way Of Adidam", in Part Three of *What, Where, When, How, Why, and <u>Who</u> To Remember To Be Happy*.

fifth stage Nirvikalpa Samadhi
The Sanskrit term "Nirvikalpa Samadhi" literally means "meditative ecstasy without form", or "deep meditative concentration (or absorption) in which there is no

perception of form (or defined experiential content)". Traditionally, this state is regarded to be the final goal of the many schools of Yogic ascent whose orientation to practice is that of the fifth stage of life. Like "Cosmic Consciousness", fifth stage conditional Nirvikalpa Samadhi is an isolated or periodic Realization. In it, attention ascends beyond all conditional manifestation into the formless Matrix of Divine Vibration and Divine Light Infinitely Above the world, the body, and the mind. And, like the various forms of Savikalpa Samadhi, fifth stage conditional Nirvikalpa Samadhi is a temporary state of attention (or, more precisely, of the suspension of attention). It is produced by manipulation of attention and of the body-mind, and is (therefore) incapable of being maintained when attention returns (as it inevitably does) to the states of the body-mind.

Avatar Adi Da's Instruction relative to fifth stage conditional Nirvikalpa Samadhi is Given in chapter forty-two of *The Dawn Horse Testament Of The Ruchira Avatar.*

Jnana Samadhi, or Jnana Nirvikalpa Samadhi "Jnana" means "knowledge". Jnana Nirvikalpa Samadhi (sixth stage Nirvakalpa Samadhi, or, simply, Jnana Samadhi) is the characteristic meditative experience in the sixth stage of life in the Way of Adidam. Produced by the intentional withdrawal of attention from the conditional body-mind-self and its relations, Jnana Samadhi is the conditional, temporary Realization of the Transcendental Self (or Consciousness Itself), exclusive of any perception (or cognition) of world, objects, relations, body, mind, or separate-self-sense—and, thereby, formless (or "nirvikalpa").

Avatar Adi Da's Instruction relative to Jnana Nirvikalpa Samadhi is Given in "The Sixth and The Seventh Stages of Life in The Way Of Adidam" in *The Lion Sutra.*

seventh stage Sahaj Samadhi, or seventh stage Sahaja Nirvikalpa Samadhi Avatar Adi Da's description of seventh stage Sahaj Samadhi is Given in Part Four of *The <u>All-Completing</u> and <u>Final</u> Divine Revelation To Mankind.*

Samraj "Samraj" (from the Sanskrit "Samraja") is a traditional Indian term used to refer to great kings, but also to refer to the Hindu gods. "Samraja" is defined as "universal or supreme ruler", "paramount Lord", or "paramount sovereign".

The Sanskrit word "raja" (the basic root of "Samraj") means "king". It comes from the verbal root "raj", meaning "to reign, to rule, to illuminate". The prefix "sam-" expresses "union" or "completeness". "Samraj" is thus literally the complete ruler, the ruler of everything altogether. "Samraj" was traditionally given as a title to a king who was regarded to be a "universal monarch".

Avatar Adi Da's Name "Adi Da Samraj" expresses that He is the Primordial (or Original) Giver, Who Blesses all as the Universal Lord of every thing, every where, for all time. The Sovereignty of His Kingdom has nothing to do with the world of human politics. Rather, it is entirely a matter of His Spiritual Dominion over all and All, His Kingship in the hearts of His devotees.

samsara / samsaric "Samsara" (or "samsaric") is a classical Buddhist and Hindu term for all conditional worlds and states, or the cyclical realm of birth and change and death. It connotes the suffering and limitations experienced in those limited worlds.

Sanctuaries Avatar Adi Da has Empowered two Hermitage-Retreat Sanctuaries and two Pilgrimage and Retreat Sanctuaries as Agents of His Divine Spiritual Transmission. The senior Hermitage-Retreat Sanctuary is Adidam Samrajashram, the Island of Naitauba in Fiji, where Avatar Adi Da usually Resides in Perpetual Retreat. It is the place where Avatar Adi Da Himself and the senior renunciate order of the Way of Adidam, the Ruchira Sannyasin Order of the Tantric Renunciates of Adidam, are established. It is the primary Seat of Avatar Adi Da's Divine Blessing Work with the entire Cosmic Mandala.

Avatar Adi Da has Spoken of the significance of this Hermitage Ashram:

AVATAR ADI DA SAMRAJ: Adidam Samrajashram was established so that I might have a Place of Seclusion in which to do My Spiritual Work. This is the Place of My perpetual Samadhi, the Place of My perpetual Self-Radiance. Therefore, this is the Place where people come to participate in My Samadhi and be further Awakened by It. My devotees come to Adidam Samrajashram to magnify their practice of right, true, and full devotion to Me, to practice the Way of Adidam as I Have Revealed and Given It for the sake of most perfectly ego-transcending Real-God-Realization.

Tat Sundaram is a small Hermitage-Retreat Sanctuary that provides a private circumstance for Avatar Adi Da and members of the Ruchira Sannyasin Order.

The two Pilgrimage and Retreat Sanctuaries (The Mountain Of Attention, in northern California, and Da Love-Ananda Mahal, in Hawaii—formerly known as "Tumomama Sanctuary") were principal sites of Avatar Adi Da's Teaching Demonstration during the years of His Divine Teaching-Work. Through His years of Blessing-Infusion of each of these Hermitage-Retreat Sanctuaries and these Pilgrimage and Retreat Sanctuaries, He has fully Empowered them for His devotees throughout all time.

Santosha "Santosha" is Sanskrit for "satisfaction" or "contentment"—qualities associated with a sense of completion. These qualities are characteristic of no-seeking, the fundamental Principle of Avatar Adi Da's Wisdom-Teaching and of His entire Revelation of Truth. Because of its uniquely appropriate meanings, "Santosha" is one of Avatar Adi Da's Names. As Santosha Adi Da, Avatar Adi Da Samraj is the Divine Giver of Perfect Divine Contentedness, or Perfect Searchlessness.

Santosha Avatar As the Santosha Avatar, Avatar Adi Da is the Very Incarnation of Perfect Divine Contentedness, or Perfect Searchlessness.

Sat-Guru "Sat" means "Truth", "Being", "Existence". Thus, "Sat-Guru" literally means "True Guru", or a Guru who can lead living beings from darkness (or non-Truth) into Light (or the Living Truth).

Satsang The Hindi word "Satsang" (from the Sanskrit "Satsanga") literally means "true (or right) relationship", "the company of Truth". In the Way of Adidam, Satsang is the eternal relationship of mutual sacred commitment between Avatar Adi Da Samraj and each formally acknowledged practitioner of the Way of Adidam.

Savikalpa Samadhi See **Samadhi**.

scientific materialism Scientific materialism is the predominant philosophy and worldview of modern humanity, the basic presumption of which is that the material world is all that exists. In scientific materialism, the method of science, or the observation of objective phenomena, is made into philosophy and a way of life that suppresses our native impulse to Liberation.

seeing See **listening, hearing, and seeing**.

self-Enquiry The practice of self-Enquiry in the form "Avoiding relationship?", unique to the Way of Adidam, was spontaneously developed by Avatar Adi Da in the course of His own Ordeal of Divine Re-Awakening. Intense persistence in the "radical" discipline of this unique form of self-Enquiry led rapidly to Avatar Adi Da's Divine Enlightenment (or Most Perfect Divine Self-Realization) in 1970.

The practice of self-Enquiry in the form "Avoiding relationship?" and the practice of non-verbal Re-cognition are the principal technical practices that serve feeling-Contemplation of Avatar Adi Da in the Devotional Way of Insight.

Self-Existing and Self-Radiant Avatar Adi Da uses "Self-Existing and Self-Radiant" to indicate the two fundamental aspects of the One Divine Person (or Reality)—Existence (or Being, or Consciousness) Itself, and Radiance (or Energy, or Light) Itself.

seven stages of life See **stages of life**.

Shakti, Guru-Shakti "Shakti" is a Sanskrit term for the Divinely Manifesting Energy, Spiritual Power, or Spirit-Current of the Divine Person. Guru-Shakti is the Power of the Guru to Liberate his or her devotees.

Shaktipat In Hindi, "shaktipat" is the "descent of Spiritual Power". Yogic Shaktipat, which manipulates natural, conditional energies or partial manifestations of the Spirit-Current, is typically granted through touch, word, glance, or regard by Yogic Adepts in the fifth stage of life, or fourth to fifth stages of life. Yogic Shaktipat must be distinguished from (and, otherwise, understood to be only a secondary aspect of) the Blessing Transmission of the Heart Itself (Hridaya-Shaktipat), which is uniquely Given by Avatar Adi Da Samraj.

Siddha, Siddha-Guru "Siddha" is Sanskrit for "a completed, fulfilled, or perfected one", or "one of perfect accomplishment, or power". Avatar Adi Da uses "Siddha", or "Siddha-Guru", to mean a Transmission-Master who is a Realizer (to any significant degree) of Real God, Truth, or Reality.

Siddha Yoga "Siddha Yoga" is, literally, "the Yoga of the Perfected One[s]".

Swami Muktananda used the term "Siddha Yoga" to refer to the form of Kundalini Yoga that he taught, which involved initiation of the devotee by the Guru's Transmission of Shakti (or Spiritual Energy). Avatar Adi Da Samraj has indicated that this was a fifth stage form of Siddha Yoga.

In "I (Alone) <u>Am</u> The Adidam Revelation", Avatar Adi Da Says:

. . . I Teach Siddha Yoga in the Mode and Manner of the <u>seventh</u> stage of life (as Ruchira Avatara Hridaya-Siddha Yoga, or Ruchira Avatara Maha-Jnana Hridaya-Shaktipat Yoga)—and always toward (or to the degree of) the Realization inherently associated with (and, at last, Most Perfectly Demonstrated and Proven by) the only-by-Me Revealed and Given seventh

stage of life, and as a practice and a Process that progressively includes (and, coincidently, <u>directly</u> transcends) <u>all</u> <u>six</u> of the phenomenal and developmental (and, necessarily, yet ego-based) stages of life that precede the seventh.

Avatar Adi Da's description of the similarities and differences between traditional Siddha Yoga and the Way of Adidam is Given in "I (Alone) <u>Am</u> The Adidam Revelation", which Essay appears in many of Avatar Adi Da's twenty-three "Source-Texts".

siddhi "Siddhi" is Sanskrit for "power", or "accomplishment". When capitalized in Avatar Adi Da's Wisdom-Teaching, "Siddhi" is the Spiritual, Transcendental, and Divine Awakening-Power That He spontaneously and effortlessly Transmits to all.

"Sila" "Sila" is a Pali Buddhist term meaning "habit", "behavior", "conduct", or "morality". It connotes the restraint of outgoing energy and attention, the disposition of equanimity, or free energy and attention for the Spiritual Process.

"simpler" (or "simplest") form of the Way of Adidam See **forms of practice in the Way of Adidam**.

sleeping See **waking, dreaming, and sleeping**.

"Source-Texts" During the twenty-seven years of His Teaching-Work and Revelation-Work (from 1972 to 1999), Avatar Adi Da elaborately described every aspect of the practice of Adidam, from the beginning of one's approach to Him to the Most Ultimate Realization of the seventh stage of life.

Avatar Adi Da's Heart-Word is summarized in His twenty-three "Source-Texts". These Texts present, in complete and conclusive detail, His Divine Revelations, Confessions, and Instructions, which are the fruits of His years of Teaching and Revelation Work. In addition to this "Source-Literature", Avatar Adi Da's Heart-Word also includes His "Supportive Texts" (comprising His practical Instruction in all the details of the practice of Adidam, including the fundamental disciplines of diet, health, exercise, sexuality, childrearing, and cooperative community), His "Early Literature" (Written during His Teaching Years), and collections of His Talks. (For a complete list of Avatar Adi Da's twenty-three "Source-Texts", see pp. 361-68.)

spinal line, spinal Yoga   The spinal (or ascending) line of the body-mind conducts the Spirit-Current of Divine Life in an upward direction from the base of the body (or perineal area) to the crown of the head, and beyond.

In the Way of Adidam, the spinal Yoga is the process whereby knots and obstructions in the subtle, astral, or the more mentally and subtly oriented dimension of the body-mind are penetrated, opened, surrendered, and released through the devotee's reception and "conductivity" of Avatar Adi Da's Transmission into the spinal line of the body-mind. This ascending Yoga will be required for practitioners of Adidam only in relatively rare cases. The great majority of Avatar Adi Da's devotees will be sufficiently purified through their practice of the frontal Yoga to proceed directly to practice in the context of the sixth stage of life, bypassing practice in the context of the "advanced" fourth stage and the fifth stage of life.

Spirit-Baptism   Avatar Adi Da often refers to His Transmission of Spiritual Blessing as His "Spirit-Baptism". It is often felt by His devotee as a Current descending in the frontal line and ascending in the spinal line. However, Avatar Adi Da's Spirit-Baptism is fundamentally and primarily His Moveless Transmission of the Divine Heart Itself. As a secondary effect, His Spirit-Baptism serves to purify, balance, and energize the entire body-mind of the devotee who is prepared to receive It.

Spiritual anatomy / esoteric anatomy
Avatar Adi Da Samraj has Revealed that just as there is a physical anatomy, there is an actual Spiritual anatomy, or structure, that is present in every human being. As He Says in *The Basket Of Tolerance*, it is

because of this structure that the "experiential and developmental process of Growth and Realization demonstrates itself in accordance with what I have Revealed and Demonstrated to be the seven stages of life".

Avatar Adi Da's extended Instruction relative to the Spiritual anatomy of Man is Given in *The Seven Stages Of Life* and *Santosha Adidam*.

Spiritual, Transcendental, Divine
Avatar Adi Da uses the words "Spiritual", "Transcendental", and "Divine" in reference to dimensions of Reality that are Realized progressively in the Way of Adidam. "Transcendental" and "Spiritual" indicate two fundamental aspects of the One Divine Reality and Person— Consciousness Itself (Which Is Transcendental, or Self-Existing) and Energy Itself (Which Is Spiritual, or Self-Radiant). Only That Which Is Divine is simultaneously Transcendental <u>and</u> Spiritual.

Sri   "Sri" is a term of honor and veneration often applied to an Adept. The word literally means "flame" in Sanskrit, indicating that the one honored is radiant with Blessing Power.

stages of life   Avatar Adi Da has Revealed the underlying structure of human growth in seven stages. The seventh stage of life is Divine Self-Realization, or Most Perfect Enlightenment.

The first three stages of life develop, respectively, the physical, emotional, and mental/volitional functions of the body-mind. The first stage begins at birth and continues for approximately five to seven years; the second stage follows, continuing until approximately the age of twelve to fourteen; and the third stage is optimally complete by the early twenties. In the case of virtually all individuals, however, failed adaptation in the earlier stages of life means that maturity in the third stage of life takes much longer to attain, and it is usually never fulfilled, with the result that the ensuing stages of Spiritual development do not even begin.

In the Way of Adidam, however, growth in the first three stages of life unfolds in the Spiritual Company of Avatar Adi Da and is based in the practice of feeling-Contemplation of His bodily (human) Form and in devotion, service, and self-discipline in relation to His bodily (human) Form. By the Grace of this relationship to Avatar Adi Da, the first three (or foundation) stages of life are lived and fulfilled in an ego-transcending devotional disposition, or (as He describes it) "in the 'original' (or beginner's) devotional context of the fourth stage of life".

The fourth stage of life is the transitional stage between the gross (bodily-based) point of view of the first three stages of life and the subtle (mind-based, or psyche-based) point of view of the fifth stage of life. The fourth stage of life is the stage of Spiritual devotion, or devotional surrender of separate self to the Divine, in which the gross functions of the being are aligned to the higher psychic (or subtle) functions of the being. In the fourth stage of life, the gross (or bodily-based) personality of the first three stages of life is purified through reception of the Spiritual Force ("Holy Spirit", or "Shakti") of the Divine Reality, which prepares the being to out-grow the bodily-based point of view.

In the Way of Adidam, as the orientation of the fourth stage of life matures, heart-felt surrender to the bodily (human) Form of Avatar Adi Da deepens by His Grace, Drawing His devotee into Love-Communion with His All-Pervading Spiritual Presence. Growth in the "basic" context of the fourth stage of life in the Way of Adidam is also characterized by reception of Avatar Adi Da's Baptizing Current of Divine Spirit-Energy, Which is initially felt to flow down the front of the body from Infinitely Above the head to the bodily base (or perineal area).

The Descent of Avatar Adi Da's Spirit-Baptism releases obstructions predominantly in what He calls the "frontal personality", or the personality typically animated in the waking state (as opposed to the dream state and the state of deep sleep). This Spirit-Baptism purifies His devotee and infuses the devotee with His Spirit-Power. Avatar Adi Da's devotee is, thus, awakened to profound love of (and devotional intimacy with) Him.

Eventually, Avatar Adi Da's Divine Spirit-Current may be felt to turn about at the bodily base and ascend up the spine to the brain core. In this case, the fourth stage of life matures to its "advanced" context, which is focused in the Ascent of Avatar Adi Da's Spirit-Baptism and the consequent purification of the spinal line of the body-mind.

In the fifth stage of life, attention is concentrated in the subtle (or psychic) levels of awareness in ascent. Avatar Adi Da's Divine Spirit-Current is felt to penetrate the brain core and rise toward the Matrix of Light and Love-Bliss Infinitely Above the crown of the head, possibly culminating in the temporary experience of fifth stage conditional Nirvikalpa Samadhi, or "formless ecstasy". In the Way of Adidam, most practitioners will not need to practice either in the "advanced" context of the fourth stage of life or in the context of the fifth stage of life, but will (rather) be Awakened, by Avatar Adi Da's Grace, directly from maturity in the fourth stage of life to the Witness-Position of Consciousness (in the context of the sixth stage of life).

In the traditional development of the sixth stage of life, a strategic effort is made to Identify with Consciousness Itself by excluding the realm of conditional phenomena. Avatar Adi Da Teaches, however, that the deliberate intention to exclude the conditional world for the sake of Realizing Transcendental Consciousness is an egoic error that must be transcended by His devotees who are practicing in the context of the sixth stage of life.

In deepest meditation in the sixth stage of life in the Way of Adidam, the knot of attention (which is the root-action of egoity, felt as separation, self-contraction, or the feeling of relatedness) dissolves, and all sense of relatedness yields to the Blissful and undifferentiated Feeling of Being. The characteristic Samadhi of the sixth stage of life is Jnana Samadhi, the temporary Realization of the Transcendental Self (or Consciousness Itself)—which is temporary because it can occur only when awareness of the world is excluded in meditation.

The transition from the sixth stage of life to the seventh stage Realization of Absolute Non-Separateness is the unique Revelation of Avatar Adi Da. Various traditions and individuals previous to Adi Da's Revelation have had sixth stage intuitions (or premonitions) of the Most Perfect seventh stage Realization, but no one previous to Avatar Adi Da has Realized the seventh stage of life.

The seventh stage Realization is a Gift of Avatar Adi Da to His devotees who have (by His Divine Grace) completed their practice of the Way of Adidam in the context of the first six stages of life. The seventh stage of life begins when His devotee Gracefully Awakens from the exclusive Realization of Consciousness to Most Perfect and Permanent Identification with Consciousness Itself, Avatar Adi Da's Divine State. This is Divine Self-Realization, or Divine Enlightenment, the perpetual Samadhi of "Open Eyes" (seventh stage Sahaj Samadhi)—in which all "things" are Divinely Self-Recognized without "difference", as merely apparent modifications of the One Self-Existing and Self-Radiant Divine Consciousness.

In the course of the seventh stage of life, there may be spontaneous incidents in which psycho-physical states and phenomena do not appear to the notice, being Outshined by the "Bright" Radiance of Consciousness Itself. This Samadhi, Which is the Ultimate Realization of Divine Existence, culminates in Divine Translation, or the permanent Outshining of all apparent conditions in the Inherently Perfect Radiance and Love-Bliss of the Divine Self-Condition (which necessarily coincides with the physical death of the body-mind).

In the context of practice of the Way of Adidam, the seven stages of life as Revealed by Avatar Adi Da are not a version of the traditional "ladder" of Spiritual attainment. These stages and their characteristic signs arise naturally in the course of practice for a fully practicing devotee in the Way of Adidam, but the practice itself is oriented to the <u>transcending</u> of the first six stages of life, in the seventh stage Disposition of Inherently Liberated Happiness, Granted by Avatar Adi Da's Divine Grace in His Love-Blissful Spiritual Company.

Avatar Adi Da's extended Instruction relative to the seven stages of life is Given in *The Seven Stages Of Life*.

Star Form   Avatar Adi Da has Revealed that He is "Incarnated" in the Cosmic domain as a brilliant white five-pointed Star, the original (and primal) conditional visible Representation (or Sign) of the "Bright" (the Source-Energy, or Divine Light, of Which all conditional phenomena and the total cosmos are modifications).

The apparently objective Divine Star can potentially be experienced in any moment and location in cosmic Nature. However, the vision of the Divine Star is not a necessary experience for growth in the Spiritual Process or for Divine Self-Realization.

Avatar Adi Da's discussion of His Star Form is found in *He-<u>and</u>-She <u>Is</u> Me*.

student-novice / student-beginner
A student-novice is an individual who is formally approaching, and preparing to become a formal practitioner of, the total practice of the Way of Adidam (as a member of the second congregation). The student-novice makes a vow of eternal commitment to Avatar Adi Da as his or her Divine Guru, and to the practice He has Given, and is initiated into simple devotional and sacramental disciplines in formal relationship to Avatar Adi Da. During the student-novice stage, the individual engages in intensive study of Avatar Adi Da's Wisdom-Teaching and adapts to the functional, practical, relational, and cultural disciplines of the Way of Adidam.

A student-beginner is a practitioner in the initial developmental stage of the second congregation of Adidam. In the course of student-beginner practice, the devotee of Avatar Adi Da, on the basis of the eternal "Bond" of devotion to Him that he or she established as a student-novice, continues the process of listening and further adaptation to the disciplines that were begun in the student-novice stage of approach.

subtle See **gross, subtle, causal**.

"Supportive Texts" Among Avatar Adi Da's "Supportive Texts" are included such books as *Conscious Exercise and the Transcendental Sun*, *The Eating Gorilla Comes in Peace*, *Love of the Two-Armed Form*, and *Easy Death*.

Swami The title "Swami" is traditionally given to an individual who has demonstrated significant self-mastery in the context of a lifetime dedicated to Spiritual renunciation.

Swami Muktananda See **Lineage, Avatar Adi Da's**.

Swami Nityananda See **Lineage, Avatar Adi Da's**.

Swami Rudrananda See **Lineage, Avatar Adi Da's**.

T

Tail of the Horse Adi Da Samraj has often referred to a passage from the ancient Indian text *Satapatha Brahmana*, which He has paraphrased as: "Man does not know. Only the Horse Knows. Therefore, hold to the tail of the Horse." Adi Da has Revealed that, in the most esoteric understanding of this saying, the "Horse" represents the Adept-Realizer, and "holding to the tail of the Horse" represents the devotee's complete dependence on the Adept-Realizer in order to Realize Real God (or Truth, or Reality).

"talking" school "'Talking' school" is a phrase used by Avatar Adi Da to refer to those in any tradition of sacred life whose approach is characterized by talking, thinking, reading, and philosophical analysis and debate, or even meditative enquiry or reflection, without a concomitant and foundation discipline of body, emotion, mind, and breath. He contrasts the "talking" school with the "practicing" school approach—"practicing" schools involving those who are committed to the ordeal of real ego-transcending discipline, under the guidance of a true Guru.

Tat Sundaram "Sundara" is the Sanskrit word for "beauty", and "Sundaram" means "something which is beautiful". "Tat" is the Sanskrit word for "it" or "that". Thus, "Tat Sundaram" means "That Which Is Beautiful" or, by extension, "All Of This Is Beautiful", and is a reference to the seventh stage Realization of the Perfect Non-Separateness and Love-Bliss-Nature of the entire world—conditional and Un-Conditional. Tat Sundaram is also the name of the Hermitage-Retreat Sanctuary reserved for Avatar Adi Da in northern California.

Teaching-Work For a description of Avatar Adi Da's Divine Teaching-Work, see pp. 15-16.

technically "fully elaborated" practice See **forms of practice in the Way of Adidam**.

technically "simpler" (and even "simplest") practice See **forms of practice in the Way of Adidam**.

three stations of the heart See **heart, stations of the heart**.

the "Thumbs" See **Samadhi**.

Thunder The Divine Sound of Thunder (which Avatar Adi Da also describes as the "Da" Sound, or "Da-Om" Sound, or "Om" Sound) is one of Avatar Adi Da's three Eternal Forms of Manifestation in the conditional worlds—together with His Divine Star of Light and His Divine Spiritual Body.

Avatar Adi Da's principal Revelation-Confession about these three forms of His Manifestation is Given in *He-and-She Is Me*.

. . . I Am conditionally Manifested (First) As The everywhere Apparently Audible (and Apparently Objective) Divine Sound-Vibration (or "Da" Sound, or "Da-Om" Sound, or "Om" Sound, The Objective Sign Of The He, Present As The Conscious Sound Of sounds, In The Center Of The Cosmic Mandala), and As The everywhere Apparently Visible (and Apparently Objective) Divine Star (The Objective Sign

Of The She, Present As The Conscious Light Of lights, In The Center Of The Cosmic Mandala), and (From That He and She) As The everywhere Apparently Touchable (or Tangible), and Apparently Objective, Total Divine Spiritual Body (The Objective, and All-and-all-Surrounding, and All-and-all-Pervading Conscious and Me-Personal Body Of "Bright" Love-Bliss-Presence, Divinely Self-"Emerging", Now, and Forever Hereafter, From The Center Of The Cosmic Mandala Into The Depths Of Even every "where" In The Cosmic Domain) . . . .

total practice of the Way of Adidam
The total practice of the Way of Adidam is the full and complete practice of the Way that Avatar Adi Da Samraj has Given to His devotees who are formal members of the first or the second congregation of Adidam (see pp. 285-91). One who embraces the total practice of the Way of Adidam conforms every aspect of his or her life and being to Avatar Adi Da's Divine Word of Instruction. Therefore, it is only such devotees (in the first or the second congregation of Adidam) who have the potential of Realizing Divine Enlightenment.

"True Prayer"   "True Prayer" is Avatar Adi Da's technical term for the various forms of the "conscious process" that are practiced by His Spiritually Awakened devotees who have chosen the Devotional Way of Faith.

Avatar Adi Da's full Instruction relative to "True Prayer" is Given in *The Dawn Horse Testament Of The Ruchira Avatar.*

Turaga   "Turaga" (Too-RAHNG-ah) is Fijian for "Lord".

"turiya", "turiyatita"   Terms used in the Hindu philosophical systems. Traditionally, "turiya" means "the fourth state" (beyond waking, dreaming, and sleeping), and "turiyatita" means "the state beyond the fourth", or beyond all states.

Avatar Adi Da, however, has given these terms different meanings in the context of the Way of Adidam. He uses the term "turiya" to indicate the Awakening to the Consciousness Itself (in the context of

the sixth stage of life), and "turiyatita" as the State of Most Perfect Divine Enlightenment, or the Realization of all arising as transparent and non-binding modifications of the One Divine Reality (in the context of the seventh stage of life).

U

ultimate   See **the advanced and the ultimate stages of life**.

Ultimate Self-Domain   "Ultimate Self-Domain" is a synonym for "Divine Self-Domain". (See **Divine Self-Domain**.)

Ultimate Source-Condition   The Divine Reality prior to all conditional arising, which is, therefore, the "Source" of all conditional worlds, beings, and things.

V

Vira-Yogi   Sanskrit for "Hero-Yogi". (See **"Heroic"**.)

Vow   For a description of the Vow and responsibilities associated with the Way of Adidam, see pp. 284-96.

W, X, Y, Z

waking, dreaming, and sleeping
These three states of consciousness are associated with the dimensions of cosmic existence.

The waking state (and the physical body) is associated with the gross dimension.

The dreaming state (and visionary, mystical, and Yogic Spiritual processes) is associated with the subtle dimension. The subtle dimension, which is senior to the gross dimension, includes the etheric (or energic), lower mental (or verbal-intentional and lower psychic), and higher mental (or deeper psychic, mystical, and discriminative) functions.

The sleeping state is associated with the causal dimension, which is senior to both the gross and the subtle dimensions. It is the root of attention, prior to any particular experience. (See also **gross, subtle, causal**.)

washing the dog   Avatar Adi Da uses the metaphor of the "dog" and "washing the dog" to Indicate the purification of the body-mind in the process of Adidam. He addresses the presumption (as in the Kundalini Yoga tradition) that the Spiritual process requires a spinal Yoga, or an effort of arousing Spiritual Energy literally at the "tail" end of the "dog" (the bodily base, or the muladhara chakra), and then drawing It up (or allowing It to ascend) through the spinal line to the head (and above). In contrast, Avatar Adi Da Samraj has Revealed (particularly in His *Hridaya Rosary*) that, in reality, the human being can be truly purified and Liberated (or the "dog" can be "washed") only by receiving His Divine Blessing-Power (or Hridaya-Shakti) and Spiritual Person downward from Infinitely Above the head to the bodily base. This Process of downward reception of Avatar Adi Da is what He calls the "frontal Yoga", because it occurs in the frontal line of the body (which is a natural pathway of descending energy, down the front of the body, from the crown of the head to the bodily base). This necessary descending Yoga of the frontal line, once completed, is sufficient to purify and Spiritually Infuse the body-mind, and, in most cases, it allows the practitioner of the Way of Adidam to bypass the ascending Yoga of the spinal line (which is the complementary natural pathway of ascending energy, up the back of the body, from the bodily base to the crown of the head). The frontal line and the spinal line are the two arcs of the continuous energy-circuit that Avatar Adi Da calls the "Circle" of the body-mind.

AVATAR ADI DA SAMRAJ: You wash a dog from the head to the tail. But somehow or other, egos looking to Realize think they can wash the "dog" from the "tail" toward the head by doing spinal Yoga. But, in Truth, and in Reality, only the frontal Yoga can accomplish most perfect Divine Self-Realization, because it begins from the superior position, from the "head" position, from My Crashing Down.

The heart-disposition is magnified by My Crashing Down in your devotional Communion with Me. And the vital,

grosser dimensions of the being are purified by this washing from the head toward the "tail". If the Process had to begin from the bodily base up, it would be very difficult, very traumatizing—and, ultimately, impossible. The "dog" is washed, simply and very directly, by your participation in My Divine Descent, by your participation in this frontal Yoga. I am Speaking now of the Spiritually Awakened stages, basically. But, even in the case of beginning practitioners in the Way of Adidam—not yet Spiritually Awakened, not yet responsible for the truly Spiritual dimension of their relationship to Me—this "wash" is, by Means of My Avataric Divine Grace, going on.

Therefore, Spiritual life need not be a traumatic course. The "dog" should enjoy being bathed. Nice gentle little guy, happy to be rubbed and touched. You talk to him, struggle a little bit, but you gentle him down. That is how it should work. And, at the end of it, the "dog" sort of "wags its tail", shakes the water off—nice and clean, happy, your best friend. That is how it should work.

If you wash the "dog" from the "tail" up, you smear the shit from his backside toward his head. Basically, that "washing from the tail toward the head" is a self-generated, self-"guruing" kind of effort. The Divine Process can only occur by Means of Divine Grace. Even the word "Shaktipat" means the "Descent (pat) of Divine Force (Shakti)". But Shaktipat as it appears in the traditions is basically associated with admonitions to practice a spinal Yoga, moving from the base up. In Truth, the Divine Yoga in My Company is a Descent—washing the "dog" from head to "tail" rather than giving the "dog" a "bone", letting it wash itself from the "tail" to the head.

DEVOTEE: It is only Your Hridaya-Shakti that does it.

AVATAR ADI DA SAMRAJ: This is why you must invest yourself in Me. And that is how the "dog" gets washed. [August 13, 1995]

Avatar Adi Da's extended Discourse relative to "washing the dog" is "Be Washed, From Head to Tail, By Heart-Devotion To Me", in *Hridaya Rosary*.

Way of "Radical" Understanding
Avatar Adi Da uses "understanding" to
mean "the process of transcending
egoity". Thus, to "understand" is to simultaneously observe the activity of the self-
contraction and to surrender that activity
via devotional resort to Avatar Adi Da
Samraj.

Avatar Adi Da has Revealed that,
despite their intention to Realize Reality
(or Truth, or Real God), all religious and
Spiritual traditions (other than the Way of
Adidam) are involved, in one manner or
another, with the search to satisfy the ego.
Only Avatar Adi Da has Revealed the Way
to "radically" understand the ego and (in
due course, through intensive formal practice of the Way of Adidam, as His formally
acknowledged devotee) to most perfectly
transcend the ego. Thus, the Way Avatar
Adi Da has Given is the "Way of 'Radical'
Understanding".

**Witness, Witness-Consciousness,
Witness-Position**   When Consciousness
is free of identification with the body-
mind, it takes up its natural "position" as
the Conscious Witness of all that arises to
and in and as the body-mind.

In the Way of Adidam, the stable
Realization of the Witness-Position is associated with, or demonstrated via, the
effortless surrender (or relaxation) of all
the forms of seeking and all the motives
of attention that characterize the first five
stages of life. However, identification with
the Witness-Position is not final (or Most
Perfect) Realization of the Divine Self.
Rather, it is the first of the three stages of
the "Perfect Practice" in the Way of
Adidam, which Practice, in due course,
Realizes, by Avatar Adi Da's Grace, complete and irreversible and utterly Love-
Blissful Identification with Consciousness
Itself.

Avatar Adi Da's extended Instruction
relative to the Witness is Given in *The
Lion Sutra*.

Yoga   "Yoga", in Sanskrit, is literally
"yoking", or "union", usually referring to
any discipline or process whereby an
aspirant attempts to unite with God.
Avatar Adi Da acknowledges this conventional and traditional use of the term, but
also, in reference to the Great Yoga of
Adidam, employs it in a "radical" sense,
free of the usual implication of egoic separation and seeking.

Yogananda, Paramahansa
Paramahansa Yogananda (Mukunda Lal
Ghosh, 1893-1952) was born in Bengal,
the child of devout Hindu parents. As a
young man, Yogananda found his Guru,
Swami Yukteswar Giri, who initiated him
into an order of formal renunciates. In
1920, Yogananda traveled to America to
attend an international conference of religions in Boston. Subsequently he settled
in the United States, attracting many
American devotees. He Taught "Kriya
Yoga", a system of practice that had been
passed down to him by his own Teacher
and that had originally been developed
from traditional techniques of Kundalini
Yoga. Yogananda became widely known
through the publication of his life-story,
Autobiography of a Yogi.

The Sacred Literature of Avatar Adi Da Samraj

Read the astounding Story of Avatar Adi Da's Divine Life and Work in *The Promised God-Man Is Here*.

The Promised God-Man Is Here:
The Extraordinary Life-Story,
The "Radical" Teaching-Work, and
The Divinely "Emerging" World-Blessing
Work Of The Divine World-Teacher
Of The "Late-Time", Ruchira Avatar
Adi Da Samraj

The profound, heart-rending, humorous, miraculous, wild—and true—Story of the Divine Person Alive in human Form. Essential reading as background for the study of Avatar Adi Da's books.

Enjoy the beautiful summary of His Message that Avatar Adi Da has written especially "for children, and everyone else".

What, Where, When, How, Why, and <u>Who</u> To Remember To Be Happy

Illustrated Children's Edition

Fundamental Truth about life as a human being, told in very simple language for

children. Accompanied by extraordinarily vivid and imaginative illustrations.

The Five Books Of
The Heart Of The Adidam Revelation

In these five books, Avatar Adi Da Samraj has distilled the very essence of His Eternal Message to every one, in all times and places.

BOOK ONE:

Aham Da Asmi
(Beloved, I <u>Am</u> Da)

The "Late-Time" Avataric Revelation Of The True and Spiritual Divine Person (The egoless Personal Presence Of Reality and Truth, Which <u>Is</u> The Only <u>Real</u> God)

The most extraordinary statement ever made in human history. Avatar Adi Da Samraj fully Reveals Himself as the Living Divine Person and Proclaims His Infinite and Undying Love for all and All.

BOOK TWO:

Ruchira Avatara Gita
(The Way Of The Divine Heart-Master)

The "Late-Time" Avataric Revelation Of The Great Secret Of The Divinely Self-Revealed Way That Most Perfectly Realizes The True and Spiritual Divine Person (The egoless Personal Presence Of Reality and Truth, Which <u>Is</u> The Only <u>Real</u> God)

Avatar Adi Da Offers to every one the ecstatic practice of devotional relationship to Him— explaining how devotion to a living human Adept-Realizer has always been the source of true religion, and distinguishing true Guru-devotion from religious cultism.

Book Three:

Da Love-Ananda Gita
(The Free Gift Of The Divine Love-Bliss)

The "Late-Time" Avataric Revelation Of The Great Means To Worship and To Realize The True and Spiritual Divine Person (The egoless Personal Presence Of Reality and Truth, Which <u>Is</u> The Only <u>Real</u> God)

Avatar Adi Da Reveals the secret simplicity at the heart of Adidam—relinquishing your preoccupation with yourself (and all your problems and your suffering) and, instead, Contemplating the "Bright" Divine Person of Infinite Love-Bliss.

Book Four:

Hridaya Rosary
(Four Thorns Of Heart-Instruction)

The "Late-Time" Avataric Revelation Of The Universally Tangible Divine Spiritual Body, Which Is The Supreme Agent Of The Great Means To Worship and To Realize The True and Spiritual Divine Person (The egoless Personal Presence Of Reality and Truth, Which <u>Is</u> The Only <u>Real</u> God)

The ultimate Mysteries of Spiritual life, never before revealed. In breathtakingly beautiful poetry, Avatar Adi Da Samraj sings of the "melting" of the ego in His "Rose Garden of the Heart".

Book Five:

Eleutherios
(The <u>Only</u> Truth That Sets The Heart Free)

The "Late-Time" Avataric Revelation Of The "Perfect Practice" Of The Great Means To Worship and To Realize The True and Spiritual Divine Person (The egoless Personal Presence Of Reality and Truth, Which <u>Is</u> The Only <u>Real</u> God)

An address to the great human questions about God, Truth, Reality, Happiness, and Freedom. Avatar Adi Da Samraj Reveals how Absolute Divine Freedom is Realized, and makes an impassioned Call to everyone to create a world of true human freedom on Earth.

The Seventeen Companions
Of The True Dawn Horse

These seventeen books are "Companions" to *The Dawn Horse Testament*, Avatar Adi Da's great summary of the Way of Adidam (p. 368). Here you will find Avatar Adi Da's Wisdom-Instruction on particular aspects of the true Spiritual Way, and His two tellings of His own Life-Story, as autobiography (*The Knee Of Listening*) and as archetypal parable (*The Mummery*).

BOOK ONE:

Real God Is The Indivisible Oneness Of Unbroken Light

Reality, Truth, and The "Non-Creator" God In The True World-Religion Of Adidam

The Nature of Real God and the nature of the cosmos. Why ultimate questions cannot be answered either by conventional religion or by science.

BOOK TWO:

The Truly Human New World-Culture Of Unbroken Real-God-Man

The Eastern Versus The Western Traditional Cultures Of Mankind, and The Unique New Non-Dual Culture Of The True World-Religion Of Adidam

The Eastern and Western approaches to religion, and to life altogether—and how the Way of Adidam goes beyond this apparent dichotomy.

BOOK THREE:

The Only Complete Way To Realize The Unbroken Light Of Real God

An Introductory Overview Of The "Radical" Divine Way Of The True World-Religion Of Adidam

The entire course of the Way of Adidam—the unique principles underlying Adidam, and the unique culmination of Adidam in Divine Enlightenment.

BOOK FOUR:

The Knee Of Listening

The Early-Life Ordeal and The "Radical"
Spiritual Realization Of The Ruchira Avatar

Avatar Adi Da's autobiographical account of the years from His Birth to His Divine Re-Awakening in 1970. Includes a new chapter, "My Realization of the Great Onlyness of Me, and My Great Regard for My Adept-Links to the Great Tradition of Mankind".

BOOK FIVE:

The Divine Siddha-Method Of The Ruchira Avatar

The Divine Way Of Adidam Is An ego-Transcending
<u>Relationship</u>, Not An ego-Centric Technique

Avatar Adi Da's earliest Talks to His devotees, on the fundamental principles of the devotional relationship to Him and "radical" understanding of the ego. Accompanied by His summary statements on His relationship to Swami Muktananda and on His own unique Teaching-Work and Blessing-Work.

BOOK SIX:

The Mummery

A Parable Of The Divine True Love

A work of astonishing poetry and deeply evocative archetypal drama. This is the story of Raymond Darling's birth, his growth to manhood, his finding and losing of his beloved (Quandra), and his ultimate resolution of the heart-breaking "problem" of mortality. *The Mummery* is Avatar Adi Da's telling of His own Life-Story in the language of parable, including His unflinching portrayal of how the unconverted ego makes religion (and life altogether) into a meaningless mummery.

BOOK SEVEN:

He-_and_-She _Is_ Me

The Indivisibility Of Consciousness and Light In The Divine Body Of The Ruchira Avatar

One of Avatar Adi Da's most esoteric Revelations—His Primary "Incarnation" in the Cosmic domain as the "He" of Primal Divine Sound-Vibration, the "She" of Primal Divine Light, and the "Son" of "He" and "She" in the "Me" of His Divine Spiritual Body.

BOOK EIGHT:

Ruchira Avatara Hridaya-Siddha Yoga

The Divine (and Not Merely Cosmic) Spiritual Baptism In The Divine Way Of Adidam

The Divine Heart-Power (Hridaya-Shakti) uniquely Transmitted by Avatar Adi Da Samraj, and how it differs from the various traditional forms of Spiritual Baptism, particularly Kundalini Yoga.

BOOK NINE:

Ruchira Avatara Hridaya-Tantra Yoga

The Physical-Spiritual (and Truly Religious) Method Of Mental, Emotional, Sexual, and Whole Bodily Health and Enlightenment In The Divine Way Of Adidam

The transformation of life in the realms of money, food, and sex. Includes: understanding "victim-consciousness"; the ego as addict; the secret of how to change; going beyond the "Oedipal" sufferings of childhood; the right orientation to money; right diet; life-positive and Spiritually auspicious sexual practice.

Book Ten:

The Seven Stages Of Life

Transcending The Six Stages Of egoic Life, and Realizing The ego-Transcending Seventh Stage Of Life, In The Divine Way Of Adidam

The stages of human development from birth to Divine Enlightenment. How the stages relate to physical and esoteric anatomy. The errors of each of the first six stages of life, and the unique egolessness of the seventh stage of life. Avatar Adi Da's Self-Confession as the first, last, and only seventh stage Adept-Realizer.

Book Eleven:

The <u>All-Completing</u> and <u>Final</u> Divine Revelation To Mankind

A Summary Description Of The Supreme Yoga Of The Seventh Stage Of Life In The Divine Way Of Adidam

The ultimate secrets of Divine Enlightenment—including the four-stage Process of Divine Enlightenment, culminating in Translation into the Infinitely Love-Blissful Divine Self-Domain.

Book Twelve:

The Heart Of The Dawn Horse Testament Of The Ruchira Avatar

The Epitome Of The "Testament Of Secrets" Of The Divine World-Teacher, Ruchira Avatar Adi Da Samraj

A shorter version of *The Dawn Horse Testament*—all of Avatar Adi Da's magnificent summary Instruction, without the details of the technical practices engaged by His devotees.

BOOK THIRTEEN:

What, Where, When, How, Why, and <u>Who</u> To Remember To Be Happy

A Simple Explanation Of The Divine Way Of Adidam (For Children, and <u>Everyone</u> Else)

A text written specifically for children but inspiring to all—with accompanying Essays and Talks on Divine Ignorance, religious practices for children and young people in the Way of Adidam, and the fundamental practice of whole bodily devotion to Avatar Adi Da Samraj. (The central text of this book is also available in a special illustrated children's edition—see p. 360.)

BOOK FOURTEEN:

Santosha Adidam

The Essential Summary Of The Divine Way Of Adidam

An extended overview of the entire course of the Way of Adidam, based on the esoteric anatomy of the human being and its correlation to the progressive stages of life.

BOOK FIFTEEN:

The Lion Sutra

The "Perfect Practice" Teachings In The Divine Way Of Adidam

Practice in the ultimate stages of the Way of Adidam. How the practitioner of Adidam approaches—and passes over—the "Threshold" of Divine Enlightenment.

Book Sixteen:

The Overnight Revelation Of Conscious Light

*The "My House" Discourses
On The Indivisible Tantra Of Adidam*

A vast and profound "consideration" of the fundamental Tantric principles of true Spiritual life and the "Always Already" Nature of the Divine Reality. The day-by-day record of Avatar Adi Da's Discourses from a two-month period in early 1998.

Book Seventeen:

The Basket Of Tolerance

The Perfect Guide To Perfectly <u>Unified</u> Understanding Of The One and Great Tradition Of Mankind, and Of The Divine Way Of Adidam As The Perfect <u>Completing</u> Of The One and Great Tradition Of Mankind

An all-encompassing "map" of mankind's entire history of religious seeking. A combination of a bibliography of over 5,000 items (organized to display Avatar Adi Da's grand Argument relative to the Great Tradition) with over 100 Essays by Avatar Adi Da, illuminating many specific aspects of the Great Tradition.

The Dawn Horse Testament Of The Ruchira Avatar

*The "Testament Of Secrets"
Of The Divine World-Teacher,
Ruchira Avatar Adi Da Samraj*

Avatar Adi Da's paramount "Source-Text", which summarizes the entire course of the Way of Adidam. Adi Da Samraj says: "In making this Testament I have been Meditating everyone, contacting everyone, dealing with psychic forces everywhere, in all time. This Testament is an always Living Conversation between Me and absolutely every one."

See My Brightness Face to Face

A Celebration of the Ruchira Avatar, Adi Da Samraj, and the First Twenty-Five Years of His Divine Revelation Work.

A magnificent year-by-year pictorial celebration of Ruchira Avatar Adi Da's Divine Work with His devotees, from 1972 to 1997. Includes a wealth of selections from His Talks and Writings, numerous Stories told by His devotees, and over 100 color photographs. **$19.95**, 8-1/2" x 11" paperback, 200 pages.

The "Truth For Real" series

Brief Essays and Talks by the Divine World-Teacher, Ruchira Avatar Adi Da Samraj

13 individual booklets on topics such as ecstasy, death, and the impulse to Happiness.
3-3/4" x 6", **$1.95** each

The Basket Of Tolerance Booklet series

6 individual essays on the religious traditions of humankind from *The Basket Of Tolerance.*
3-3/4" x 6", **$1.95** each

In addition to Avatar Adi Da's 23 "Source-Texts", the Dawn Horse Press offers many other publications by and about Avatar Adi Da Samraj, as well as videotapes and audiotapes of Avatar Adi Da's Wisdom-Teaching. Dawn Horse Press publications are distributed by the Adidam Emporium, a devotee-operated business offering a wide array of items for meditation, sacred worship, health and well-being, and much more.

For more information or a free catalog:

**CALL THE ADIDAM EMPORIUM
TOLL-FREE 1-877-770-0772**
(Outside North America call 707-928-6653)

Visit online at
www.adidam.com

Or e-mail:
emporium@adidam.com

Or write:
**ADIDAM EMPORIUM
10336 Loch Lomond Road
PMB #306
Middletown, CA 95461
USA**

INDEX

NOTE TO THE READER: Page numbers in **boldface** type refer to the Scriptural Text of the *Da Love-Ananda Gita*. All other page numbers refer to the introductions, endnotes, and the back matter.

G

Index

I do not simply recommend or turn men and women to Truth. I *Am* Truth. I Draw men and women to Myself. I *Am* the Present Real God, Desiring, Loving, and Drawing up My devotees. I have Come to Be Present with My devotees, to Reveal to them the True Nature of life in Real God, which is Love, and of mind in Real God, which is Faith. I Stand always Present in the Place and Form of Real God. I accept the qualities of all who turn to Me, dissolving those qualities in Real God, so that *Only* God becomes the Condition, Destiny, Intelligence, and Work of My devotees. I look for My devotees to acknowledge Me and turn to Me in appropriate ways, surrendering to Me perfectly, depending on Me, full of Me always, with only a face of love.

I am waiting for you. I have been waiting for you eternally.

Where are you?

AVATAR ADI DA SAMRAJ

1971